THE MOST ACTIVIST
SUPREME COURT IN HISTORY
THE ROAD TO MODERN
JUDICIAL CONSERVATISM
THOMAS M. KECK

The University of Chicago Press

CHICAGO AND LONDON

Thomas M. Keck is assistant professor
of political science at the Maxwell School of Citizenship
and Public Affairs at Syracuse University.

The University of Chicago Press, Chicago 60637
The University of Chicago Press, Ltd., London
© 2004 by Thomas M. Keck
All rights reserved. Published 2004
Printed in the United States of America
13 12 11 10 09 08 07 06 05 04   1 2 3 4 5

ISBN: 0-226-42884-2 (cloth)
ISBN: 0-226-42885-0 (paper)

Library of Congress Cataloging-in-Publication Data

Keck, Thomas Moylan.
The most activist supreme court in history : the road to modern judicial
conservatism / Thomas M. Keck.
p.   cm.
Includes bibliographical references and index.
ISBN: 0-226-42884-2 (cloth : alk. paper) — ISBN: 0-226-42885-0 (pbk. : alk. paper)
1. United States. Supreme Court. 2. Rehnquist, William H., 1924 –
3. Conservatism — United States. 4. Law and politics. I. Title.
KF8748.K43 2004
347.73'26 — dc22

2004005108

⊗ The paper used in this publication meets the minimum requirements
of the American National Standard for Information Sciences — Permanence of
Paper for Printed Library Materials, ANSI Z39.48-1992.

THE MOST ACTIVIST
SUPREME COURT
IN HISTORY

FOR JULIE EVE GOZAN

CONTENTS

List of Tables   ix

Preface   xi

Introduction: The Supreme Court and Modern Judicial Conservatism   1

PART I
The Roots of Modern Judicial Conservatism, 1937–1969

1. The New Deal Revolution and the Reconstruction of Constitutional
   Law, 1937–1949   17
2. Frankfurter's Failure: The Rise and Decline of Judicial Self-Restraint,
   1949–1962   38
3. The Warren Court and Its Critics, 1962–1969   67

PART II
The Court and the Conservative Turn in American Politics, 1969–1994

4. The Nixon Court and the Conservative Turn, 1969–1980   107
5. The Reagan Court and the Conservative Ascendance, 1980–1994   156

PART III
The Rehnquist Court and the Splintering of Judicial Conservatism, 1994–2003

6. Activism and Restraint on the Rehnquist Court   199
7. Law and Politics on the Rehnquist Court   254

Conclusion: Modern Conservatism and Judicial Power   284

Notes   297
Cases Cited   327
References   339
Index   357

TABLES

2.1. Decisions striking down federal statutes on constitutional grounds   40

2.2. Decisions striking down state and local statutes on constitutional grounds   41

3.1. Frequency of dissent, 1962–1968 terms   70

3.2. Interagreement with Black during Warren era   86–87

4.1. Frequency of solo dissent during Burger era   116–17

4.2. Interagreement with Rehnquist during Burger era   118

6.1. Support for liberal and conservative activism on the Rehnquist Court   200

6.2. Frequency in majority during late Rehnquist era   202

6.3. Federal statutes ruled unconstitutional by the Supreme Court   204–7

6.4. State and local statutes ruled unconstitutional by the Supreme Court   209–14

6.5. Support for judicial review on the late Rehnquist Court   251

PREFACE

The defining political development during my lifetime has been the conservative turn in American politics. I was born during the Nixon era, first participated in a political event of my own choosing during the Reagan era, and first voted in the election that brought George H. W. Bush to office. During that first Bush presidency, I began to study politics at Oberlin College, and in 1994, when the Republican Party recaptured the House of Representatives for the first time in forty years, I was a graduate student in political science at Rutgers University.

For as long as I can remember, my parents, Donna Poggi Keck and Jim Keck, encouraged my love of learning and my commitment to politics, and for this I thank them. A long list of teachers in the Baltimore City public schools encouraged these passions on a daily basis as well. I thank all of them, but Mr. Alpern and Ms. Moxon in particular. At Oberlin, yet another long list of teachers helped me continue on this path, and here I'd like to single out Ron Kahn, Chris Howell, Chandra Mohanty, and Linda Carty for thanks. Perhaps even more importantly, my fellow students — my classmates and friends — in both Baltimore and Oberlin helped to shape me into the person who wrote this book.

I don't know exactly when I first developed an interest in courts, though I do remember one election day in the 1970s with my mom, as we worked the polls to support a proposed rent control ordinance, and I remember her effort some time later to explain that we had won the election, but that the law had been struck down by the courts. In hindsight at least, that small event seems to have played some role in setting me on the path that led to this book. In any event, I began to study the Supreme Court and constitutional law while at Oberlin, and again in hindsight, it's clear that I was already grappling with the questions at the heart of this book: whether and how conservatives had succeeded in transforming the modern Court into an institution that would actively promote conservative ends.

This book was a long time in writing, and it is a great pleasure finally to thank the many friends and colleagues who helped along the way. In the early stages of the project, Susan Lawrence, Milton Heumann, Michael Paris, and Ron Kahn (again) provided unwavering support and consistently helpful comments and criticisms for a graduate student whose reach sometimes exceeded his grasp. Several other professional colleagues generously lent their time and insight at the beginning as well. Since these encounters were sometimes fleeting, these colleagues may not know how helpful their feedback was. In this light, I'd like to thank my fellow panel members at several annual meetings of the American Political Science Association, the Western Political Science Association, and the Northeastern Political Science Association. Of particular assistance and support were Keith Whittington, Susan Burgess, Ken Sherrill, Harry Hirsch, Sue Davis, Pam Brandwein, Kevin McMahon, and especially Howard Gillman, who truly went above and beyond the call of duty.

Somewhat later, Ron Peters, Bob Cox, Don Maletz, Ann Marie Szymanski, Allen Hertzke, Amanda Winkler, Nina Cooke John, and David Rodgers read and commented on portions of the manuscript. Karen Orren and Mike McCann did so as well, pushing me to sharpen my argument in ways that proved very helpful. And toward the very end, Mark Graber and an anonymous reviewer read the entire manuscript not once but twice. Their pointed comments, questions, and criticisms have made this a much better book, though they of course bear no responsibility for any faults that remain. At the University of Chicago Press, it has been a pleasure to work with Matt Avery, David Bemelmans, Ashley Cave, Anne Ford, Leslie Keros, Bonny McLaughlin, Rodney Powell, and especially John Tryneski, who never stopped prodding me to make the book better and always conveyed his confidence that the effort would be worthwhile.

I could not have completed the book without extensive support, both intellectual and financial, from Rutgers University, the University of Oklahoma, and Syracuse University. In particular, I'd like to thank my department chairs at Oklahoma and Syracuse, Ron Peters (again) and Jeff Stonecash; the countless librarians at these three institutions, and also at the Library of Congress and Georgetown University, who provided much-needed help along the way; and my research assistants, Brian Blaho, Stephanie Youngblood, and Akin Owoso. My thanks also to Sara Benesh and Harold Spaeth for the use of their U.S. Supreme Court Databases, available at the Program for Law and Judicial Politics at Michigan State University. I am grateful to *Polity* for permission to adapt parts of an earlier article, "Activism and Restraint on the Rehnquist Court: Timing, Sequence, and Conjuncture in Constitutional Development," which appeared in the Fall 2002 issue.

Having thanked those who helped most directly with the completion of the book, I'd like to turn to the many friends and family members who helped in less direct ways, principally by getting me to forget about the book for a few hours at a time. Sasha Rachel Gozan-Keck arrived only at the end, but she has been particularly good at this. Besides Sasha, my thanks to Jeffrey Kliman, Cathie Keck, John and Chris and Sara and Ellen Poggi, Moshe and Robbin Imel (and Sol and Omar!), Rachel Schwartz and Lauren Howerdd (and Leo!), Makela Spielman, John McKiernan-Gonzalez, James Kennedy, Jun Coue, Retsu Takahashi, Aaron Stark, Erin Korff, Jess Dobkin and Sandra Smith, Courtney Standish, Jill and Andrew Tao, Brian Taylor and Renee de Nevers (and Lucian and Anatol!), Ari and Lesley Kelman, Adam and Julie Cohen (and Will and Theo!), Josh Piker and Francesca Sawaya, Rick and Debbie Poland, David Ray and Tim Miller, Cindy Simon Rosenthal, Ben Alpers and Karin Schutjer, Randy Lewis and Circe Sturm, Mark Lewellen, Alice Anderton, Vickie Wolfe, Dave Charlson, Adrianne Johnson, Mark Griffin and Joy Pendley, Jerry Messick, Lorna Caraway, Norman Kutcher and Richard Wallach, Dan Fassett and Sarah Harwell (and Hannah!), Keith Bybee and Jennifer Champa (and Evan!), Elizabeth Cohen, Emily Lee, Rogan Kersh, and Suzanne Mettler.

Some of these folks were friends and neighbors in Washington, Norman, or Syracuse as I worked on the book, but just one person was with me in all three places. Just one person had to live with me, and hence with this book, every day for the past eight years. This book is for Julie Gozan. I couldn't have done it without you.

INTRODUCTION

THE SUPREME COURT AND MODERN JUDICIAL CONSERVATISM

On December 12, 2000, the U.S. Supreme Court decided the outcome of the nation's presidential election by a single judicial vote. In *Bush v. Gore*, the Court's five most conservative justices halted the ongoing ballot recount in Florida — a recount that, so far as anyone knew at the time, might well have resulted in Democrat Al Gore's election. The conservative justices called the contest to a close, ruling that the Equal Protection Clause of the Fourteenth Amendment prohibited the recount from continuing. This decision was surprising to many observers because these same conservative justices had long been known for their critique of "government by judiciary," and because vote-counting in a democratic election represents precisely the sort of "political thicket" that conservatives had long urged courts to avoid.

For decades, in fact, the standard conservative view of the Supreme Court has amounted to a critique of liberal "judicial activism" and a call for "judicial restraint." These terms have not always been used with precision, but if judicial restraint means anything in the context of the long conservative critique of the Warren Court and its legacy, it must mean a relative unwillingness to declare constitutional limitations on government, or a relative unwillingness to become involved in heated political questions, or as federal judge Richard Posner has defined it, the "belie[f] that the power of [the] court system relative to other branches of government should be reduced" (1996:314). As *Bush v. Gore* makes clear, however, the Rehnquist Court simply cannot be understood as a tribunal committed to such restraint. In a wide variety of doctrinal contexts, the justices of the Rehnquist Court have proven willing both to declare constitutional limitations on government and to become involved in heated political questions. In its view toward federal legislative power, in particular, the later Rehnquist Court has been the least deferential of any in the history of the U.S. Supreme Court, striking down thirty provisions of federal law from 1995 to 2001. As some scholars have begun to recognize, and as I spell out in some detail, the current Court has developed a distinctive new style of conservative judicial activism (Seidman 1996; Rosen 2000c). Consider, for example, the series of recent decisions in which the Court has revived the federalism-based limits on national legislative power, striking down provisions of the Gun Free School Zones Act, the Brady Bill, the Violence against Women Act, the Age Discrimination in Employment Act, the Americans with Disabilities Act, and a variety of other congressional statutes that, just ten years ago, would have been deemed perfectly constitutional without any serious question.

How is it that a judicial conservatism born in reaction to the liberal judicial activism of the Warren Court has come to create not judicial restraint but instead its own version of judicial activism? Why would the Rehnquist Court, led by ostensibly conservative justices, engage in such widespread judicial activism? And if these justices are engaged in such activism, how can they continue to maintain that they are committed to the ideal of restraint? This book is an effort to answer these questions.

A New Conservative Constitutional Order?

One possible explanation is a legalistic one. The apparent tension between the conservatives' activism and their own long-standing demand for restraint might be resolved by the written Constitution itself. This is the explanation that many conservatives themselves would offer — that the justices actively enforce limits on governmental power where the original meaning of the constitutional text tells them to do so, and that they defer to the political branches where the original meaning of the constitutional text is "silent." As I argue later in the book, this account is incomplete at best. While some of the Rehnquist Court's judicial activism has been rooted in plausible readings of the original Constitution, much of it has not. As I show, much of the recent conservative activism has been rooted in New Right constitutional commitments that have emerged over the past three decades. These commitments have been built on both modern conservative political discourse and long-standing American constitutional traditions, but the conservatives' effort to tie their specific modern constitutional doctrines to the 1787 Constitution has been both inconsistent and unsuccessful. And so it cannot be the mere text of our fundamental law that explains why conservatives have denounced certain forms of liberal judicial activism while engaging in a distinctive variety of conservative activism themselves.

An alternative explanation is a political one. Perhaps contemporary conservatives are simply engaged in rank instrumentalism, in the sense that they were never actually committed to judicial restraint in the first place, and that they quickly abandoned this purported commitment upon taking control of the federal judiciary. Political scientists Jeffrey Segal and Harold Spaeth, for example, argue that the doctrine of judicial restraint is nothing more than a rhetorical cover for judicial "deference" to policies that a justice happens to agree with (1993:300–327). Some scholars have advanced the related argument that the justices, like other political actors, seek to enact policies that benefit their constituents, and that the vagueness and flexibility of the Constitution's language allow them significant leeway to do so. Martin Shapiro, for example, has argued that the Warren Court's decisions were an effort to benefit the New Deal coalition of the working class, racial minorities, and liberal intellectuals, and Mark Tushnet has suggested, in turn, that the decisions of the Burger and Rehnquist Courts represent the "triumph of country-club Republicanism." [1]

These political explanations are rooted in a long-standing effort by political scientists to debunk an overly legalistic understanding of the Court. Some of these scholars have followed Robert Dahl's suggestion that the justices are themselves members of the "national law-making majority," in that they are drawn from, and appointed by, the dominant governing coalition, and hence that their decisions can generally be explained by reference to the policy preferences of the president who appointed them (Dahl 1957). Thus, these scholars have sometimes described constitutional development in terms of a series of temporally distinct "constitutional orders," by which they mean both the "reasonably stable set of institutions through which a nation's fundamental decisions are made over a sustained period, and the principles that guide those decisions." [2] Tushnet's description of the displacement of "the New Deal/Great Society constitutional order" during the 1980s and 1990s, for example, clearly fits with Dahl's account of the Court. In this narrative, periodic partisan realignments in national politics produce personnel changes on the Court, which in turn produce a transition to a new constitutional order.

Like the purely legalistic explanation, however, this narrowly political approach is also incomplete. In particular, it cannot explain the mixed pattern
of conservative influence on modern constitutional law. While the Rehnquist
Court has reshaped constitutional law in a conservative direction in many areas, it has surprisingly reaffirmed and even extended a number of landmark
liberal precedents from the Warren and early Burger years — precedents like
Miranda v. Arizona, Shapiro v. Thompson, Frontiero v. Richardson, and most
notably, *Roe v. Wade.* If the Court's decisions are shaped solely by partisan
change, the appointment of new justices, and the justices' own political preferences, then it is hard to understand why a Court with seven Republican appointees has so utterly failed to overturn *Roe,* one of the key targets of conservative critique for the past thirty years. If we have made the transition
from the New Deal/Great Society constitutional order to a subsequent conservative one, then why have conservatives been unwilling or unable to displace some of the key elements of the prior regime?

The reason is that constitutional development does not in fact proceed by
means of the smooth, wholesale replacement of an existing constitutional
order with an emergent one. Rather, like political change more generally,
all constitutional change "proceeds upon a prior ground, a site, of political
arrangements, rules, leaders, ideas, practices, attitudes, and so on, already in
existence" (Orren and Skowronek 2000:4). Those scholars who have described the Rehnquist Court's jurisprudence as part of a "new constitutional
order" have sometimes recognized this point, but their accounts have still
tended to suggest a sharper transformation than is actually the case (Tushnet
2003; Balkin and Levinson 2001). Partisan change can and often does lead to
the displacement of an existing constitutional order, but the process occurs
by means of a slow, halting transition, never a clean break with the past. New
constitutional ideas are layered upon, or intertwined with, preexisting ones,
rather than replacing them altogether.

The New Deal/Great Society constitutional order ran from roughly 1937
to 1969, as justices like Stone, Warren, and Brennan led the modern Court in
staking out an expansive role of defending individual liberty and minority
rights. From the beginning, critics like Felix Frankfurter and Alexander
Bickel denounced this expanded judicial role as illegitimate, but a particular
version of liberal judicial activism was clearly the dominant motif, especially
during the Warren Court's heyday from 1962 to 1969. Richard Nixon's 1968
presidential campaign, during which he ran against the liberal Warren Court
almost as much as his actual opponent, marked the beginning of a conserva-

tive shift in American politics, and the justices appointed by Republican Presidents Nixon, Reagan, and Bush have transformed constitutional law in many ways. By the time conservatives came to power, however, important elements of the previous order had already become entrenched and would not easily be dislodged. Most significantly, while Frankfurter's vision of judicial restraint had been an open possibility following the New Deal, the Warren Court had rejected it in favor of rights-based judicial activism. This decision by the Court during the 1950s and 1960s marked a "critical juncture," after which Frankfurter's alternative would be much more difficult to recover. When conservatives came to power after 1968, they continued to advance their critique of judicial activism, but given the path that was open, they also began to articulate their own conservative versions of rights-based constitutionalism, rooted in their New Right vision of limited government.

Perhaps the clearest way to understand these competing strains in modern conservatism is in terms of the shifting targets of conservative critique.[5] At the close of the Warren era in 1969, the key target of constitutional conservatives was "government by judiciary," but by the close of the twentieth century, that target had in large measure been supplanted by modern liberalism itself. In the interim, conservative intellectuals and political leaders had articulated a broad New Right critique of liberalism as the source of cultural decay, economic stagnation, and American decline. During the 1970s and 1980s, for example, the Court was increasingly influenced by an emerging neoconservative critique of the welfare state and "liberal social engineering." Thus, while the initial conservative objection to New Deal constitutionalism had focused on the Court's broad rights-based judicial activism, constitutional conservatives subsequently articulated a critique of the second major tenet of New Deal constitutionalism as well — namely, the Court's broad deference to the authority of the national welfare-regulatory state. In short, modern conservatives have emphasized both judicial restraint and limited government, two principles that have sometimes pulled in different directions.

These principles are rooted in two different constitutional orders, and the conservative effort to reconcile them has dramatically shaped modern constitutional development. In certain areas of constitutional law, the New Right critique of liberalism has simply reinforced the preexisting conservative demand for judicial restraint, but in other areas, these separate critiques have created a sharp tension within constitutional conservatism. In the civil rights context, for example, conservatives began during the 1970s to emphasize an individualistic conception of merit that they saw as threatened by liberal egalitarian policies. In constitutional terms, this came to be expressed as a "color-blind" vision of Fourteenth Amendment equality, and there was in fact a long-standing (though sharply contested) constitutional tradition ascribing such a color-blind reading to the Equal Protection Clause. In the desegregation context, this principle of color-blindness reinforced the conservative critique of judicial overreaching, as conservatives denounced the school busing decisions both because they adopted race-conscious pupil assignment policies and because those policies were judicially imposed. When affirmative action started to displace school desegregation as the key constitutional debate in the area of racial equality, however, the logic of these two conservative principles diverged. Rejected white university applicants, and others who believed themselves victims of affirmative action, began turning to the courts to demand that they strike down race-conscious policies that had been adopted by democratically accountable government institutions (and not by the courts themselves). The conservative justices began to heed these arguments despite any countervailing concern for judicial restraint, which might have suggested that university admissions policies and government contracting decisions were not generally to be second-guessed by unelected judges.

During this same period, a new style of conservative activism was also emerging in response to the conservative critique of the welfare state. During the New Deal/Great Society era, the Court had largely abandoned the traditional limits on government regulatory authority that had been rooted in the original constitutional principles of federalism and property rights (Gillman 1999b). During the 1970s, however, in a political context in which the Republican Party was making increasingly successful appeals to public distrust of government, constitutional conservatives sought to recover and enforce such pre–New Deal conceptions of limited government, again despite any countervailing concern for restraint. In other words, as Republican political leaders were denouncing "tax and spend" liberalism and intrusive government regulation of the private economy, conservative judges were mining our constitutional traditions for judicially enforceable limits on the modern welfare-regulatory state. In these areas and others, then, conservatives sought to constitutionalize their emerging New Right commitments, and where elected institutions rather than courts were enacting liberal policies, the conservatives were now in a position to appeal to the federal courts to strike those policies down. They could only do so, however, if they were willing to abandon (or cabin) their commitment to restraint.

The conservative justices of the Rehnquist Court have thus been faced with the task of reconciling these competing constitutional commitments. Broadly speaking, they have adopted two different strategies for doing so, and the line between these competing strategies represents the key conflict on the current Court. The conjuncture of the post–New Deal development of rights-based constitutionalism and the post-1968 conservative realignment presented these justices with a crucial opportunity to shape constitutional development. This opportunity, however, was itself shaped and constrained by the inherited traditions of constitutional discourse, which left the justices with three broad options for transforming constitutional law. First, they could have attempted to maintain a consistent commitment to judicial restraint, exercising substantial deference to the elected branches across the board. This option, however, had been rendered much less attractive by the time they came to power, as the very mission of an independent Supreme Court had come to be identified — in the minds of ordinary citizens, elite opinion makers, and the justices themselves — with the enforcement of rights-based limits on political action. For them to abandon this role would be to call into question the very justification for their office. Second, the conservative justices could have chosen to abandon the protection of liberal constitutional rights associated with the Warren Court tradition, while articulating a new set of conservative rights claims that they were willing to defend. This is essentially what Justices Scalia, Thomas, and Rehnquist have done. Third and finally, they could have preserved the liberal, rights-based activism of the Warren Court, while also endorsing the newer conservative activism. It is this last choice, made by Justices O'Connor and Kennedy, that explains why the Rehnquist Court has dramatically transformed constitutional law in a conservative direction in some areas, while reaffirming and even expanding landmark liberal precedents in others.

Thus, in the most immediate sense, O'Connor and Kennedy have been responsible for the two most striking elements of the Rehnquist Court's constitutional jurisprudence: the survival of liberal activism, on the one hand, and the emergence of conservative activism, on the other. In characterizing these decisions as "activist," I mean simply to suggest the opposite of a commitment to judicial restraint — in other words, a relative willingness to exercise judicial power, principally (though not exclusively) in the form of striking down state or federal statutes as unconstitutional. The Court's willingness to do so has expanded and contracted throughout its long history, and as a

growing number of scholars have recognized, the current Court falls at the
activist end of the spectrum. Since the term "activist" is generally perceived
as an epithet, the justices of the Rehnquist Court would not accept this characterization of their own decisions. Scalia and Thomas, for instance, would
argue that the Court should be considered activist only when it is striking
down democratically enacted statutes *without a firm constitutional basis for
doing so,* and hence that their own exercises of judicial review, rooted in the
original constitutional text, have not been activist.[4] The problem with this
definition is that all justices urge the Court to exercise judicial power in certain contexts, and they all insist that such exercises, in such contexts, are required by the Constitution. They differ on what those contexts are — abortion rights for liberals, property rights for conservatives — but the term
"activism" does not draw a useful distinction in this regard. They also differ
on how often and how boldly they are willing to assert the Court's power, and
it is this variance in perceptions of the Court's role that I mean to capture
with the terms "activism" and "restraint."[5]

Timing, Sequence, and Conjuncture in Constitutional Development

The patterns in contemporary constitutional doctrine that I have described
cannot be explained by reference either to disembodied legal categories or to
partisan shifts in the political system alone. It is, rather, the conjuncture of
these relatively autonomous processes that has shaped constitutional development. The justices appointed by the Republican presidential coalition have
been influenced by modern conservative political ideas and interests, but
they have all sought to reconcile these emergent demands with the inherited
traditions of constitutional discourse. Thus, we can best understand this dynamic by attending to the interaction between the logic of partisan political
order, on the one hand, and the institutionalized pattern of ideas associated
with constitutional interpretation, on the other.

In recent years, a number of political scientists have highlighted the importance of such "conjunctures of separately determined processes" in shaping patterns of political development (Skocpol 2000:674). Karen Orren and
Stephen Skowronek, for example, have emphasized that the political system
is made up of multiple institutions, whose origins are nonsimultaneous,
whose trajectories of development are relatively autonomous from each
other, and whose interaction can explain broad patterns of political order
and change. Given the tendency of particular political institutions to persist,

"at any [one] time several different sets of rules and norms are likely to be operating simultaneously. . . . Such a perspective directs the analyst to the disjointed character of political development and to the tensions among relatively independent institutional orderings as these become formative of political action." As Orren and Skowronek note, "[t]he persistence of institutions implies that the objectives they pursue at any given moment will reflect the resolution of earlier encounters, and that new purposes and procedures will accumulate over time. Analysis in this frame is therefore drawn back to the circumstances in which the different rules in play originated, and individual institutions themselves will be described as a layering of divergent experiences and imperatives" (1996:111–12, 139). To capture this view of political development, Orren and Skowronek have suggested the image of a matrix, with "several patterns moving alongside one another, each with its own rhythms and different points of inception and termination" (2002:753; see also Lieberman 2002).

For example, while Supreme Court justices are members of the national lawmaking majority, as Dahl suggested, they are also the leading members of the community of constitutional interpreters, made up of federal judges, constitutional scholars, and public commentators on the Constitution. These two separate communities are at times closely linked — in the context of judicial appointment, for example — but they are also relatively autonomous from each other. The institutional features of the Court, moreover, generally compel the justices to adhere to standards of legitimacy drawn from each of these two communities. In other words, while the Court's rules, norms, and traditions allow (or even require) the justices to act on and respond to political ideas and interests, broadly understood, they generally discourage them from simply manipulating constitutional arguments to achieve their preferred results or to advance the policies of the president who appointed them.[6]

In addition, the Court is just one of several political institutions that together shape constitutional development. As Keith Whittington has noted, "constitutional authority and meaning [are] shaped through the interaction of different institutions. Constitutional meaning emerges from the interplay of multiple actors, rather than through the abstracted reasoning of an isolated judiciary" (1998a:13). The justices' actions, motives, and conceptions of the possible are all shaped in large part by the interaction between preexisting jurisprudential traditions and emerging constellations of political ideas and interests that reach the Court through the process of judicial appointment, governmental and interest group litigation, and other external pressures. The Supreme Court is not free to elaborate the meaning of the Constitution in a political vacuum, but neither can a newly elected president freely recreate the constitutional order in his own image — not even a popular two-term president like Ronald Reagan. In this light, the only way to make sense of the particular pattern in which conservatives have been able to reshape constitutional law in certain areas but not others is to attend to the conjuncture of these two relatively autonomous institutional dynamics.

This attention to conjuncture, moreover, foregrounds questions of timing and sequence in political development. Modern rights-based constitutionalism became embedded in American law and politics prior to the post-1968 conservative shift in national party politics, and this sequence of development has rendered it more difficult for contemporary conservatives to articulate a persuasive case for the abandonment of judicial power. Constitutional conservatives are most noted for denouncing the system of "government by judiciary" that they see as the legacy of the Warren Court; but despite ten consecutive Republican appointments from 1969 to 1992, the Rehnquist Court has failed to overturn the landmark decisions that defined that legacy. Where conservative justices have sought not to abandon judicial power but to redirect its active use in conservative directions, however, they have been much more influential. Insisting, for example, that affirmative action policies violate the individual right to race-neutral treatment by the government, the Court's five most conservative justices have significantly transformed constitutional law during the past decade. As I have already noted, they have also revived a pre–New Deal conception of federalism, proving increasingly willing to strike down federal statutes as illegitimate infringements on state authority. In other words, while their critique of "government by judiciary" has been influential in certain contexts, constitutional conservatives have been relatively more successful where they have articulated an alternative other than the simple abandonment of judicially enforceable constitutional rights.

The layering of multiple institutional commitments is characteristic of political development more generally, but particularly so with an institution like the Supreme Court. The Court's formal and informal rules of operation, after all, expressly direct the justices' attention to past decisions, a dynamic that can lead to the entrenchment of particular sets of constitutional ideas long after their creators have left the Court. As with other institutions, "institutional rules and purposes shape the behavior of their incumbents," and so any accurate explanation of constitutional development must take account of the prevailing legal ideas and jurisprudential traditions to which the justices themselves have sought to respond (Orren and Skowronek 1996:140). Inherited, institutionalized norms — such as particular conceptions of the constitutional order and the judicial role — operate to shape and constrain subsequent patterns of political behavior and legal development. The institutionalized practice of constitutional adjudication fosters particular understandings of professional duty and the bounds of legitimate action, and these understandings have a meaningful and observable impact on what judges do. In fact, we cannot hope to explain what judges are doing when they decide a constitutional case without reference to their own understandings of what may legitimately be done. As Howard Gillman and Cornell Clayton have noted, this sort of institutional analysis is valuable both because we cannot make sense of individual behavior without attention to context — since institutions "structure one's ability to act on a set of beliefs" — and because institutions "are also a source of distinctive political purposes, goals and preferences." For Supreme Court justices, these institutional purposes might well include "a sense of duty or obligation about their responsibilities to the law and . . . a commitment to act as judges rather than as legislators" (1999b:4–5).

After all, if "ideas affect human behavior," they "will be particularly important for an institution like the judiciary," as Malcolm Feeley and Edward Rubin have observed. Along with the judges' own political views, one set of ideas that is likely to influence judicial decisionmaking is "existing legal doctrine." Though never determinative on its own, such "doctrine constrains as one element in a dynamic, interacting process; the need to maintain contact with existing doctrine, to stretch it without snapping it, is one of several conditions for effective judicial policy making" (1998:24–25, 355). In the particular context of constitutional adjudication, judges are faced with the task of combining and reconciling rights principles — that is, legally enforceable individual entitlements against the state — with what Ronald Kahn has called "polity principles," by which he means "deeply held ideas about where decisionmaking power should be located when deciding questions of constitutional significance" (1994:20–22). Contemporary conservatives have strived to reconcile the polity principle of judicial restraint with a variety of conservative rights principles that call for judicial activism.

If this account is persuasive, then the process of constitutional development can be examined only by means of interpretive methods that allow the researcher to uncover the meaning that legal ideas have for legal practitioners themselves. If the development of modern constitutional law has reflected

the efforts of conservative justices (and others) to fashion and maintain a coherent constitutional vision out of their competing political and legal commitments, then we must pay careful attention to the evolution of competing doctrinal arguments and broader constitutional rhetorics over the past
generation. Again, while these developments must be situated within their
broader political contexts, we should also remember that constitutional development represents a relatively autonomous feature of American politics,
shaped at all times by the peculiar logic of legal interpretation. Gillman has
argued that while judicial decisionmaking is clearly related to the justices' political views, broadly understood, "[a] careful reading of texts and contexts
often uncovers a process that more closely resembles principled (albeit politically charged) acts of interpretation than unrestrained acts of legislation"
(1994b:877). Constitutional interpretation certainly requires the exercise of
political judgment, but, like all institutionalized processes, it is governed by
a set of norms and standards that guide and constrain its legitimate practice.
Legal principles and constitutional provisions are themselves indeterminate,
but it is nonetheless true that within given contexts and communities, these
principles settle down (temporarily) into coherent and observable patterns.[7]

    If we are to decipher the particular mechanisms by which prevailing con-
stitutional norms come to shape judicial decisionmaking, then, as Stephen
Griffin observes, "we must necessarily investigate how the justices themselves
understand their role" (1996:135–36). As Mark Graber notes, "[j]udicial decisions cannot be adequately explained or assessed in the absence of fairly
thick descriptions of the legal arguments, political constraints, and strategic
maneuvers open to judicial actors at particular historical times. Moreover, . . . the strategic and policy choices justices make are largely but not fully
constrained by the legal arguments that can plausibly be made at a given
time" (1999:30). If it is true that particular constellations of legal ideas tend
to become temporarily entrenched within constitutional discourse and that,
once entrenched, these ideas shape both the preferences of, and the strategic
constraints facing, subsequent constitutional interpreters, then what I am
calling "modern judicial conservatism" represents just such a constellation of
legal ideas. In addition, such legal ideas have to come from somewhere, and
the attention to sequence and conjuncture highlights their roots in broader
political-historical processes.

• • •

In the chapters that follow, I account for the mixed pattern of conservative success on the Rehnquist Court by reference to the interaction between relatively autonomous legal ideas and partisan developments in national politics. In the aftermath of the New Deal constitutional revolution of 1937, having abandoned long-standing constitutional conceptions of limited government in order to make way for the modern welfare-regulatory state, the justices faced a crucial choice. They either had to abandon the idea of judicially enforceable limits on government power altogether or else had to reconstruct a new set of foundations for preserving the notion of constitutional liberty in the context of the modern state. The liberal justices of the Warren Court made the latter choice, entrenching a particular vision of rights-based constitutionalism into the American polity for the foreseeable future. Justice Frankfurter and his disciples in the legal academy often agreed with the political results of the Warren Court's decisions, but they nonetheless denounced such activism as illegitimate. Once Frankfurter retired, Justices Harlan and Black emerged as the Court's leading dissenters, and the modifications they made to Frankfurter's critique would influence constitutional conservatives for years to come. Once the GOP gained control of the presidency in 1968, a series of Republican presidents brought their power to bear on the Court, principally by replacing the liberal justices of the Warren Court with constitutional conservatives. Like their predecessors, the conservative justices of the Rehnquist Court have faced a crucial choice. One of the defining features of modern conservatism had been a critique of judicial power, but now that they themselves had taken over the Court, they faced a strong incentive to put that institution to work on their own behalf.

Beginning with the widely noted affirmative action and Tenth Amendment cases of the 1970s, the New Right demand for limited government reached the Court. Not until the conservative justices consolidated their control in the 1990s, however, did it become fully apparent that the call for conservative judges to enforce limits on the liberal state was in tension with the long-standing conservative commitment to restraint. The origins of contemporary judicial conservatism, then, can be found both in the ideological demands advanced by contemporary conservative political movements and in the critique of liberal activism, particularly as modified by Harlan and Black during the Warren years. The conservative justices of the Rehnquist Court have been forced to negotiate the tensions among these cross-cutting commitments, and their competing efforts to do so have produced a Court that is playing an ever-broader role in the American political system.

Some of these developments have been noted by scholars and journalists, but they have not been well understood. Conversations about the Court, both in legal scholarship and in the public arena, have too often equated judicial activism with the work of the Warren Court, and judicial restraint with critiques of the Warren Court. We need a new and better conversation about what the contemporary Supreme Court is doing. This book is an effort to promote that conversation.

THE ROOTS OF
MODERN JUDICIAL
CONSERVATISM
1937–1969

CHAPTER ONE

THE NEW DEAL REVOLUTION
AND THE RECONSTRUCTION
OF CONSTITUTIONAL LAW
1937–1949

Though modern judicial conservatism has roots that reach back to the adoption of the original Constitution, its principal lines of development began with the founding moment of modern constitutional law, the New Deal "switch in time" of 1937. By that time, the pre–New Deal Court's active enforcement of constitutional limits on state and federal legislative authority had led many judges and scholars to conclude that such sweeping judicial power was illegitimate in a democratic political system. As President Franklin D. Roosevelt's appointees took over the Court during the late 1930s, they abandoned the preexisting constitutional conceptions of limited government — rooted primarily in notions of federalism and property rights — in order to legitimize the modern welfare-regulatory state. Having done so, they would either have to abandon the idea of judicially enforceable limits on government power altogether, or else reconstruct a new set of foundations for preserving the notion of constitutional liberty in the context of the modern state.

The Court eventually chose the latter course, marking out a new, modern judicial activism in defense of civil liberties and minority rights, a vision of rights-based constitutionalism that is now firmly entrenched in the American political system. This choice, however, was not fully made until the second half of the Warren era. In the years immediately following the New Deal, the outcome of these constitutional debates was truly in doubt, with pitched battles waged over the future direction of American constitutionalism. In this chapter, I explore the new constitutional foundations marked out by three particularly influential New Deal appointees: Felix Frankfurter, Harlan Fiske Stone, and Hugo Black.[1] Frankfurter insisted that the lesson to be gleaned from the New Deal conflict is that unchecked judicial power is incompatible with democratic governance, and hence that the unelected Court must exercise an extreme form of deference to legislative decisions. Black and Stone agreed that the Court should ordinarily defer to the democratic will on issues of economic regulation, but they each sought to identify a particularly important set of constitutional rights and liberties that the Court should actively protect against infringement by democratic majorities. In this regard, Black emphasized the importance of enforcing the specific provisions of the original Bill of Rights, while Stone sought to protect those "preferred freedoms" (such as the freedom of speech) that are essential to the democratic political process, and to ensure equal treatment for those groups (such as racial minorities) who are likely to be mistreated by elected political institutions. The judicial opinions during the late 1930s and 1940s of Frankfurter, Black, and Stone shaped constitutional debate for the generation that followed, laying key foundations for both modern liberal and conservative constitutionalism.

In short, during the immediate post–New Deal period, the justices faced a key choice point, with a number of alternative visions of the judicial role available to them. The establishment of modern rights-based constitutionalism was far from inevitable, and the Court's choices at this critical juncture would have far-reaching consequences. Students of political development have often noted that particular decisions at crucial moments can have lasting effects, both intended and unintended. As Paul Pierson and Theda Skocpol have described this process, "[o]utcomes at a critical juncture [can] trigger feedback mechanisms that reinforce the recurrence of a particular pattern into the future. . . . Political alternatives that were once quite plausible may become irretrievably lost. Thus, events or processes occurring during and immediately following critical junctures emerge as crucial" (2002:699– 700). Like all political evolution, constitutional development is a "path dependent" historical process; the particular sequence by which competing norms become entrenched within constitutional discourse has a substantial effect on subsequent events. Once we recognize, with Pierson, that "today's policymakers operate in an environment fundamentally shaped by policies inherited from the past," it becomes clear that ongoing lines of development are sometimes difficult to reverse (1996a:179, 175; see also 2000a). To understand political order and change, then, it is often necessary to trace the longterm interaction between slow, secular trends, such as the growth of the modern state, and more rapid and cyclical developments, such as the rise and fall of partisan regimes (Skowronek 1993).

In the constitutional context, it is difficult to specify precisely the significance of entrenched traditions because the justices have a substantial degree of freedom to pick up on one or another such "path" in a variety of contexts. Nonetheless, it is clear that particular jurisprudential traditions at particular historical moments become entrenched in ways that render them resistant to change. Moreover, the particular paths that unfold may change the legal and political terrain in such a way as to alter the preferences of individual legal interpreters. In this light, the key persistent trend in modern constitutional development has been the steady entrenchment of rights-based constitutionalism and the corresponding expansion of judicial power.

The notion of judicially enforceable liberty is not, of course, new; the American Bill of Rights is over two hundred years old and was itself built upon deep foundations in Anglo-American law. Nonetheless, our contemporary conception of individual liberty and minority rights, enforceable by the unelected judiciary against the wishes of democratic majorities, is in large part a modern development. In the shadow of the New Deal and World War II, the Court, led by Justice Stone in particular, began to articulate judicially enforceable guarantees of free expression, religious freedom, racial equality, and the like. As Gillman has observed, "[h]aving abdicated the responsibility of determining whether legislation was rationally related to a legitimate public purpose, judges created for themselves a new role in the political system, one that involved identifying those 'preferred freedoms' or 'suspect classifications' that might provide a basis for trumping the otherwise unrestrained power of the modern legislature" (1993:202–3). During this period, Stone and his fellow justices developed innovative conceptions of fundamental rights in an effort to preserve the Constitution's balance between individual liberty and democratic government.

The New Deal Conflict and the Abandonment of Original Foundations

Again, however, this rights-based vision did not fully develop until the Warren Court years. When FDR was struggling with the conservative Court over the constitutionality of New Deal legislation, he demanded that the justices defer to the will of the elected institutions. When he proposed his Court-packing plan in 1937, for example, he complained that "[w]hen the Congress has sought to stabilize national agriculture, to improve the conditions of labor, to safeguard business against unfair competition, to protect our national resources, and in many other ways to serve our clearly national needs, the majority of the Court has been assuming the power to pass on the wisdom of these acts of the Congress — and to approve or disapprove the public policy written into these laws." FDR argued that the Court had "improperly set itself up as a third House of the Congress — a super-legislature, as one of the justices has called it — reading into the Constitution words and implications which are not there, and which were never intended to be there."[2] Though Roosevelt lost the Court-packing battle in 1937 — his own Democratic allies in Congress rejected his proposal to expand the size of the Court — he won the larger war. Having served a full term already with no opportunity for a Supreme Court appointment, he appointed eight new justices over the next seven years, justices who were fully expected to exercise their power more sparingly.

FDR's call for judicial restraint had been supported by Justices Oliver Wendell Holmes and Louis Brandeis on the Court, and also by Professor Frankfurter at Harvard Law School, each of whom argued that changing social facts require changing laws and that the Constitution should not be construed to stand in the way of such change. In this sense, FDR and his supporters were calling for the abandonment of original constitutional foundations to allow a much greater degree of judicial deference to the democratic will.

For Holmes, the Court's stubborn enforcement of long-standing constitutional principles of limited government represented a vain and illegitimate effort to thwart the will of current majorities. In his famous dissent in *Lochner v. New York,* for example, he chastised the Court for deciding the case "upon an economic theory which a large part of the country does not entertain." He also insisted that "the word liberty in the Fourteenth Amendment is perverted when it is held to prevent the natural outcome of a dominant opinion, unless it can be said that a rational and fair man necessarily would admit that the statute proposed would infringe fundamental principles as they have been understood by the traditions of our people and our law."[3] Dissenting from a decision extending *Lochner* eighteen years later, Holmes insisted that "[t]he criterion of constitutionality is not whether we believe the law to be for the public good. We certainly cannot be prepared to deny that a reasonable man reasonably might have that belief in view of the legislation of Great Britain, Victoria and a number of the States of this Union," all of which had minimum wage statutes similar to the one at issue in this case.[4] Seven years after that, dissenting in *Baldwin v. Missouri*, he expressed his "anxiety . . . at the ever increasing scope given to the Fourteenth Amendment in cutting down what I believe to be the constitutional rights of the States." In light of the Court's recent decisions, he saw "hardly any limit but the sky to the invalidating of those rights if they happen to strike a majority of this Court as for any reason undesirable. I cannot believe that the Amendment was intended to give us carte blanche to embody our economic or moral beliefs in its prohibitions."[5] In these widely influential dissenting opinions, Holmes elaborated on the views of Harvard's James Bradley Thayer, articulating what would become the modern doctrine of judicial restraint, rooted in a majoritarian conception of American democracy that he carried so far as to threaten an abandonment of constitutionalism itself (Thayer 1893).

Because this approach represented a significant departure from long-standing constitutional traditions, Holmes sought to justify it by reference to a "living," or evolutionary, conception of constitutionalism. In *Missouri v. Holland*, for example, writing for the Court in upholding an early congressional conservation law against a federalism-based challenge, he noted that "[w]hen we are dealing with words that are a constituent act, like the Constitution of the United States, we must realize that they have called into life a being the development of which could not have been foreseen completely by the most gifted of its begetters. . . . The case before us must be considered in the light of our whole experience and not merely in that of what was said a hundred years ago."[6] Six years earlier, he had observed that "the provisions of the Constitution are not mathematical formulas having their essence in their form; they are organic, living institutions transplanted from English soil. Their significance is vital, not formal; it is to be gathered not simply by taking the words and a dictionary, but by considering their origin and the line of their growth."[7] Holmes's early-twentieth-century opinions influenced an entire generation of legal scholars, including the founders of the "legal realist" movement, who argued that legal rules were indeterminate, that judicial discretion was vast, and that judicial decisions could be explained almost wholly by the particular preferences and prejudices of individual judges.

Holmes retired in 1932, but as the Court came into increasing conflict with the elected branches during the 1930s, Justices Brandeis, Hughes, Cardozo, and Stone continued to advocate his vision of judicial restraint. Concurring in *Ashwander v. TVA*, for example, Brandeis articulated what Alexander

Bickel would later call the "passive virtues," insisting that the Court should avoid constitutional decisions whenever possible. Because the exercise of judicial review was presumptively illegitimate, Brandeis insisted that "[w]hen the validity of an act of the Congress is drawn in question, and even if a serious doubt of constitutionality is raised, it is a cardinal principle that this Court will first ascertain whether a construction of the statute is fairly possible by which the question may be avoided." When no such statutory construction is possible, the Court should still avoid the issue on jurisdictional or justiciability grounds if it can. In other words, Brandeis insisted, the Court should only confront a substantive constitutional question when it is forced to do so, and even then, it should issue as narrow a rule as possible.[8] Brandeis did not invent these "passive virtues" — as Mark Graber (1995) has noted, such judicial strategies date to the Marshall Court — but he and his colleagues during the 1930s defended them more forthrightly than anyone before. Just a month before the *Ashwander* decision, Stone had dissented from the Court's decision invalidating FDR's 1933 Agricultural Adjustment Act, observing that "while unconstitutional exercise of power by the executive and legislative branches of the government is subject to judicial restraint, the only check upon our own exercise of power is our own sense of self-restraint. For the removal of unwise laws from the statute books appeal lies not to the courts but to the ballot and to the processes of democratic government."[9]

Off the Court, the most influential advocate of this vision of restrained judicial power was Professor Frankfurter. Throughout the *Lochner* era and the early New Deal period, in his public writings and private letters, Frankfurter advocated the doctrine of judicial restraint, denounced the Court for thwarting the majority will, and went so far as to endorse the constitutional repeal of the Due Process Clauses of the Fifth and Fourteenth Amendments (Gunther 1994:375–78). As Mark Silverstein has noted, "[w]ith Justices Holmes and Brandeis providing leadership from the high court and academics like Frankfurter training a new generation of lawyers, judicial restraint coupled with strict application of the rules of justiciability emerged as the defining characteristic of judicial liberalism and progressive politics on the eve of the New Deal" (1994:45). The Court adopted the Holmesian approach in *West Coast Hotel v. Parrish*, making its famous "switch in time that saved nine" — so named because the Court saved itself from political reprisal by abandoning a series of unpopular doctrines.

In response to this switch, the Court's conservatives continued to defend their active enforcement of constitutional limits on legislative power, and they did so on what we would now call "originalist" grounds. In *West Coast Hotel,* for example, Justice Sutherland insisted in dissent that "[t]he suggestion that the only check upon the exercise of the judicial power . . . is the judge's own faculty of self-restraint, is both ill considered and mischievous. Self-restraint belongs in the domain of will and not of judgment. The check upon the judge is that imposed by his oath of office, by the Constitution and by his own conscientious and informed convictions." Sutherland insisted that the courts must enforce the limits imposed by the Constitution and that they cannot legitimately adopt a more restrained approach simply because those limits appear to be outmoded. In his view, "the meaning of the Constitution does not change with the ebb and flow of economic events. . . . [T]o say . . . that the words of the Constitution mean today what they did not mean when written — that is, that they do not apply to a situation now to which they would have applied then — is to rob that instrument of the essential element which continues it in force as the people have made it until they, and not their official agents, have made it otherwise." [10]

Similarly, when the Court rejected a Contract Clause challenge to a Minnesota mortgage moratorium statute designed to provide debt relief to impoverished farmers, Sutherland noted in dissent that "it is hardly necessary to say" that a "provision of the Constitution . . . does not mean one thing at one time and an entirely different thing at another time." Insisting that the meaning of a constitutional provision is "changeless," he observed that "[c]onstitutional grants of power and restrictions upon the exercise of power are not flexible as the doctrines of the common law are flexible. . . . The whole aim of construction, as applied to a provision of the Constitution, is to discover the meaning, to ascertain and give effect to the intent, of its framers and the people who adopted it." As far as the framers were concerned, the redistribution of property to benefit a particular class was not a legitimate end of the state, and for Sutherland, the courts were not at liberty to change that view. [11] As Gillman has observed, "[f]or these justices, the evolving Constitution amounted to little more than the vanishing Constitution, for if the Constitution did not stand against debtor relief then it did not stand against anything" (1997:225).

The terms of this debate have sometimes been obscured for modern readers because, as Gillman notes, the Court "abandon[ed] the inherited tradition [but] suffered a failure of nerve in the form of an unwillingness to make a case for the irrelevance or impracticality of originalist constitutionalism" (1997:238). Similarly, Morton Horwitz observes that while the claim was doubtful, the victorious New Deal coalition successfully "portray[ed] its triumph not as constitutional revolution, but as constitutional restoration" (1993:56–57). The Court came closest to acknowledging its willingness to ignore the original meaning of the Constitution in the mortgage moratorium case, *Home Building and Loan Association v. Blaisdell,* but stopped short even there. Writing for a bare majority, Chief Justice Hughes responded to Sutherland by going a long way toward acknowledging that the Constitution must evolve over time, and that the Court might sometimes be justified in abandoning outmoded constitutional limits. In support of this approach, he cited the Holmes passage from *Missouri v. Holland* quoted above, and also Chief Justice Marshall's famous statements that "[w]e must never forget that it is a constitution we are expounding" and that it is a "constitution intended to endure for ages to come, and consequently, to be adapted to the various crises of human affairs." [12] Though the *Blaisdell* opinion is one of the Court's most candid statements that it need not abide by the framers' specific intentions, Hughes failed to explicitly address the problematic legitimacy of judicially crafted constitutional change.

In sum, while the Court never fully acknowledged the fact, it enacted a constitutional revolution in 1937.[13] As Sutherland's dissenting opinions make clear, the Court abandoned its enforcement of long-standing constitutional limits on legislative power, limits rooted in fundamental principles of limited government and private property rights. In place of these limits, many New Deal constitutionalists offered the Holmesian doctrine of majoritarian democracy and judicial self-restraint. As Stephen Griffin observes, "[t]he New Deal experience appeared to show the folly of the Court trying to stand against the considered judgment of a massive and persistent electoral majority and the wisdom of judicial self-restraint. This was the lesson Justice Felix Frankfurter, his clerk Bickel, and subsequent generations of constitutional scholars drew from the New Deal" (1996:106).

Stone, Frankfurter, and the Limits of Restraint

After the New Deal "switch in time," Roosevelt sought to consolidate the new constitutional order by making a series of what Bruce Ackerman (1998) has called "transformative judicial appointments." Of these, Frankfurter is the model example. Appointed for his intellectual ability and his firm support of New Deal constitutionalism, rather than the more narrowly political criteria that often influence such decisions, he immediately set out to embed his restrained vision of judicial power into the law. Though adhering consistently to his long-standing view, Frankfurter moderated his proposed remedies. Rather than seeking the repeal of the Fourteenth Amendment, something he had suggested as a law professor, he settled on the effort to develop a jurisprudence of self-restraint that, now on the Court himself, he was best in a position to implement.[14] In almost every area of constitutional law, Frankfurter followed Thayer's "doctrine of the clear mistake" — which held that the Court should strike down only those laws that unambiguously violated the Constitution on any reasonable interpretation — and he regularly encouraged his judicial colleagues to read the influential 1893 article in which Thayer had articulated this doctrine (Hirsch 1981).[15] As Frankfurter and the other New Deal appointees took their seats, it appeared that they would quickly usher in a philosophy of broad judicial deference to the national welfare-regulatory state.

For example, the Court made a series of rapid changes in its approach to the Constitution's federalism-based limits on congressional power. In 1935 and 1936, the Court had repeatedly struck down New Deal statutes on the grounds that they exceeded Congress's enumerated powers under the original Constitution. In *Carter v. Carter Coal*, the Court struck down the 1935 Bituminous Coal Conservation Act, with Sutherland conceding that stabilizing the coal industry was an "object[ ] of great worth," but insisting that "the attainment of [such an end] has [not] been committed by the Constitution to the federal government." Sutherland emphatically rejected "[t]he proposition . . . that the power of the federal government inherently extends to purposes affecting the nation as a whole with which the states severally cannot deal or cannot adequately deal, and the related notion that Congress, entirely apart from those powers delegated by the Constitution, may enact laws to promote the general welfare."[16] FDR and his supporters made clear that these constitutional limits were preventing the federal government from responding to pressing national needs, and the Court eventually acquiesced. Shortly after its "switch in time" in *West Coast Hotel*, and by the same 5-4 vote, the Court upheld the National Labor Relations Act against a federalism-based constitutional challenge. Abandoning a longtime constitutional distinction between local manufacturing and interstate commerce, Chief Justice Hughes held that Congress could regulate the Jones and Laughlin Steel Corporation's manufacturing operations because they bore "a close and substantial relation to interstate commerce."[17] Once FDR's appointees took over the Court, they pushed these changes even further. In *United States v. Darby*, the

Court unanimously upheld the 1938 Fair Labor Standards Act, which imposed nationwide regulation of wages and hours, and in *Wickard v. Filburn,* the Court upheld the secretary of agriculture's imposition of quotas for wheat production, even as applied to a small farmer who grew wheat for home consumption.

FDR had remade the Court, and its deference to the economic policies of the modern welfare-regulatory state was now virtually complete. And for Frankfurter at least, this deference should apply even in the face of denials of civil liberties. His opinion for the Court in *Minersville School District v. Gobitis,* in particular, revealed that his own long-standing civil libertarianism would not translate into judicial activism. Just over a year after joining the Court, Frankfurter held that the compulsory recitation of the Pledge of Allegiance in public schools was constitutionally legitimate, observing that "[e]xcept where the transgression of constitutional liberty is too plain for argument, personal freedom is best maintained — so long as the remedial channels of the democratic process remain open and unobstructed — when it is ingrained in a people's habits and not enforced against popular policy by the coercion of adjudicated law."[18] Only Justice Stone dissented from this opinion, and Frankfurter tried to persuade him to make the judgment unanimous:

> For resolving such [a] clash [of rights] we have no calculus. But there is for me, and I know also for you, a great make-weight for dealing with this problem, namely, that we are not the primary resolvers of the clash. We are not exercising an independent judgment; we are sitting in judgment upon the judgment of the legislature. . . .
>
> What weighs with me strongly in this case is my anxiety that . . . we do not exercise our judicial power unduly, and as though we ourselves were legislators by holding too tight a rein on the organs of popular government. In other words, I want to avoid the mistake comparable to that made by those who we criticized when dealing with the control of property.

Stone held firm, publishing his dissent and reading it aloud from the bench.[19]

With the constitutional ground unsettled, and the future role of the Court undecided, Stone and some of his colleagues recognized that Frankfurter's approach threatened to abandon the notion of constitutional limits on government power. They therefore sought to construct a somewhat different vision of the new constitutional order. In *DeJonge v. Oregon,* for example, the Court unanimously struck down Oregon's Criminal Syndicalism Law, throwing out Dirk DeJonge's conviction (and seven-year prison term) for speaking at a Communist Party meeting. Citing a number of pre–New Deal decisions in which Holmes and Brandeis had begun to suggest the preferred position of the freedom of speech, Chief Justice Hughes held that "[t]he greater the importance of safeguarding the community from incitements of our institutions by force and violence, the more imperative is the need to preserve inviolate the constitutional rights of free speech, free press and free assembly in order to maintain the opportunity for free political discussion, to the end that government may be responsive to the will of the people and that changes, if desired, may be obtained by peaceful means. Therein lies the security of the Republic, the very foundation of constitutional government." While the First Amendment protects the freedom of speech (and the associated right to assemble peaceably) only against infringement by the federal government, the Court held that these same rights were included within the constitutional "liberty" that the Fourteenth Amendment protects against violation by the states. Hughes reached this conclusion because these rights "cannot be denied without violating those fundamental principles of liberty and justice which lie at the base of all civil and political institutions." [20]

During the Supreme Court term that followed, while upholding a murder conviction and death sentence for a man who had been tried twice for the same offense, Justice Cardozo rejected the argument that the Fourteenth Amendment made all of the specific provisions of the original Bill of Rights applicable against the states, choosing instead to expand on Hughes's suggestion that it protects only those liberties that are particularly fundamental. Writing for the Court in *Palko v. Connecticut,* Cardozo recognized that identifying such liberties would require significant judgment, and he offered several abstract formulations designed to guide that judgment. He asked whether the particular rights at issue were "of the very essence of a scheme of ordered liberty," such that "neither liberty nor Justice would exist if they were sacrificed"; whether their deprivation would amount to "a hardship so acute and shocking that our polity will not endure it"; and whether the rights could be found amidst those "'principle[s] of justice so rooted in the traditions and conscience of our people as to be ranked as fundamental.'" The liberties contained in the First Amendment, for example, have been "brought within the Fourteenth Amendment by a process of absorption" — and hence protected against infringement by the states — because the freedom of speech and thought represent "the matrix, the indispensable condition, of nearly every other form of freedom."[21]

During this same period, the Court began to give life to the principle of constitutional equality as well. In *Missouri ex rel. Gaines v. Canada,* for example, the NAACP won its first victory in the Supreme Court when Hughes held that Missouri's provision of a public law school for whites but none for African Americans was an obvious failure to provide "separate but equal" facilities, and hence a violation of the Equal Protection Clause. In *Edwards v. California,* the Court struck down a California statute prohibiting persons from knowingly bringing indigents into the state, observing that while this type of law may "enjoy[ ] a firm basis in English and American history," "the theory of the Elizabethan poor laws no longer fits the facts."[22] The following year, in *Skinner v. Oklahoma,* the Court struck down a state statute providing for the involuntary sterilization of "habitual criminals" but exempting certain white-collar crimes. Writing for the Court, Justice William O. Douglas coined the term "strict scrutiny," holding that such "scrutiny of the classification which a State makes in a sterilization law is essential, lest unwittingly, or otherwise, invidious discriminations are made against groups or types of individuals in violation of the constitutional guarantee of just and equal laws."[23] Two years later, the Court coined a second key term in modern equal protection doctrine, when Justice Black held that "all legal restrictions which curtail the civil rights of a single racial group are immediately suspect." As with Cardozo's description of constitutional liberty in *Palko,* this statement came in the context of the Court's rejection of a fairly substantial claim of constitutional right — here, the equal protection challenge to the wartime internment of Japanese Americans in *Korematsu v. United States.*[24] Still, while judicial deference remained for the time being the general rule, it was increasingly clear that where either a "preferred freedom" or a "suspect classification" was involved, the Court might be willing to apply a higher level of judicial scrutiny.

It was Justice Stone who provided the most influential, albeit tentative, suggestions about both what this new judicial role might look like and why it should be considered legitimate. Though he had advocated judicial self-restraint in cases like *Butler,* Stone now recognized the need for new constitutional foundations to support the judicial protection of individual liberty and minority rights against an increasingly powerful modern state.[25] He wrote separately in *Skinner,* for example, to emphasize that "[t]here are limits to the extent to which the presumption of constitutionality can be pressed, especially where the liberty of the person is concerned." [26] He supported this claim with a citation to a footnote he had written four years earlier, a footnote that has since exerted a wide influence on constitutional development.

Writing for the Court in *United States v. Carolene Products,* Stone had upheld a 1923 public health law that prohibited companies from diluting milk products with other compounds. In doing so, he observed that the Court would afford extraordinary deference to legislative judgments with respect to most matters of economic regulation, but in a three-paragraph footnote, he suggested several circumstances in which this presumption of constitutionality might not apply.[27] Each of these suggestions was tentative: First, "[t]here may be narrower scope for operation of the presumption of constitutionality when legislation appears on its face to be within a specific prohibition of the Constitution, such as those of the first ten amendments." Second, "[i]t is unnecessary to consider now whether legislation which restricts those political processes which can ordinarily be expected to bring about repeal of undesirable legislation" — such as a restriction on the right to vote or on political speech — "is to be subjected to more exacting judicial scrutiny." [28] And third, the Court need not now "enquire whether similar considerations enter into the review of statutes directed at particular religious, or national, or racial minorities: whether prejudice against discrete and insular minorities may be a special condition, which tends seriously to curtail the operation of those political processes ordinarily to be relied upon to protect minorities, and which may call for a correspondingly more searching judicial inquiry." [29]

Stone's footnote has come to stand for two crucial propositions in modern constitutional law, each of which influenced the Warren Court's rights revolution. First, the *Carolene Products* approach directs the Court to single out for heightened judicial scrutiny those particular preferred freedoms or fundamental rights that are essential either to the democratic process or to individual human dignity. And second, it directs the Court to single out those minority groups who are in need of judicial protection from majoritarian political processes and to consider legislative classifications that disadvantage these groups to be similarly suspect.

Two years after *Carolene Products,* Stone built on these propositions in his masterful opinion in *Gobitis.* Dissenting alone, and rejecting Frankfurter's entreaties to join the rest of the Court, Stone cited his earlier footnote and observed that most "infringements of personal liberty by the state" have been directed at "politically helpless minorities." Frankfurter made a nod to Stone's approach by suggesting that "the remedial channels of the democratic process [must] remain open and unobstructed," but this requirement of formal access was inadequate for Stone, who replied by emphasizing the risk of "surrender[ing] . . . the constitutional protection of the liberty of small minorities to the popular will." The plaintiffs in *Gobitis* were Jehovah's Witnesses who refused to salute the flag on the grounds of religious freedom and who faced widespread intolerance, discrimination, and even violence as a result. In this context, Stone elaborated his view that "[t]he Constitution expresses more than the conviction of the people that democratic processes must be preserved at all costs. It is also an expression of faith and a command that freedom of mind and spirit must be preserved, which government must obey, if it is to adhere to that justice and moderation without which no free government can exist."[30]

Within three years, Stone had persuaded a majority of his colleagues. Writing for the Court in *West Virginia v. Barnette,* Justice Robert Jackson overturned *Gobitis,* observing that "[t]he very purpose of a Bill of Rights was to withdraw certain subjects from the vicissitudes of political controversy, to place them beyond the reach of majorities. . . . One's right to life, liberty and property, to free speech, a free press, freedom of worship and assembly, and other fundamental rights may not be submitted to vote; they depend on the outcome of no elections."[31] This dramatic change did not occur simply because of the intellectual power of Stone's arguments. The *Gobitis* decision had been sharply criticized in the press, in large part because of the widespread mob violence directed against Jehovah's Witnesses and, more generally, the dawning awareness in 1943 of the dangers of racial and religious hatred (Peters 2000; Simon 1989:113–16). Following Stone, Jackson recognized that the judicial protection of certain fundamental liberties and minority rights may well be necessary if the democratic process is to have any meaning. The issue in *Gobitis* and *Barnette,* after all, was an effort by the public schools to enforce national unity, and Jackson pointed to the "[u]ltimate futility of such attempts . . . from the Roman drive to stamp out Christianity . . . , [to] the Inquisition, . . . down to the fast failing efforts of our present totalitarian enemies."[32] For the justices, as for the rest of the world, 1943 was a markedly different time from 1940, and the need to defend individual liberty and minority rights was becoming increasingly clear. The important point, however, is that unlike Frankfurter, most of the justices were willing to take on such a role, and their written opinions from this period laid key foundations that shaped the development of that role for decades to come.

For Frankfurter, this willingness was a crucial mistake, yet another example of the Court's unaccountable justices aggrandizing power to themselves. His default rule was judicial deference, and in sharp contrast to Stone, he was determined to adhere to this rule even when it meant sacrificing important constitutional rights. Even when the remedial channels of the democratic process were obstructed, Frankfurter was convinced that the costs of judicial activism generally outweighed its benefits. A few years after *Barnette*, he wrote for a three-justice plurality in *Colegrove v. Green*, rejecting a constitutional challenge to a substantially unequal pattern of legislative apportionment because it raised a nonjusticiable political question. Noting that "[t]he one stark fact that emerges from a study of the history of Congressional apportionment is its embroilment in politics, in the sense of party contests and party interests," Frankfurter held that "the Constitution has conferred upon Congress exclusive authority to secure representation by the States in the popular House and left to that House determination whether States have fulfilled their responsibility. If Congress failed in exercising its powers, whereby standards of fairness are offended, the remedy ultimately lies with the people." Some of his colleagues were beginning to wonder how the people could appeal to their elected representatives themselves for a remedy to the problem of inadequate representation, but Frankfurter was firmly convinced that "[c]ourts ought not to enter this political thicket."[33]

Similarly, in *Barnette*, Frankfurter's colleagues were concerned that judicial deference was inappropriate because they were dealing with discrimination against an unpopular minority and the denial of a particularly important "preferred freedom," but from his perspective, they were simply "writing [their own] private notions of policy into the Constitution." For Frankfurter, judicial restraint was "equally necessary whenever an exercise of political or legislative power is challenged. . . . In no instance is this Court the primary protector of [constitutional] liberty."[34] The flag salute cases, raising fundamental issues of patriotism and dissent during the height of World War II, crystallized the justices' debates over their proper role in a constitutional democracy. Frankfurter had gotten further than any of his colleagues in elaborating an account of that role that was consistent with the spirit of the New Deal, but Stone was already making clear that other options were on the table.

Black, Frankfurter, and the Original Bill of Rights

Stone's alternative, moreover, was not the only one that Frankfurter was forced to combat during this period. Justice Black shared Stone's suspicion of Frankfurter's near-abandonment of judicially enforceable constitutional liberty, but he also shared Frankfurter's suspicion of unconstrained judicial power. Hoping to reconcile these concerns, Black turned to a strict reading of the constitutional text in an effort to cabin judicial discretion while still preserving a robust conception of constitutional rights. While he had joined Frankfurter's opinion in *Gobitis*, for example, he almost immediately had second thoughts, telling Justice Douglas less than three months later that he had reconsidered (Hirsch 1981:152). He first had a chance to make this reconsideration public in *Jones v. Opelika*, another case involving Jehovah's Witnesses, in which Stone was now joined by Black, Douglas, and Frank Murphy in dissent. It was in this case that Stone coined the term "preferred position" to describe the constitutional status of the freedoms of speech and religion, and the other three dissenters wrote separately to note that they now thought *Gobitis* had been "wrongly decided." In their newly developing view, "our democratic form of government, functioning under the historic Bill of Rights, has a high responsibility to accommodate itself to the religious views of minorities, however unpopular and unorthodox those views may be." Concurring in *Barnette*, Black again emphasized the importance of the First Amendment freedom of religion.[35]

It was with regard to another First Amendment guarantee, however, that Black would make his name, as he would soon come to be known as the Court's most active defender of the freedom of speech. In the 1940s, he had not yet developed his theory of free speech "absolutism," but it was already clear that he valued this first freedom quite highly. In *Bridges v. California*, for example, a case pitting the constitutional values of free speech and fair trial against one another, Frankfurter initially appeared to have the support of six justices for his opinion weighing the balance in favor of fair trial. During the course of the Court's deliberations, however, McReynolds and Hughes retired, and Murphy changed his vote. After reargument the following term, Jackson (one of the two new justices) sided with Black, giving him a majority for his holding that labor leader Harry Bridges could not constitutionally be held in contempt for publicly criticizing a trial court about a pending case. In support of this holding, Black noted that "[n]o purpose in ratifying the Bill of Rights was clearer than that of securing for the people of the United States much greater freedom of religion, expression, assembly, and petition than the people of Great Britain had ever enjoyed." [36]

Black and Frankfurter would continue this First Amendment debate in the years to come, but their principal conflict during the 1940s centered on whether the Court should apply the original Bill of Rights to the states. Those fundamental rights guarantees had originally been designed as limits on the federal government, but as Black observed in 1940, there had long been "a current of opinion — which this court has declined to adopt in many previous cases — that the Fourteenth Amendment was intended to make secure against state invasion all the rights, privileges and immunities protected from federal violation by the Bill of Rights." [37] Over the next several years, Justice Black became the leading advocate of this theory that the Court should read the abstract provisions of the Fourteenth Amendment as having "incorporated" the specific provisions of the first eight amendments and thus applied them to the states. He adopted this approach because he viewed the chief alternative — Cardozo's and Frankfurter's open-ended interpretation of the abstract provisions themselves — as an invitation to unrestrained judicial lawmaking. Rather than attempting to figure out whether state criminal proceedings had met some vague standard of "fundamental fairness," Black asked whether they had met all the specific guarantees of the Bill of Rights. In *Betts v. Brady*, for example, he urged the Court to hold that the Due Process Clause incorporated the Sixth Amendment right to counsel, and in *Adamson v. California*, he made the same argument with respect to the Fifth Amendment privilege against self-incrimination. But all of these arguments were in dissent, as the Court repeatedly held that only "such provisions of the Bill of Rights as were 'implicit in the concept of ordered liberty' became secure from state interference by the [due process] clause." [38]

In defending his theory of incorporation, Black undertook the modern Court's first extensive excavation of the original understanding of the Fourteenth Amendment, urging the justices to place themselves "as nearly as possible in the condition of the men who framed that instrument." He did so in an effort to expand the Court's protection of constitutional liberty, but the style of argument he developed would influence conservative critiques of such liberal activism for many decades to come. After all, the key features of what would come to be called "constitutional originalism" were both present in Black's opinions from this period: (1) the insistence that in the absence of an explicit textual command, the Court has no legitimate authority to thwart the popular will; and (2) the effort to decipher such textual commands by reference to their historical origins. In a twenty-five-page dissenting opinion in *Adamson,* followed by a thirty-one-page historical appendix on the drafting and adoption of the Fourteenth Amendment, which he had spent the previous summer studying in preparation, Black argued that "the language of [that] Amendment . . . was thought by those responsible for its submission to the people, and by those who opposed its submission, sufficiently explicit to guarantee that thereafter no state could deprive its citizens of the privileges and protections of the Bill of Rights."[39]

The Court had abandoned this original understanding, Black insisted, in an effort to expand its own power. Rather than reading §1 of the Fourteenth Amendment in terms of the original Bill of Rights, the Court was instead acting as if it were "endowed by the Constitution with boundless power under 'natural law' periodically to expand and contract constitutional standards to conform to the Court's conception of what at a particular time constitutes 'civilized decency' and 'fundamental liberty and justice.'" He acknowledged that the exercise of judicial review requires a process of interpretation, but insisted that

> to pass upon the constitutionality of statutes by looking to the particular standards enumerated in the Bill of Rights and other parts of the Constitution is one thing; to invalidate statutes because of application of "natural law" deemed to be above and undefined by the Constitution is another. In the one instance, courts proceeding within clearly marked constitutional boundaries seek to execute policies written into the Constitution; in the other, they roam at will in the limitless area of their own beliefs as to reasonableness and actually select policies, a responsibility which the Constitution entrusts to the legislative representatives of the people.

Black concluded that "the 'natural law' formula which the Court uses to reach its conclusion in this case should be abandoned as an incongruous excrescence on our Constitution."[40]

Frankfurter responded by arguing that Black's approach would lead to excessive judicial interference with the operation of state criminal law, and he reiterated the Court's duty to exercise its power with self-restraint. For Frankfurter, moreover, Black's literalist approach represented a naive attempt to avoid the unavoidable exercise of judgment that lies at the heart of constitutional adjudication. Frankfurter had made these arguments before, but he developed them most fully in his lengthy concurring opinion in *Adamson.*[41] He complained that Black was "disregard[ing] the historic meaning of 'due process,'" which had always imposed an independent limit on state criminal proceedings. Frankfurter's abstract requirement of decency, fairness, and justice would be broader than the specific guarantees of the Bill of Rights in some instances, but narrower in others. Following Cardozo, he fully acknowledged the need for judgment in interpreting such limits, but he insisted that it would not be judgment without guides: "These standards of justice are not authoritatively formulated anywhere as though they were prescriptions in a pharmacopoeia. But 'neither does the application of the Due Process Clause imply that judges are wholly at large. The judicial judgment in applying the Due Process Clause must move within the limits of accepted notions of justice and is not to be based upon the idiosyncracies of a merely personal judgment." In Frankfurter's view, Black's effort to avoid judicial discretion altogether would only "lead[ ] . . . to a warped construction of specific provisions of the Bill of Rights to bring within their scope conduct clearly condemned by due process but not easily fitting into the pigeon-holes of the specific provisions."[42]

Frankfurter also took up the historical debate that Black had opened, noting that the "[r]emarks of a particular proponent of the Amendment, no matter how influential, are not to be deemed part of the Amendment. What was submitted for ratification was his proposal, not his speech." If the framers of the Fourteenth Amendment were attempting to provide "that every State must thereafter initiate prosecutions through indictment by a grand jury, must have a trial by a jury of twelve in criminal cases, and must have trial by such a jury in common law suits where the amount in controversy exceeds twenty dollars," he insisted, then the language which they adopted in the due process clause was "a strange way of saying it. It would be extraordinarily strange for a Constitution to convey such specific commands in such a roundabout and inexplicit way." Noting that almost half of the States in 1868 did not adhere to the Fifth Amendment's grand jury requirement, he found it implausible "that by ratifying the Amendment they [had] uprooted their established methods for prosecuting crime and fastened upon themselves a new prosecutorial system."[43] Frankfurter posed the historical question in a way that is now familiar on the Court: To what extent can a particular modern rights claim — say, the right to serve on a jury, or to desegregated schools, or to choose to have an abortion — fairly be found within the scope of Fourteenth Amendment liberty and equality as understood in 1868?

Black opened this debate in *Adamson*. Frankfurter responded in that very case, and constitutional scholar Charles Fairman supported Frankfurter two years later in a widely influential article in the *Stanford Law Review*. After an extended review of the same historical record, Fairman concluded that Black's reading was wholly without merit. He elaborated on Frankfurter's argument by documenting that many of the states that ratified the Fourteenth Amendment had statutes on the books in 1868 that were inconsistent with one or more provisions of the Bill of Rights. The fact that these state legislatures ratified the amendment without any discussion of, say, their laws allowing criminal indictments without a grand jury, and that they continued enforcing such laws after 1868, was, for Fairman, conclusive evidence of the text's original meaning. Still further evidence was the fact that the very Congress that drafted and proposed the amendment also formally accepted a number of new state constitutions that were inconsistent with the Bill of Rights (1949:84–132).

Fairman's lengthy attack on Black's incorporation argument quickly became the dominant view among constitutional scholars, holding that place at least until the publication of revisionist accounts by Michael Kent Curtis (1986) and Akhil Reed Amar (1998) in the 1980s and 1990s.[44] Fairman's work also influenced similar historical debates beyond the incorporation issue. Like Alexander Bickel in the 1950s, and Raoul Berger in the 1960s and 1970s, Fairman sought to intervene in an ongoing constitutional debate by means of a detailed account of Reconstruction history. His 135-page article was devoted almost entirely to the historical undertaking, but he concluded by arguing that "the record of history is overwhelmingly against" Justice Black and that Cardozo's "ordered liberty" formulation "comes as close as one can to catching the vague aspirations that were hung upon the privileges and immunities clause" (1949:139).[45] As Pamela Brandwein (1999) has shown, William Crosskey's contemporary response to Fairman provided extensive historical evidence that the Reconstruction Republicans did indeed intend to incorporate the original Bill of Rights, but Crosskey's argument was largely rejected at the time (Crosskey 1954). Due in large part to Frankfurter's efforts, Fairman's account became institutionalized on the Court and served as an important resource for critics of Warren Court activism.

Black disagreed with Fairman and Frankfurter on the history, but even more importantly, he read their flexible and restrained approach as an abandonment of the very purpose of a written Constitution. Noting that the provisions of the Bill of Rights "may be thought outdated abstractions by some," and that "they were [indeed] designed to meet ancient evils," Black emphasized that the same kind of human evils . . . have emerged from century to century wherever excessive power is sought by the few at the expense of the many. In my judgment the people of no nation can lose their liberty so long as a Bill of Rights like ours survives and its basic purposes are conscientiously interpreted, enforced and respected so as to afford continuous protection against old, as well as new, devices and practices which might thwart those purposes. I fear to see the consequences of the Court's practice of substituting its own concepts of decency and fundamental justice for the language of the Bill of Rights as its point of departure in interpreting and enforcing that Bill of Rights.

Frankfurter's approach led the Court to apply some of the provisions of the Bill of Rights to the states, and Black acknowledged that this was better than nothing, but he reiterated that "the original purpose of the Fourteenth Amendment [was] to extend to all the people of the nation the complete protection of the Bill of Rights."[46]

The Court's leading justices were at loggerheads. Frankfurter remained convinced that Black's approach would lead to excessive activism, and so he continued to emphasize his alternative of judgment and self-restraint. Black remained convinced that Frankfurter was abandoning his duty to enforce the written Constitution, and Stone was at the same time developing his broad justification for judicially enforceable democratic liberties and minority rights. This breakdown of constitutional consensus during the 1940s led to a dramatic decline in the Court's tradition of unanimity and a corresponding rise in the frequency of concurring and dissenting opinions (Kelsh 1999). Black and Stone posed a significant challenge to Frankfurter — particularly on the issues of minority rights, speech, and incorporation — but for the time being, their views usually remained in dissent. More often than not, Frankfurter persuaded his colleagues to defer to legislative judgments and to avoid "political thickets." Justice Jackson, for example, increasingly joined Frankfurter, despite his votes in *Barnette* and *Bridges,* a development that was influenced at least in part by Jackson's sharp personality conflict with Black (Hutchinson 1989). When Murphy and Wiley Rutledge both died in 1949, it appeared that Frankfurter had won the war. They had regularly supported the active enforcement of constitutional liberties, and it quickly became clear that their replacements — Truman appointees Tom Clark and Sherman Minton — would not.

CHAPTER TWO

FRANKFURTER'S FAILURE:
THE RISE AND DECLINE
OF JUDICIAL SELF-RESTRAINT
1949–1962

In the wake of the New Deal, the justices of the U.S. Supreme Court faced three options in reconstructing constitutional foundations for the modern American state. Despite some suggestions of a new liberal constitutional order emphasizing the judicial protection of preferred freedoms, described in different ways by Harlan Stone and Hugo Black, Felix Frankfurter fully expected to lead the Court in adopting a sweeping posture of deference to the democratic process. The Warren Court would ultimately reject his vision of judicial restraint, marking a crucial turning point in constitutional development, but this turn was not fully made until after Frankfurter's retirement in 1962. When Tom Clark and Sherman Minton replaced Frank Murphy and Wiley Rutledge in 1949, Stone's and Black's arguments for rights-based activism receded and Frankfurter's vision appeared to control the Court throughout the 1950s.

Even as Frankfurter's doctrine of restraint became dominant, however, there were continued signs that the modern Court might follow the lead of Stone and Black in adopting a distinctive new activist role. Most notably, Earl Warren joined the Court in 1953 and quickly marshaled his colleagues to their unanimous decision in *Brown v. Board of Education*. The school desegregation cases were significant both because they foreshadowed the decline of Frankfurterian deference and because they led the Court to once again grapple with Fourteenth Amendment history. The Warren Court would eventually reject both Frankfurter's restraint and the emerging originalist vi-

sion of the Fourteenth Amendment, but modern conservatives would remember each of them in the years to come.

Frankfurter and the Height of Holmesian Self-Restraint

While the Hughes and Stone Courts had laid the foundations for modern
civil liberties jurisprudence, these decisions remained the exception rather
than the rule. After striking down fourteen provisions of federal law during
the New Deal battles of 1932 to 1936, for example, the Court failed to strike
down a single federal statute from 1937 to 1942; struck down only three between 1943 and 1953; and then struck down seven during the early years of the
Warren Court, 1954 to 1962. None of the three decisions prior to the start of
the Warren era raised an issue of civil rights or civil liberties, while all seven
of the decisions during the early Warren years did so. As table 2.1 makes clear,
the period from the New Deal "switch in time" to the full emergence of the
Warren Court marked a sharp, but temporary, downturn in the twentieth-
century Court's willingness to impose constitutional limits on the federal
government.[1] Table 2.2 reveals a similar, though less stark, pattern with regard to judicial review of state and local statutes.

Led by Frankfurter, the Court continued to exercise a sweeping deference
to state and federal legislatures in the context of economic regulation. In cases
such as *Railway Express Agency v. New York, Lincoln Federal Labor Union v.
Northwestern Iron and Metal Company,* and *Williamson v. Lee Optical,* the
Court repeatedly held that regulatory statutes need not be perfectly drawn to
be constitutional: "It is enough that there is an evil at hand for correction,
and that it might be thought that the particular legislative measure was a rational way to correct it. The day is gone when this Court uses the Due Process Clause of the Fourteenth Amendment to strike down state laws, regulatory of business and industrial conditions, because they may be unwise,
improvident, or out of harmony with a particular school of thought."[2]

Even outside the area of business regulation, moreover, Frankfurter led
the Court in exercising a striking degree of deference to state and federal
laws that curtailed individual liberty and minority rights. In his concurring opinion in *Kovacs v. Cooper,* for example, he explicitly rejected Stone's
defense of rights-based activism, observing that "'the preferred position of
freedom of speech' . . . is a phrase that has uncritically crept into some recent opinions of this Court. I deem it a mischievous phrase, if it carries the
thought, which it may subtly imply, that any law touching communication

TABLE 2.1 *Decisions Striking Down Federal Statutes on Constitutional Grounds*

Historical Period	Years	Number	Annual Average
Early Court	1789–1863	2	0.03
Chase Court	1864–1873	8	0.80
Waite Court	1874–1888	7	0.47
Fuller Court	1888–1910	14	0.64
White Court	1910–1921	12	1.09
Taft Court	1921–1930	11	1.38
Hughes Court, pre–"switch in time"	1930–1936	14	2.00
Roosevelt Court	1937–1953	3	0.18
Early Warren Court	1954–1962	7	0.78
Late Warren Court	1963–1969	16	2.29
Burger Court	1969–1986	32	1.88
Early Rehnquist Court	1986–1994	7	0.78
Late Rehnquist Court	1995–2003	33	3.67

Source: Congressional Research Service, *The Constitution of the United States of America: Analysis and Interpretation* and *2000 Supplement* (Washington, D.C.: Government Printing Office, 1996, 2000), updated by author.

is infected with presumptive invalidity." Noting that "[a] footnote hardly seems to be an appropriate way of announcing a new constitutional doctrine" and that Stone's *Carolene Products* opinion "did not have the concurrence of a majority of the Court," he insisted that the regulation of public expression was, like most other constitutional questions, primarily a matter for the legislative judgment.[3]

Two years later, Frankfurter concurred in the Court's 1951 decision upholding the convictions of several members of the Communist Party under the Smith Act, which made it illegal for any person "to knowingly or willfully advocate, abet, advise, or teach the duty, necessity, desirability, or propriety of overthrowing or destroying any government in the U.S. by force or violence." Concurring in the judgment in *Dennis v. United States*, Frankfurter argued that the interest of free speech must be balanced against that of national security, and that the "[p]rimary responsibility" for weighing that bal-

TABLE 2.2 *Decisions Striking Down State and Local Statutes on Constitutional Grounds*

Historical Period	Years	Number	Annual Average
Early Court	1789–1864	39	0.51
Chase Court	1864–1873	33	3.67
Waite Court	1874–1888	65	4.64
Fuller Court	1888–1910	89	4.05
White Court	1910–1921	124	11.27
Taft Court	1921–1930	129	14.33
Hughes Court, pre–"switch in time"	1930–1936	65	9.29
Roosevelt Court	1937–1953	108	6.35
Early Warren Court	1954–1962	73	8.11
Late Warren Court	1963–1969	113	16.14
Burger Court	1969–1986	309	18.18
Early Rehnquist Court	1986–1994	85	10.63
Late Rehnquist Court	1995–2003	43	4.78

Source: Congressional Research Service, *The Constitution of the United States of America: Analysis and Interpretation* and *2000 Supplement* (Washington, D.C.: Government Printing Office, 1996, 2000), updated by author.

ance belongs to Congress. He insisted that the Court should "set aside the judgment of those whose duty it is to legislate only if there is no reasonable basis for it" and that "[f]ull responsibility for the choice cannot be given to the courts. Courts are not representative bodies. They are not designed to be a good reflex of a democratic society."[4] Frankfurter urged his colleagues to "remember that this Court's power of judicial review is not an exercise of the powers of a super-legislature," and he reiterated that "[f]ree speech cases are not an exception to the principle that we are not legislators, that direct policymaking is not our province."[5]

For Justice Frankfurter, the core principle of American constitutional democracy was majoritarianism and the chief danger was judicial tyranny. When the actions of the federal legislative or executive branches were challenged on constitutional grounds, those coordinate branches of the federal government were owed significant deference by the Court. Dissenting in

Trop v. Dulles, for example, Frankfurter insisted that the national government was constitutionally free to revoke an individual's citizenship for deserting the military during wartime. Emphasizing the framers' belief that "[a]ll power is . . . of an encroaching nature," he noted that "[j]udicial power is not immune against this human weakness." Acknowledging that "[i]t is not easy to stand aloof and allow want of wisdom to prevail," he reiterated that "it is not the business of this Court to pronounce policy. It must observe a fastidious regard for limitations on its own power, and this precludes the Court's giving effect to its own notions of what is wise or politic. That self-restraint is of the essence in the observance of the judicial oath, for the Constitution has not authorized the judges to sit in judgment on the wisdom of what Congress and the Executive Branch do." Frankfurter concluded by noting that "the whole of [Justice Holmes's] work during his thirty years of service on this Court should be a constant reminder that the power to invalidate legislation must not be exercised as if, either in constitutional theory or in the art of government, it stood as the sole bulwark against unwisdom or excesses of the moment."[6]

Following Louis Brandeis, Frankfurter also emphasized that one of the best ways for the justices to restrain their own power was to avoid constitutional decisions altogether, and during the 1950s and early 1960s, he often persuaded the Court to go along with him. Writing for a four-justice plurality in *Poe v. Ullman,* for example, he refused to hear a constitutional challenge to Connecticut's anti-contraception law because the plaintiffs faced no actual threat of prosecution. Quoting *Ashwander v. TVA,* Frankfurter provided a lengthy discussion of the passive virtues, noting that "[t]he various doctrines of 'standing,' 'ripeness,' and 'mootness,' which this Court has evolved . . . are but several manifestations — each having its own 'varied application' — of the primary conception that federal judicial power is to be exercised to strike down legislation . . . only at the instance of one who is himself immediately harmed, or immediately threatened with harm, by the challenged action."[7] A few years earlier, writing for the Court in *United States v. United Auto Workers,* he had called on his fellow justices to heed the lesson of *Dred Scott v. Sandford,* in which "the Court, forgetting 'the fallibility of the human judgment,'" had settled a constitutional question when it was unnecessary to do so, and thus suffered a "self-inflicted wound."[8]

With respect to state and local legislation, Frankfurter's majoritarianism was buttressed by the constitutional doctrine of federalism. Judicial deference was particularly important in the context of criminal procedure, he continued to insist, because "the bulk of authority to legislate on what may be compendiously described as criminal justice, which in other nations belongs to the central government, is under our system the responsibility of the individual States."[9] Though Justice Black repeatedly challenged this conclusion, Frankfurter continued to prevail. Two years after *Adamson v. California,* Frankfurter wrote for the Court in *Wolf v. Colorado,* holding that the Fourth Amendment's exclusionary rule does not apply to the states since it is not an indispensable element of due process. He reiterated that "[t]he real clue to the problem confronting the judiciary in the application of the Due Process Clause is not to ask where the line is once and for all to be drawn but to recognize that it is for the Court to draw it by the gradual and empiric process of 'inclusion and exclusion.'" Laying out an evolutionary conception of due process that Justice Harlan would develop more fully in the coming years, he characterized it as a "living principle" that "conveys neither formal nor fixed nor narrow requirements. It is the compendious expression for all those rights which the courts must enforce because they are basic to our free society." In Frankfurter's view, privacy in the home was protected by the Due Process Clause, but the exclusionary rule was just one particular means of enforcing that value. He noted that thirty-one states had rejected this particular means and concluded that it was not an essential component of fair judicial process.[10]

As noted in chapter 1, Frankfurter's position was strengthened by the publication of Charles Fairman's influential *Stanford Law Review* article in 1949. Ten years later, for example, Frankfurter wrote for the Court in *Bartkus v. Illinois,* rejecting a double jeopardy challenge to an Illinois criminal conviction. Observing that the Court had "held from the beginning and uniformly that the Due Process Clause . . . does not apply to the States any of the provisions of the first eight amendments as such," he cited Fairman and insisted that "[t]he relevant historical materials . . . demonstrate conclusively that Congress and the members of the legislatures of the ratifying States did not contemplate that the Fourteenth Amendment was a short-hand incorporation of the" original Bill of Rights. Frankfurter supported this claim with an eight-page table, compiled directly from Fairman's article, documenting the numerous state laws on the books in 1868 that were inconsistent with the jury provisions of the Fifth, Sixth, and Seventh Amendments.[11]

Though he is more often remembered for his exercise of judicial deference, Frankfurter's flexible "fundamental fairness" approach did sometimes lead him to enforce constitutional limits on government power. In *Rochin v.*

California, for example, he held that forcibly pumping a suspect's stomach to retrieve evidence that had been swallowed violated "those canons of decency and fairness which express the notions of justice of English-speaking peoples." In light of these standards, he concluded "that the proceedings by which this conviction was obtained do more than offend some fastidious squeamishness or private sentimentalism about combating crime too energetically. This is conduct that shocks the conscience." [12] In other words, when state action threatened what Frankfurter believed to be a truly fundamental constitutional value, he was willing to make an exception to the principle of judicial deference.

From the beginning, this posture has led some scholars to conclude that Frankfurter's restraint was not genuine; that he, like other justices, proclaimed adherence to restraint whenever he agreed with the policy being challenged, but abandoned that restraint when he did not. In fact, this reading of Frankfurter's constitutional decisions played a significant role in the development of the "attitudinal model," the claim by some political scientists that Supreme Court decisions are rooted almost entirely in the justices' individual political preferences (Ulmer 1960; Spaeth 1964). It is certainly true that, like all other justices, Frankfurter believed there were some instances in which the Constitution called for the active exercise of judicial power and others in which it did not. His substantive constitutional commitments that called for judicial activism, however, were not identical to his own political preferences. Frankfurter's political and legal activities before joining the Court make clear that he was a committed civil libertarian who would have rejected the policies at issue, for example, in *Minersville School District v. Gobitis, West Virginia v. Barnette,* and *Dennis v. United States* — namely, mandatory flag salutes and the Smith Act — if he had believed it was his job to do so (Hirsch 1981:65–98; Alexander 2001:71–125; Simon 1989:21–65). Since he was not an elected member of either a local school board or the federal Congress, however, it was not his job. Thus, when political scientist Harold Spaeth argued shortly after Frankfurter's retirement that the justice's so-called restraint had simply been a cover for his conservative pro-business bias, Wallace Mendelson replied that "[b]usinessmen might have difficulty swallowing this, considering that Frankfurter spent a major part of his life in a successful fight against the labor injunction — to say nothing of his landmark opinions which all but exempted unions from the anti-trust laws; destroyed one of the last vestiges of the sweat shop; required employers, who have refused to hire men because of their union membership, to give them not only jobs but back pay; and, finally, his dissenting view that neither Congress nor Constitution bars a union from spending dues for political purposes" (Mendelson 1963:599; see Spaeth 1964). Though his vision of the Constitution and the judicial role has influenced modern constitutional conservatism a great deal, Frankfurter himself was no conservative.

For Frankfurter, the essence of the judicial function was the exercise of judgment in balancing competing values. While the scales should include a great deal of deference to the elected institutions, that deference would sometimes be outweighed, as when those institutions undertook actions that "shock the conscience." In *Sweezy v. New Hampshire,* for example, he noted that his holding rested on "a judicial judgment in balancing two contending principles — the right of a citizen to political privacy, as protected by the Fourteenth Amendment, and the right of the State to self protection." He continued:

> [S]triking the balance implies the exercise of judgment. This is the inescapable judicial task in giving substantive content, legally enforced, to the Due Process Clause, and it is a task ultimately committed to this Court. It must not be an exercise of whim or will. It must be an overriding judgment founded on something much deeper and more justifiable than personal preference. As far as it lies within human limitations, it must be an impersonal judgment. It must rest on fundamental presuppositions rooted in history to which widespread acceptance may fairly be attributed. Such a judgment must be arrived at in a spirit of humility when it counters the judgment of the State's highest court. But, in the end, judgment cannot be escaped — the judgment of this Court.

In this case, Frankfurter was arguing that the state could not force a professor to disclose his political associations in a way that would inhibit his freedom to teach as he saw fit. A former professor himself, Frankfurter considered academic freedom an important constitutional value in the defense of which he was willing to exercise judicial power.[13]

Frankfurter's faith in judicial judgment should not be surprising. James Bradley Thayer, after all, had acknowledged that in the face of an unambiguous constitutional violation, the Court must be willing to exercise judicial review, and Frankfurter was particularly confident in his own ability to discern such "unambiguous" violations. He was confident that he could articulate a reasoned resolution of any particular political or legal conflict that would bring all well-meaning people to agreement. His "shocks-the-conscience" test, for example, required what he elsewhere called the inescapable "instance-by-instance, case-by-case application of [the Due Process Clause] in all the varieties of situations that come before this Court."[14] He never gave a very clear definition to such tests — and indeed he believed that such an *a priori* articulation of definitive standards was neither possible nor desirable — but he did identify a number of substantive constitutional values that he was willing to defend quite actively. These were obviously values that he himself held to be important, but they were not reducible to a list of his own preferred results on particular issues.

The most important of these values for Frankfurter were the Fourth Amendment right to privacy; the separation of church and state; and racial equality. In Frankfurter's view, these values were firmly rooted in Anglo-American legal traditions, and it was fully within the legitimate scope of judicial power to defend them. Dissenting from William O. Douglas's decision upholding a seizure of private papers in *Davis v. United States,* for example, he had emphasized "one of the great chapters in the historic process whereby civil liberty was achieved and constitutionally protected against future inroads." Characterizing John Adams's description of James Otis's 1761 argument against writs of assistance in *Paxton's Case* as the spark igniting the American Revolution, Frankfurter insisted that it was this "living experience" with the necessity of personal privacy and the danger of police excesses that Madison wrote into the Fourth Amendment.[15] Once having identified the substantive constitutional value, moreover, Frankfurter was willing to defend that value even against new threats. On the distinctly modern Fourth Amendment issue of electronic eavesdropping, for example, he followed Brandeis's privacy-protecting dissent in *Olmstead v. United States.*[16]

Similarly, in the Establishment Clause context, Frankfurter urged the Court actively to defend a high wall of separation between church and state. In the landmark case of *Everson v. Board of Education of Ewing Township,* Justice Black held for the Court that the framers did indeed erect such a wall in the First Amendment, but that New Jersey was nonetheless permitted to reimburse parents for the cost of busing their children to private parochial schools. In Black's view, so long as the funding policy was neutral among religions and had a secular purpose, it did not violate the Establishment Clause merely because it indirectly benefited some religious organizations. Justices Robert Jackson and Rutledge both dissented in *Everson,* insisting that the policy was unconstitutional, and Frankfurter joined each of their opinions. As in *Korematsu v. United States,* Black had written for a Court that was will-

ing to adopt fairly sweeping, rights-protecting rhetoric, but was not yet willing to enforce that rhetoric in actual practice. Over the next few years, the
Court would come to enforce the Establishment Clause more actively, with
Frankfurter consistently encouraging these efforts. In *McCollum v. Board of
Education,* for example, the Court ruled that an Illinois school board could
not constitutionally administer a so-called released time policy, under which
outside teachers were brought in to provide religious instruction during regular school hours within the public schools. Writing separately, Frankfurter
supported this conclusion with a lengthy review of the history of such gov-
ernment-supported religious education in the United States. This history, in
his view, counseled that "[t]he great American principle of eternal separation . . . is one of the vital reliances of our Constitutional system for assuring
unities among our people stronger than our diversities. It is the Court's duty
to enforce this principle in its full integrity."[17] Four years later, when the
Court distinguished *McCollum* in upholding a similar policy allowing students to be released from public school to attend religious classes off-site,
Frankfurter dissented, urging the Court to strike down this policy as well.[18]
In his view, "the principle that a government must neither establish nor sup-
press religious belief" was deeply rooted in Anglo-American legal traditions
and hence was included within the broad concept of due process liberty.[19]

In the area of racial equality, Frankfurter provided ambivalent but consistent support for the Court's emerging protection of the rights of racial minorities under the Reconstruction amendments. In a series of civil rights
cases brought by the NAACP during the 1930s and 1940s, the Court had
slowly chipped away at the legal foundations of racial segregation. Frankfurter was not yet on the Court for the NAACP's first victory, in *Missouri
ex rel. Gaines v. Canada,* but from 1939 to 1948, he had joined the Court in
striking down Oklahoma's racially discriminatory "grandfather clause" for
voting rights; the white primary in Texas; racially restrictive covenants in residential real estate contracts; and the University of Oklahoma School of Law's
whites-only admissions policy.[20] In both *McLaurin v. Oklahoma State Regents
for Higher Education* and *Sweatt v. Painter,* Frankfurter joined Chief Justice
Fred Vinson's unanimous opinions in support of racial equality but worked
successfully to keep the decisions narrow (Simon 1989:216–18). Three years
later, he concurred in the Court's judgment that the Texas Democratic Party's
continued effort to hold a whites-only primary election was unconstitutional, but he again sought to narrow the grounds of the Court's decision.[21]

During this same period, Frankfurter persistently urged his fellow justices to delay action in *Brown v. Board of Education*, in the hopes of keeping the decision narrow and unanimous. When the Court decided to postpone the decision for a year, after initially hearing arguments during the 1952 term, it was Frankfurter and his law clerk, Alexander Bickel, who drafted the five questions for reargument. When the Court finally did decide the merits in 1954, it was Frankfurter who came up with the idea of postponing the decision on remedy still further, and it was he who proposed that the Court order desegregation "with all deliberate speed" (a phrase borrowed from Holmes) the following year. In sum, Frankfurter supported the Court's single most activist endeavor during his tenure — because he believed that racial equality was a fundamental constitutional value — but he consistently urged the Court to move forward with as much caution and restraint as possible.

The Dawn of the Warren Court
and the Birth of Modern Originalism

The Warren Court's effort to dismantle a centuries-old system of legally enforced racial segregation clearly represented a departure from Frankfurter's vision of the judicial role. The justices were turning away from his emphasis on history and self-restraint and turning toward a new American democracy of rights, though this change would not be complete until the 1960s. With the Court struggling to mark out a new, more modern vision of the judicial role, Justice Black was making the case for a strict adherence to the original meaning of the constitutional text (as he understood it). The Court had rejected this approach in *Adamson*, however, and in 1954, as David Garrow has observed, *Brown* inaugurated the modern Court's "dramatically expansive — and aggressively anti-historical — reading and application of the Fourteenth Amendment's Equal Protection and Due Process Clauses" (1997:75). Though its full articulation was yet a long way off, *Brown* contained the seeds of the modern liberal conception of the "living Constitution" — the idea that the Constitution's abstract rights provisions must be interpreted in light of changing historical conditions and moral understandings, a constitutional vision that would eventually find its most influential advocate in Justice William Brennan and its most comprehensive theorist in Ronald Dworkin (Brennan 1986; Dworkin 1996b; 1978). As Garrow (1997) notes, this expansive vision was particularly apparent in *Brown*'s companion case, *Bolling v. Sharpe*, in which the Court held that constitutionally protected liberty was "not confined to mere freedom from bodily restraint. Liberty under law extends to the full range of conduct which the individual is free to pursue, and it cannot be restricted except for a proper governmental objective. Segregation in public education is not reasonably related to any proper governmental objective, and thus it imposes on Negro children in the District of Columbia a burden that constitutes an arbitrary deprivation of their liberty in violation of the Due Process Clause." [22]

While the Court was ostensibly moving away from a strictly historical reading of the Constitution, however, the structure of the segregation debate — as with the incorporation debate a few years earlier — produced a preoccupation with the original meaning of the Fourteenth Amendment that would prove influential on constitutional conservatives for many years to come. Confronted with the undeniable fact that Jim Crow segregation violated the spirit of equality enshrined in the Fourteenth Amendment, the justices recognized that holding this segregation unconstitutional would represent a dramatic constitutional change requiring some substantial explanation. Supporters of segregation would certainly point out that the constitutional text had never before been held to prohibit segregation and that the text itself was no different in 1954 than it had been in 1868. Thus, when the Court ordered that the *Brown* case be reargued during the 1953 term, it directed the parties to focus largely on the original understanding of the amendment with respect to school segregation. After this exhaustive historical review, the new Chief Justice Warren held that while the historical sources "cast some light," they were ultimately "inconclusive." [23] In fact, by the time of reargument, a research memo prepared by Bickel had "firmly directed the Justices away from any potential history-based solution to their American dilemma" (Garrow 1997:76).

In his opinion for the Court, Warren made this rejection of history clear, holding that "we cannot turn the clock back to 1868 when the Amendment was adopted, or even to 1896 when *Plessy v. Ferguson* was written. We must consider public education in the light of its full development and its present place in American life throughout the Nation. Only in this way can it be determined if segregation in public schools deprives these plaintiffs of the equal protection of the laws." The amendment's history was inconclusive, Warren held, because the role of public education in society and politics had changed so dramatically between 1868 and 1954. Since this role had been so narrow during the Reconstruction era, "it is not surprising that there should be so little in the history of the Fourteenth Amendment relating to its intended effect on public education." Moreover, Warren observed, the various members

of Congress and the state legislatures who had been responsible for the adoption of the Fourteenth Amendment in 1868 had no consistently shared intentions about its reach.[24] In the face of this inconclusive history, the Warren
Court was willing to hold that segregation violated an abstract constitutional
principle of equality, a principle whose meaning had evolved significantly
since first being enshrined in the text.

Because the stakes were so high in the desegregation context, all nine justices acquiesced in this potentially dramatic expansion of the Court's role.
This judicial consensus, however, did not prevent the emergence of sharp denunciations from a number of quarters, and most of these immediate critical
reactions emphasized the question of history and original meaning. In 1956,
for example, nineteen U.S. senators and seventy-seven representatives signed
"The Southern Manifesto: A Declaration of Constitutional Principles," in
which they pledged "to use all lawful means to bring about a reversal of this
decision which is contrary to the Constitution and to prevent the use of force
in its implementation." Though the manifesto relied in part on the despica-
ble claim that the *Brown* decision was "destroying the amicable relations between the white and Negro races that have been created through 90 years of
patient effort by the good people of both races," it also emphasized that
"[t]he original Constitution does not mention education" and that "[t]he debates preceding the submission of the 14th amendment clearly show that
there was no intent that it should affect the system of education maintained
by the States." The manifesto proceeded to point out that "[t]he very Congress which proposed the amendment subsequently provided for segregated
schools in the District of Columbia," and that most of the state legislatures
that ratified the amendment provided for segregated schools in their own ju-
risdictions as well. In this light, the manifesto complained, it was clear that
the justices of the Warren Court were "exercis[ing] their naked judicial
power and substitut[ing] their personal political and social ideas for the established law of the land."[25]

Relying on similar constitutional claims, eight southern state legislatures
formally "nullified" *Brown.* South Carolina declared that "[t]his action of the
Court ignored the principle that the meaning of the Constitution and of
its Amendments does not change. It is a written instrument. That which
the Fourteenth Amendment meant when adopted it means now." Similarly,
the Alabama legislature resolved that the *Brown* decision was, "as a matter of
right, null, void, and of no effect; and . . . [that] this State is not bound to
abide thereby," unless and "until the issue between the State of Alabama and

the General Government is decided by the submission to the states, pursuant to Article V of the Constitution, of a suitable constitutional amendment that would declare, in plain and unequivocal language, that the states do surrender their power to maintain public schools and other public facilities on a basis of separation as to race." [26]

These originalist arguments had first taken shape in the segregation cases leading up to *Brown,* with the State of Texas's brief in *Sweatt v. Painter* playing a particularly significant role. As Mark Tushnet has noted, the Texas brief had "compiled a fair amount of information indicating that, no matter how 'radical' the Republicans were, when they wrote the Fourteenth Amendment they did not seem bothered by school segregation. The most dramatic evidence, of course, was that Congress created segregated schools in the District of Columbia around the time it proposed the Fourteenth Amendment." On the basis of extensive archival research, Tushnet found that Justice Jackson was particularly "impressed by the Texas brief, which established to his satisfaction that most proponents of the Fourteenth Amendment did not intend to 'interfere with the state school systems on the question of segregation,' and that 'even those who wanted to see that accomplished acknowledged that it was not accomplished by the Amendment. . . .' For Jackson, this meant that the question for the Court was not whether to 'fill gaps or construe the Amendment to include matters which were unconsidered,' but was 'whether we will construe it to include what was deliberately and intentionally excluded'" (1994:171, 143). [27] In light of this Reconstruction history, it is no surprise that the defenders of segregation, both before and after *Brown,* made extensive reference to the original meaning of the Fourteenth Amendment.

Significantly, this historicist critique of *Brown* was soon echoed by a number of distinguished constitutional scholars. In 1955, the *Harvard Law Review* published a revised version of Bickel's research memo for Frankfurter. While Bickel's primary purpose had been to buttress Warren's argument that the Court need not be bound by history, his article was most influential for its apparent demonstration that the Fourteenth Amendment had not originally been understood to apply to school segregation (or to jury service, suffrage, or anti-miscegenation statutes, either). Bickel began by noting that even if the "historical materials . . . are inconclusive and . . . the clock cannot be turned back," they can still "cast some light" on the matter, and so, endorsing Fairman on the incorporation question, he undertook a similar analysis of the Thirty-ninth Congress on the issue of segregation. He concluded that if the Court were bound to adhere to the specific intentions of the framers, then it would be "foreclosed from applying [the Fourteenth Amendment] to segregation in public schools. The evidence of congressional purpose is as clear as such evidence is likely to be, and no language barrier stands in the way of construing the section in conformity with it" (1955:4–6, 58–59). In the cover letter to the justices, attached to his original memo, he had stated this conclusion even more plainly, insisting that "it is impossible to conclude that the 39th Congress intended that segregation be abolished; impossible also to conclude that they foresaw it might be, under the language they were adopting" (*quoted in* Kluger 1975:654).

Bickel took pains to insist, however, that since the Court was interpreting an expansive set of constitutional rights guarantees, it should "aim to discover what if any thought was given to the long-range effect, under future circumstances, of provisions necessarily intended for permanence." In this light, he hypothesized that the framers of the amendment adopted language that "was sufficiently elastic to permit reasonable future advances," a hypothesis that credited the framers with "an awareness . . . that it was *a constitution* they were writing, which led to a choice of language capable of growth." The Reconstruction Republicans had deferred the crucial question of the extent of the amendment's guarantees "to be decided another day . . . . [T]here is no indication of the way in which anyone thought the decision would go on any given specific issue." Thus, the *Brown* Court "was able to avoid the dilemma [between upholding segregation or explicitly repudiating clear evidence of original intent] because the record of history, properly understood, left the way open to, in fact invited, a decision based on the moral and material state of the nation in 1954, not 1866" (1955:59–65). This would not be the last time Bickel set out to defend Warren Court activism but ended up buttressing its critics.

Interestingly, Fairman followed Frankfurter and Bickel in endorsing the Court's anti-historical approach in *Brown,* though the segregationists appeared to have originalist evidence just as weighty as his own evidence on incorporation (Fairman 1956). His task in the incorporation piece had been primarily a negative one — to disprove Black's claim that the Reconstruction Republicans intended to incorporate the Bill of Rights. And if Warren had tried to make such an originalist claim in *Brown,* Fairman might well have tried to debunk that one too. But Warren made no such effort, and like Frankfurter and Bickel (and Holmes before them), Fairman believed that the Court could legitimately depart from the Constitution's original meaning if it did so in support of an important constitutional value. Racial equality was such a value, and so all three of these advocates of restraint supported the Court's activism in *Brown*.

Of more immediate concern to the justices than these scholarly assessments, however, was the increasing hostility that the Court faced from Congress. As Lucas Powe has noted, southern segregationists were joined by many northerners and moderates in denouncing the Warren Court after a series of controversial domestic security decisions. During the 1956 term, the Court heard twelve cases involving communists, and it decided all twelve of them against the government, culminating on June 17, 1957, when it announced its decisions in *Service v. Dulles, Watkins v. United States, Sweezy v. New Hampshire,* and *Yates v. United States.* After "Red Monday," as this day quickly became known, the Court faced a serious political threat, with Congress considering a variety of bills designed to restrict the Court's power either by altering the procedures for judicial appointment or by removing certain categories of cases from the Court's jurisdiction. During the summer of 1958, in particular, the congressional attacks reached a level almost "comparable to Roosevelt's Court-packing plan twenty-one years earlier." As Powe notes, "[t]he anti-Court measures, though not as all-encompassing as the Court-packing plan, had come far closer to passage than Roosevelt's initiative. Black, Frankfurter, and Douglas had been there in 1937 and had joined the Court shortly thereafter. They knew, or should have known, what Congress was saying" (Powe 2000:127, 133; see also Murphy 1962).

In the face of these attacks, the Court retreated, essentially abandoning the field of school desegregation for a time, and reversing much of the domestic security law established during the 1956 term. With help from his newest and closest ally on the Court — the second Justice Harlan, appointed by Eisenhower in 1955 — Frankfurter helped to quell congressional hostility by persuading the Court to exercise restraint. In *Barenblatt v. United States,* for example, the Court upheld Lloyd Barenblatt's six-month sentence for contempt of Congress for refusing to answer questions posed by the House Un-American Activities Committee. Writing for the Court, Harlan emphasized that constitutional liberty must always be balanced against pressing public needs, prompting a sharp dissent from Black reiterating his free speech absolutism. Black continued this debate in his James Madison lecture at NYU Law School the following year, arguing that the balancing approach of Frankfurter and Harlan — which held that liberties admittedly part of the Bill of Rights could nevertheless be abridged in favor of a superior public interest — would inevitably lead to the infringement of liberty in times of crisis. In Black's view, this "approach to basic individual liberties assumes to legislatures and judges more power than either the framers or I myself believe should be entrusted, without limitation, to any man or group of men" (1960:866–67). Justice Black therefore continued trying to constrain judicial power by binding it tightly to the constitutional text. For the time being, he was still mobilizing this originalist approach in favor of activism and against Frankfurter's restraint, but that would soon start to change.

The Scholarly Critique and Frankfurterian Self-Restraint

Though the Court backtracked for a time during the late 1950s in the face of congressional hostility, it soon regained its footing, moving cautiously forward to defend constitutional liberty and equality ever more actively. Meanwhile, Frankfurter continued his efforts on the Court to curtail this sort of activism, and his allies off the Court struck back whenever his fellow justices failed to heed him. Due in part to Frankfurter's enormous influence, for example, the American Bar Association, the Conference of State Chief Justices, the country's leading federal circuit judge, and a number of distinguished members of the scholarly community all criticized the Court's activism during the late 1950s. In 1957, the American Bar Association's Committee on Communist Strategy attacked the Court so sharply at a meeting attended by Chief Justice Warren that he resigned his membership in the ABA, and the following year, the state chief justices adopted a report expressing "grave concern" that the justices' "individual views of . . . what is wise or desirable [were] unconsciously overrid[ing] a more dispassionate consideration of what is or is not constitutionally warranted. . . . It is our earnest hope that that great Court exercise to the full its power of judicial self-restraint by adhering firmly to its tremendous, strictly judicial powers and by eschewing, so far as possible, the exercise of essentially legislative powers" (Powe 2000:100, 139–40).

Within just a few years, moreover, Bickel would be the leading member of a group of scholarly critics who repeatedly denounced the Warren Court's activism, including the *Brown* decision. Though now widely praised as a landmark fulfillment of judicial duty, the *Brown* case initially "produced a sharply critical reaction among elite legal thinkers" who had been heavily influenced by Frankfurter, "for it challenged at the deepest levels their effort to re-establish a neutral, value-free system of constitutional doctrine" (Horwitz 1992:258; see also Peller 1988; Kalman 1996:30–32). Unlike the segregationist arguments that I have already canvassed, these scholarly critiques did not rely primarily on an appeal to the original meaning of the Fourteenth Amendment. The Court itself had clearly rejected such an approach in both *Adamson* and *Brown,* and most of the scholarly critics in the late 1950s and early 1960s did not disagree on this point. Instead, they denounced the Court on the very Frankfurterian grounds of deference to democratic majorities.

In February 1958, for example, with the attack on the Court at its height, Second Circuit judge Learned Hand delivered the annual Holmes Lectures at Harvard Law School. Reflecting the restrained approach that he had followed throughout his career, Hand insisted that the power of judicial review had no constitutional foundation and urged judges to refuse to enforce the Bill of Rights. He advanced this argument in part by questioning the Court's decision in *Brown,* which he saw as the revival of an illegitimate pre–New Deal conception of judicial power. In his view, the *Brown* Court had simply overruled "the 'legislative judgment' of states by its own reappraisal of the relative values at stake" (Hand 1958:54–55; see Gunther 1994:651–55). The nation's most distinguished jurist not on the Supreme Court, Hand had consistently exercised judicial restraint during his half-century on the federal bench, and with these lectures, he temporarily turned the constitutional critique of *Brown* away from the question of the fixed meaning of the text and toward the proper limits of judicial power.[28] Like Holmes and Frankfurter, Hand had been heavily influenced by Professor Thayer while a student at Harvard. In the words of Hand's biographer, Gerald Gunther, "[t]he result of Thayer's approach to constitutional law, as Hand once put it, 'was to imbue us with a skepticism about the wisdom of setting up courts as the final arbiters of social conflicts, [a skepticism] which many of [us] always retained.' . . . And what [Hand] found 'most original' was that Thayer saw 'pretty plainly what would result if the courts [made] themselves into what is really a legislative body with a veto. He foresaw that and said that the only way for them to behave was to hold back and have a certain moderation.'" Like Frankfurter, Hand had been sharply critical of the Court's activism during the *Lochner* era, going so far as to propose repealing the Constitution's Due Process Clauses or requiring a two-thirds vote for the exercise of judicial review (Gunther 1994:51, 247–52, 374–75). And like Frankfurter and Holmes, Hand rejected a strict originalist approach to constitutional interpretation, insisting that contemporary majorities could not be constrained by outmoded constitutional limits.[29]

The core of Hand's constitutional vision, as articulated in the Holmes Lectures, was that the power of judicial review was probably not intended by the framers. He granted that the power could nevertheless be inferred on pragmatic grounds, because it was "essential to prevent the defeat of the venture at hand." In other words, the American political system had come to rely on judicial review, and it could not now be abandoned. However, "since this power is not a logical deduction from the structure of the Constitution but only a practical condition upon its successful operation, it need not be exercised whenever a court sees, or thinks that it sees, an invasion of the Constitution. It is always a preliminary question how importunately the occasion demands an answer." In this light, he followed Brandeis and Frankfurter in insisting that the Court should often refuse to decide a constitutional conflict with which it is presented. As a prime example of such restraint, Hand cited the political questions doctrine, under which the Court had so far refused to decide whether inegalitarian legislative apportionment practices violated the Constitution (1958:10–11, 14–16).

Hand insisted that while the federal courts should continue to enforce the Constitution's division of governmental powers — principally by means of the nondelegation doctrine — they should regard the Due Process Clauses and the Bill of Rights as merely "admonitory or hortatory." In this way, the courts would prevent the legislature from abdicating its legislative authority to someone else, but would not interfere with how it chose to exercise that authority. Thus, following Frankfurter, Hand rejected the modern Court's invention of the "double standard," which had very nearly reversed this principle by elevating certain provisions of the Bill of Rights to a preferred constitutional status (1958:34, 48–51, 29–30). As Gunther notes, Hand's "doubts about judicial activism had increased during his last years. Hostility to judges' tendency to pour their personal preferences into vague constitutional phrases was Hand's most consistent, deep-seated feeling about courts, and . . . the due-process clauses had long been his special target," but "his skepticism produced a prescription of self-restraint — indeed, near abdication — that went well beyond his earlier views" (1994:664–65). In other words, in reaction against the Warren Court's emerging activism, Hand carried his critique of judicial power so far as to threaten the abandonment of judicially enforceable constitutional rights altogether.

Hand's 1958 lectures were particularly significant because they provided the critique of judicial power with both public exposure and intellectual legitimacy. His argument that judges generally "wrap up their veto in a protective veil of adjectives . . . , whose office usually . . . is to disguise what they are doing and impute to it a derivation far more impressive than their personal preferences, which are all that in fact lie behind the decision," has since become quite familiar. And his most famous passage — that "[f]or myself it would be most irksome to be ruled by a bevy of Platonic Guardians, even if I knew how to choose them, which I assuredly do not" — is still quoted to this day (1958:70, 73–74). At the time, these arguments were quickly picked up by southern editorial writers, congressional advocates of Court-curbing legislation, and other Warren Court critics, and for those who supported the Court's activism, or at least hoped to preserve some realm of judicially enforceable constitutional liberty, Hand's lectures posed a sharp challenge (Gunther 1994:659–62; Powe 2000:129–32).

The most famous response was provided by constitutional scholar Herbert Wechsler in the Holmes Lectures at Harvard the following year. Wechsler began by noting that unlike Hand, he had "not the slightest doubt respecting the legitimacy of judicial review" and that this power "is grounded in the language of the Constitution and is not a mere interpolation." He saw Hand's call for the courts to avoid deciding constitutional cases as a dereliction of judicial duty, and he set about to articulate a set of standards to govern the practice of constitutional adjudication. In doing so, he sought a middle ground for the Court between a strict originalist approach and unconstrained judicial legislation, "a middle ground consisting of judicial action that embodies what are surely the main qualities of law, its generality and its neutrality." Wechsler explicitly rejected the use of constitutional adjudication to achieve preferred results, decrying as illegitimate the position of any constitutional interpreter who "know[s] he disapproves of a decision when all he knows is that it has sustained a claim put forward by a labor union or a taxpayer, a Negro or a segregationist, a corporation or a Communist." He argued that "the main constituent of the judicial process is precisely that it must be genuinely principled, resting with respect to every step that is involved in reaching judgment on analysis and reasons quite transcending the immediate result that is achieved." He acknowledged that courts are inevitably faced with political questions, but insisted that they are only allowed to give certain kinds of answers, which is why they are required to support their "choice of values by the type of reasoned explanation that . . . is intrinsic to judicial action" (1959:2–3, 6–9, 12, 15–16).

Wechsler's defense of judicial power, then, rested not on the authority of the constitutional text or its original meaning — each of which he rejected as inadequate guides — but on "the role of reason and of principle in the judicial" process. Following Frankfurter, he insisted that in exercising judicial review, the courts "are bound to function otherwise than as a naked power organ; they participate as courts of law." As such, legal decisions that are properly principled must "rest[ ] on reasons with respect to all the issues in the case, reasons that in their generality and their neutrality transcend any immediate result that is involved. When no sufficient reasons of this kind can be assigned for overturning value choices of the other branches of the Government or of a state, those choices must, of course, survive" (1959:16, 19).

Though Wechsler sought through this approach to defend modern judicial power from Hand's critique, his application of the approach revealed its limits. Like Hand, Wechsler argued that the Warren Court had not adequately justified its decision in *Brown*. He repeatedly insisted that he agreed with the result, but complained that it did not rest on neutral principles. He was not concerned that the Court had overturned its own precedents or had departed from the original meaning of the Fourteenth Amendment, but thought the Court simply had not provided adequate reasoning in support of its elaboration of constitutional principle. On his reading, "the question posed by state-enforced segregation is not one of discrimination at all" since the separate school facilities were, hypothetically, equal to each other. The question, rather, involved the freedom of association, and "[g]iven a situation where the state must practically choose between denying the association to those individuals who wish it or imposing it on those who would avoid it," he could find no "basis in neutral principles for holding that the Constitution demands that the claims for association should prevail" (1959:27, 34, 31–32).

The Hand–Wechsler debate helped spawn a distinctive new style of scholarly critique of the Court. Both Wechsler and (to a lesser extent) Hand denounced the Court's work on the grounds of legal craftsmanship. In their view, the opinions of the Warren Court were poorly reasoned, incompetently drafted, result-oriented, unprincipled, and even irrational. Hand also called for the Court to refrain from exercising judicial review whenever possible and criticized the current Court for its eagerness to declare constitutional limitations on government action. A number of prominent scholars advanced these arguments during the Warren years, but it was Alexander Bickel who would develop them most fully. Like Wechsler, Bickel responded to Hand's sharp critique of constitutionalism with a defense of judicial power, and like Wechsler, Bickel settled on an approach that remained suspicious of Warren Court activism.

In addition to the Holmes Lectures, the principal institutional outlet for this emerging scholarly critique was the *Harvard Law Review*'s annual foreword, in which a prominent scholar would review the Court's previous term. In 1959, for example, Henry Hart used his foreword to criticize the Warren Court for failing to measure up to even "minimal standards of craftsmanship and intellectual responsibility" (1959:122).[30] After a lengthy analysis of a recent habeas corpus decision, he complained that "the Court gave gratuitous aid and comfort to the most extreme of its critics who say that it twists facts and words at its pleasure in order to reach the results it wants to reach." He insisted, moreover, "that these failures are threatening to undermine the professional respect of first-rate lawyers for the incumbent Justices of the Court" (1959:110, 101). Hart attributed this failing to the alleged fact that the justices lacked adequate time to study, deliberate on, and decide the number of cases with which they were faced each year, a notion he drew from a Frankfurter dissent in an insurance case from the previous term. "Regretfully and with deference," Hart noted, "it has to be said that too many of the Court's opinions are about what one would expect could be written in twenty-four hours." Hence, he concluded, the justices should exercise restraint by deciding fewer cases (1959:100–101).[31]

Two years later, Bickel built on Hart's argument in his own *Harvard Law Review* foreword, articulating the doctrine by which the Court could legitimately avoid deciding some of the cases with which it was presented. Following Hand's suggestion that the power of judicial review "need not be exercised whenever a court sees, or thinks that it sees, an invasion of the Constitution," Bickel urged the justices to exercise the "passive virtues." He emphasized that in any given constitutional case, the Court had not two but three options: it could uphold the law or it could strike it down, but it could also do neither, and he urged the Court to remember this option of forbearance. To aid the Court in doing so, he drew from Brandeis's opinion in *Ashwander* and expounded at some length on the doctrines of jurisdiction, standing, ripeness, mootness, and political questions. As an exemplary instance of the use of such doctrines, Bickel called attention to *Poe v. Ullman*, in which, as I noted earlier, Frankfurter refused to hear a constitutional challenge to Connecticut's anti-contraception law (Bickel 1961:58–64; Hand 1958:14–16; see also Freund 1952; Bickel and Wellington 1957).

These Warren Court critics were part of a broader postwar scholarly movement whose advocates emphasized the varying "institutional competencies" of judicial, legislative, administrative, and private lawmaking institutions. For these "legal process" scholars, the duty of elected legislatures was to determine the substantive content of the law, while the particular institu-

tional competence of courts was to engage in the "reasoned elaboration" of
legal principles. Both the terms "legal process" and "reasoned elaboration"
were coined by Hart and his Harvard Law School colleague Albert Sacks in
their casebook *The Legal Process: Basic Problems in the Making and Application of Law*. Though never actually published during their lifetimes, the
mimeographed 1958 "tentative edition" was, in legal historian Morton Horwitz's words, "[t]he most influential and widely used text in American law
schools during the 1950s" (1992:254).[32]

For Hart and Sacks, one of the first questions a court should ask about any
dispute with which it is presented is whether "the legislature as an institution
[is] a more appropriate agency of settlement than a court." Only if the dispute is susceptible to resolution by reference to some preexisting legal rule or
principle — even if that rule or principle requires significant elaboration to
decide the extant case — does it fall within the institutional competence of
the courts. After all, "it is an integral part of the concept of adjudication . . .
that decision is to be arrived at by reference to impersonal criteria of decision
applicable in the same fashion in any similar case." In Hart and Sacks's view,
a legal interpreter must always elaborate the particular legal provision at issue "in a way which is consistent with other established applications of it.
And he must do so in the way which best serves the principles and policies it
expresses." Thus, "the magistrate is obliged to relate his decision in some reasoned fashion to the . . . [legal provision] out of which the question arises. He
is not to think of himself as in the same position as a legislator taking part in
the enactment of the statute in the first place" (1994:341, 643, 147, 143).

Hart and Sacks did not discuss constitutional interpretation extensively in
their casebook, but Wechsler's "neutral principles" formulation was clearly
drawn from their broader approach.[33] As with Wechsler's neutral principles,
Hart and Sacks's notion of "reasoned elaboration" represented a middle
ground between a mechanical vision of legal rules, on the one hand, and an
overtly political vision of unbridled judicial discretion, on the other: "In the
difficult and delicate enterprise of trying to control the future [by means of
law], choice does not have to be made between the rigors of a perfected
rule . . . and the looseness of unbuttoned discretion" (1994:144). These scholars were all reacting against the legal realist movement by acknowledging that
"general directives often do not transparently tell officials and citizens what
to do in specific situations, . . . [but] nevertheless disput[ing] the realist
claims that the official simply imposes a political interpretation on the general directive and that law is a prediction of how the official will exercise his

discretion" (Eskridge and Frickey 1994:xcii). According to the legal process scholars, "judges neither found law in the old-fashioned sense nor made it in the sense of the Realists; they reasoned toward it and then articulated their reasoning processes." For these scholars, then, it was crucial "to impress upon the Court's members a sense of the kinds of controversies which were justiciable and which sorts of analytical processes were likely to produce respected opinions" (White 1978b:144, 148–49).

Like Wechsler, Bickel followed Hart and Sacks in defending judicial power while still emphasizing the importance of judicial restraint. He expanded on the argument of his Harvard foreword in his monumental book *The Least Dangerous Branch: The Supreme Court at the Bar of Politics,* which began by articulating what was fast becoming the defining preoccupation of modern constitutional theory: "The root difficulty is that judicial review is a counter-majoritarian force in our system" and hence "a deviant institution in the American democracy." Despite this stark formulation, Bickel sought to follow Wechsler in mapping out a middle ground that stopped short of Hand's abandonment of constitutionalism:

> The search must be for a function which might (indeed, must) involve the making of policy, yet which differs from the legislative and executive functions; which is peculiarly suited to the capabilities of the courts; which will not likely be performed elsewhere if the courts do not assume it; which can be so exercised as to be acceptable in a society that generally shares Judge Hand's satisfaction in a "sense of common venture"; which will be effective when needed; and whose discharge by the courts will not lower the quality of the other departments' performance by denuding them of the dignity and burden of their own responsibility.[34]

Bickel had been grappling toward such a middle ground ever since his initial response to Hand's lectures in 1958. Writing in *The New Republic* that year, he had characterized Hand's argument as "a radical doctrine of judicial restraint" and noted that the Court had never "adhered to quite so uncompromising a position." In Gunther's words, "Bickel struggled to state a function that somehow managed to assign to the courts 'the weighing of choices,' yet 'which differs from the legislative and executive functions.' He found an answer that satisfied him by insisting on Supreme Court decisions 'properly attuned to our people's traditions and aspirations and resting on deeply felt first principles,' an approach he argued was distinguishable from 'more personal or group preferences.' In short, he tried to solve the conundrum by allying himself with an essentially Frankfurterian restrained approach, which he thought distinguishable from the even greater judicial abstinence advocated by Hand" (Gunther 1994:663, quoting Bickel 1958:16). As Edward Purcell has noted, *The Least Dangerous Branch* was Bickel's effort to reconcile his support for restraint with his support for *Brown,* the same task of reconciliation that Frankfurter himself faced (1976:532–36).

Like Wechsler, Bickel sought to craft this defense of judicial power on the basis of "the need . . . for an institution which stands altogether aside from the current clash of interests, and which, insofar as is humanly possible, is concerned only with principle." He argued that "government should serve not only what we conceive from time to time to be our immediate material needs but also certain enduring values," and that the Supreme Court might serve as "the pronouncer and guardian of such values." While legislative assemblies were ordinarily disposed to act on the basis of expediency and "the pressure for immediate results," Bickel thought that courts would have a greater "capacit[y] for dealing with matters of principle. . . . Judges have, or should have, the leisure, the training, and the insulation to follow the ways of the scholar in pursuing the ends of government." Moreover, he insisted, "[t]heir insulation and the marvelous mystery of time give courts the capacity to appeal to men's better natures, to call forth their aspirations, which may have been forgotten in the moment's hue and cry."[35]

Given this approach, of course, the crucial question was "[h]ow and whence do nine lawyers, holding lifetime appointments, devise or derive principles which they are prepared to impose without recourse upon a democratic society?" Like Hand and Wechsler, Bickel rejected any simplistic reliance on the constitutional text or its original meaning, noting that such materials are no more than "sources of inspiration" or reflection. Building on the foundation laid down by Frankfurter and Hand, moreover, he suggested that "[t]he function of the Justices . . . is to immerse themselves in the tradition of our society and of kindred societies that have gone before, in history and in the sediment of history which is law, and, as Judge Hand once suggested, in the thought and the vision of the philosophers and the poets." Having done so, "[t]he Justices will then be fit to extract 'fundamental presuppositions' from . . . the evolving morality of our tradition. . . . Only through this effort . . . can the conscientious judge himself be assured that he is not at sea, buffeted by the wavelets of his personal predilections" (1986:235–37). In Bickel's view, while the life of the law had not been logic, it had been "reason"— a principled process of analysis, argument, judgment, and rhetoric.

Bickel recognized that this "forum of principle" approach was potentially open-ended, and he sought to constrain it by insisting that the "Court should declare as law only such principles as will — in time, but in a rather immediate and foreseeable future — gain general assent. . . . The Court is a leader of opinion, not a mere register of it, but it must lead opinion, not merely impose its own; and — the short of it is — it labors under the obligation to succeed." [36] In this way, "[i]t may . . . be that if the process is properly carried out, an aspect of the current — not only the timeless, mystic — popular will finds expression in constitutional adjudication. The result may be a tolerable accommodation with the theory and practice of democracy." As exemplars of this judicial application of reason, he pointed to Brandeis's dissent in *Olmstead* — arguing that the principle of privacy underlying the Fourth Amendment prohibited unauthorized wire-tapping — and the Court's decision in *Brown* (Bickel 1986:28). Bickel's argument here represented the apex of his long and influential effort to articulate a principled defense of modern judicial power that was consistent with democratic theory, an effort he would ultimately abandon as a failure.

As legal historian Laura Kalman has noted, Bickel and his fellow postwar constitutional theorists rendered democracy "a central legitimating concept in constitutional law," but the normative vision of democracy that they adopted was a fairly complacent one: "Without any evidence, Bickel assumed that the legislature pursued a majoritarian perspective, reflective of the popular will" (Kalman 1996:39–41; see also Horwitz 1993). As Gary Peller has observed, "the fifties constitutional law theorists who made the 'counter-majoritarian difficulty' the centerpiece of their entire theoretical approach never bothered to consider the legitimacy of legislative action" (1988:611). Instead, these scholars took that legitimacy for granted, in large part because of what Purcell has described as "the spreading status quo orientation that marked social thought during the two decades after World War II." Postwar social scientists and legal scholars tended to treat the existing American system as the ideal example of a practically workable democracy and thus "to gloss over the glaring discrepancies of wealth and power that existed in American society" (Purcell 1973:253, 261). As Ronald Kahn has noted, Bickel and Wechsler relied on the contemporary political science scholarship of Robert Dahl and David Truman, which emphasized that America's pluralist "political system was quite open to political change." The leading scholars of American politics during the Warren era tended to abandon the "traditional moral, critical function" of democratic theory and to "gloss[ ] over the glaring discrepancies of wealth and power that existed in American society."[37] Thus, while the adherents of legal process saw their own approach as "liberal and progressive, inspired by an authentic devotion to democracy and the rule of law and posed against the forces of dictatorship and oppression," it was actually "the effect of a particular, and benign, view of American society within which the possibility of social domination had been defined away." In particular, Wechsler's neutral principles article "made clear that the 'rule of law' that would symbolize the free world in the post-War era was perfectly consistent with broad-scale social domination" (Peller 1988:606–7, 621–22). In this way, the postwar legal academy's vision of the constitutional order was closely linked to an uncritical, even apologetic, view of the normal operation of the American democratic system (Purcell 1973:259–66).

Most importantly, as Kahn has noted, the Warren Court was familiar with this complacent vision of American politics and firmly rejected it. The justices simply did not share the scholars' faith in the democratic character of ordinary politics, their "faith that state and local governments, voluntary organizations, and interest group politics were respectful of minorities." Bickel's espousal of judicial prudence and the passive virtues and Wechsler's requirement that the Court articulate neutral principles as the basis for its decisions both had the effect of demanding great deference to the choices made by the political branches. The justices of the Warren Court rejected this deferential stance because they had adopted a much more critical interpretation of American politics. Having disavowed the scholars' "benign view of the normal American political system," the justices considered an activist Court both necessary and legitimate (Kahn 1994:95, 36, 73–76, 91). As Hart and Sacks's posthumous editors later acknowledged, "the legal process materials, the classic exposition of the post-war consensus in public law, were being drafted at the very point when the Warren Court's constitutional activism was posing a systematic challenge to elements of that consensus" (Eskridge and Frickey 1994:xcviii; see also Kersch 2003).

In this light, the oft-repeated scholarly complaints about the Court during the 1950s and early 1960s — Hart's derisive insistence, for example, that if only the justices had more time (and were better lawyers) they would produce more well-reasoned opinions — were based on a fundamental misreading of the Warren Court's constitutional jurisprudence. The problem was not that the Court's opinions were poorly reasoned, but that they were based on reasons that the scholarly critics rejected.[38] Because the Court rejected the apologetic pluralist vision of the political system then regnant among legal and political elites, moreover, Frankfurter's academic allies were unable to help him put a stop to the Court's newfound liberal activism. In *The Least Dangerous Branch,* for instance, Bickel identified Frankfurter's use of the political questions doctrine in *Colegrove v. Green* as a shining example of judicial self-restraint. But Bickel's book was published in 1962, just as the Warren Court was moving in a more activist direction. Earlier that same year, Brennan had written for the Court in *Baker v. Carr,* overturning *Colegrove* and holding that malapportionment was a justiciable question after all. Bickel did his best to characterize *Baker* as simply the opening of a "colloquy" with the elected political institutions — in which the Court was prodding the state legislatures to act without actively trying to constrain the manner in which they did so — but he could not have been more wrong (1986:189–96). Just one year later, in *Gray v. Sanders,* the Court would announce the principle of "one person, one vote," thereby commanding the reapportionment of virtually every state and federal legislative district in the country.

Frankfurter recognized the new dawn more clearly than Bickel. His fifty-five-page dissenting opinion in *Baker* was magisterial, but it was almost literally his dying gasp. The Court rejected his argument, and he suffered a stroke two weeks later. Justice Frankfurter retired in August 1962, just as the Court was turning decisively away from his New Deal vision of judicial restraint and toward a newer, rights-based vision of liberal constitutionalism. This shift caused so much conflict among New Deal liberal constitutionalists that the legal process wing now looks, from our twenty-first century vantage, like a precursor of modern conservatism.

• • •

In sum, the Warren Court responded to the New Deal constitutional revolution not by abandoning judicial power but by articulating a new set of constitutionally protected rights and liberties. This choice rendered Frankfurter's vision of judicial deference a relic of the past; the Court might someday recover it, but that was unlikely for the foreseeable future. Here as elsewhere, the Court's doctrines articulate commitments, both individual and institutional, and the abandonment of these commitments can impose significant costs. Thus, as rights-based constitutionalism became entrenched in the American polity, it would prove increasingly difficult to dislodge. In this light, the influential group of postwar constitutional scholars who responded to the Warren Court's activism by questioning the very legitimacy of judicial power were fighting a rearguard action that would not succeed. As Martin

Shapiro has observed, the New Deal conflict had been the formative experi-ence for the Warren-era commentators, which is why "we heard endlessly about judicial self-restraint, that central theme of the Rooseveltian Court cri-sis, long after the Warren Court had rendered the debate obsolescent by firmly choosing the path of activism" (1983:218). Having made this choice, advocates of restraint were left with the smaller, though still significant, task of constraining this newfound activism at the margins, an effort that fell largely to the Court's internal critics — the dissenting justices of the Warren Court.

CHAPTER THREE

THE WARREN COURT
AND ITS CRITICS
1962–1969

The Warren Court's abandonment of restraint in the reapportionment context was one of a dramatic series of doctrinal innovations expanding the scope of constitutional rights during the 1960s. In many of these decisions, the Supreme Court overturned a precedent that Felix Frankfurter himself had authored, and in all of them, it turned away from his sweeping vision of deference to democratic majorities. Frankfurter left the Court in 1962, hoping to be replaced by a distinguished scholar committed to his own vision of restraint, such as Harvard law professor Paul Freund, but President Kennedy instead chose his own secretary of labor, Arthur Goldberg (Simon 1989:254–55). When Goldberg sided consistently with the Court's activist wing, Frankfurter's deferential approach was buried for the foreseeable future. Henceforward, a majority of the justices saw the active defense of constitutional liberty and equality as the very justification for the Court's existence, and with Frankfurter gone, John Marshall Harlan and Hugo Black emerged as the leading critics of this expanding liberal activism.

Justice Harlan's dissenting role was to be expected, as he had been closely allied with Frankfurter since his appointment in 1955, but Black's refusal to join the Warren Court majority was more surprising. As I have shown, Black had been known as a great liberal activist himself, and his free speech and incorporation opinions of the 1940s and 1950s had laid the groundwork for many of the Warren Court's landmark decisions of the 1960s. He supported some key elements of the Court's rights revolution — in the areas of free speech, reapportionment, and desegregation, most notably — but as this revolution unfolded, he increasingly denounced it for going too far. He was particularly critical, for example, of the Court's enforcement of an unenumerated right to privacy in cases like *Griswold v. Connecticut*. More generally, his continued emphasis on the original constitutional text led him to actively enforce those specific principles of liberty and equality that he found therein, but as the Court followed Harlan Stone in protecting rights not clearly specified in the text, Black stubbornly adhered to the line that he had always drawn. In short, during his last decade on the Court, the liberal majority of both the justices and the nation pushed past him, and his strict textualist approach became a conservative force.

Justice Harlan also supported some of the Court's activist holdings. Following the tradition marked out by Benjamin Cardozo and Frankfurter, he emphasized the unavoidability of "reasoned judgment" in constitutional adjudication, insisting that that judgment be tempered by history and self-restraint. In his hands, however, this approach seemed to authorize a greater degree of judicial activism, particularly in defense of due process liberty. Still, when his colleagues failed to exercise the requisite restraint, when they ignored the historical limits on the judicial role, or when they dragged the Court into political thickets, Harlan followed Frankfurter in denouncing what they saw as aggrandizements of power. In sum, Harlan's and Black's distinctive approaches to constitutional adjudication led each of them to support certain elements of the rights revolution — not, generally, the same ones — but they remained sharply critical of others, and they were, in fact, the leading dissenters during the heyday of the Warren Court.

Playing these dissenting roles during a time of great public attention on the Court, Harlan and Black each made important modifications to the Frankfurterian critique. In their influential dissenting opinions throughout the 1960s, they supplemented Frankfurter's deference with more explicit appeals to constitutional text and history, to their own reasoned judgment, and to an emerging critique of liberal egalitarianism — all of which would influence conservative critiques of the Court for years to come. For example, given the majority's increasingly innovative use of the Fourteenth Amendment, both Harlan and Black were led to denounce the Court for departing from the amendment's original meaning. As I have shown in chapters 1 and 2, this "originalist" approach to the Fourteenth Amendment had been present in constitutional discourse since the 1940s, though it had yet to be named as such. Black himself had turned in 1947 to a detailed excavation of the records of the Thirty-ninth Congress to argue that the Due Process Clause incorporated the individual provisions of the Bill of Rights, and the Court later called attention to this same history on the question of school segregation.[1] Through 1962, however, this historical approach had never been adopted by the post–New Deal Court — it was explicitly rejected in both *Adamson v. California* and *Brown v. Board of Education* — and it had not even very often been advanced as a respectable criticism of the Court's newfound liberal activism. Prior to this point, most critics of the Warren Court had relied instead on the Frankfurterian doctrine of deference to contemporary democratic majorities. In short, it was the dissenting opinions of the Warren Court that for the first time made originalism an acceptable part of the conservative critique of judicial power.

After Frankfurter's retirement, as table 3.1 shows, Harlan and Black were the Warren Court's first and third most frequent dissenters, respectively, but they were not the only justices who questioned some of the Court's activist holdings during the 1960s. Byron White and Tom Clark each wrote a number of influential dissenting opinions, particularly in the area of criminal procedure, and Potter Stewart dissented even more frequently than Black. Appointed by Eisenhower in 1958, Stewart often agreed with Harlan, regularly criticizing the Warren Court for ignoring the historical meaning of the Constitution, but he also revealed a pragmatic tendency to support some innovative constitutional interpretations. In the reapportionment context, for example, he broke with Frankfurter and Harlan in *Baker v. Carr*, deliberating for some time before casting the decisive vote for judicial intervention (Lewis 1997). When the Court extended the "one person, one vote" principle so far as to invalidate a districting scheme that had been approved by a majority of voters in a statewide initiative, however, he joined Harlan in dissent.[2] In the privacy rights context, Stewart first agreed with Black, but later reconsidered, dissenting in *Griswold* but then joining the Court majority in *Roe v. Wade*. Stewart also joined Harlan in dissenting from the Court's landmark criminal procedure decisions in *Escobedo v. Illinois* and *Miranda v. Arizona*, and he was the only justice to dissent from the landmark school prayer decisions in *Engel v. Vitale* and *Abingdon School District v. Schempp*.

While Justices Harlan and Black were not alone in dissenting from the Warren Court revolution, they articulated the two most well developed, coherent, and sustained critiques. These two critiques were fundamentally incompatible — like Frankfurter and Black, Harlan and Black rarely agreed with each other — but each has played a crucial role in the development of constitutional conservatism. So long as they were offering a dissenting cri-

TABLE 3.1 *Frequency of Dissent, 1962–1968 Terms**

Term/Justice	Black	Douglas	Warren	Brennan	Harlan	Clark	Stewart	White	Goldberg	Fortas	Marshall
1962	13.6	16.4	6.5	4.5	38.5	23.1	30.0	13.2	9.7	—	—
1963	16.5	14.2	5.5	4.7	36.4	17.4	19.4	15.7	14.3	—	—
1964	24.7	23.6	5.8	2.2	21.6	6.7	18.4	8.0	13.8	—	—
1965	22.0	20.2	3.3	2.1	30.1	6.4	20.4	13.2	—	10.7	—
1966	18.6	28.9	14.6	9.6	33.0	14.0	31.6	10.9	—	23.1	—
1967	22.0	14.4	6.5	2.8	26.9	—	17.6	17.4	—	8.4	1.8
1968	31.3	19.8	7.4	2.1	29.5	—	31.3	15.8	—	14.3	4.7
Total	21.0	19.4	7.1	4.0	31.1	14.0	24.1	13.6	12.5	13.9	3.5

Source: Original U.S. Supreme Court Database, with orally argued citation as unit of analysis.

*Percentage of formally decided full opinion cases in which each justice dissented.

tique as opposed to a governing philosophy, moreover, this incompatibility was inconsequential. Harlan and Black each accused their colleagues of ignoring the proper limits on the Court's role and rewriting the Constitution to suit their own ends. That they advanced these accusations on different grounds did not, for the moment, seem to matter.

The Warren Court and the American Democracy of Rights

The Warren Court had pointed toward its newfound liberal activism as early as *Brown,* but during the 1950s, that case could be viewed as an exceptional response to America's most blatant and long-standing constitutional violation. The *Brown* decision, after all, was sharply denounced by Frankfurter's followers, and the Court had moved very cautiously in the area of desegregation during the subsequent decade. Not until after Frankfurter's retirement did it become clear that the country was witnessing the birth of a new constitutional order. For this reason, Lucas Powe (2000) has referred to the last seven terms of Warren's tenure as "history's Warren Court."

To appreciate the sweeping reach of the Warren Court's rights revolution, consider the series of landmark decisions during the Court's 1963 term. In *New York Times Co. v. Sullivan,* Justice William Brennan dramatically expanded the reach of the First Amendment, ruling for the first time that it imposed a limit on state libel law, and inserting the Court into the ongoing civil rights conflict in the process. Just a few months later, the Court revealed its continuing concern for free speech by overturning an obscenity conviction and seizure from Ohio and Kansas, respectively.[3] In the civil rights context, the Court also ratcheted up its enforcement of *Brown* by holding that Prince Edward County, Virginia could not constitutionally close its public schools to avoid desegregating them, and threw out the state trespass convictions of twelve African American students for staging a sit-in at a segregated restaurant.[4] In *Escobedo,* a sharply divided Court condemned the system of police interrogations and criminal confessions used in all fifty states, laying the groundwork for the sweeping *Miranda* decision two years later. And in *Wesberry v. Sanders, Lucas v. Forty-fourth General Assembly,* and *Reynolds v. Sims,* the Court extended the "one person, one vote" principle to almost every electoral district in the country. As if that were not enough, the Court also struck down two federal statutes — one authorizing the revocation of citizenship for certain foreign-born citizens living abroad and one providing for the denial of passports to all members of Communist organizations.[5]

As this brief review makes clear, Black's defense of the Bill of Rights had laid an important jurisprudential foundation for the Warren Court's activism, although he himself denounced much of this later activism as illegitimate. Even more important were the foundations laid by Stone in the late 1930s and 1940s, as much of the Warren Court's activism was designed to police the democratic process and to protect minority rights. Some years later, constitutional scholar John Hart Ely would offer a magisterial defense of Warren Court jurisprudence on precisely these grounds, and both contemporary critics and subsequent historians have described the Warren Court by reference to Stone's influential footnote from *United States v. Carolene Products* as well (Ely 1980; Wechsler 1965:1002–3; Blum 1991:188–217).

Building on these jurisprudential foundations, the Court was leading the nation toward a new American democracy of rights.[6] As Powe has noted, the Warren Court overruled precedents in forty-five separate cases, and in forty-four of these moved the law in a more liberal direction (2000:405). As tables 2.1 and 2.2 made clear, moreover, "history's Warren Court" declared federal, state, and local statutes unconstitutional more frequently than during any previous period of the Court's history. Thus, the 1960s marked a critical juncture, a crucial fork in the nation's long road toward the ever firmer establishment of rights-based constitutionalism. Having considered and rejected the political and constitutional vision proffered by Frankfurter and the scholarly critics — the claim that the American political system faithfully represented the majority will and adequately protected minority rights — the justices of the Warren Court set out to police the democratic process, to prevent majoritarian discrimination, and to preserve civil liberties. In doing so, they would spark a critical backlash, and the lines of this critique would generally begin with the Court's own dissenting justices.

DUE PROCESS LIBERTY AND THE BILL OF RIGHTS

The year before Frankfurter's retirement, the Court had begun what would prove a revolution in the constitutional law of criminal procedure, holding in *Mapp v. Ohio* that the Fourth Amendment exclusionary rule applied to state criminal proceedings, thus overruling Frankfurter's opinion for the Court in *Wolf v. Colorado*. Two years later, in *Gideon v. Wainwright,* the Court held that the Sixth Amendment required the states to provide counsel for indigent criminal defendants, overturning *Betts v. Brady,* in which Frankfurter had joined Justice Owen Roberts in reaching the opposite conclusion.

In *Mapp* and then *Gideon,* the Court reopened the incorporation debate and rejected Frankfurter's long-standing argument that the Due Process Clause did not apply the Bill of Rights to the states. The Court also rejected Black's demand for total incorporation, choosing instead to incorporate the various provisions of the Bill of Rights one at a time. Over the next few years, Brennan led the Court in doing so with the privilege against self-incrimination, the right to confront witnesses, the right to a speedy trial, the right to compulsory process for obtaining witnesses, the right to a jury trial, and the prohibition on double jeopardy — this last one occurring on the final day of the Warren Court and representing a reversal of Cardozo's landmark holding in *Palko v. Connecticut.*[7] Most controversial were the cases dealing with police interrogations and confessions, *Escobedo* and *Miranda,* in which the Court famously held that before questioning a criminal suspect, the police must inform him of his rights to remain silent and to the assistance of counsel.

Throughout these cases, Black continued to urge the total incorporation of the Bill of Rights, but he was happy to go along with Brennan's second-best alternative. Harlan continued to follow Charles Fairman's and Frankfurter's historical arguments and to criticize the Court for wrongly imposing federal constitutional norms on the state governments. In *Escobedo* and *Miranda,* for example, Harlan objected to the Court's dramatic expansion of the constitutional limits on police interrogations, an expansion that Black supported, and in *Duncan v. Louisiana* he dissented from the Court's incorporation of the right to trial by jury, insisting that "[t]he overwhelming historical evidence marshalled by Professor Fairman demonstrates, to me conclusively, that the Congressmen and state legislators who wrote, debated, and ratified the Fourteenth Amendment did not think they were 'incorporating' the Bill of Rights." Citing Holmes, Frankfurter, and Cardozo for support, Harlan reiterated that the Due Process Clause was an independent guarantee of fundamental fairness, the content of which should be determined by reference to the nation's legal history and traditions.[8]

This independent guarantee, on Harlan's reading, was not to be stretched by the Court to impose overly restrictive limits on the operation of state criminal law, but it did retain a significant substantive content of its own. Outside the incorporation context, for example, Harlan articulated a vision of Fourteenth Amendment liberty that was much more expansive than Frankfurter's. In *Poe v. Ullman,* when Frankfurter had avoided the constitutional issue by appealing to the passive virtues, Harlan had offered a broad substantive due process rationale for striking down Connecticut's criminal contraception statute:

> [T]he full scope of the liberty guaranteed by the Due Process Clause cannot be found in or limited by the precise terms of the specific guarantees elsewhere provided in the Constitution. This "liberty" is not a series of isolated points pricked out in terms of the taking of property; the freedom of speech, press, and religion; . . . and so on. It is a rational continuum which, broadly speaking, includes a freedom from all substantial arbitrary impositions and purposeless restraints, . . . and which also recognizes, what a reasonable and sensitive judgment must, that certain interests require particularly careful scrutiny of the state needs asserted to justify their abridgment.

Harlan's approach to due process liberty was clearly indebted to Frankfurter, but he was simply more willing to enforce such liberty in particular cases. Like Frankfurter, he was confident that the Court's broad discretion in doing so would be adequately constrained by the exercise of reasoned "judgment and restraint." By attending to legal history and traditions, in the manner of the common law, Harlan hoped to prevent himself and his colleagues from "roam[ing] where unguided speculation might take them." While the content of due process liberty could not "be determined by reference to any code," Harlan insisted that the Court could find guidance in "the balance which our Nation, built upon postulates of respect for the liberty of the individual, has struck between that liberty and the demands of organized society. . . . The balance of which I speak is the balance struck by this country, having regard to what history teaches are the traditions from which it developed as well as the traditions from which it broke. That tradition is a living thing."[9]

Having outlined such a sweeping vision of constitutional liberty, Harlan easily concluded in *Poe* that Connecticut's contraception statute was invalid. After all, "the statute allows the State to enquire into, prove and punish married people for the private use of their marital intimacy," thus invading "the privacy of the home in its most basic sense." In his view, it was "difficult to imagine what is more private or more intimate than a husband and wife's marital relations," and such marital privacy had been so uniformly recognized throughout our nation's history as to be included within the Fourteenth Amendment's guarantee of liberty against state infringement. He acknowledged that the home could be "made a sanctuary for crime," and hence that "[t]he right of privacy most manifestly is not an absolute." This new-found liberty, he insisted, did not include the right to engage in "adultery, homosexuality, fornication and incest . . . , however privately practiced."[10] Despite these efforts to limit its reach, however, Harlan's *Poe* opinion has spawned a long line of cases extending constitutional protection to a wide variety of unenumerated rights, including some that Harlan himself would have rejected.[11]

This result confirmed Black's assessment of the dangers of such a flexible, Frankfurterian approach, and when the Court followed Harlan's lead four years later in *Griswold,* Black objected in a biting dissent. Given Black's argument in particular, and the continuing legacy of the New Deal conflict more generally, the *Griswold* majority was unwilling to openly endorse Harlan's expansive conception of substantive due process. Writing for the Court, Justice William O. Douglas sought to draw a line between economic liberty and privacy rights, declining the "invitation" to follow *Lochner* and observing that "[w]e do not sit as a super-legislature to determine the wisdom, need, and propriety of laws that touch economic problems, business affairs, or social conditions. This law, however, operates directly on an intimate relation of husband and wife and their physician's role in one aspect of that relation." Douglas's evasiveness here produced a notoriously convoluted opinion, which rested on the holding that "specific guarantees in the Bill of Rights have penumbras, formed by emanations from those guarantees that help give them life and substance." In other words, Douglas went out of his way to try to link the newly recognized privacy right to the words of the original constitutional text, and thus to avoid Black's charge of judicial lawmaking. Despite Douglas's best efforts, however, the Court's holding has subsequently been read as an endorsement of Harlan's expansive vision of substantive due process liberty. In a separate concurring opinion, Justice Harlan reiterated that the Due Process Clause protects rights beyond those "assured by the letter or penumbra of the Bill of Rights" and he, Douglas, and Goldberg all cited his *Poe* opinion in support.[12]

Both Black and Stewart dissented, agreeing with Douglas that "the day has long passed since the Due Process Clause was regarded as a proper instrument for determining 'the wisdom, need and propriety' of state laws," and insisting that the justices were thereby bound to uphold the Connecticut statute no matter how strongly they objected to it.[13] After all, they noted, the Court had been consistently rejecting due process challenges to state economic regulations for several years. Just two years earlier, every justice except

Harlan had joined Black's opinion in *Ferguson v. Skrupa,* holding that "[t]he doctrine that prevailed in *Lochner, Coppage, Adkins, Burns,* and like cases — that due process authorizes courts to hold laws unconstitutional when they believe the legislature has acted unwisely — has long since been discarded. We have returned to the original constitutional proposition that courts do not substitute their social and economic beliefs for the judgment of legislative bodies, who are elected to pass laws." Upholding a Kansas statute outlawing the debt-adjusting business, Black had added that "relief, if any be needed, lies not with us but with the body constituted to pass laws for the State of Kansas." [14] Black rejected the post–New Deal "double standard" — which distinguished "personal rights" from "property rights" — and hence saw no constitutional difference between Connecticut's contraception statute and Kansas' debt-adjusting statute.

Dissenting in *Griswold,* Black declared that he liked his privacy as well as anyone else, but that he was "nevertheless compelled to admit that government has a right to invade it unless prohibited by some specific constitutional provision." In Black's view, the *Griswold* holding was simply an effort "to claim for this Court . . . power to invalidate any legislative act which the judges find irrational, unreasonable or offensive. . . . If these formulas based on 'natural justice,' or others which mean the same thing, are to prevail, they require judges to determine what is or is not constitutional on the basis of their own appraisal of what laws are unwise or unnecessary. The power to make such decisions is of course that of a legislative body." Citing Hand's aphorism comparing the justices to "a bevy of Platonic Guardians," he insisted that the post-1937 Court had rightly repudiated this characteristic *Lochner*-era reasoning. Here, as elsewhere, Black rejected the notion that the Court should be the engine of a living Constitution that changes to meet changing circumstances, and insisted that if the substantive due process decisions were wrong in 1905, they remained wrong sixty years later. The Article V amendment procedures, Black emphasized, remained the only legitimate mode of constitutional change: "That method of change was good for our Fathers, and being somewhat old-fashioned I must add it is good enough for me." [15]

Black and Harlan were both concerned with the arbitrary and undemocratic exercise of judicial power — the problem of "government by judiciary" — but they both also sought to preserve an important realm of judicially enforceable constitutional liberty. They each sought to resolve this tension by appealing to history, though their particular understandings of history, interpretation, and legal judgment remained far apart. Black's fear of judicial tyranny led him to exercise restraint not just in the due process context, but with respect to any constitutional provision that was (on his reading) so vague that it was not subject to principled interpretation and application. Harlan and Frankfurter fundamentally disagreed with Black on this point, as they thought that history could constrain the Court even where the text was open-ended. While Frankfurter had considered Fourth Amendment privacy one of the most important principles enshrined in the Constitution, for example, Black essentially ignored this provision because he found its prohibition of "unreasonable searches and seizures" irredeemably vague. In *Rochin v. California,* for example, Black had fully agreed that forcible stomach pumping to retrieve evidence was unconstitutional, but had sharply rejected the "shocks the conscience" test that Frankfurter had used to reach that holding. Frankfurter had insisted that this test did not refer to his own individual conscience, and had offered a number of verbal formulations designed to guide the Court's judgment — the "decencies of civilized conduct," "the compelling traditions of the legal profession," "the traditions and conscience of our people," and the like — but Black had found these "evanescent" and "nebulous" standards essentially meaningless. With recent decisions like *Dennis v. United States* as evidence, Black had good reason to worry that Frankfurter's approach would "inevitably imperil" constitutional liberty, but as the Warren Court pushed past him in the 1960s, he spent more time denouncing it for going too far in defense of constitutional liberty and less time criticizing it for not going far enough.[16]

In *Katz v. United States,* for example, Black dissented from the Court's holding that the Fourth Amendment applied to wiretaps used by law enforcement officers without a warrant because he did "not believe that the words of the Amendment will bear the meaning given them by today's decision," and he did "not believe that it is the proper role of this Court to rewrite the Amendment in order to . . . reach a result that many people believe to be desirable." Emphasizing the text's explicit reference to "persons, houses, papers, and effects," all of which are "tangible things with size, form, and weight," he insisted that "[a] conversation overheard by eavesdropping . . . is not tangible and, under the normally accepted meanings of the words, can neither be searched nor seized." Black acknowledged that the framers had been unfamiliar with wiretapping, but noted that they were certainly aware of eavesdropping and insisted that "if they had desired to outlaw or restrict the use of evidence obtained [in such a manner], . . . they would have used the appropriate language to do so. . . . They certainly would not have left such a task to the ingenuity of language-stretching judges." Applying his characteristically fixed conception of constitutional meaning, Black criticized Harlan's concurring opinion as yet another "illustrat[ion of] the propensity of some members of the Court to rely on their limited understanding of modern scientific subjects in order to fit the Constitution to the times and give its language a meaning that it will not tolerate." [17]

Harlan and Black continued this debate through their last years on the Court. Dissenting in *In re Winship,* for example, Black reiterated his objections to a broad, unwritten concept of substantive due process, providing yet another indication that Harlan's approach would sometimes prove a more robust defense of constitutional liberty. [18] In *Winship,* Black objected to the Court's extension of the requirement of proof beyond a reasonable doubt to state juvenile court proceedings because the constitutional guarantee of due process has no content beyond the specific provisions of the Bill of Rights, and those provisions do not include the "reasonable doubt" requirement. In contrast, Harlan insisted that to allow the conviction of juveniles on the basis of the less rigorous standard of preponderance of the evidence "offends the requirement of fundamental fairness embodied in the Due Process Clause." Noting his "continued bafflement at . . . Black's insistence that due process . . . does not embody a concept of fundamental fairness as part of our scheme of constitutionally ordered liberty," Harlan objected that Black's "thesis flies in the face of . . . an unbroken line of opinions that have interpreted due process to impose restraints on the procedures government may adopt in its dealing with its citizens." Here, Harlan cited his own opinion in *Poe,* as well as Charles Fairman's "uncontroverted scholarly research . . . respecting the intendment of the Due Process Clause." Black's familiar response was to reiterate his "belief that [the constitutional] document itself should be our guide, not our own concept of what is fair, decent, and right." As always, he rejected "the 'natural law due process' notion by which this Court frees itself from the limits of a written Constitution and sets itself loose to declare any law unconstitutional that 'shocks its conscience,' deprives a person of 'fundamental fairness,' or violates the principles 'implicit in the concept of ordered liberty.'" For Black, these phrases were nothing more than euphemisms for Harlan's own individual judgment and opinion, and they served neither to justify nor to constrain the Court's activism. [19]

POLICING THE POLITICAL PROCESS

Harlan rejected Black's simplistic textualism, but he too turned to constitutional history when he thought the Court was illegitimately revising the Constitution. While he led the Court in expanding the scope of judicially enforceable constitutional rights in the area of substantive due process, for example, he stood as a firm opponent of such an expansion in the equal protection context. Harlan sought to explain this distinction by insisting that the Court was wrongly interpreting the Equal Protection Clause to include principles that the framers had expressly considered and rejected — such as "one person, one vote" — but rightly interpreting the Due Process Clause merely to apply to new and unforeseen questions. In one of his many reapportionment dissents, for example, Harlan observed that:

> This is not a case in which the Court vindicates the kind of individual rights that are assured by the Due Process Clause of the Fourteenth Amendment, whose "vague contours" of course leave much room for constitutional developments necessitated by changing conditions in a dynamic society. Nor is this a case in which an emergent set of facts requires the Court to frame new principles to protect recognized constitutional rights. The claim for judicial relief in this case strikes at one of the fundamental doctrines of our system of government, the separation of powers. In upholding that claim, the Court attempts to effect reforms in a field which the Constitution, as plainly as can be, has committed exclusively to the political process.[20]

A few years later, Harlan noted that "[t]his resurgence of the expansive view of 'equal protection' carries the seeds of more judicial interference with the state and federal legislative process, much more indeed than does the judicial application of 'due process' according to traditional concepts, about which some members of this Court have expressed fears as to its potentialities for setting us judges 'at large.'"[21] In Harlan's view, the long-standing legal traditions associated with due process liberty would effectively constrain judicial discretion, while the unbounded principle of equality would leave judges free to impose their own idiosyncratic preferences. This distinction was not altogether persuasive to his colleagues. Justice Douglas often made the opposite argument — that "[t]he Due Process Clause . . . has proven very elastic in the hands of judges . . . [while] rather definite guidelines have been developed" governing the reach of the Equal Protection Clause — and Black regularly insisted that both clauses were elastic warrants for arbitrary judicial discretion.[22] Nonetheless, Harlan appears to have taken this distinction seriously, and it led him to fill Frankfurter's shoes as the Court's leading advocate of restraint in the equal protection context.

Frankfurter's dissenting opinion in *Baker* had combined his familiar call for judicial deference with an appeal to history, in what has since become a prominent mode of conservative constitutional argument. The unelected judiciary, this argument runs, has no business enforcing a "constitutional" value that in fact bears no connection to the historical meaning of the constitutional text, particularly where doing so would require a substantial interference with the decisions of the democratic branches. As Frankfurter put it, "[t]he notion that representation proportioned to the geographic spread of population is so universally accepted as a necessary element of equality between man and man that it must be taken to be the standard of a political equality preserved by the Fourteenth Amendment . . . is, to put it bluntly, not true. . . . It was not the English system, it was not the colonial system, it was not the system chosen for the national government by the Constitution, it was not the system exclusively or even predominantly practiced by the States at the time of adoption of the Fourteenth Amendment, it is not predominantly practiced by the States today." To hold otherwise, he had insisted, would be for "the judges of this Court . . . to make their private views of political wisdom the measure of the Constitution — views which in all honesty cannot but give the appearance, if not reflect the reality, of involvement with the business of partisan politics so inescapably a part of apportionment controversies."[23] As far as Frankfurter was concerned, malapportioned state legislative districts could not possibly be held to violate the Equal Protection Clause because an unbroken legal tradition accepting such districts stretched from the colonial era to the present.

Harlan joined Frankfurter's dissent in *Baker,* endorsing its demonstration of "the abrupt departure the majority makes from judicial history by putting the federal courts into this area of state concerns." He also wrote separately, squarely rejecting the claim that "[t]he Equal Protection Clause requires that each vote cast in state legislative elections be given approximately equal weight." Endorsing Frankfurter's reading of the original intentions, he insisted that "there is nothing in the Federal Constitution to prevent a State, acting not irrationally, from choosing any electoral legislative structure it thinks best suited to the interests, temper, and customs of its people." The very existence of the U.S. Senate, he noted, makes clear that our system of democratic representation does not require districts of equal population. He concluded that "[t]hose observers of the Court who see it primarily as the last refuge for the correction of all inequality or injustice, no matter what its nature or source, will no doubt applaud this decision and its break with the past. Those who consider that continuing national respect for the Court's authority depends in large measure upon its wise exercise of self-restraint and discipline in constitutional adjudication, will view the decision with deep concern."[24] Thus, Harlan followed Frankfurter in mobilizing constitutional history to buttress his claim for judicial deference.

The following year, in *Gray v. Sanders,* the Court struck down Georgia's county unit system of election for statewide offices, a system that had the result of weighing rural votes significantly more heavily than urban votes. It was here that Justice Douglas coined the phrase, "one person, one vote," and with Frankfurter gone, it fell to Harlan to object that this standard "surely flies in the face of history." In Harlan's view, the mere numerical disparities in voting strength among the counties did not make the system irrational, and it was only "by judicial fiat" that the Court could say otherwise. He noted that "[t]he disproportions in the Georgia County Unit System are indeed not greatly out of line with those existing under the Electoral College count for the Presidency" and insisted that the Court had unwisely "turned its back" on its "steadfast pre–*Baker v. Carr* refusal 'to enter [the] political thicket.'" In light of these difficulties, Harlan argued that the Court should exercise restraint — in the form of Bickel's passive virtues — by waiting for a fully developed trial record before addressing this issue.[25]

Like Frankfurter, Harlan buttressed his calls for restraint with appeals to either federalism (when he was urging deference to the states) or the separation of powers (when he was urging deference to Congress or the president). In *Baker,* he argued that the Court's holding "strikes deep into the heart of our federal system" because it "would require us to turn our backs on the regard which this Court has always shown for the judgment of state legislatures and courts on matters of basically local concern." Citing *Williamson v. Lee Optical,* Harlan insisted that the Court should exercise the same sort of self-restraint in this context — "when what is involved is the freedom of a State to deal with so intimate a concern as the structure of its own legislative branch" — as it does "[w]ith respect to state tax statutes and regulatory measures."[26] And in *Wesberry v. Sanders,* when the Court extended the "one person, one vote" requirement to congressional districting, he denounced his colleagues for "declar[ing] constitutionally defective the very composition of a coordinate branch of the Federal Government."[27]

While most of the debates between Harlan and Black over constitutional history centered on the Fourteenth Amendment, the *Wesberry* decision produced a similar debate regarding the original 1789 Constitution. Writing for the Court, Black emphasized Article I's command that representatives be chosen "by the People of the several States," noting that "[i]t would defeat the principle solemnly embodied in the Great Compromise — equal representation in the House for equal numbers of people — for us to hold that, within the States, legislatures may draw the lines of congressional districts in such a way as to give some voters a greater voice in choosing a Congressman than others. The House of Representatives, the Convention agreed, was to represent the people as individuals, and on a basis of complete equality for each voter." In dissent, Harlan conducted his own extensive review of the debates at the Constitutional Convention and concluded, quite at odds with Black, that "[w]hatever the dominant political philosophy at the Convention, one thing seems clear: it is in the last degree unlikely that most or even many of the delegates would have subscribed to the principle of 'one person, one vote.'" His review of *The Federalist* and of the state ratifying conventions convinced him likewise, and he insisted that both the constitutional text and "the relevant history" were "in strong and consistent direct contradiction of the Court's holding. [Thus, t]he constitutional right which the Court creates is manufactured out of whole cloth."[28]

Harlan's historical claims here were largely persuasive, and Black's argument simply masked the fact that the Court was abandoning history as the primary source of constitutional authority. Douglas's opinion in *Gray* the previous year had made this development more clear, with its holding that "[t]he conception of political equality from the Declaration of Independence, to Lincoln's Gettysburg Address, to the Fifteenth, Seventeenth, and Nineteenth Amendments can mean only one thing — one person, one vote."[29] As Rogers Smith has noted, Douglas was arguing "that America's constitutional development showed a declining acceptance of the types of inegalitarian devices defended by the *Federalist*" (1985:135). The Warren Court majority saw the framers' narrow vision of constitutional liberty and equality as outmoded and was convinced that it could legitimately be abandoned in the course of national progress. Thus, when Warren wrote for the Court in *Reynolds,* he ignored history altogether, holding that the Fourteenth Amendment "demands no less than substantially equal state legislative representation for all citizens, of all places as well as of all races." On these grounds, he held that "the Equal Protection Clause requires that the seats in

both houses of a bicameral state legislature must be apportioned on a population basis." [30] In *Gray, Wesberry,* and now *Reynolds,* the Court had applied
the "one person, one vote" principle to elections for statewide office, then
congressional districting, and finally state legislative districting. Frankfurter's
aggrieved concern that the Court had no business in this area had been left
far behind.

The justices of the Warren Court fundamentally disagreed on whether
they were authorized to police the democratic process in this way. In Harlan's
view, the "unstated premise" of the Court's holdings in these cases was "quite
obviously . . . that the Congress has not dealt, and the Court believes it will
not deal, with the problem of . . . apportionment in accordance with what the
Court believes to be sound political principles." This premise was in his view
irrelevant, since the Court did not have "blanket authority to step into every
situation where the political branch may be thought to have fallen short."
Following Thayer, Harlan argued that such active judicial intervention was
not only illegitimate, but also unwise, because it would "encourage popular
inertia in efforts for political reform through the political process, with the
inevitable result that the process is itself weakened. By yielding to the demand
for a judicial remedy in this instance, the Court . . . does a disservice both to
itself and to the broader values of our system of government." [31] Chief Justice
Warren acknowledged Harlan's warning "about the dangers of entering into
political thickets and mathematical quagmires," but replied that "a denial of
constitutionally protected rights demands judicial protection; our oath and
our office require no less of us." [32]

Justice Harlan dissented throughout the reapportionment cases, but he
provided his fullest account of the original understanding of the Fourteenth
Amendment in *Reynolds.* Beginning with the text itself, he insisted that its
words "speak as clearly as may be against the construction which the majority puts on them," since §2 of the amendment explicitly references the states'
power to deny the right to vote in state elections. Turning next to the intentions of the amendment's framers, he reviewed the debates in the Thirty-
ninth Congress, finding "conclusive evidence that neither those who proposed nor those who ratified the amendment believed that the Equal
Protection Clause limited the power of the States to apportion their legislatures as they saw fit. Moreover, the history demonstrates that the intention to
leave this power undisturbed was deliberate and was widely believed to be essential to the adoption of the Amendment." Building on Frankfurter's argument in *Baker,* Harlan also made extensive reference to the traditional prac-

tices of the state governments in 1868 and subsequent years. He observed that fifteen of the twenty-three loyal states that ratified the amendment prior to 1870 had constitutional provisions that applied principles other than population in apportionment, and he found it unlikely "that the legislatures of these States . . . would have ratified an amendment which might render their own States' constitutions unconstitutional."[33] Echoing Fairman's reading of the incorporation history and Justice Robert Jackson's on segregation, Harlan observed that "[t]here is here none of the difficulty which may attend the application of basic principles to situations not contemplated or understood when the principles were framed. The problems which concern the Court now were problems when the Amendment was adopted. By the deliberate choice of those responsible for the Amendment, it left those problems untouched." And finally, he insisted that historical developments over the nearly one hundred years since 1868 confirmed his account of the original meaning. After all, he noted, a majority of the states continued in 1964 to "recognize[ ] bases of apportionment other than geographic spread of population, and to . . . favor[ ] sparsely populated areas by a variety of devices."[34]

Thus, in leading the Court's dissenters in these voting rights cases, Harlan articulated the conservative conception of judicial restraint in its modern form, sharply stated as an attack on illegitimate judicial power and closely linked to a historical reading of the commands of the Fourteenth Amendment.[35] Harlan's historical argument was essentially irrelevant at the time; since the Court was abandoning history, it did not matter how much historical evidence he amassed. It would not be long, however, before such arguments were constraining the Court's activism more effectively. For one thing, Harlan's and Black's opinions fostered the continued, but still quite sporadic, scholarly attention to constitutional history. Following the justices' lead, several scholars began mobilizing constitutional history in an effort to resolve contemporary constitutional conflicts. Some of these scholars used their historical research to support the Warren Court's rights-protecting decisions, but most of them built on Fairman's pioneering work to denounce the Court for departing from the original meaning of the Fourteenth Amendment.[36]

In a widely noted article on "Clio and the Court," for example, Alfred Kelly criticized all of the justices except Frankfurter for engaging in "law office history," the instrumental search through the historical record for evidence to support a preconceived result. Kelly disagreed with many of Harlan's historical arguments, but he too was seeking to mobilize Reconstruction history in the service of judicial restraint. Insisting that the Court's historical claims had been "most dubious in those instances in which an appeal to the past has been recruited for activist purposes of interventionist political implications," he argued that "the present turbulence over the Court's use and abuse of history is in reality only a part of a much larger problem: that raised by the present Court's apparent determination to carry through a constitutional equalitarian revolution" (1965:157–58). Like Harlan, Kelly was suspicious of the Court's emerging egalitarianism, and like Harlan, he buttressed this substantive concern by resorting to a constitutional history that allegedly demonstrated the novelty and illegitimacy of the Warren Court's values. Constitutional scholars were divided over whether either Black or Harlan had offered plausible historical readings, but following the Court's lead, they were increasingly preoccupied with the historical origins of the Fourteenth Amendment.[37]

Harlan continued to elaborate his own reading of Fourteenth Amendment history through his last years on the Court. A year after the Warren era had ended, for example, when the Court held in *Oregon v. Mitchell* that Congress could constitutionally lower the voting age from twenty-one to eighteen for federal, but not for state and local, elections, Harlan published a sixty-seven-page separate opinion (not counting the lengthy appendix) arguing that "the Fourteenth Amendment was never intended to restrict the authority of the States to allocate their political power as they see fit and therefore that it does not authorize Congress to set voter qualifications, in either state or federal elections." Since he found "no other source of congressional power to lower the voting age as fixed by state laws," Congress could only do so by means of a constitutional amendment.[38] His opinion was so lengthy because he continued the thorough review of Reconstruction history that he had begun in *Reynolds*. Again relying heavily on Fairman's account, he insisted that the historical evidence was clear beyond argument that "Section 1 of the Amendment did not reach discriminatory voter qualifications." He also paused to express his continued "astonishment" at his colleagues' position that such history was irrelevant. Acknowledging that the Court must "apply[ ] the Constitution in changing circumstances, and [that] as conditions change the Constitution in a sense changes as well," he nevertheless insisted that "when the Court gives the language of the Constitution an unforeseen application, it does so, whether explicitly or implicitly, in the name of some underlying purpose of the Framers." If this were not true, the unelected ju-

TABLE 3.2 *Interagreement with Black during Warren Era**

Term/ Justice	Minton	Reed	Burton/ Stewart	Clark	Warren	Douglas	Jackson/ Harlan
1953	53.3	53.6	55.0	65.5	70.7	84.5	56.6
1954	70.3	57.3	65.8	82.7	85.1	83.8	61.5
1955	66.3	62.5	61.3	80.8	97.5	91.3	53.1
1956	—	55.6	50.0	59.8	86.4	86.8	49.4
1957	—	—	50.5	54.5	92.9	91.1	44.6
1958	—	—	60.5	66.3	89.2	89.4	58.7
1959	—	—	56.7	67.8	92.1	80.2	48.3
1960	—	—	62.6	58.4	91.3	79.6	57.3
1961	—	—	70.4	73.2	90.1	81.7	53.8
1962	—	—	57.3	72.2	87.9	80.9	49.1
1963	—	—	65.4	71.3	85.2	84.8	41.6
1964	—	—	68.2	74.4	73.5	70.9	60.5
1965	—	—	70.0	75.8	79.3	79.1	61.9
1966	—	—	68.4	73.9	66.7	71.9	63.7
1967	—	—	69.4	—	73.8	73.1	65.7
1968	—	—	52.6	—	73.4	65.3	61.5
Total	64.0	57.9	61.6	69.4	83.6	80.8	55.7

(continued)

diciary would be seeking "to establish the norms for the rest of society," and thus "violat[ing] the constitutional structure which it is its highest duty to protect."[39]

LIBERAL EGALITARIANISM AND WELFARE RIGHTS

Justices Harlan and Black began from very different premises, but they had each come to emphasize the Court's duty to adhere to "the express intent and understanding of the Framers."[40] While they regularly disagreed on the specific lessons to be drawn from that history, moreover, their shared dissenting position brought them closer together over time. As table 3.2 makes clear, from 1955 through 1963, Harlan and Black never voted together more than 60 percent of the time during any given term. From 1964 through 1968,

TABLE 3.2 *(Continued)*

Frankfurter	Whitaker	Brennan	White	Goldberg/ Fortas	Marshall
61.7	—	—	—	—	—
78.4	—	—	—	—	—
63.6	—	—	—	—	—
58.0	53.8	75.9	—	—	—
45.0	53.5	83.8	—	—	—
56.2	55.8	80.0	—	—	—
43.3	47.8	83.7	—	—	—
56.3	51.5	84.5	—	—	—
57.9	63.6	82.9	83.3	—	—
—	—	84.5	74.5	78.6	—
—	—	81.9	72.9	82./	—
—	—	77.0	75.3	70.2	—
—	—	75.8	70.8	71.3	—
—	—	71.3	73.9	68.1	—
—	—	76.9	78.9	74.8	67.3
—	—	66.7	64.5	69.1	70.6
56.9	53.1	78.9	73.3	74.2	69.3

Source: Original U.S. Supreme Court Database, with orally argued citation as unit of analysis.

Note: Burton served through the 1957 term and was replaced by Stewart beginning with the 1958 term; Jackson served through the 1953 term and was replaced by Harlan beginning with the 1954 term; Goldberg served through the 1964 term and was replaced by Fortas beginning with the 1965 term.

*Percentage of formally decided full opinion cases in which each justice voted with Black.

however — and, in fact, through their final term two years later — they never voted together less than 60 percent of the time.

As Black was voting with Harlan more frequently, he was also voting with Warren, Brennan, and Douglas less frequently. Though he had often been condemned as a liberal judicial activist himself, his ceaseless appeal to the authority of the original constitutional text was fast becoming a limit on, rather than a prop for, such activism. Black had always insisted that "to pass upon the constitutionality of statutes by looking to the particular standards enumerated in the Bill of Rights and other parts of the Constitution is one thing; to invalidate statutes because of application of 'natural law' deemed to be above and undefined by the Constitution is another," and he adhered to this distinction to the end of his days.[41] While he was standing still, the Warren Court pushed past him, and his strict textualism, once a force for rights-based judicial activism, became a call for restraint. As table 3.1 shows, Black dissented almost as often as Harlan during the last five years of the Warren Court, even surpassing him during the 1964 and 1968 terms.

In an increasingly significant line of cases dealing with economic equality and welfare rights, for example, Harlan and Black often found themselves together in dissent. Beginning in the mid-1950s, the Warren Court issued a series of decisions prohibiting discrimination against the poor in state judicial processes and in the electoral arena, coming close to declaring that the poor were, like racial minorities, a "suspect class" worthy of heightened judicial protection (Bussiere 1997:85–91; Kahn 1994:41–45). The most sweeping of these decisions was *Harper v. Virginia State Board of Elections,* in which the Court struck down the poll tax in federal elections, casually and firmly rejecting an originalist approach in the process. Writing for the Court, Justice Douglas held that "the Equal Protection Clause is not shackled to the political theory of a particular era. In determining what lines are unconstitutionally discriminatory, we have never been confined to historic notions of equality, any more than we have restricted due process to a fixed catalogue of what was at a given time deemed to be the limits of fundamental rights. Notions of what constitutes equal treatment for purposes of the Equal Protection Clause do change."[42]

Black had gone along with the early cases in this line, but Harlan had dissented from the very beginning, and by 1966, they were both objecting to what they saw as unconstrained judicial lawmaking. When the Court held in *Griffin v. Illinois* that the right to appeal a criminal conviction could not be denied for failure to pay court costs, Black joined the majority, but Harlan objected that "no economic burden attendant upon the exercise of a privilege bears equally upon all" and insisted that there was "no reason to import new substance into the concept of equal protection to dispose of the case." He argued that the question should instead be analyzed under the due process standards of *Palko* and *Betts v. Brady,* and he concluded that the failure to provide a cost-free right of appeal did not constitute a "denial of fundamental fairness, shocking to the universal sense of justice."[43] When the Court extended *Griffin* in *Douglas v. California,* Black again joined the majority, and Harlan again criticized it for invalidating a law "of general applicability" solely because it "may affect the poor more harshly than it does the rich."[44] In *Harper,* Harlan continued to denounce the Court's "depart[ure] from long-established standards governing the application of" the Equal Protection Clause, and this time Black joined him in dissent. Unlike race, Harlan insisted, indigency was not "a 'neutral fact,' irrelevant or suspect for purposes of legislative classification." Hence, the Court should scrutinize legislative classifications in this context only to ensure that they rest on some rational basis. Since "[p]roperty qualifications and poll taxes have been a traditional part of our political structure," he noted, it was no more than judicial "fiat" to say "that there can be no rational debate as to their advisability." As Black noted in his own dissent, their fellow justices appeared to believe that fidelity to the original Constitution was "an intolerable and debilitating evil; that our Constitution should not be 'shackled to the political theory of a particular era,' and that to save the country from the original Constitution the Court must have constant power to renew it and keep it abreast of this Court's more enlightened theories of what is best for our society." For Harlan and Black, this approach represented "an attack . . . on the [very] concept of a written constitution which is to survive through the years as originally written unless changed through the amendment process which the Framers wisely provided."[45]

The most significant aspect of these decisions for the development of constitutional conservatism was that Harlan began supplementing these appeals to constitutional history with a more explicit critique of the substantive value that he saw as his colleagues' chief motivation. He objected to the Court's decisions in *Griffin, Douglas,* and *Harper* because the Court was exceeding the legitimate bounds of its power, but also because it was adopting an unrestrained egalitarianism foreign to American values. In *Douglas,* for example, he noted that a state requirement that criminal defendants pay a modest fee before appealing their convictions did "not deny equal protection to the less fortunate for one essential reason: the Equal Protection Clause does not impose on the States an affirmative duty to lift the handicaps flowing from differences in economic circumstances. To so construe it would be to read into the Constitution a philosophy of leveling that would be foreign to many of our basic concepts of the proper relations between government and society."[46]

Harlan and his liberal colleagues had very different perceptions of the contemporary operation of American democracy; he followed Bickel and Dahl's pluralist view, while the Warren Court majority was much more critical. As a result, Harlan was convinced that the Court's egalitarianism represented illegitimate judicial tinkering with the natural outcomes of the economic and political order. This nascent suspicion of the New Deal/Great Society welfare state was analytically distinct from his narrow vision of the scope of judicial power. It was the latter critique that was most clearly understood at the time — and that Harlan himself would have emphasized as most important — but the former would also prove influential on a generation of judicial conservatives to come.

Harlan's nascent critique of egalitarianism explains how he could be both a leading advocate of judicially enforceable constitutional liberty and a leading critic of judicially enforceable constitutional equality. He was simply more supportive of the former than the latter as a substantive constitutional value. He complained that the *Harper* decision reflected the simple fact that poll taxes were "not in accord with current egalitarian notions of how a modern democracy should be organized," but his own decisions invalidating restrictive anti-contraception laws appeared to rest on the claim that such regulations were not in accord with current libertarian notions of how a modern democracy should be organized. It was clear to Harlan that "the Equal Protection Clause [did not] rigidly impose upon America an ideology of unrestrained egalitarianism," but others would denounce his own vision of the Due Process Clause for imposing an ideology of unrestrained libertarianism.[47] After all, the two clauses were often used to achieve the same results. When the Court extended *Griffin* and *Douglas* to the civil court context in *Boddie v. Connecticut,* for example, holding that a state could not condition the right to a divorce on the payment of a filing fee, Harlan ignored Brennan's argument that the Equal Protection Clause prohibited discrimination against the indigent, but nonetheless struck the statute down on the basis of a *Griswold*-like concern for marital rights, rooted in the Due Process Clause.[48]

Since the Court's expansive and evolving egalitarian vision sometimes led Black and Harlan to agree in dissent, and since they were at times able to persuade some of their colleagues, the liberal majority was on notice that its activism could be pushed only so far. Harlan and Black remained in the Court's minority in the early wealth discrimination cases, but their arguments proved more influential in the welfare rights cases that came a few years later. By the end of the Warren era, liberal constitutional scholars such as Charles

Reich and Frank Michelman were building on the Court's doctrinal innovations to urge the recognition of a constitutional right to welfare assistance, with Reich famously describing welfare benefits as a form of "new property" (Reich 1964; Michelman 1969). The Court never carried this line of doctrine so far, however, because Harlan's and Black's persistent critiques of judicial power reflected a concern shared to varying degrees by all of the justices.

In *Shapiro v. Thompson,* for example, the Court struck down state residency requirements on the receipt of welfare benefits, but refused to recognize a Fourteenth Amendment right to welfare assistance as such. As Elizabeth Bussiere has noted, when the Court ordered the case reargued in the fall of 1968, the welfare rights lawyers concluded that they "had pushed too abruptly for a constitutional welfare right" and that "[a] more modest approach was necessary." Thus, Archibald Cox, arguing on behalf of the welfare recipients, came up with the idea that the residency requirements infringed on the "right to travel," successfully providing the Court with a narrower ground on which to reach its decision. In Bussiere's view, this move by Cox was crucial in persuading Justice Brennan, who had been unwilling to declare a broad constitutional right to welfare, but who cast the deciding vote in favor of Cox's narrower argument (1999:162–63).[49]

The justices were not yet willing to recognize a constitutional right to livelihood, but as Powe notes, Brennan's *Shapiro* opinion left the door open for such a holding. It was here that Brennan brought his "compelling state interest" approach into the equal protection context, suggesting that denials of the necessities of life might be constitutionally suspect, and hence illegitimate unless narrowly tailored to serve a compelling state interest (Powe 2000:453–55). The following year, with the Warren era now ended, Brennan was willing to go still further in this regard, holding in *Goldberg v. Kelly* that the Due Process Clause requires an evidentiary hearing before the termination of welfare benefits. Citing Reich's "new property" argument in a footnote, he observed that "[i]t may be realistic today to regard welfare entitlements as more like 'property' than a 'gratuity,'" and he repeatedly emphasized that welfare benefits provide "the basic demands of subsistence" and "the very means by which to live." Nonetheless, he avoided the substantive constitutional issue, holding only that "[s]uch benefits are a matter of statutory entitlement for persons qualified to receive them," and hence that they cannot be terminated without due process.[50]

Though the Court declined to read a right to welfare into the Fourteenth Amendment in these cases, Harlan and Black were not any happier with the

approach that it did adopt. Harlan went along with the procedural due process ruling in *Goldberg,* but in *Shapiro* he objected that the compelling state
interest doctrine represented an unwarranted and "increasingly significant
exception to the long-established rule that a statute does not deny equal protection if it is rationally related to a legitimate governmental objective." He
granted that the doctrine "is sound when applied to racial classifications," but
rejected its extension to classifications that affect a "fundamental right," such
as the right to interstate travel at issue in *Shapiro.* After all, "[v]irtually every
state statute affects important rights. . . . When the right affected is one assured by the Federal Constitution, any infringement can be dealt with under
the Due Process Clause. But when a statute affects only matters not men-
tioned in the Federal Constitution and is not arbitrary or irrational, . . . I
know of nothing which entitles this Court to pick out particular human activities, characterize them as 'fundamental,' and give them added protection
under an unusually stringent equal protection test." Harlan concluded by
observing yet again that the Court was acting as if it "possesses a peculiar wisdom all its own whose capacity to lead this Nation out of its present troubles
is contained only by the limits of judicial ingenuity in contriving new constitutional principles to meet each problem as it arises."[51] Black joined Warren's
dissent in *Shapiro,* and unlike Harlan, also dissented in *Goldberg,* objecting
that the justices were using "judicial power for legislative purposes."[52]

Harlan's and Black's dissenting opinions throughout the 1960s articulated
a series of trenchant critiques of the Court's liberal activism, and as Bruce
Ackerman has noted, when even "one or two Justices are willing to elaborate
a doctrinal tradition," the principles associated with that tradition "remain a
vital part of the living constitution":

> Not only does a constant stream of dissenting opinions testify to the con-
> tinuing relevance of the tradition, but practicing lawyers will continue to
> study them with painstaking care — if only because dissenters vote and
> may make a difference when splits in the majority ranks appear. Over the
> long haul, the dissenters may have a larger impact. Their ongoing critique
> may subtly influence the opinions expressed by the dominant majority.
> No less important, they will serve as a priceless resource should a new
> president come into office responsive to the constitutional values the dis-
> senting tradition emphasizes. If he convinces the Senate to support his
> nominations to the Supreme Court, the new appointments can reinforce
> a living tradition of constitutional discourse, already containing a familiar

and elaborate critique of the prevailing doctrine. Through a gradual process of evolutionary reinterpretation, the dissenting doctrine will begin increasingly to shape the path of the law (1998:373).[53]

As the Court was announcing these liberal, rights-protecting decisions, it was often supported by dominant political interests, but the signs of disaffection were already apparent. Once the conservative backlash developed, Harlan's and Black's dissenting critiques would be a vital source for those looking to articulate an alternative vision of the judicial role.

The Court and the Political System in the 1960s

As Lucas Powe has noted, the Warren Court's rights revolution was rooted both in the judicial ideology of Stone's *Carolene Products* footnote and in the contemporary political ideology of Kennedy–Johnson liberalism, both of which sought to better defend the rights of "those most in need of help" (2000:489). While the Warren Court's landmark, rights-protecting decisions are often described as countermajoritarian, the justices saw themselves as working in active partnership with the Democratic Congress and president (Powe 2000; Shapiro 1983). Thus, while the Warren Court was "activist" in at least one sense of the word, it did not seek to impose its own constitutional (or political) vision on the coordinate branches of the national government.[54] As Powe (2000) has shown, much of the Court's work during the 1960s was an effort to enforce widely held national values against infringement by local outliers. With the support of a national majority — particularly after LBJ's sweeping electoral mandate in 1964 — the Court was willing to stamp out unacceptable southern practices regarding racial equality, the rights of criminal defendants, and religious freedom, and also the overly restrictive regulation of contraception and obscenity in the Catholic Northeast. In short, while the justices were motivated in part by jurisprudential concerns, they were also seeking to promote the political values of the New Deal/Great Society coalition, of which they themselves were enthusiastic members.

From the very beginning, however, some of the Warren Court's activist decisions were challenged as undemocratic and illegitimate. The school prayer decisions, for example, prompted newspaper headlines declaring, "Court outlaws God," and attacks from southern congressmen complaining that the justices had first "put Negroes in the school and now they've driven God out."[55] The public reaction to the Court's religion and obscenity cases, in fact, helped spark the growth of the religious Right, though it was not yet apparent that this would become a significant force in national politics. The Court's criminal justice cases also sparked a strong backlash, as conservative (and even liberal) political leaders blamed *Mapp* and *Miranda* for increasing crime rates and demanded a return to "law and order." During the 1964 presidential campaign, both Democrat George Wallace and Republican Barry Goldwater lambasted the Warren Court, emphasizing the criminal procedure and civil rights cases (Blum 1991:156–60; Powe 2000:391–92). While Wallace's campaign for the Democratic nomination was short-lived, and Goldwater won only six states in the general election against LBJ, their campaigns served nonetheless to launch a profound conservative shift in national electoral politics, and more specifically, a political backlash against the liberal activism of the Warren Court.

Perceived as a failure at the time, Goldwater's 1964 campaign planted the seeds for many successful conservative efforts to come.[56] Most importantly, it was the vehicle by which southern and western conservatives captured the GOP from its more moderate, northeastern wing. A young senator from Arizona, Goldwater had become popular with his party's conservative activists, who drafted him in what seemed like an impossible mission to steal the GOP nomination from Nelson Rockefeller and the party's other moderate, establishment candidates (Perlstein 2001:3–60). Goldwater's frequent criticisms of the Supreme Court were part of a more general denunciation of the New Deal/Great Society Democratic order, a denunciation that he had spelled out in a successful book published four years earlier. Ghost-written and produced by the conservative party activists who were hoping to draft him for a presidential run as early as 1960, Goldwater's *The Conscience of a Conservative* denounced the welfare state as a threat to individual liberty, "a Leviathan, a vast national authority out of touch with the people, and out of their control." Bluntly stating the emerging conservative critique of the Great Society, Goldwater observed: "I have little interest in streamlining government or making it more efficient, for I mean to reduce its size. I do not undertake to promote welfare, for I propose to extend freedom. My aim is not to pass laws, but to repeal them. It is not to inaugurate new programs, but to cancel old ones that do violence to the Constitution, or that have failed in their purpose, or that impose on the people an unwarranted financial burden." He characterized the Constitution's purpose as limited government, fingered the state itself as the chief threat to individual liberty, and defined politics "as the art of achieving the maximum amount of freedom for individuals that is consistent with the maintenance of social order." In a series of short chapters, he criticized the federal government for abandoning these principles in the areas of civil rights, agriculture policy, labor policy, taxation and spending, welfare policy, and education. He also devoted a full chapter to the Cold War struggle against "the Soviet menace," the one area in which he did support a strong and active federal government. For Goldwater, the internal and external threats to the nation were linked because federal policies such as Social Security and even the income tax amounted to a form of "Socialism-through-Welfarism" that was tyrannical and un-American (Goldwater 1960:20–23, 13–16, 70). As historian Lisa McGirr has noted, Goldwater's central message, repeated again and again, was that "[g]overnment is not your master, it must be your servant" (2001:134; see also Blum 1991:156–60; Perlstein 2001; Powe 2000:391–92).

Goldwater's supporters at the 1964 convention in San Francisco built on this central theme of limited government in drafting the GOP platform, which emphasized states' rights and the virtues of free enterprise, along with anti-communism. The platform also criticized the nation's "moral decline and drift," insisted on the right to pray in public places, and called for greater regulation of obscenity. On the issue of civil rights, it supported the 1964 Civil Rights Act, but opposed "federally-sponsored inverse discrimination whether by the shifting of jobs or the abandonment of neighborhood schools for reasons of race." The most notorious lines to emerge from the convention were in Goldwater's acceptance speech, in which he declared that "[e]xtremism in the defense of liberty is no vice. Moderation in the pursuit of justice is no virtue." As McGirr notes, this "strident rhetoric . . . not only failed to appeal to a broader constituency but also scared many people." Unable to shake "his image as a warmonger and the man who would ruin Social Security," Goldwater received only 39 percent of the popular vote (2001: 140–42).

In defeat, however, southern and western conservatives took control of the Republican Party, laying the groundwork for Ronald Reagan's 1966 election as governor of California and, fourteen years later, as president of the United States. Reagan himself burst onto the scene with a fall 1964 television address in support of Goldwater, which Steve Hess and David Broder characterized as "[t]he most successful national political debut since William Jennings Bryan electrified the 1896 Democratic convention with his 'Cross of Gold' speech" (1967:253). Articulating a number of arguments that he would use in the coming years, Reagan criticized the federal government's burdensome taxation, excessive spending, and overly intrusive regulation of the private economy; denounced LBJ's War on Poverty as wasteful; called for the defense of private property rights against government planners and bureaucrats; and advocated the partial privatization of Social Security. In support of this last point, he insisted that the nation's founding fathers "knew that outside of its legitimate functions, government does nothing as well or as economically as the private sector of the economy." In Reagan's view, the welfare state was both inefficient and unjust; he repeatedly criticized the policies of liberal "do-gooders" both because they were not working and because they were trying to "trade our freedom for the soup kitchen of the welfare state." As Goldwater himself had done, Reagan also linked these domestic failures of the liberal state with the nation's greatest external threat, the Soviet Union. The liberals were losing the Cold War, Reagan insisted, because the nation had "been weakened from within spiritually, morally, and economically" (Reagan 1964).

More clearly than any prominent political figure to date, including Goldwater himself, Reagan articulated the emerging conservative libertarian streak in American political culture, with its hostility to the federal government's welfare state and the liberal elites who were running it. "Somewhere a perversion has taken place," he insisted. "Our natural, unalienable rights are now considered to be a dispensation of government, and freedom has never been so fragile, so close to slipping from our grasp as it is at this moment." For Reagan, the issue of the 1964 election was "[w]hether we believe in our capacity for self-government or whether we abandon the American Revolution and confess that a little intellectual elite in a far-distant capital can plan our lives for us better than we can plan them ourselves" (Reagan 1964; see Branch 1998:520–21).

A few weeks before Reagan's speech, Senator Strom Thurmond of South Carolina had also given a widely noted television address in support of Goldwater, denouncing his own Democratic Party for "abandon[ing] the people" and announcing that he was switching to the GOP. Sounding themes similar to Reagan's, Thurmond had complained that the Democratic Party "has repudiated the Constitution of the United States"; "has rammed through Congress unconstitutional, impractical, unworkable, and oppressive legislation which invades inalienable personal and property rights of the individual"; "has encouraged lawlessness, civil unrest, and mob actions"; "has succored and assisted our Communist enemies"; "has adopted the practice of taking your money by taxation and then using that money to attempt to buy your votes"; and "has encouraged, supported, and protected the Supreme Court in a reign of judicial tyranny." If the Democrats prevail, Thurmond warned, "freedom as we have known it in this country is doomed, and individuals will be destined to lives of regulation, control, coercion, intimidation, and subservience to a power elite who shall rule from Washington." [57] To the liberal elites who were running the country in 1964, Thurmond, Reagan, and Goldwater appeared merely to be tilting at windmills. But Goldwater's campaign appealed to a whole generation of conservatives — including three young lawyers named William Rehnquist, Sandra Day O'Connor, and Robert Bork — and Richard Nixon was watching closely, as he planned his own presidential bid for 1968 (Perlstein 2001:418).

The Sharpening of the Scholarly Critique

While the Court's own dissenting justices remained its most influential critics for the time being, there was an emerging political backlash against the Warren Court, and the Court's familiar scholarly critics continued to sharpen their own critique as well. One of Frankfurter's last acts had been to urge Bickel and his fellow law professors to criticize the Court publicly, which Bickel was already doing with some regularity in *The New Republic*.[58] The scholarly critics were still sounding their principal New Deal theme of judicial deference, but their work was starting to reflect some of the newer critiques as well. As the Warren Court became increasingly bold, for example, Bickel became ever more critical of judicial power. In *The Least Dangerous Branch*, he had defended a restrained vision of the judicial role, but had still maintained that the courts should actively enforce the fundamental, longterm principles of the American polity. Unlike Hand and Wechsler, Bickel had firmly supported the *Brown* decision, but as the Warren Court began to enforce such rights-based principles more regularly, he became increasingly critical, and in 1969, he followed tradition by using Harvard's Holmes Lectures to attack the Court.[59] Speaking just five months after the Warren era had ended, he began by reviewing the Court's record of liberal activism in the areas of desegregation, reapportionment, school prayer, obscenity, and criminal procedure. By this time, he had become much more pessimistic, coming "to doubt in many instances the Court's capacity to develop 'durable principles' and to doubt, therefore, that judicial supremacy can work and is tolerable in broad areas of social policy." In making these arguments, Bickel subjected the Court's desegregation and reapportionment decisions to particularly sustained criticism. He characterized these two lines of doctrine as the Court's "noblest" and "most popular" enterprises, respectively, but insisted that they were "heading toward obsolescence, and in large measure abandonment" (1970:99, 173).[60]

As he and his fellow scholarly critics had been doing since the mid-1950s, Bickel continued to critique the Warren Court's work on the grounds of craftsmanship. In his view, the Court had been willfully misinterpreting history in the equal protection context, refusing to give any reasons at all in the obscenity context, and generally failing to act as a body committed to the reasoned elaboration of principle. He balanced this demand for principle, however, with a continued commitment to expediency, urging the Court once again to remember the passive virtues (1970:47–100, 72–73). As Gerald Gunther had characterized Bickel's approach a few years earlier, his call was a "100% insistence on principle, 20% of the time" (1964:3). Elaborating on an argument that had been suggested by Hart and Sacks, and that would be developed more fully by neoconservative policy analysts in the 1970s, Bickel also insisted that courts lacked the institutional capacity to effectively make and implement social policy (1970:175).

Bickel's increasingly critical stance was rooted in the Court's widening divergence from his own pluralist vision of American politics. Following Dahl, he was convinced that "[i]n the political process, groups sometimes lose out, but so long as the process is operational and both diffuses power and allows majorities ultimately to work their will, no group that is prepared to enter into the process and combine with others need remain permanently and completely out of power" (1970:37). In one of the most influential contemporary responses to Bickel's lectures, D.C. Circuit judge J. Skelly Wright rejected this "faith in the pluralistic political process," particularly because it failed to account for the inequality of power among various groups. Denouncing Bickel and his colleagues as "self-appointed scholastic mandarins," Wright asserted that their quarrel with the Warren Court represented "a fundamental dispute over the good society as well as over judicial method." Only such a fundamental divide could explain the severity of Bickel's substantive attack on the Court, Wright noted, his "apparent[ ] feel[ing] that he must show the Warren Court to be not simply overly activist, but consciously demonic" (1971:772, 783–84, 787–90).

As I noted in chapter 2, the scholarly critics had been denouncing the Court with exceedingly sharp rhetoric since the 1950s, and Bickel's was by no means the sharpest. While he compared the Warren Court justices to social-ist planners and levelers, he did so elliptically — denouncing the justices' "tendency . . . to circumscribe and displace private ordering, to legalize the society, to rationalize it in the sense in which the great industrial consolida-tors spoke of rationalizing the economy" (1970:104). Some of his colleagues and heirs drew these comparisons more explicitly, with Philip Kurland emerging as the most vociferous. In an essay on "Egalitarianism and the War-ren Court," for example, Kurland observed that "[t]hose too young to re-member what happened to Europe immediately prior to World War II, as country after country fell under the thrall of equality, may yet find the alle-gory of Orwell's *Animal Farm* instructive and frightening" (1970a:682). Like Bickel, Kurland had clerked for Frankfurter, and like Bickel, he had made his name with a widely noted annual foreword in the *Harvard Law Review* (1964). Also like Bickel, he too had the chance to look back on the Warren era in a distinguished series of lectures, the 1969 Cooley Lectures at the Univer-sity of Michigan, which he used to call attention to the Court's limited insti-tutional capacity in general and the Warren Court's inferior craftsmanship and reasoning ability in particular.[61] The sharpness of their rhetoric repre-sented yet another way in which Bickel's and Kurland's arguments presaged a generation of conservative attacks on the Court.

Ultimately, Bickel and Kurland were so critical of the Warren Court be-cause it was enforcing a constitutional value that they rejected. Like Harlan, they read the Court's decisions as a single-minded pursuit of an "egalitarian revolution," and like Harlan, they rejected this principle as wrong-headed and unjust (Kurland 1964:145; see also Bickel 1970:13–14). Emphasizing the Court's desegregation, reapportionment, and criminal procedure decisions, Kurland complained that "[i]n constitutional terms, 'equality' has become the first freedom" (1970a:629). In his view, the Court's egalitarian revolution was both dangerous and illegitimate because the justices failed to recognize that equality conflicts with other important constitutional values — princi-pally liberty, federalism, and judicial restraint (1964; 1970a). As I have already suggested, the scholarly critics understood the Court's egalitarianism to be a rigid judicial imposition on the nation because they saw the policies that the Court was invalidating as products of a basically fair and just democratic pro-cess. This perception was not shared by the Warren Court majority, who saw much of their work as an effort to correct the various, sometimes glaring, de-fects in the practice of American democracy. Following Stone, the liberal justices were struggling to define a role for the Court in enhancing the democratic character of the political process, a role that the scholarly critics could not see as either necessary or legitimate.[62]

Despite their disagreements, the justices and the scholarly critics were unwilling to ignore each other altogether, and they continued to share certain fundamental assumptions. The legal academy did not completely abandon its support for the Warren Court because, as Ronald Kahn observes, "the Court's critical view of government extended no further than formal access, [and so] it was not far outside the pluralist equilibrium model" (1994:92). Bickel, for example, supported many of the Court's decisions guaranteeing the right to vote, or otherwise removing formal barriers to access, while raising questions when the Court reached beyond these initial goals. He firmly supported the Court's efforts to end *de jure* segregation in the schools, but was increasingly skeptical of the Court's efforts to end *de facto* racial imbalance. Moreover, in contrast to the political scientists who viewed the Court simply as a political institution like any other, the legal scholars "kept alive the idea that law and the Court were independent of politics [and] accepted the Supreme Court as a definer of fundamental rights" (Kahn 1994:82; see Bickel 1965; 1970). For this reason, the dialogue between the Court and its scholarly critics was preserved, and the critics were able to impose some limits on the Court's doctrinal innovations.

The scholarly critique was never accepted by the Court as a whole, but it did influence a number of the justices, and it would have a dramatic influence on a generation of Court critics to come. Moreover, because the Warren Court was initially faced with such a vast array of formal barriers to access to the political system — particularly the disenfranchisement of African Americans — it did not have to move much beyond the pluralist framework. When the Court did attempt to move beyond such formal requirements, "as when it raised issues of the relationship between economic and social inequality and public economic policies such as welfare," the widely accepted pluralist vision imposed sharp limits on the Court's efforts (Kahn 1994:93).

Put another way, the long-standing critique of judicial power and the emerging critique of liberal egalitarianism — each advanced by critics both on and off the Court — had the effect of constraining the Warren Court's activism at the margins. For example, the Court's brief, and ultimately aborted, effort to create a constitutional right to welfare signals the lengths to which Warren Court activism might have reached if it had not faced such withering critiques from the political system, the legal academy, and the Court's own dissenting justices.

While the critics of modern judicial power helped curtail the Warren Court's rights revolution, however, they were going to have a difficult time actually reversing it. By the end of the Warren era, judicially enforceable constitutional rights had become entrenched as a core feature of modern American democracy. Kurland closed his 1969 Cooley lectures by observing that "[t]he Nixon Court has awesome tasks before it. To match the Warren Court attainments in the protection of individuals and minorities that today justifies the Court's existence; to restore the confidence of the American public in the rule of law. One or the other is not enough" (1970b:206). Kurland had long criticized the Warren Court's rights revolution for undermining the rule of law, but he recognized that this revolution could not easily be reversed, even if conservatives took over the Court. As I show in chapters 4 and 5, Nixon's appointees did stop the rights revolution short in some areas, but the Court continued to push forward in others.

After all, once the rights revolution had begun, influential political constituencies emerged in its support. As Charles Epp (1998) has noted, the "support structure" for rights advocacy — rights-advocacy organizations, rights-advocacy lawyers, and sources of funding for rights-based litigation — played a key role in fostering the twentieth-century rights revolution. The litigation efforts of civil rights organizations like the NAACP and the ACLU, along with the federal Justice Department, were crucial in forcing rights issues onto the judicial agenda. Without the NAACP, there would have been no *Brown* decision, just as without the grassroots civil rights movement of the 1950s and 1960s, there would have been no 1964 Civil Rights Act. And as Frederick Lewis (1999) has argued, such organized interests helped to ensure the survival of rights-based judicial activism even as American politics took a conservative turn. Whether Congress and the White House have been in the hands of liberals or conservatives, the modern Court has progressively expanded the sphere of judicially enforceable rights and liberties.

Many scholars have noted how the civil rights movement profoundly transformed American democracy, producing "a growing inclination of people and organized groups to define politics in terms of rights, a growing willingness of the federal government to enforce individuals' claims to constitutional rights, and a widening of the domain of 'politics' propelled by rights-consciousness" (Schudson 1998:242). Contemporary American political debate is often conducted in the language of rights, a language that carries significant weight in a wide variety of contexts. Ronald Dworkin (1978:184) observed as early as the late 1970s that "the language of rights now dominates political debate in the United States," and Mary Ann Glendon later made this argument more extensively (and more critically) in *Rights Talk: The Impoverishment of Political Discourse* (1993). Stephen Griffin has described the modern American polity as a "democracy of rights," in which the political branches support the courts, and sometimes even advance beyond the courts, in seeking "to create, promote and enforce important constitutional rights" (2002:288, 291).

In the decades following the New Deal revolution, several paths of constitutional development had been open, and Frankfurter's sweeping vision of judicial deference was the road not taken. The Court (and the nation) chose to embark on the path of rights-based constitutionalism, and the results of this choice have become entrenched and reproduced over time. Of course, old constitutional arguments can sometimes be recovered, and contemporary arguments are not locked in for perpetuity. The justices are free to articulate new arguments (or to revive ancient ones), but they cannot do so without making reference to the multiple jurisprudential traditions that they have inherited. "In this respect," states Mark Graber, "doctrinal evolution resembles institutional development. . . . Although existing state structures can be modified in many ways, they shape prevalent political reforms because the old forms must implement the new" (1991:220). Moreover, the "new" arguments that the justices sometimes articulate have to come from somewhere — generally, the broader political system, as I emphasize in the chapters to come.

• • •

Harlan and Black left the Court together in September 1971, shortly after the end of the Warren era, bequeathing a legacy that subsequent conservative justices have used to great effect. The modern conservative critique of judicial power, in fact, hails more directly from their dissenting opinions than from any other source. They sustained the critique of liberal activism as a submerged constitutional tradition, available for subsequent conservative justices to build upon. Even more importantly, they modified this tradition in influential ways. Black and especially Harlan rejected the Court's emerging egalitarianism, as it violated their fundamental conceptions of individualism and limited government. And while they disagreed on many things, they both responded to their colleagues' increasing advocacy of a "living constitu-tion" by insisting that the Court pay greater attention to constitutional his-tory and, more specifically, that the long-standing existence of a particular law or policy suggested its compatibility with constitutional limits. In fact, the emphasis on Article V amendment procedures as the primary mode of constitutional change was probably the single trope used most frequently by both Harlan and Black.

Thus, one clear legacy of their dissenting arguments during this period was the full emergence of modern constitutional originalism. By the end of the Warren era, these ideas had begun to influence academic constitutional theory, and it would be only a few short years before they would lead to an explosion of scholarly interest in constitutional history and a more explicit articulation of the conservative philosophy of originalism. During the 1970s, constitutional scholars like Robert Bork and Raoul Berger would develop these arguments more fully, and during the 1980s the Reagan administration would publicly endorse a "jurisprudence of original intentions." When post-1968 political developments created the opportunity, the Court's conserva-tives would pick up on these submerged strains and begin to enact them into law. Again and again, the conservative justices of the Burger and Rehnquist Courts would look to Harlan and Black to buttress their critiques of "gov-ernment by judiciary."

In doing so, these justices would be confronted with a number of difficult questions: Whose historical arguments were more accurate, Harlan's or Black's? Is fidelity to the original meaning of the Constitution an indepen-dent value in its own right or merely a rhetorical device used to buttress the claim for judicial deference? Which would more effectively, and realistically, constrain judicial power — the literal meaning of the constitutional text or our nation's evolving legal traditions? Which would serve as a more secure guarantee of constitutional liberty? At the close of the Warren era, these ques-tions remained unanswered, but the Court would be forced to confront them by two developments that were on a collision course: the entrenchment of rights-based constitutionalism as a core feature of American democracy, on the one hand, and the conservative turn in national politics, on the other. If dominant national political forces started to agree with Harlan's and Black's dissenting critique, the Court was in for a bruising fight.

PART II

THE COURT
AND THE CONSERVATIVE TURN
IN AMERICAN POLITICS
1969–1994

CHAPTER FOUR

THE NIXON COURT
AND THE CONSERVATIVE TURN
1969–1980

The Warren era came to a sudden end during the 1968 presidential election. Following the assassination of Democratic presidential candidate Robert Kennedy in June, Chief Justice Earl Warren concluded that Richard Nixon was likely to be elected. Warren immediately submitted his resignation, hoping to allow Lyndon Johnson, the lame-duck president, the opportunity to name his successor. Johnson, in turn, announced his intention to promote Justice Abe Fortas to chief justice and to nominate Fifth Circuit judge Homer Thornberry to take Fortas's seat. Both Fortas and Thornberry were perceived as Johnson cronies, which reinforced the perception that Warren and Johnson were maneuvering to deny Nixon the chance to appoint the chief justice. Within hours of Johnson's announcement, Nixon was insisting that a new president should be allowed to make the nomination after the election, and the Warren Court's opponents quickly mobilized to block Fortas's confirmation, even though the Senate had succeeded in doing so only once before in the twentieth century.

When Fortas's confirmation hearings started later that summer, Republican senators on the Judiciary Committee angrily questioned him about the Warren Court's liberal activism. Led by South Carolina's Strom Thurmond, the senators hounded Fortas to defend the Court's decisions on criminal procedure and obscenity, for which they charged him with supporting rapists and pornographers. Later that summer, Fortas's opponents discovered that he had not fully disclosed either his extensive contacts with the president while he was a sitting justice or a sizeable teaching fee he had received from

American University. These revelations were the final "nails in the coffin," as Laura Kalman later noted, and after a divided committee vote and a Republican filibuster, Johnson withdrew the nomination. The rights revolution had made the Court an attractive political target, and it would be Nixon, not LBJ, who would name Warren's successor.[1]

Even before Fortas's nomination, Nixon had been making the Court's liberal activism a key theme in his campaign. In May, he had released a campaign paper entitled "Toward Freedom from Fear," blaming both the Warren Court and the Johnson administration for the nation's dramatic increase in violent crime.[2] After the Fortas rejection, Nixon emphasized this issue even more. James Simon reports that Thurmond "told Nixon two months before the Republican convention that there was no stronger issue, in the South at least, than what Governor George Wallace called that 'sorry, lousy, no-account outfit,' better known as the U.S. Supreme Court." Nixon sought to capitalize on this antagonism by denouncing the Court for judicial lawmaking, and Wallace was even more strident in his third-party campaign (Simon 1973:8). Nixon's victory in November was a narrow one, but he and Wallace together polled 56.9 percent of the vote, signaling widespread public dissatisfaction with the Warren Court in particular and the New Deal Democratic order more generally.

Following the account of Robert Dahl (1957), we might have expected this new conservative governing majority to remake the Court and the Constitution, perhaps after a brief time lag due to slow turnover on the Court. During the campaign, Nixon had promised to appoint "strict constructionists" to the bench, and four vacancies opened on the Court during his first term, giving him ample opportunity to do so. The four Nixon appointees certainly influenced constitutional development in many ways, but fifteen years after Nixon's election, the leading scholarly description of the Burger Court emphasized "the counter-revolution that wasn't" (Blasi 1983). Nixon's four appointees marked the beginning of a long Republican effort to stack the high Court with conservative justices, but the conservative transformation of constitutional law evolved more slowly and inconsistently than might have been expected. The Nixon appointees began laying jurisprudential foundations for the ascendance of constitutional conservatism, but much of this work remained in dissent.

As I have noted, when the conservative turn began in the late 1960s, rights-based constitutionalism was already entrenched in the American political system, a sequence that altered the preferences of, and the strategic constraints faced by, post-1968 constitutional conservatives. Rhetorically, conservatives were still preoccupied with denouncing liberal activism, but without much acknowledgment, they were beginning to develop a distinctive judicial activism of their own. The roots of the Rehnquist Court's conservative activism lie with Burger era decisions on affirmative action and the Tenth Amendment. Those Burger Court decisions, in turn, had been rooted in the contemporaneous emergence of a broad New Right critique of modern liberalism.

Throughout the Burger years, while conservatives continued to criticize "government by judiciary," they also began to articulate a substantive critique of modern liberalism itself. They were increasingly critical, for example, of the New Deal/Great Society welfare state; of the immorality of post-1960s norms regarding gender and sexuality; and of the liberal egalitarianism spawned by the civil rights movement. This comprehensive critique of liberalism has borne significant rhetorical weight and political force, particularly where it has tapped into emerging New Right political movements such as the libertarian tax revolt and the religious Right. Thus, when conservatives came to power in the federal judiciary after 1968, they were faced with a difficult choice: they could abandon liberal activism in favor of judicial restraint, or they could use their newfound control of the courts to help dismantle the edifice of modern liberalism. As the Burger era progressed, they continued to advance their critique of judicial power, but given the path that was open, they also began to articulate their own conservative versions of rights-based constitutionalism, rooted in this New Right critique of liberalism.

In this chapter, I describe the doctrinal influence of these political developments throughout the 1970s. I look first at the uncertain fate of liberal activism during these years. The rights-protecting constitutional doctrines of the Warren Court were now buffeted by the conservative critiques of both judicial power and modern liberalism itself, but they were also increasingly entrenched as a core feature of contemporary American democracy. As I show, the Burger Court curtailed the Warren Court's expansive liberal activism in some areas, but reaffirmed and even extended it in others. Because the conservative justices were so often still in the minority, moreover, they did not yet realize that their various critiques of Warren Court activism were inconsistent with each other. For the time being, these arguments could serve simply as alternative critiques of the reigning doctrines of liberal constitutionalism, but once the conservatives were in a position to settle the law themselves, their efforts would be fractured by these simmering tensions. I then turn to the early signs of a newer style of conservative judicial activism, as Nixon's appointees began articulating constitutional principles designed to impose some limits on the modern liberal state. Providing little explanation for these departures from their ostensible commitment to restraint, the Nixon justices led the Court in striking down democratically enacted policies in cases like *Regents of the University of California v. Bakke* and *National League of Cities v. Usery*, decisions that would influence the Court for many years to come.

The Rise of Conservative Republicans

Nixon's 1968 campaign built heavily on the inroads made by the Goldwater campaign four years earlier. The GOP had lost badly in 1964, but just two years later, the party had gained forty-seven seats in the House and three in the Senate, and Reagan had been elected governor of California in a landslide victory over liberal Democrat Edmund "Pat" Brown. Campaigning in the shadow of Berkeley and Watts — the 1964 free speech demonstrations on campus and the 1965 riots in Los Angeles — Reagan had emphasized law and order with great success. Nixon had been making use of the same issue himself, traveling the country that year to stump for Republican congressional candidates (McGirr 2001:187–210; Blum 1991:270). By the summer of 1968, after three years of widespread urban riots and the assassinations of Martin Luther King Jr. and Robert Kennedy that spring, Nixon knew that violent crime was at the forefront of national consciousness. In his standard stump speech that year, he would declare that "[i]n the past forty-five minutes this is what happened in America. There has been one murder, two rapes, forty-five major crimes of violence, countless robberies and auto thefts." As usual, Wallace was even blunter, insisting in his own stump speech that "[i]f you walk out of this hotel tonight and someone knocks you on the head, he'll be out of jail before you're out of the hospital, and on Monday morning they'll try the policeman instead of the criminal" (Powe 2000:408–10).

Both Nixon and Wallace found it politically useful to blame the Supreme Court for rising crime rates and for the nation's ever-increasing antiwar activism and ongoing racial unrest. As historian John Blum has observed, conservatives successfully "link[ed] the issue of law and order to the disruptions caused by other questions agitating and dividing the American people, particularly race, poverty, and war" (1991:214). Throughout the 1968 campaign, Nixon repeatedly declared that the Warren Court's criminal procedure decisions "have had the effect of seriously hamstringing the peace forces in our society and strengthening the criminal forces. . . . From the point of view of the criminal forces, the cumulative impact of these decisions has been to set free patently guilty individuals on the basis of legal technicalities. The tragic lesson of guilty men walking free from hundreds of courtrooms across the country has not been lost on the criminal community."[3] He had borrowed some of these arguments from a 1967 speech delivered by D.C. Circuit judge Warren Burger, who complained that *Miranda* and other high Court decisions had made it "often very difficult to convict even those who are plainly guilty" (Burger 1967:70; see Blum 1991:335–36; Yalof 1999:101–2). Feeling the political pressure that summer, Congress passed the Omnibus Crime Control and Safe Streets Act, a sweeping law-and-order measure that, among other things, purported to overrule *Miranda* by making confessions admissible so long as they were voluntary (and whether or not the "*Miranda* warnings" had been read).

Nixon's successful 1968 campaign marked the birth of a victorious GOP electoral coalition, at least at the presidential level. Following his infamous "southern strategy," he was able to break the New Deal/Great Society coalition and begin forming a new Republican majority. Described by Nixon campaign aide Kevin Phillips in a 1969 book presciently titled *The Emerging Republican Majority*, the southern strategy was an effort to use indirect racial appeals to attract the white, conservative southerners who had always been Democrats because the only alternative was the party of Lincoln. In Nixon's hands, the strategy was a weaker, or at least more coded, version of the arguments that Wallace and Goldwater had been making for several years. Reagan had also used such arguments in his 1966 gubernatorial campaign, successfully appealing to white, working-class conservatives by blaming urban blacks for the state's breakdown in law and order and by criticizing welfare recipients as lazy and irresponsible (McGirr 2001:200–202). As historians Lisa McGirr and Michael Kazin have noted, Nixon and Reagan sought to appeal to "Middle America" — to the "forgotten man" and the "silent majority" — and they developed a new style of middle-class, populist conservatism in the process. To appeal to these voters, Nixon repeatedly denounced both the liberal elites who were running the welfare state — including the unelected justices of the Supreme Court — and the unruly urban masses who were threatening the peace and quiet of the suburbs (McGirr 2001:214–15; Kazin 1995:248–55).

Issues of race and civil rights constituted a crucial element of Nixon's conservatism. His law-and-order rhetoric was clearly racially charged, and the

other constitutional issue that he most often emphasized was school desegregation. At the 1968 Republican convention, he appealed to a group of
southern delegates by insisting, "I want men on the Supreme Court who are
strict constitutionalists, men that interpret the law and don't try to make the
law. . . . I know there are a lot of smart judges, believe me — and probably a
lot smarter than I am — but I don't think there is any court in this country,
any judge in this country, either local or on the Supreme Court — any court,
including the Supreme Court of the U.S. — that is qualified to be a local
school district and to make the decisions as your local school board." Later
that fall, in a television interview in Charlotte, North Carolina, he expressed
support for the *Brown v. Board of Education* decision, but noted that he would
not "go beyond that and say it is the responsibility of the federal government,
and the federal courts, to, in effect, act as local school districts in determining how we carry that out, and then to use the power of the federal treasury
to withhold funds or give funds in order to carry it out." In his view, "that
kind of activity should be scrupulously examined and in many cases . . .
would be rescinded. . . . I think that to use that power on the part of the federal government to force a local community to carry out what a federal administrator or bureaucrat may think is best for that local community — I
think that is a doctrine that is a very dangerous one" (*quoted in* Edsall and Edsall 1992:75–76). As with his law-and-order arguments, Nixon "staked out a
position lending comfort to racial conservatives, while remaining publicly
committed to racial equality" himself (Edsall and Edsall 1992:76; see also Silverstein 1994:31; Blum 1991:313; Frymer and Skrentny 1998; Berlet and Lyons
2000).

Once in office, Nixon quickly acted on these campaign themes. One of his
first acts was to propose a bill for reorganizing the D.C. courts that included
a number of provisions designed to be tough on crime (several of which were
later invalidated by the federal courts). Throughout his first term in office, he
urged congressional action to limit judicial power in the desegregation context, and his administration almost immediately began supporting the re-
quests of segregated school districts for continued delay in achieving integration. Through his control of the Justice Department's civil rights litigation
and HEW's education funding, Nixon withdrew federal pressure for local desegregation in general and race-conscious busing in particular (Orfield 1978;
Simon 1973:125–26; Blum 1991:332–36). Despite these efforts during his first
term, however, the Court's liberal activism continued in full bloom, ensuring
that Nixon and the Court would remain in conflict, and more generally that

the Court would remain a focal point for conservative denunciations of governing liberal elites. Thus, in an effort to capture the same conservative white voters for his reelection bid in 1972, Nixon sharply criticized the Burger Court's liberal decisions on school busing and the death penalty (Blum 1991:409–14). As new constitutional issues arose over the next twenty years, Republican presidents would continue to focus on the Court as a key target in their ongoing southern strategy, garnering political support for their criticism of judicial decisions on affirmative action, abortion, school prayer, and the like. By emphasizing such social and cultural issues, Republicans manufactured a new category of conservative voters, soon to be known as "Reagan Democrats," shattering the class-based New Deal Democratic coalition in the process.

The Nixon Court?

Nixon's most important campaign pledge in 1968 regarding the Court was to appoint conservative southerners and "strict constructionists," and he quickly had four opportunities to do so, as Justices Earl Warren, Abe Fortas, Hugo Black, and John Harlan all retired during his first term in office.[4] For chief justice, Nixon quickly settled on Warren Burger, the conservative federal judge whose views on the Warren Court had drawn his attention during the campaign. After his successful appointment of Burger, however, the Senate blocked his first two choices to fill Fortas's seat. Urging his legal advisers to find judicial nominees from "the meat and potatoes law schools" of the South, Midwest, and West, Nixon had settled on federal judges Clement Haynsworth and then G. Harrold Carswell, but the Democratic Senate rejected each of them, leading Nixon to announce, in 1970, "I have reluctantly concluded, with the Senate presently constituted, I cannot nominate to the Supreme Court any federal appellate judge from the South who believes as I do in the strict construction of the Constitution" (*quoted in* Edsall and Edsall 1992:82–83; see Yalof 1999:98–112). It was only after these defeats that Nixon settled on Burger's "Minnesota twin," Eighth Circuit judge Harry Blackmun. (Burger and Blackmun had been childhood friends in St. Paul, Minnesota.) In short, Nixon faced significant political constraints when he replaced Fortas, but he still sought assurances that Blackmun was "at bottom a strict constructionist," and Blackmun's judicial record was indeed conservative, though less so than Haynsworth's and Carswell's (Yalof 1999:112–14).

The following year, Black and Harlan announced their retirements within a week of each other, forcing the Court to begin its 1971 term with only seven justices. In a nationally televised press conference in October, Nixon announced his nominations of Lewis Powell and William Rehnquist directly to the American people, sounding the themes he had developed during the 1968 campaign:

> As far as judicial philosophy is concerned, it is my belief that it is the duty of a judge to interpret the Constitution and not to place himself above the Constitution or outside the Constitution. He should not twist or bend the Constitution in order to perpetuate his personal political and social views. . . . You will recall, I am sure, that during my campaign for the Presidency, I pledged to nominate to the Supreme Court individuals who shared my judicial philosophy, which is basically a conservative philosophy. . . . As a judicial conservative, I believe some court decisions have gone too far in the past in weakening the peace forces as against the criminal forces in our society. In maintaining, as it must be maintained, the delicate balance between the rights of society and defendants accused of crimes, I believe the peace forces must not be denied the legal tools they need to protect the innocent from criminal elements.[5]

Both Powell and Rehnquist were confirmed in December, as Nixon was now having greater success in appointing southern conservatives. Powell was a moderate, establishment candidate, particularly on civil rights, but he was nonetheless a prominent conservative lawyer from the South. Rehnquist was an even bigger coup — a young, brilliant, committed, conservative activist from within the administration itself.[6]

Nixon continued to campaign against the Warren Court in his bid for reelection in 1972, praising his four appointees because they "can be expected to give a strict interpretation of the Constitution, and protect the interests of the average law-abiding American." He insisted that they had "shifted the balance away from protection of the criminal to the protection of law-abiding citizens," and he pledged that if reelected, he would appoint "not reactionary judges but men who are constitutional conservatives" (*quoted in* Simon 1973:253, 291). Nixon was reelected, of course, but his second term was cut dramatically short. The Watergate scandal forced him to resign in disgrace, and the 1974 midterm elections gave the Democrats a twenty-four-seat margin in the Senate, leaving his successor to face severe political constraints when liberal stalwart Justice William O. Douglas retired in 1975. Aware of his limited options, and rejecting a number of more conservative candidates (including Robert Bork), President Ford nominated John Paul Stevens, a moderate northern Republican from the Seventh Circuit, known as an advocate of judicial restraint (Yalof 1999:125–31).

Thanks to Harlan and Black, these new conservative justices had a variety of rhetorics available for criticizing the Warren Court. As soon as he took his seat on the bench in 1972, for example, Rehnquist became the Court's leading advocate of both judicial restraint and a fixed conception of the written Constitution. In his judicial opinions and his public lectures, he complained that advocates of a "living Constitution" made "possible an individual's persuading one or more appointed federal judges to impose on other individuals a rule of conduct that the popularly elected branches of government would not have enacted and the voters have not and would not have embodied in the Constitution." Such an approach, he insisted, was "genuinely corrosive of the fundamental values of our democratic society" (1976:703–6). He rejected the notion that the Constitution should be understood as a charter of individual rights and insisted that it is better for the Court to fail to protect an individual's liberty than to wrongly thwart the majority will.[7] Applying this constitutional vision of majoritarianism and originalism, Rehnquist consistently adopted a narrow conception of the Fourteenth Amendment and denounced the expansive rights-protecting decisions that the Burger Court continued to make.

At the same time, Rehnquist began urging the Court to exercise its power quite actively in defense of federalism, limited government, and property rights. As Keith Whittington has noted, Rehnquist fully rejected Stone's constitutional vision, arguing instead for a strong presumption of constitutionality for state and local laws challenged on individual rights grounds, particularly if the alleged rights were not clearly rooted in the constitutional text. But when federal legislation was challenged for interfering with state authority, or when state and local legislation violated certain fundamental principles of limited government, Rehnquist was willing to use judicial power to impose some constitutional limits (Whittington 2003). The relevant line for Rehnquist was whether or not a judicially enforceable limit could be found in the original Constitution.

If it had been up to Rehnquist alone, the Burger Court would have made sweeping changes in constitutional doctrine. Whether he was trying to curtail liberal activism or to expand conservative activism, however, Rehnquist

TABLE 4.1 *Frequency of Solo Dissent during Burger Era**

Term/ Justice	Black	Douglas	Harlan	Brennan	Stewart	White
1969	3	2	1	1	0	0
1970	3	9	2	0	3	0
1971	—	11	—	0	0	0
1972	—	8	—	1	0	2
1973	—	16	—	1	1	0
1974	—	11	—	1	1	0
1975	—	—	—	2	1	0
1976	—	—	—	3	1	1
1977	—	—	—	0	1	1
1978	—	—	—	3	0	1
1979	—	—	—	1	0	0
1980	—	—	—	1	3	0
1981	—	—	—	1	—	2
1982	—	—	—	0	—	0
1983	—	—	—	1	—	0
1984	—	—	—	1	—	0
1985	—	—	—	2	—	1
Annual average	3.00	9.50	1.50	1.12	0.92	0.47

(continued)

could not influence the Court by himself, and his fellow Nixon appointees did not always join him. From the beginning, in fact, he had an unusual propensity for dissenting alone, as table 4.1 makes clear. During Rehnquist's first three full terms on the Court, no one could match Douglas, who was issuing solo dissents at an unprecedented rate, but Rehnquist was the second most frequent solo dissenter in each of those years.[8] During six of the next seven terms, moreover, with Douglas's having retired, Rehnquist was the Court's most frequent solo dissenter.[9]

Burger was Rehnquist's closest ally during the 1970s, but he was more inclined to join a majority he disagreed with in an effort to narrow the opin-

TABLE 4.1 (Continued)

Marshall	Burger	Blackmun	Powell	Rehnquist	Stevens	O'Connor
0	1	—	—	—	—	—
0	0	0	—	—	—	—
0	3	0	0	1	—	—
0	0	1	0	3	—	—
1	0	1	0	4	—	—
1	1	1	1	6	—	—
0	0	0	0	3	1	—
1	1	0	1	0	6	—
0	0	2	2	5	0	—
3	0	0	0	4	2	—
?	0	2	0	6	2	—
3	0	1	1	3	3	—
1	3	1	0	3	3	0
6	1	0	1	3	5	2
2	0	1	1	3	6	1
0	0	0	0	5	6	1
2	0	1	0	2	8	0
1.29	0.59	0.69	0.47	3.40	3.82	0.80

Source: Original U.S. Supreme Court Database, with orally argued citation as unit of analysis.
*Number of formally decided full opinion cases in which each justice dissented alone.

ion's reach, while Rehnquist was more willing to write dissenting opinions that spoke to the future. The other Republican appointees — Powell, Blackmun, and Stevens — broke with Rehnquist even more often than Burger did, as table 4.2 makes clear. Powell proved to be a moderate conservative, often casting deciding votes as the Court's swing justice in the 1970s and 1980s. Blackmun and Stevens played similar roles during their early years and developed over time into leading judicial liberals. When Rehnquist urged his colleagues to dramatically scale back the Warren Court's liberal activism, Powell, Blackmun, and Stevens often proceeded more cautiously, sometimes tempering that activism at the margins, but refusing to abandon it altogether.

TABLE 4.2 *Interagreement with Rehnquist during Burger Era**

Term/Justice	Douglas	Brennan	Stewart	White	Marshall	Burger	Blackmun	Powell	Stevens	O'Connor
1971	43.9	56.9	73.7	82.8	53.4	93.1	91.1	88.2	—	—
1972	37.6	44.5	65.4	80.9	47.3	85.0	77.1	80.2	—	—
1973	36.9	46.3	79.7	73.9	49.2	89.6	84.8	86.6	—	—
1974	42.9	54.5	72.1	80.3	59.0	87.7	82.8	78.1	—	—
1975	100.0	44.1	77.8	77.8	47.6	88.2	78.4	80.6	67.2	—
1976	—	43.1	82.0	75.5	45.5	91.2	82.2	82.0	63.6	—
1977	—	46.5	68.1	59.2	50.4	80.0	60.8	66.1	67.8	—
1978	—	48.4	79.5	69.9	47.6	87.1	72.6	80.1	64.2	—
1979	—	37.6	74.1	69.0	37.0	80.3	62.4	75.9	59.5	—
1980	—	54.1	78.9	77.7	48.6	88.3	70.3	82.6	68.5	—
1981	—	48.9	—	66.9	49.6	85.3	61.2	81.3	64.9	88.0
1982	—	60.4	—	79.3	52.2	83.6	65.7	86.0	65.2	89.2
1983	—	56.3	—	83.9	54.7	87.5	73.6	84.0	66.2	89.0
1984	—	55.9	—	82.8	55.0	89.7	74.6	76.6	65.4	88.9
1985	—	49.3	—	83.3	46.7	89.2	57.6	84.4	56.2	83.2
Total	39.7	49.9	75.1	76.2	49.7	86.9	72.3	80.9	64.3	87.7

Source: Original U.S. Supreme Court Database, with orally argued citation as unit of analysis.

Note: During the 1975 term, Douglas participated in only one case.

* Percentage of formally decided full opinion cases in which each justice voted with Rehnquist.

And when Rehnquist urged them to actively enforce conservative principles of limited government, they often followed him to a point, while exhibiting a reluctance to interfere with the political branches too severely.

The Uncertain Fate of Liberal Activism

When the Burger era began, many scholars predicted that the new conservative justices would eviscerate the Warren Court's legacy of constitutional rights and liberties, but their actual impact proved more complex. As with Harlan's and Black's dissenting arguments during the Warren years, the now fully developed conservative critique of judicial power served to constrain the Burger Court's liberal activism at the margins, preventing certain expansions of constitutional liberty and equality that might otherwise have occurred. This impact could be quite significant — the Burger Court declined, for example, to rule capital punishment unconstitutional after initially appearing ready to do so — but it never amounted to an abandonment of judicially enforceable constitutional rights altogether. In 1973, for example, the Court's decision in *Roe v. Wade* signaled just how fully judicial activism and the "living Constitution" had been entrenched. The Nixon justices often criticized this liberal activism, and in some areas, the Court became less willing to expand the scope of constitutional rights and liberties, but this conversation was taking place at the margins, not challenging the rights revolution itself.

One of the first areas in which the Burger Court successfully halted its predecessor's line of liberal activism was that of economic equality. The extent to which the Warren Court had been prepared to extend its welfare rights holdings is a matter of some scholarly dispute, but the direction in which it had been moving was clear.[10] Warren himself had never supported the Court's strides toward a constitutional guarantee of economic equality, but in cases like *Shapiro v. Thompson* and *Goldberg v. Kelly,* his fellow liberals had cautiously pushed ahead without him. In fact, as Mark Graber (1997) has pointed out, the jurisprudential foundations of poverty rights were stronger in 1969 than those of abortion rights. Nonetheless, the Nixon appointees quickly made clear that they were skeptical of this sort of innovative liberal activism. Dissenting in a companion case to *Goldberg,* for example, the new Chief Justice Burger noted that the federal Department of Health, Education, and Welfare was already in the process of revising the procedures for welfare termination and objected that the Court should not legislate "via constitutional fiat when an apparently reasonable result has been accomplished administratively."[11] Just two weeks later, still the only Nixon appointee to have joined the Court, Burger concurred in the Court's rejection of a welfare rights claim in *Dandridge v. Williams.* Writing for the Court, Justice Potter Stewart emphasized the modern practice of judicial deference to "state regulations in the social and economic field" and insisted that the "intractable economic, social, and even philosophical problems presented by public welfare assistance programs are not the business of this Court." He argued that to recognize a "fundamental right" to welfare "would be far too reminiscent of" the *Lochner* era, when the justices had usurped the power to strike down laws with which they disagreed.[12]

In *Harper v. Virginia State Board of Education, Shapiro,* and *Goldberg,* the Court had been reading a modern egalitarian vision into the Constitution, but as Powe has noted, it had been doing so with the support of the elected branches and the popular will. Just as *Shapiro* and *Goldberg* were being decided, however, the political branches were withdrawing this support, and the Court aborted its welfare rights effort in the early 1970s (Powe 2000:445–55). In 1973, with the four Nixon appointees now on the bench, the Court rejected a constitutional challenge to Texas's system of public school financing, despite substantial funding inequalities between wealthy and poor districts. Writing for the Court in *San Antonio Independent School District v. Rodriguez,* Justice Powell signaled a narrowing of the scope of Fourteenth Amendment rights and an unwillingness to continue down the path toward constitutionally guaranteed economic equality. Reading the Warren Court precedents narrowly, he concluded that residents of poor school districts did not constitute a suspect class worthy of heightened judicial protection. He also followed Alexander Bickel and Philip Kurland in emphasizing the limits of judicial capacity, and he noted at the end of his opinion that "[w]e are unwilling to assume for ourselves a level of wisdom superior to that of legislators, scholars, and educational authorities in 50 States, especially where the alternatives proposed are only recently conceived and nowhere yet tested. The constitutional standard under the Equal Protection Clause is whether the challenged state action rationally furthers a legitimate state purpose or interest." In response to the claim that Texas was depriving poor students of a judicially enforceable "right to education," Powell insisted that "[i]t is not the province of this Court to create substantive constitutional rights" or to assess "the relative societal significance of education as opposed to subsistence or housing," but merely to "assess[ ] whether there is a right to education explicitly or implicitly guaranteed by the Constitution."[13]

Just two months after supporting the Court's landmark decision in *Roe v. Wade,* Powell relied here on principles of federalism and judicial restraint and evinced a significant sense of caution regarding the judicial expansion of constitutional rights and liberties. This disjuncture was characteristic of the Burger Court's approach to the liberal rights-protecting doctrines it inherited. Under both the Equal Protection and Due Process Clauses, the Court slowed or reversed the line of development in some contexts while maintaining or advancing it in others.

In the area of school desegregation, the Burger Court initially followed the Warren Court's trajectory of supporting increasingly expansive (and controversial) remedial decrees, but soon put on the brakes. Prior to 1966, virtually all federal judges had assumed that *Brown* required simply an end to purposeful discrimination and the adoption of nondiscriminatory school assignment policies, but the Warren Court had suggested during its final years that school officials must take affirmative steps to achieve schools that were in fact racially mixed.[14] This "affirmative duty" to integrate would prove to require both extensive judicial supervision of school boards and the use of race-conscious measures to achieve racially balanced schools. In *United States v. Montgomery County,* the Court affirmed federal district judge Frank Johnson's desegregation order requiring racial quotas in faculty assignment, thus, in the view of some scholars, "sanction[ing] minimum racial quotas in the public workplace without any independent discussion of the merits of such a course" (Wilkinson 1979:118–19).

Four months later, now led by Burger, the Court rejected the Justice Department's request for a further three-month delay in desegregating Mississippi schools, sending a sharp rebuke to the Nixon administration.[15] And in *Swann v. Charlotte-Mecklenburg Board of Education,* the Court issued its broadest desegregation holding to date, insisting that schools must "achieve the greatest possible degree of actual desegregation" and endorsing the use of race-conscious busing. The Court explicitly affirmed that school boards were free to conclude "that in order to prepare students to live in a pluralistic society each school should have a prescribed ratio of Negro to white students reflecting the proportion for the district as a whole."[16] In a companion case, the Court struck down a North Carolina statute requiring color-blind student assignments because it "exploit[ed] an apparently neutral form to . . .

render illusory the promise of *Brown*." [17] In all of these cases, the Court purported to be requiring remedies only for prior purposeful discrimination, but placed increasing emphasis on concrete results as the measure of whether such discrimination had been eliminated.

Before long, however, Nixon's appointees began to chip away at the Court's expansive efforts in this area. The first cracks in the Court's sixteen-year-old tradition of unanimity in desegregation cases appeared in *Carter v. West Feliciana Parish School Board,* as Burger and Stewart offered a brief dissent from the Court's holding requiring immediate steps toward integration, regardless of any difficulties or disruptions that this might entail. The Court's public face of unanimity returned the following year in *Swann,* but only because of Burger's strategic decision that rather than dissenting, he would vote with the majority, assign the opinion to himself, and attempt to provide some limits on the Court's approval of racial quotas and race-conscious busing (Woodward and Armstrong 1979:119–28; Schwartz 1986:100–185, 1996a: 56–58, 135–40; Graglia 1976:104–44; Wilkinson 1979:147–48; Douglas 1980: 232–33). Though the substance of the Court's holding remained quite broad, Burger inserted some significant limiting language in the opinion, holding that "the nature of the [constitutional] violation determines the scope of the remedy"; that court-ordered busing decrees should be sensitive to practical difficulties; that while racial quotas could serve as a "useful starting point," there is no "substantive constitutional right [to] any particular degree of racial balance or mixing"; that "the existence of some small number of one-race, or virtually one-race, schools within a district is not in and of itself the mark of a system that still practices segregation by law"; and that "[n]either school authorities nor district courts are constitutionally required to make year-by-year adjustments of the racial composition of student bodies once . . . racial discrimination through official action is eliminated from the system." [18]

After *Swann,* the Court would no longer have even superficial unanimity in this area. Five months after Powell and Rehnquist joined the Court in 1972, all four Nixon appointees dissented in *Wright v. Council of City of Emporia.* In *Wright,* the Court held that the city of Emporia, Virginia could not constitutionally withdraw from the surrounding Greensville County school district because doing so would have increased the percentage of black students in the county, thus impeding the process of desegregation. Burger insisted in dissent that the Court's "result far exceeds the contemplation of *Brown,* and all succeeding cases." Relying on his own narrow statements from the *Swann* opinion, he objected to the Court's focus on "racial ratios" and "racial balance" and observed that "[t]here is no basis for concluding . . . that Emporia's decision to operate a separate school system was the manifestation of a discriminatory purpose." He insisted that "[s]ince the goal is to dismantle dual school systems rather than to reproduce in each classroom a microcosmic reflection of the racial proportions of a given geographical area, there is no basis for saying that a plan providing a uniform racial balance is more effective or constitutionally preferred." Burger also emphasized the importance of judicial restraint, noting that "the invocation of remedial jurisdiction is not equivalent to having a school district placed in receivership. . . . A local school board plan that will eliminate dual schools, stop discrimination, and improve the quality of education ought not be cast aside because a judge can evolve some other plan that accomplishes the same result, or what he considers a preferable result, with a two percent, four percent, or six percent difference in racial composition." [19]

Like Burger, Powell and Rehnquist also challenged the Court's broad, activist, race-conscious efforts to integrate the public schools. Before joining the Court, Powell had submitted an *amicus curiae* brief arguing against court-ordered busing in *Swann,* and two years later, now on the Court himself, he dissented in part from his colleagues' extension of busing into northern cities (Jeffries 1994:284–89). Dissenting in *Keyes v. School District No. 1, Denver, Colorado,* he noted his "profound misgivings" regarding *Swann*'s apparent requirement of "large-scale or long-distance transportation in our metropolitan school districts." In his view, "[n]othing in our Constitution commands or encourages any such court-compelled disruption of public education." While Powell opposed race-conscious busing, he insisted that if the federal courts were going to impose such remedies on the South, they should extend them to the North as well. He presciently saw that such an extension would ultimately lead the nation to abandon the effort. [20]

Rehnquist also dissented in *Keyes,* going farther than Powell in both substance and rhetoric. He objected to the District Court's imposition of a "federal receivership" on the Denver schools, complaining that the Court's more recent decisions had "represented a marked extension of the principles of *Brown.* . . . To require that a genuinely 'dual' system be disestablished, in the sense that the assignment of a child to a particular school is not made to depend on his race, is one thing. To require that school boards affirmatively undertake to achieve racial mixing in schools where such mixing is not achieved in sufficient degree by neutrally drawn boundary lines is quite obviously

something else." Rehnquist insisted that the Court had no warrant for reading this "affirmative duty to integrate" into the Constitution, and in dissenting opinions over the next several years, he continued to accuse his colleagues
of "total substitution of judicial for popular control of local education" and
of pursuing a policy of "integration *über alles.*"[21]

Like Justice Harlan before them, Burger, Powell, and Rehnquist objected
to the Court's activist decisions for two reasons: because they were undemocratic and because they were rooted in wrongheaded efforts at liberal social
engineering. Over time, these dissenting arguments proved influential on the
Court. In *Milliken v. Bradley,* for example, Stewart joined the four Nixon appointees to hold that the courts could not forcibly include suburban school
districts in an urban desegregation order simply to achieve a better racial balance. The Court's holding that the scope of the remedy must be limited by the
scope of the constitutional violation was influenced both by Burger's opinion
in *Swann* and by Solicitor General Bork's argument as *amicus curiae* (Jeffries
1994:313–14). Two years later, in *Pasadena Board of Education v. Spangler,*
these five justices, now joined also by Byron White, held that the District
Court's requirement of annual adjustments in student assignment to prevent
any school from having a majority of minority students surpassed the limits
set in *Swann.* In subsequent cases, the Court made the proof of constitutional
violations increasingly difficult and the scope of remedial action increasingly
narrow. In *Dayton Board of Education v. Brinkman,* for example, Rehnquist
held that "[t]he finding that the pupil population in the various Dayton
schools is not homogenous, standing by itself, is not a violation of the Fourteenth Amendment in the absence of a showing that this condition resulted
from intentionally segregative actions on the part of the Board." He proceeded to reject the remedy imposed by the Court of Appeals as "entirely out
of proportion to the constitutional violations found," and while he had been
making similar arguments for several years, he now spoke for a majority of
the Court.[22] It would be several more years before the Court adopted these
arguments consistently, but it was now moving steadily toward the conviction that once school systems had ceased segregating students by law, the federal courts should withdraw their "intrusive" supervision of those systems.[23]

The conservative arguments in the school cases were paralleled in a separate line of equal protection decisions holding that racially neutral statutes
were not unconstitutional merely because they had some unintended discriminatory effect. In *Washington v. Davis,* for example, the Nixon appointees were again joined by White, and now by Stevens as well, in holding that

"the invidious quality of a law claimed to be racially discriminatory must ultimately be traced to a racially discriminatory purpose." In so holding, Justice White emphasized the need for judicial restraint, observing that the application of strict scrutiny to all laws with a discriminatory impact "would be far reaching and would raise serious questions about, and perhaps invalidate, a whole range of tax, welfare, public service, regulatory and licensing statutes that may be more burdensome to the poor and to the average black than to the more affluent white."[24] Prior to this decision, the Court had appeared willing to ignore these concerns and enforce a broader conception of racial equality. In *Griggs v. Duke Power Co.,* for example, a unanimous Court had held that a utility company's requirement of an intelligence test as a condition of employment violated Title VII of the 1964 Civil Rights Act because it had a disparate impact on African American job applicants. Though *Griggs* was limited to the statutory context, several lower federal courts had subsequently extended it to the constitutional context, holding that the Equal Protection Clause prohibits *de facto* as well as *de jure* discrimination. As in the school desegregation cases, the conservative justices cut short this effort to outline an expansive role for the federal courts in pursuing a broad substantive vision of racial equality.

Following a similar, though even more dramatic, pattern, the Burger Court initially appeared ready to declare capital punishment unconstitutional, but as the Nixon appointees gained their footing, they halted this judicial revolution. As Burger was taking the reins from Warren, the justices' competing interpretations of the Cruel and Unusual Punishment Clause were picking up where the prior generation's debates over the Due Process Clause had left off. In his final term, for example, Justice Harlan wrote for the Court in rejecting a constitutional challenge to California's use of absolute jury discretion in capital sentencing decisions, holding that "the Federal Constitution, which marks the limit of our authority in these cases, does not guarantee trial procedures that are the best of all worlds, or that accord with the most enlightened ideas of students of the infant science of criminology, or even those that measure up to the individual predilections of the members of this Court. The Constitution requires no more than that trials be fairly conducted and that guaranteed rights of defendants be scrupulously respected." Applying his long-standing conception of due process, Harlan found it "quite impossible to say that committing to the untrammeled discretion of the jury the power to pronounce life or death in capital cases is offensive to anything in the Constitution."[25]

As the Court had not yet addressed the constitutionality of capital punishment per se, however, it was clear that this divisive constitutional conflict would return. William Brennan and his fellow liberal constitutionalists insisted that the evolving standards of decency protected by the Constitution were violated by the continued practice of state-sponsored murder. Conservatives responded by noting that several provisions of the constitutional text explicitly reference capital punishment; that the framers had clearly not intended to abolish it; and that any suggestion to the contrary amounted to a blatant usurpation of legislative power. This debate broke into the open in February of 1972, as the California Supreme Court struck down the death penalty on state constitutional grounds, providing Governor Reagan with another opportunity to denounce the courts for "setting themselves up above the people and the legislature."[26] Four months later, the Burger Court followed suit, striking down the Georgia and Texas death penalty statutes in a case that fractured the Court so badly that the justices issued a brief *per curiam* opinion announcing the judgment, followed by nine separate opinions expressing their individual views of the matter.

All four Nixon appointees dissented in this case, *Furman v. Georgia,* with Rehnquist stating the issue most plainly in his short opinion. Observing that the case "brings into sharp relief the fundamental question of the role of judicial review in a democratic society," Rehnquist reminded his colleagues that "[t]he very nature of judicial review, as pointed out by Justice Stone in his dissent in the *Butler* case, makes the courts the least subject to Madisonian check in the event that they shall, for the best of motives, expand judicial authority beyond the limits contemplated by the Framers. It is for this reason that judicial self-restraint is surely an implied, if not an expressed, condition of the grant of authority of judicial review. The Court's holding in these cases has been reached, I believe, in complete disregard of that implied condition." Similarly, Powell denounced the Court's decision for "the shattering effect [it would have] on the root principles of *stare decisis,* federalism, judicial restraint and — most importantly — separation of powers." Relying extensively on Oliver Wendell Holmes and Felix Frankfurter, Powell emphasized that the appropriateness of capital punishment "is the very sort of judgment that the legislative branch is competent to make and for which the judiciary is ill-equipped. . . . I can recall no case in which, in the name of deciding constitutional questions, this Court has subordinated national and local democratic processes to such an extent." For Powell, the judicial review of legislative decisions — always a grave and delicate duty — was that much graver "when we are not asked to pass on the constitutionality of a single penalty under the facts of a single case but instead are urged to overturn the legislative judgments of 40 state legislatures as well as those of Congress." He complained that the Court's decision revealed "a basic lack of faith and confidence in the democratic process" and that "impatience with the slowness, and even the unresponsiveness, of legislatures is no justification for judicial intrusion upon their historic powers."[27]

The dissenting conservative justices were building on a long line of arguments here, insisting that they had carefully excluded their own preferences or predilections from consideration, but suggesting that their more liberal colleagues had succumbed to the "temptation" of enacting their own views into law. They buttressed these arguments for restraint with appeals to the constitutional text, the intentions of the framers, and the Court's precedents. As Powell noted, "whatever punishments the Framers of the Constitution may have intended to prohibit under the 'cruel and unusual' language, there cannot be the slightest doubt that they intended no absolute bar on the Government's authority to impose the death penalty." This was clear, Powell insisted, because the Fifth Amendment itself makes three references to capital punishment, and because the first Congress, which adopted the Bill of Rights, also provided for the death penalty in the first Crimes Act of 1790.[28] As conservatives had been arguing for some time, the dissenters protested that there was no legitimate way for the Court to make the Constitution mean the opposite of what it had meant for the past two hundred years. As Justice Blackmun commented, "[i]t is comforting to relax in the thoughts — perhaps the rationalizations — that . . . we are less barbaric than we were in 1879, or in 1890, or in 1910, or in 1947, or in 1958, or in 1963, or a year ago, in 1971, when *Wilkerson, Kemmler, Weems, Francis, Trop, Rudolph,* and *McGautha* were respectively decided," but such arguments "ma[de] sense only in a legislative and executive way" and should not influence the Court's interpretation of our written Constitution.[29]

The Nixon justices had plumbed every available argument for judicial restraint, but they were unable, in 1972, to convince the Court. The justices in the majority could not agree on a constitutional rationale, but they invalidated all then-existing death penalty statutes nationwide. Brennan and Thurgood Marshall insisted that the death penalty was fully prohibited by the Eighth Amendment, while Stewart, White, and Douglas held that it was currently being administered in an unconstitutionally arbitrary, capricious, or discriminatory fashion. Because only two justices appeared willing to invalidate capital punishment altogether, state legislatures throughout the country responded to *Furman* not by abolishing the death penalty but by attempting to make it less arbitrary in operation. Within four years, Stewart, White, and Stevens (Douglas's replacement) joined the four Nixon appointees in allowing the resumption of capital punishment throughout the nation, upholding most of the newly revised death penalty statutes. In his plurality opinion in *Gregg v. Georgia,* Stewart reiterated the need for restraint that the *Furman* dissenters had emphasized, and he observed that developments during the past four years had undercut the anti-death-penalty arguments even further. It was "now evident," he noted, "that a large proportion of American society continue[d] to regard [capital punishment] as an appropriate and necessary criminal sanction." For Stewart, the fact that thirty-five states had enacted new death penalty statutes since *Furman* undercut the "evolving standards of decency" argument that he had been willing to entertain in the earlier case.[30]

In this context, then, the conservative critique of judicial power forestalled the Court from undertaking what would have been a significant expansion of constitutional liberty. As in the desegregation cases, the conservatives' demand for restraint was buttressed here by their opposition to the liberal policy agenda (i.e., race-conscious desegregation decrees or abolition of the death penalty). In another similarity, the conservatives closed off the liberal development, but did not succeed in returning the law to its original position. Never again would states be free to impose the death penalty as they saw fit, just as they would not be free to assign students to public schools in a discriminatory fashion. In one of *Gregg*'s companion cases, for example, the Court held that statutes that impose mandatory death sentences are unconstitutional, and it has continued to impose some constitutional limits on capital punishment ever since.[31]

While Justice Rehnquist and his fellow conservatives' narrow vision of constitutional liberty was widely influential in the death penalty context, it remained almost exclusively in dissent with regard to abortion rights. Following *Griswold v. Connecticut,* the Court had been forced to determine the limits of the new right to privacy that it had found implicit in the Constitution. When the Warren Court held state miscegenation laws unconstitutional in 1967, for example, it had relied primarily on the Equal Protection Clause but had also observed that "[t]he freedom to marry has long been recognized as one of the vital personal rights essential to the orderly pursuit of happiness by free men."[32] Two years later, the Court struck down a conviction for possession of obscene films, holding that the First Amendment was buttressed here by the "fundamental . . . right to be free, except in very limited circumstances, from unwanted governmental intrusions into one's privacy."[33] In *Eisenstadt v. Baird,* the Burger Court continued on this path, extending *Griswold* by holding that "the right of privacy . . . is the right of the individual, married or single, to be free from unwarranted governmental intrusion into matters so fundamentally affecting a person as the decision whether to bear or beget a child."[34] According to some accounts, Brennan inserted this language in the opinion with the then-pending abortion cases in mind, and the following year, a seven-justice majority held that "[t]his right of privacy . . . is broad enough to encompass a woman's decision whether or not to terminate her pregnancy."[35]

Picking up where Justice Black had left off in *Griswold,* Rehnquist protested in *Roe* that "[t]o reach its result, the Court necessarily has had to find within the scope of the Fourteenth Amendment a right that was apparently completely unknown to [its] drafters." Unlike Black, he acknowledged that the "liberty" protected by the Due Process Clause "embraces more than the rights found in the Bill of Rights," but he insisted that when faced with the alleged deprivation of a nontextual "liberty interest" such as this one, the Court should inquire only whether the challenged statute had "a rational relation to a valid state objective." In Rehnquist's view, the Court's much stricter "compelling state interest" test intruded upon the democratic prerogatives of the states and was not justified by the original meaning of the Fourteenth Amendment. He reiterated his opposition to this heightened scrutiny in the equal protection context, and objected to the Court's novel effort to transpose it to the due process context as well. His short dissenting opinion ended with two lengthy footnotes documenting the thirty-six state or territorial laws limiting abortion that had been on the books in 1868 and the twenty-one such laws that remained in effect in 1973. His argument here recalled the segregationist critique of *Brown,* as well as Frankfurter's and Harlan's dissenting opinions in *Baker v. Carr* and *Reynolds v. Sims,* and it foreshadowed many similar Fourteenth Amendment arguments to come.[36] It was clear by this point that while Douglas had articulated the constitutional right to privacy in an effort to avoid reliance on substantive due process, this line of doctrine had in fact developed into a species of that argument.[37] It was clear, moreover, that Rehnquist and White, at least, were unwilling to go along with what they saw as an illegitimate expansion of judicial power. As table 4.2

shows, White did not always agree with Rehnquist, but he did so more often than the Burger Court's other Democratic appointees (Douglas and Marshall) and its surprisingly liberal Republican appointees (Brennan, Blackmun, and Stevens).

Throughout the 1970s, before President Reagan had elevated opposition to *Roe* to a "litmus test" for judicial nominees, Rehnquist and White were the most influential of the abortion dissenters. Dissenting in *Roe*'s companion case, *Doe v. Bolton,* White rejected the Court's argument as "an improvident and extravagant exercise of the power of judicial review" and noted that he could "find nothing in the language or history of the Constitution to support the Court's judgment." The "upshot" of the Court's decision, he complained, was "that the people and the legislatures of the 50 States [were] constitutionally disentitled to weigh the relative importance of the continued existence and development of the fetus, on the one hand, against a spectrum of possible impacts on the mother, on the other hand." [38] Three years later, Rehnquist and White again dissented in *Planned Parenthood of Missouri v. Danforth,* reiterating their opposition to the Court's "difficult and continuing venture in substantive due process" and insisting that "[t]hese are matters which a State should be able to decide free from the suffocating power of the federal judge, purporting to act in the name of the Constitution." [39]

Chief Justice Burger was less consistent, but he too came to oppose *Roe* over time. He had first expressed his reservations regarding the new substantive due process in his dissenting opinion in *Eisenstadt.* Declining to challenge *Griswold,* "despite its tenuous moorings to the text of the Constitution," he had distinguished that precedent on the grounds that it dealt with a prohibition on the use of contraceptives, while the Court here faced only a regulation of their distribution. He had complained, moreover, that "[b]y relying on *Griswold* in the present context, the Court has passed beyond the penumbras of the specific guarantees into the uncircumscribed area of personal predilections," and had argued that the Court's holding "seriously invade[s] the constitutional prerogatives of the States and regrettably hark[s] back to the heyday of substantive due process." [40] While he joined the liberal majority the following year in *Roe,* he quickly reconsidered, joining White's dissent in *Danforth,* then sitting on the fence for several years before finally declaring in 1986 that *Roe* should be reexamined. [41]

The justices' sharp divisions in the abortion cases reflected a jurisprudential split that reached more broadly, and Rehnquist, White, and Burger were usually, though not always, outvoted in other contexts as well. The year before *Roe,* White had held for the Court that there is no constitutionally guaranteed right to adequate housing, reiterating that "the Constitution does not provide judicial remedies for every social and economic ill"; but five years later, he and Rehnquist were joined by Burger and Stewart in dissenting from the Court's recognition of a constitutionally protected right for a family to live together.[42] The year after that, White joined the Court's decision protecting the right to marry in *Zablocki v. Redhail,* with Rehnquist dissenting alone. As in the abortion context, Rehnquist was in dissent in all of these cases because his fellow Nixon appointees refused to join him. While he and White were following Hugo Black in offering a narrow vision of constitutional liberty, Powell was following John Harlan in asserting that the Court's history counseled caution and self-restraint but not the abandonment of substantive due process altogether.

During this same period, Rehnquist was persistently urging judicial restraint in the equal protection context, and outside the domain of racial equality, at least, his arguments usually remained in dissent here as well. When he joined the Court, it had already begun tentatively extending equal protection scrutiny to statutes that discriminated on the basis of illegitimacy, alienage, and gender. In his view, the liberal justices had failed to provide either a convincing rationale for these extensions or a workable standard for deciding what other sorts of discrimination were prohibited.

In his first term, for example, Rehnquist dissented in *Weber v. Aetna Casualty & Surety Co.,* objecting to the Court's extension of a vaguely defined form of heightened scrutiny to legislative classifications that discriminate against illegitimate children. Relying heavily on Harlan's dissent from a similar decision four years earlier, he insisted that except where race was involved, the Court should uphold all legislative classifications that rest on some rational basis. He described the Court's holding as "devoid . . . of any historical or textual support in the language of the Equal Protection Clause" and as "an extraordinary departure" from both the original intentions of the framers and "the traditional presumption of constitutionality accorded to legislative enactments." He complained, moreover, that the modern Court's equal protection decisions, like the *Lochner* Court's due process decisions, amounted to "an invitation for judicial exegesis over and above the commands of the Constitution, in which values that cannot possibly have their source in that instrument are invoked to either validate or condemn the countless laws enacted by the various States."[43]

Rehnquist reiterated these arguments in the alienage context, criticizing

the Court for extending heightened judicial solicitude to any minority group
that the justices perceived to be politically powerless. Dissenting in *Sugarman
v. Dougall,* he followed Frankfurter in complaining that neither the language
of the Fourteenth Amendment nor any evidence of the framers' intentions
"would suggest to the slightest degree that . . . it was designed in any way to
protect 'discrete and insular' minorities other than racial minorities." After
quoting Frankfurter's critique of *United States v. Carolene Products* in *Kovacs
v. Cooper,* Rehnquist observed:

> [O]ur society, consisting of over 200 million individuals of multitudinous
> origins, customs, tongues, beliefs, and cultures is, to say the least, diverse.
> It would hardly take extraordinary ingenuity for a lawyer to find "insular
> and discrete" minorities at every turn in the road. Yet, unless the Court can
> precisely define and constitutionally justify both the terms and analysis it
> uses, these decisions stand for the proposition that the Court can choose
> a "minority" it "feels" deserves "solicitude" and thereafter prohibit the
> States from classifying that "minority" differently from the "majority." I
> cannot find, and the Court does not cite, any constitutional authority for
> such a "ward of the Court" approach to equal protection.[44]

As in the school desegregation context, Rehnquist followed Harlan in rejecting the modern Court's egalitarian reading of the Constitution both because
it called for illegitimate liberal social engineering and because it called for that
social engineering to be imposed by unelected judges.

Rehnquist elaborated this critique of modern equal protection doctrine a
few years later in *Trimble v. Gordon,* objecting that the Court seemed "to regard the Equal Protection Clause as a cat-o'-nine-tails to be kept in the judicial closet as a threat to legislatures which may, in the view of the judiciary,
get out of hand and pass 'arbitrary,' 'illogical,' or 'unreasonable' laws. Except
in the area of the law in which the Framers obviously meant it to apply —
classifications based on race or on national origin, the first cousin of race —
the Court's decisions can fairly be described as an endless tinkering with legislative judgments, a series of conclusions unsupported by any central
guiding principle." Rehnquist repeatedly derided the Court's decisions as illegitimate usurpations of legislative authority, observing that "[t]he Civil War
Amendments did not make this Court into a council of revision, and they did
not confer upon this Court any authority to nullify state laws which were
merely felt to be inimical to the Court's notion of the public interest." He also

complained that "[w]ithout any antecedent constitutional mandate, we have created on the premises of the Equal Protection Clause a school for legislators, whereby opinions of this Court are written to instruct them in a better understanding of how to accomplish their ordinary legislative tasks."[45]

Rehnquist dissented from the Court's early gender equality decisions as well. In *Frontiero v. Richardson,* Justice Brennan held for a four-justice plurality that "classifications based upon sex, like classifications based upon race, alienage, and national origin, are inherently suspect and must therefore be subjected to close judicial scrutiny." Four other justices agreed that the classification at issue was unconstitutional, but refused to join Brennan's sweeping opinion, and so three years later, in *Craig v. Boren,* the Court settled on a compromise standard of "intermediate scrutiny," under which gender classifications "must serve important governmental objectives and must be substantially related to achievement of those objectives."[46] Rehnquist dissented in both cases, insisting that gender classifications should be upheld so long as they rationally furthered some legitimate interest and complaining that the Court's stricter standards apparently came "out of thin air" and were "so diaphanous and elastic as to invite subjective judicial preferences or prejudices relating to particular types of legislation."[47]

Rehnquist's efforts in this context were dramatically unsuccessful throughout the 1970s. In *Weber, Sugarman,* and *Frontiero,* he was the only justice to dissent, and in *Trimble* and *Craig,* his fellow dissenters refused to join his opinion. His influence did grow over time, but he never persuaded his colleagues to limit the reach of the Equal Protection Clause as sharply as he hoped. As I show in the chapters to come, even he eventually came to acknowledge that a meaningful standard of review must be applied to state-sponsored discrimination against women, though he continued to object to any other expansions of the equal protection principle.

In sum, while the Court took a conservative turn in the 1970s, the Nixon appointees were either unwilling or unable to dislodge the constitutional order they had inherited. Rather than ending with Warren's retirement, the rights revolution continued in full bloom even as conservatives joined the Court. For this reason, some scholars have suggested that the transition from the Warren to the Burger era was relatively inconsequential, and that we might instead think of the whole period from roughly 1962 to 1981 as "the Brennan Court" (Hutchinson 1983:923; McCloskey 1994:150). The Brennan Court's continued support for rights-based activism during the 1970s, more-

over, sparked liberal constitutional scholars to articulate an increasingly explicit justification for this modern vision of judicial power. Perhaps the most
influential of these scholars has been Ronald Dworkin, who argued as early
as 1972 that "[o]ur constitutional system rests on a particular moral theory,
namely, that men have moral rights against the state. The difficult clauses of
the Bill of Rights, like the due process and equal protection clauses, must be
understood as appealing to moral concepts rather than laying down particular conceptions; therefore a court that undertakes the burden of applying
these clauses fully as law must be an activist court, in the sense that it must be
prepared to frame and answer questions of political morality."[48] Constitutional conservatives had long criticized such liberal activism as undemocratic, and they were increasingly challenging it on other grounds as well.

The Emerging Critique of Modern Liberalism

The 1970s witnessed a dramatic conservative shift in the nation's political and
intellectual life, a shift marked by the full emergence of a distinctive conservative critique of modern liberalism. A "New Right" was coming to dominate
national politics, representing a combination of two distinct but overlap-
ping sets of conservative voters, leaders, and ideas. First, the libertarian, free
market conservatism that Goldwater and Reagan had articulated so clearly in
the 1960s continued to grow in the following decade. As McGirr (2001) has
noted, western conservatives in particular developed an anti-government
ethos, in part because their geographical distance from Washington made it
easier to think of federal bureaucrats as an unaccountable governing elite.
These western conservatives pulled both the Republican Party and the nation
as a whole to the right. While Nixon had fundamentally accepted the New
Deal/Great Society welfare state, for example, a wide variety of conservative
activists, political leaders, and intellectuals began to adopt a much more critical stance. The conservative hostility to the federal government developed
into a sharp critique of the national welfare-regulatory state in particular, but
also taxation and government bureaucracy in general, even at the state and
local level.

The most striking political manifestation of this burgeoning libertarianism was the so-called taxpayer revolt of the 1970s, which began in Nixon's and
Reagan's home state of California. After the state Supreme Court required
equal funding of public schools in 1971, conservative activist Howard Jarvis

launched an anti-tax campaign that culminated in the 1978 passage of Proposition 13, amending the state constitution to limit local property taxes to 1 percent of property value (McGirr 2001:237–39). Proposition 13's success led to a series of similar tax-limitation campaigns throughout the country, and just two years later, Reagan rode into the presidency on his promise to "get the government off the backs of the American people" (Edsall and Edsall 1992:129–31; McWilliams 1995:75; see also Brinkley 1994). Just as he had insisted in his 1964 speech for Goldwater, Reagan continued to maintain that government was the chief threat to individual liberty, and hence that we should reduce the powers and resources at the government's disposal.[49]

As this libertarian, anti-government ethos rose to prominence, a second group of conservatives was also mobilizing to influence national politics for the first time: the Christian Right. Though religious fundamentalism has deep roots in American history, the rapid and dramatic growth of conservative evangelical churches in the 1970s and 1980s represented a cultural movement of tremendous significance. The religious broadcasting industry, to take just one example, had been expanding throughout the twentieth century, but it truly took off during this period. By 1979, Pat Robertson's Christian Broadcasting Network had an annual budget of $50 million and millions of viewers for its conservative talk show, the *700 Club*, and during the 1980s, a new breed of "televangelists" such as Jerry Falwell and Jim Bakker would begin drawing a mass audience (Diamond 1995:162–65).

Sparked by a backlash against what they saw as the nation's moral decline during the 1960s, this new religious Right became increasingly politicized. Responding in particular to the sexual revolution, the women's movement, and the emerging gay rights movement, religious conservatives called for greater government regulation of obscenity and a return to traditional gender roles. Particularly significant campaigns during the 1970s included Phyllis Schlafly's successful opposition to the national Equal Rights Amendment; Anita Bryant's successful effort to repeal a gay rights ordinance in Miami-Dade County in 1977; and the variety of pro-life movements that emerged throughout the country in response to *Roe v. Wade. Roe* was just one of many liberal activist decisions of the Warren and Burger Courts that proved popular targets, as religious conservatives opposed the school prayer, obscenity, and sexual privacy decisions as well. The support for organized prayer in the public schools, moreover, was part of a broader concern with undue liberal influence on education that played a crucial role in the development of the religious Right. Many conservative activists cut their teeth in local campaigns against sex education, the teaching of evolutionary biology, and more generally, "what they perceived to be the inculcation of morally relativist values by liberal educators" (McGirr 2001:181; see also id. at 179–258; Diamond 1995: 166–72; Berlet and Lyons 2000:208–13; Foner 1998:307–32).

During the 1970s and 1980s, these New Right social movements of antigovernment libertarians and religious conservatives would play an increasing role in Republican electoral successes, even though they were (and remain) in significant tension with each other. As many observers have noted, the former calls for a minimalist, "night watchman" state, while the latter calls for active government intervention to promote traditional morality. In actual political practice, however, the two have united in the face of a common enemy. Particularly when they were not yet in power themselves, as McGirr points out, "the contradictions between the two strands of right-wing thought did not come to matter decisively. Both were united in a common opposition to liberalism, and it was that liberalism that the movement set out to fight." During the 1950s and early 1960s, the "symbolic glue" that bonded various conservatives had been anti-communism, but as the communist threat receded during the 1970s, conservatives remained united in their shared hostility to liberal elites, particularly government bureaucrats, the national media, and east coast intellectuals (McGirr 2001:168, 35–36, 102–3).

While members of the religious Right criticized liberal elites for trying to impose what they saw as an immoral lifestyle on the nation, economic conservatives regularly criticized liberal "social engineering" for interfering with economic liberty and the free market (Keen and Goldberg 1998:107–11; Berlet and Lyons 2000). Libertarians and religious conservatives shared the belief that "America's problems were not the result of any inherent limitations of a capitalist economy or inequalities in American life, but rather were due to liberal tampering with an otherwise harmonious, self-sustaining system. Capitalism, this argument went, would run smoothly if not for an overgrown state. Family, morality, and religion would be intact if liberal elites had not encouraged permissiveness and secularism" (McGirr 2001:151). As Kevin Phillips recognized in his perceptive analysis of the 1968 election, the nation was witnessing "a populist revolt of the American masses who have been elevated by prosperity to middle-class status and conservatism. Their revolt is against the caste, policies and taxation of the mandarins of Establishment liberalism" (1969:470). In this conservative narrative, judges were always presented as part of the broader liberal governing elite, and sometimes as a particularly objectionable part, given their anti-democratic authority to strike down any morally just laws that happened to make it through the majoritarian political process.

Some of the key foundations for the New Right critique of liberalism were laid out by a distinctive group of intellectuals, intensely focused on national politics, who emerged in the 1970s and came to be known as "neoconservatives." Among the most influential of these "neocons" were Irving Kristol and Daniel Bell, co-editors of *The Public Interest,* a quarterly journal of social policy that they founded in 1965; Norman Podhoretz, editor of the monthly opinion journal *Commentary;* Nathan Glazer, a frequent contributor to both journals; Daniel Patrick Moynihan, who brought neoconservative ideas into the Nixon administration and then the Senate; and academic social scientists James Q. Wilson, Edward Banfield, and Seymour Martin Lipset (Diamond 1995:178–204; Epstein 1973). The core tenets of neoconservatism, as articulated by Kristol in 1976, included a critique of the welfare state and the Great Society; a strong belief in "the power of the market to respond efficiently to economic realities while preserving the maximum degree of individual freedom"; a rejection of liberal egalitarianism; and a respect for those "traditional values and institutions: religion, the family, the 'high culture' of Western civilization," which were threatened by the 1960s counterculture (1976: 17; see Young 1996:249; Harrington 1973). In other words, these scholars and policy analysts sought to develop more fully the visceral critique of liberalism that Goldwater, Nixon, and especially Reagan had been exploiting so well.

The neoconservative critique of the welfare state was intellectually rooted in Friedrich Hayek's influential 1944 book *The Road to Serfdom.* While Hayek's original concern had been with the central economic planning that he took as the key feature of true socialism — and that represented the "road to serfdom" of the title — he had later extended the critique to the liberal democratic welfare state as well.[50] Following Hayek, neoconservatives insisted that the welfare-regulatory state was inherently unjust because it sapped individuals of freedom and responsibility. For example, Kristol "approve[d] of those social reforms that [operated] with a minimum of bureaucratic intrusion in the individual's affairs [but was] skeptical of those social programs that create[d] vast and energetic bureaucracies to 'solve social problems'" (1976:17).

Even if the welfare state were not a threat to liberty, moreover, the neoconservatives insisted that its policies were unlikely to work. Perhaps the single goal that preoccupied them the most was to demonstrate that government has a limited capacity for bringing about social change. Moynihan, the only leading neoconservative with actual experience working within the welfare state, was a persistent advocate of this argument. With the federal government undertaking "an unprecedented range of social initiatives designed to put an end to racial and ethnic discrimination, to poverty, and eventually also to unequal levels of achievement as among groups variously defined by race, class, religion, national origin, and sex," Moynihan insisted that it was bound to fail: "The modern welfare state was getting into activities no one understood very well. It had not reached the point of picking every man a wife, but it was getting close enough to other such imponderables to find itself increasingly held to account for failure in areas where no government could reasonably promise success" (1973:53; see also Moynihan 1969). In Moynihan's view, government was inherently inferior to the market in providing services, and he was convinced that welfare policies like Aid to Families with Dependent Children (AFDC), Medicaid, and especially the "community action" programs of LBJ's Great Society created a culture of poverty and dependence among their recipients. In his estimation, the primary effect of the welfare state was to create jobs for social workers and other liberal elites, for it had done little to actually help the poor.[51] The culmination of this neoconservative critique of the War on Poverty came in Charles Murray's *Losing Ground: American Social Policy, 1950-1980*, published in 1984 with support from Kristol and the conservative Manhattan Institute.

What began as a critique of the details of the Great Society, moreover, developed into a full-fledged rejection of government regulation and social services in general. In a particularly influential, but representative, article in *The Public Interest*, Robert Martinson surveyed the existing empirical studies of prison reform efforts designed to reduce recidivism through rehabilitation. The title of the article was "What Works?" and his answer was, essentially, "nothing" (1974). Articles in *The Public Interest* and *Commentary* regularly sought to demonstrate that the unintended consequences of government action overwhelmed the intended consequences. In a 1971 article "The Limits of Social Policy," for example, Glazer noted that while social welfare policies were intended "to deal with the breakdown of traditional ways of handling distress," such as the family, the neighborhood, and the church, those policies had in fact further weakened these traditional institutions: "There is, then, no sea of misery against which we are making steady headway. Our efforts to deal with distress themselves increase distress" (1971:52). The neoconservatives insisted that social welfare and regulatory policies were a threat to individual liberty and represented a hopeless effort to solve unsolvable social problems — often exacerbating the very problems they were trying to solve — and hence that the government should generally refrain from such efforts.

One of the key areas of social policy that the neoconservatives rejected was what Glazer called "the revolution of equality [which] not only expresses a demand for equality in political rights and in political power [but] also . . . in economic power, in social status, in authority in every sphere" (1971:53). In the neoconservative view, a wide variety of emerging egalitarian policies violated fundamental principles of individual liberty and limited government, and, moreover, were unlikely to work. Most notable were the race-conscious affirmative action policies increasingly being used in the university admissions and government contracting contexts. In an article on "meritocracy and equality," for example, Daniel Bell denounced racial quotas as an attack on merit and criticized the ongoing cultural and political redefinition of equality from the "liberal ethic" of equality of opportunity to the "socialist ethic" of equality of result: "The principle of equality of opportunity derives from a fundamental principle of classical liberalism: that the individual — and not the family, the community, or the state — is the basic unit of society, and that the purpose of social arrangements is to allow the individual the freedom to fulfill his own purposes. . . . It was assumed that individuals will differ . . . and that the institutions of society should establish procedures for regulating fairly the competition and exchanges necessary to fulfill these diverse desires and competences [sic]." By imposing equal outcomes on all groups within society, the liberal state was violating the freedom of each individual "to achieve a place commensurate with his talents" (1972:48, 40). As Kristol observed, "[n]eo-conservatism affirms the traditional American idea of equality, but rejects egalitarianism — the equality of condition for all citizens — as a proper goal for government to pursue. . . . [T]he encouragement of equality of opportunity is always a proper concern of democratic government. But it is a dangerous sophistry to insist that there is no true equality of opportunity unless and until everyone ends up with equal shares of everything" (1976:17).

The emerging conservative critique of affirmative action can thus be seen

as part and parcel of a broader demand for limited government. When Jeane
Kirkpatrick criticized affirmative action in 1979, for example, she did so on
precisely these grounds:

> The distribution of scarce resources on the basis of race or sex not only vi-
> olates widely shared beliefs concerning just rewards, it violates the tradi-
> tional relationships between state and society. It commits government to
> use coercion to impose new practices on a reluctant society. New liberals
> argue that this use of government's power serves the cause of social justice.
> Traditional liberals see it as an unwarranted use of regulatory power which
> progressively narrows the scope of individual freedom, undermines the
> society's most basic values, and intrudes government's heavy hand into
> many subjects remote from its appropriate concern — from school bus-
> ing to boys' choirs; from hiring and firing to football. (1979:30)

The effort of the liberal welfare state to guarantee "equal shares of everything," the neocons insisted, was a misguided attempt at "social engineering," an effort by unrepresentative liberal elites to remake society and even
human nature in their own image. In an essay "About Equality," Kristol described these liberal elites as a "new class" of intellectuals "engaged in a class
struggle with the business community for status and power," and he and his
allies set out to debunk their pretensions to expertise (1972:43).

As far as the courts were concerned, the neocons initially joined their fellow conservatives in criticizing judicial power, emphasizing that the courts
lacked the institutional capacity to administer complex governmental institutions and to achieve broad social reform. If the federal legislature and bureaucracy could not do so successfully, they insisted, the federal courts certainly were not going to be up to the task. For example, in an influential 1975
critique of the "imperial judiciary" in *The Public Interest,* Glazer complained
that the courts "now reach into the lives of the people, against the will of the
people, deeper than they ever have in American history." Noting that the
justification usually offered for judicial activism was that the other branches
had failed to act, Glazer claimed that the political branches often refused to
address particular social problems because they had correctly concluded that
there was no clear knowledge of how government should go about doing so.
In expanding the reach of government, then, the courts were ignoring the
fact that it was "already grossly expanded beyond its capacity to perform"
(1975a:106, 118–19).

Constitutional scholars like Bickel and Kurland had been noting the limited institutional capacity of the courts for several years, but the neoconservative social policy analysts developed this argument more fully. Glazer argued that legislatures and executives had more resources than courts to determine how best to respond to public problems and that when they refused to respond, it was "because no one knows how to, or [because] there is not enough money to cover everything, or because the people simply don't want it. These strike me as valid considerations in a democracy, but they are not considered valid considerations when issues of social policy come up as court cases for judgment" (1975a:118–19). This emerging neoconservative critique of judicial policymaking emphasized both the undemocratic character of "government by judiciary" and the wrongheadedness of the liberal social engineering in which the courts were engaged. When Donald Horowitz published a book-length version of this argument for the Brookings Institution in 1977, for example, he provided four case studies of allegedly ineffective judicial policymaking, and all four were exemplars of post 1960s liberal egalitarianism.[52]

Perhaps the most frequent target of this criticism was the Burger Court's approval of compulsory busing as a means of school integration. For neocons like Nathan Glazer, this line of doctrine was part of a troublesome pattern in which the federal courts were undertaking ever broader efforts to reform governmental institutions such as schools, prisons, mental hospitals, and the juvenile justice system. Among the more distinctive characteristics of modern liberal activism was the wide-ranging use of equitable remedies and consent decrees to prevent present and future constitutional violations, and the neocons objected to such judicial "usurpations" of executive authority just as strongly as they objected to judicial interference with legislative authority.

For example, in a 1975 book titled *Affirmative Discrimination: Ethnic Inequality and Public Policy,* along with articles in *Commentary* and *The Public Interest,* Glazer argued that the busing decisions were "arguably the most disruptive decisions ever made by the courts" and that they had transformed "a legitimate, moral, and constitutional effort to eliminate the unconstitutional separation of the races . . . into something else — an intrusive, costly, painful, and futile effort to stabilize proportions of races in the schools." He insisted that "the judges have gone far beyond what the Constitution can reasonably be thought to allow or require in the operation of this complex process [and that they] should now stand back and allow the forces of political democracy in a pluralist society to do their proper work." He acknowledged that the courts' path had begun "with an effort to expand freedom [by holding that] no black child shall be excluded from any public school because of his race," but complained that it had "ended up with as drastic a restriction of freedom as we have seen in this country in recent years: No child, of any race or group, may 'escape' or 'flee' the school to which that child has been assigned on the basis of his or her race" (1975a:105; 1975b:83, 129, 109, 116–17; see also Glazer 1972, Graglia 1976). In short, Glazer rejected court-ordered busing both because it was judicially imposed and because it represented the paternalistic policy of an overbearing liberal state.

Thus, while the initial conservative objection to modern liberal activism had emphasized the undemocratic character of judicial power, 1970s conservatives supplemented this argument with an analytically distinct critique of modern liberalism itself. For the time being, moreover, conservatives did not carefully distinguish these two separate critiques. In the 1978 founding issue of the *Harvard Journal of Law and Public Policy,* for example, the editors announced that while there would be no "litmus test" for the new journal's conservative editorial perspective, the "[g]eneral philosophical premises which are widely accepted within the organization . . . include judicial restraint, limited government, and the rule of law" (Abraham and Eberhard 1978; see Kalman 1996:81). It was not fully clear at the time, but the conservative demands for judicial restraint and limited government would sometimes pull in different directions. If busing policies were illegitimate because they were race conscious, then they were illegitimate whether imposed by unelected judges or elected legislators. And if it was modern liberalism itself to which conservatives objected, then they might sometimes call on the courts to restrain the illegitimate liberal policies adopted by other institutions.

As neoconservatives developed their arguments for limited government and against social engineering — and as they strategized about how best to impose some operative limits on the welfare state — they would soon start to recognize the federal courts as a potential ally. After all, when conservatives began to take control of the federal judiciary, rights-based constitutionalism was already firmly entrenched in the American polity. Given the path that was open, it should not be surprising that they increasingly drew on their principles of limited government to craft their own conservative justifications for the exercise of judicial power. The Court was not the only liberal institution of which the conservatives were suspicious, and if it was Congress or the federal bureaucracy that was responsible for an objectionable policy, the Court might be in a position to impose some limits. Thus, while the neocons had buttressed the long-standing demands for judicial restraint — by documenting the alleged weakness of courts as policymaking institutions — they had also begun to articulate a new argument for judicial activism.

The religious conservatives did not at first join the libertarians and neocons in this latter effort, as they generally continued to counsel judicial deference to majoritarian morality. While they were slower to realize the potential to which judicial power could be pressed, however, they too would eventually come around. By the turn of the twenty-first century, as I show in the coming chapters, conservative religious organizations would be calling on the federal courts to protect their freedom of speech, to guarantee their right of equal access to state resources, and to defend their exclusionary membership policies against interference by state and federal anti-discrimination laws.

The Birth of Conservative Activism

In the shadow of this New Right critique of liberalism, the conservative justices of the Burger Court began urging the active exercise of judicial power in several areas of constitutional doctrine. They did not succeed in pushing this conservative activism very far during the 1970s, but they planted important seeds to be harvested once they consolidated their control of the Court. In the affirmative action and Tenth Amendment contexts, most notably, the conservative justices made successful initial efforts to impose some constitutional limits on the policies of the liberal state, limits that they would be able to develop more fully in later years. Without acknowledging it, the conservative justices who made these decisions, and the scholars like Bickel and Kurland who supported them, were abandoning their long-standing commitment to restraint. This tension would prove significant, not least because some members of the Court's conservative majority in these cases would express concern with the decisions' activist implications. In both the affirmative action and the Tenth Amendment cases, the centrist justices with the deciding votes would indicate a reluctance to carry the new conservative activism too far.

In the area of racial equality, as I have noted, conservatives had been emphasizing an individualistic, meritocratic conception of equality of opportunity, which they saw as threatened by liberal egalitarian policies. In the constitutional context, this came to be expressed as a "color-blind" vision of the Equal Protection Clause, a guarantee that the state treat all persons as individuals and not on the basis of racial stereotypes. When the Court was preoccupied with school desegregation, the conservative constitutional principles of judicial restraint and color-blindness pointed in the same direction: toward the curtailment of judicially imposed, race-conscious remedial efforts. During the mid-1970s, however, the principal constitutional conflict in the area of racial equality shifted from desegregation to affirmative action, and in this area the logic of the two conservative principles diverged. The principle of color-blindness suggested that government may never classify persons on the basis of race, not even to remedy the effects of past and present racial inequality or to promote diversity in our public institutions; but the doctrine of judicial restraint suggested that government contracting rules or university admissions policies were exactly the sorts of decisions that should be made by elected political leaders or appointed educational experts and not by the federal courts. Whether they were aware of the fact or not, the affirmative action debates brought the conservatives' critique of liberal social engineering and their demand for judicial restraint into sharp conflict.

By the mid-1970s, a number of state university systems, along with many other public and private institutions, had adopted race-conscious policies designed to increase the representation of racial minorities in various sectors of social and economic life. From the beginning, some whites who felt disadvantaged by these programs challenged them on equal protection grounds, and it was by no means clear how the courts would respond to these claims. In 1973, the Washington Supreme Court upheld the University of Washington School of Law's preferential admissions program, observing that the U.S. Supreme Court's desegregation decisions had "made it clear that in some circumstances a racial criterion *may* be used — and indeed in some circumstances *must* be used — by public educational institutions in bringing about racial balance." The court reviewed the affirmative action plan under strict scrutiny, but found that it was necessary to advance the compelling state interests in promoting integration in public education; in eradicating the continuing effects of past racial discrimination; in producing a diverse student body for educational purposes; and in increasing the ranks of minority lawyers.[53] The Supreme Court agreed to review this decision in *DeFunis v. Odegaard,* but then called on one of Bickel's "passive virtues" to duck the constitutional issue, ruling that the case was moot since the plaintiff had been admitted pending the outcome of the litigation and was now completing his final term of law school. Only Justice Douglas saw fit to address the merits, and his opinion made clear that the policies of post-1960s liberalism would sometimes divide the New Deal coalition. He had long been the Court's most stalwart liberal, but he insisted that "[w]hatever his race, [Marco DeFunis] had a constitutional right to have his application considered on its individual merits in a racially neutral manner." Rejecting the new liberal social engineering, Douglas argued that "[t]he Equal Protection Clause commands the elimination of racial barriers, not their creation in order to satisfy our theory as to how society ought to be organized. The purpose of the University of Washington cannot be to produce black lawyers for blacks, Polish lawyers for Poles, Jewish lawyers for Jews, Irish lawyers for Irish." [54] Since Douglas failed to persuade his colleagues, however, the constitutional question remained to be answered another day.

Perhaps the most significant aspect of the *DeFunis* case in terms of constitutional development is that it provided the opportunity for Alexander Bickel himself to articulate his views on affirmative action. As I have noted, his scholarship had laid some of the key intellectual foundations of modern constitutional conservatism, and by 1974, he had become a sharp critic of Warren Court liberalism. Together with Philip Kurland, he authored an *amicus curiae* brief on behalf of the Anti-Defamation League (ADL) of B'nai B'rith, arguing that "[a]ny racial classification by a state is presumptively invalid," except perhaps in the case of efforts "to cure racial discrimination imposed by the party against whom the remedy is ordered." Even in these cases, however, race-conscious remedial measures could not be justified on the basis of "[g]eneralized historical assertion about conditions somewhere in the United States some time in the past. . . . If such a predicate were allowed to replace careful, specific findings of discrimination as the necessary condition for maintaining reverse discrimination, such state racial preferences would be constitutionally sanctioned in a wide range of circumstances that would denigrate if not destroy the concept of racial equality specified in the Equal Protection Clause." They insisted that a "racial quota derogates the human dignity and individuality of all to whom it is applied. . . . A quota by any other name is still a divider of society, a creator of castes, and it is all the worse for its racial base especially in a society desperately striving for an equality that will make race irrelevant, politically, economically, and socially." [55] This last part just quoted was incorporated in substantially similar form in Bickel's *The Morality of Consent*, published the following year, in which he argued further:

The lesson of the great decisions of the Supreme Court and the lesson of contemporary history have been the same for at least a generation: dis-

crimination on the basis of race is illegal, immoral, unconstitutional, inherently wrong, and destructive of democratic society. Now this is to be
unlearned and we are told that this is not a matter of fundamental principle but only a matter of whose ox is gored. Those for whom racial equality was demanded are to be more equal than others. Having found support
in the Constitution for equality, they now claim support for inequality under the same Constitution. (1975:133)

This passage continues to be widely quoted, and along with Bickel's and Kurland's argument regarding "careful, specific findings of discrimination," it
has clearly influenced the conservative critique of affirmative action.

What is most striking about the arguments by Bickel and Kurland is that
these long-time critics of Warren Court activism were now urging the Court
to invalidate the considered choices of public university administrators.
Some scholars have attempted to reconcile the color-blind principle with
judicial restraint by arguing that it is necessary to prevent unaccountable
federal judges from approving whatever racial classifications they view as
reasonable (Kull 1992; Posner 1974). But if we understand restraint to require
a significant degree of deference to the political branches, then it is clearly
in tension with the judicial enforcement of color-blind law (Bybee 1996).
In the face of this tension, constitutional conservatives might well have chosen to adhere to the doctrine of restraint, but their color-blind principles instead trumped this long-standing commitment. Kurland, for example, had
insisted a few years earlier that elected legislatures — in contrast to the unelected courts — were constitutionally free to adopt race-conscious affirmative action policies, but when he wrote again on behalf of the ADL in a subsequent case, he argued that even if a public university's admissions policy
represented the majority will of the state electorate, the Equal Protection
Clause still prohibited any consideration of race.[56] This brief advanced essentially the same argument as the earlier one, buttressed now by citations to
Douglas's *DeFunis* opinion, Bickel's *The Morality of Consent,* and Glazer's *Affirmative Discrimination.*

This time, moreover, the Court was persuaded to confront the constitutional issue it had ducked in *DeFunis.* In his opinion announcing the Court's
judgment in *Regents of the University of California v. Bakke,* Justice Powell authored a famous judicial compromise that wrote the conservative vision of
color-blind equality into law, but nonetheless allowed some race-conscious
affirmative action policies to survive. With four justices to his left and four to

his right — seeking a sweeping decision for and against affirmative action's legality, respectively — Powell sought to balance the twin conservative commitments to color-blindness and judicial deference. He struck down the strict quota system used for medical school admissions by the University of California–Davis and ordered rejected white applicant Allan Bakke to be admitted, but he also insisted that some more carefully designed affirmative action programs would survive constitutional scrutiny.

The constitutional reasons that Powell offered for striking down the quota system were essentially those offered by Bickel, Kurland, and Glazer. He quoted Bickel's "whose ox is gored" passage, and he appeared to have been influenced by Glazer's critique of egalitarianism as well. Rejecting the *Carolene Products* argument that affirmative action policies were constitutional because they did not burden the rights of a powerless minority, Powell insisted that "[t]he guarantees of the Fourteenth Amendment extend to all persons" and that they "cannot mean one thing when applied to one individual and something else when applied to a person of another color. If both are not accorded the same protection, then it is not equal." Like Glazer, he observed that we live in "a Nation of minorities," in which "the white 'majority' itself is composed of various minority groups, most of which can lay claim to a history of prior discrimination at the hands of the State and private individuals." As a result, he insisted, "[i]t is far too late to argue that the guarantee of equal protection to all persons permits the recognition of special wards entitled to a degree of protection greater than that accorded others."[57] As Keith Bybee notes, Powell's rejection of the *Carolene Products* model — because "[t]here is no principled basis for deciding which groups would merit 'heightened judicial solicitude' and which would not" — was rooted in a rather uncritical pluralist vision of the American political system in which "[t]here are no fixed majorities and minorities, but only fleeting 'majorities' and 'minorities,' shifting in composition as tides of prejudice rise and fall" (Bybee 1996: 10; see also Bybee 2000; Koppelman 1996: 49).

While Powell urged the Court to read the Fourteenth Amendment as a guarantee of color-blind law, he was also concerned to avoid the active judicial supervision of university admissions procedures that such a guarantee might be thought to require. He had advocated judicial restraint in the equal protection context before, particularly in the school desegregation, school finance, and gender equality cases.[58] He had also insisted that judicial deference was particularly appropriate with regard to the academic decisions of a public university. Concurring in *Board of Curators of the University of Mis-*

souri v. *Horowitz,* for example, Powell had just recently noted that "[u]niversity faculties must have the widest range of discretion in making judgments as to the academic performance of students and their entitlement to promotion or graduation."[59] Several years later, in *Regents of the University of Michigan v. Ewing,* he would again emphasize "the respect and deference that courts should accord academic decisions made by the appropriate university authorities. . . . Judicial review of academic decisions, including those with respect to the admission or dismissal of students, is rarely appropriate, particularly where orderly administrative procedures are followed."[60] Powell was thus faced with two competing commitments, which he sought to balance in the course of case-by-case decisionmaking. As his biographer has put it, "[f]aced with two intellectually coherent, morally defensible, and diametrically opposed positions, Powell chose neither" (Jeffries 1994:469). Such a balancing effort was typical for him, and over the next several years, he continued to lead the Court in straddling the fence on the question of affirmative action's constitutionality.

While Justice Rehnquist did not play a prominent role in these early affirmative action cases, he was the Court's leading advocate of the new style of conservative activism emerging in response to the New Right critique of the welfare state. As I have noted, New Right conservatives were increasingly objecting to what they saw as a tyrannical national government, and they quickly recognized a variety of pre–New Deal constitutional traditions to which they could appeal for judicially enforceable limits on federal regulatory authority. In this political and scholarly context, the conservative justices proved willing to abandon their commitment to restraint in an effort to enforce what they saw as fundamental principles of limited government.

During the 1970s, for example, while Rehnquist was urging judicial restraint in his frequent dissenting opinions in fundamental rights cases, he insisted from the beginning that this deference did not apply to the Court's supervision of federalism (Whittington 2003). In a wide variety of doctrinal contexts, in fact, he urged his fellow justices to once again enforce the federalism-based limits on congressional power. In 1975, Rehnquist was the sole dissenter in a case upholding the application of federal wage controls to state employees, a decision fully consistent with the Court's long-standing deference to congressional regulatory authority, irrespective of any incidental limits on state sovereignty. He objected that this deference represented a "danger to our federal system" and insisted that since the allocation of authority between the national and state governments was such a "fundamental constitutional question," the command of *stare decisis* should not be controlling.[61]

Within a year, Rehnquist had persuaded the Court. In *National League of Cities v. Usery,* he wrote for a bare majority in holding that the Tenth Amendment, like the other provisions of the Bill of Rights, imposed an affirmative limitation on Congress's otherwise plenary authority to regulate interstate commerce. He insisted that "there are attributes of sovereignty attaching to every state government which may not be impaired by Congress, not because Congress may lack an affirmative grant of legislative authority to reach the matter, but because the Constitution prohibits it from exercising the authority in that manner." On these grounds, he invalidated the application of the federal Fair Labor Standards Act to state employees, holding that the power to determine the wages of public employees was an "undoubted attribute of state sovereignty."[62]

In dissent, Justice Brennan adopted Herbert Wechsler's 1954 argument regarding "the political safeguards of federalism," insisting that the constitutional limits on national legislative power would be best enforced through the states' own representation in the national political process, rather than through active judicial enforcement. Denouncing the Court's exercise of "raw judicial power," Brennan predicted that the majority's theory of state sovereignty would "astound scholars of the Constitution" and that its "essential-function test" for determining whether a given state statute was a core exercise of sovereignty would prove unworkable. Each of these predictions proved accurate, and in the face of the critical scholarly response and the immense difficulty the lower courts had in applying the Court's standard, Blackmun almost immediately began having second thoughts.[63] Just as Powell sought to balance the active judicial enforcement of constitutional principle with his commitment to judicial deference in the affirmative action context, some of the Court's centrist conservatives would support Rehnquist's revival of federalism to a point, while remaining reluctant to unduly limit the decisions of the elected branches.

This Tenth Amendment holding was the most important federalism decision of the 1970s, but Rehnquist was spelling out his vision of limited government in other doctrinal contexts as well. When his colleagues allowed California residents to proceed with a tort suit in California's courts against the State of Nevada for injuries caused by a Nevada-owned vehicle on a California highway, Rehnquist objected on the grounds of state sovereign immunity. The Eleventh Amendment provides that a state cannot be sued against its will in federal court by a citizen of another state, but in *Nevada v. Hall* Rehnquist urged the extension of this immunity to state courts as well. Appealing to the original understanding of sovereign immunity, the purposes underlying the Eleventh Amendment, the Court's long history of recognizing such immunity, and the very structure of the Constitution in which the states had retained a measure of sovereignty, he argued that "Article III and the Eleventh Amendment are built on important concepts of sovereignty that do not find expression in the literal terms of those provisions, but which are of constitutional dimension because their derogation would undermine the logic of the constitutional scheme."[64] In this area, as in many others, Rehnquist would later lead the Court in writing his dissenting view into law.

Rehnquist also narrowly construed Congress's power, granted by §5 of the Fourteenth Amendment, "to enforce" the Due Process and Equal Protection Clauses "by appropriate legislation." In *City of Rome v. United States,* he voted to strike down a provision of the 1965 Voting Rights Act as an illegitimate congressional exercise of this §5 power. Since Congress was here trying to prohibit a state practice that the Court had already found consistent with the Fourteenth Amendment — the adoption of an at-large districting system for local elections — he insisted that it could not be said to be "enforcing" the provisions of that amendment. Powell and Stewart joined Rehnquist in dissent, but they were outvoted by the Court's liberal majority.

During this same period, Rehnquist also urged the Court to renew its attention to constitutional property rights as yet another set of judicially enforceable limits on state and federal regulatory authority. As in the federalism context, the post–New Deal Court had largely abandoned such constitutional limits in favor of a broad doctrine of judicial deference, but the rising tide of libertarian conservatism in the 1970s led some judges and litigators to recover those constitutional traditions that supported their vision of limited government. Toward the end of the decade, Rehnquist began insisting that the modern Court's abandonment of property rights had been mistaken, and he urged the Court to stop shirking its constitutional duty to protect such rights. Dissenting in *Penn Central Transportation Co. v. New York City,* for example, he argued that the New York Landmark Preservation Commission could not constitutionally prohibit the owners of Grand Central Station from building a fifty-five-story office building on top of the historic landmark. In Rehnquist's view, this zoning regulation amounted to a "regulatory taking" — that is, a regulation that had such an adverse effect on the value or use of private property as to amount to an unconstitutional taking of that property without compensation.[65] That same year, he also joined Stewart's opinion for the Court in *Allied Structural Steel Co. v. Spannaus,* holding that "the Contract Clause remains part of the Constitution. It is not a dead letter. . . . If the Contract Clause is to retain any meaning at all, it must be understood to impose *some* limits upon the power of a State to abridge existing contractual relationships, even in the exercise of its otherwise legitimate police power."[66]

In response to these developments, the Court's more liberal justices warned that the reinvigoration of constitutional property rights was unwise, undemocratic, and unjustified, and that Rehnquist and his colleagues were simply trying to protect those property interests that they themselves valued. In other words, the Court's nascent conservative activism in defense of limited government immediately provoked a liberal response emphasizing the conservatives' own long-standing arguments for judicial deference. These liberal demands for restraint made clear that all of the justices, both liberal and conservative, believed that there are certain constitutional contexts that call for active judicial intervention and others that call for restraint. As Rehnquist himself would put the matter some years later, the judicial task is one of "hold[ing] true the balance between that which the Constitution puts beyond the reach of the democratic process and that which it does not."[67] The liberal justices generally struck this balance by reference to some version of Stone's *Carolene Products* jurisprudence, but Rehnquist was beginning to develop the originalist approach as a viable alternative. By the end of the 1970s, he had been insisting with some regularity that the line between those contexts that called for restraint and those that called for the exercise of judicial power was drawn by the original meaning of the constitutional text. It would fall to constitutional scholars in the legal academy, however, to fully articulate the premises of this emerging doctrine.

The Scholarly Critique and the Turn to History

One of the earliest and most influential of such works was a 1971 *Indiana Law Journal* article by Robert Bork, entitled "Neutral Principles and Some First Amendment Problems." As the title suggests, Bork was building on Wechsler's Holmes Lectures, insisting that if the Court was not to be a "naked power organ," then its decisions must be controlled by the neutral application of constitutional principle. Borrowing heavily from Bickel as well, Bork noted that this "requirement . . . arises from the resolution of the seeming anomaly of judicial supremacy in a democratic society." In Bork's view, the American people had consented to be ruled undemocratically only within certain areas defined by "enduring principles believed to be stated in, and placed beyond the reach of majorities by, the Constitution." Thus, the Court's countermajoritarian "power is legitimate only if it has . . . a valid theory, derived from the Constitution, of the respective spheres of majority and minority freedom. If it does not have such a theory but merely imposes its own value choices, or worse if it pretends to have a theory but actually follows its own predilections, the Court violates the postulates of the Madisonian model that alone justifies its power." As far as Bork was concerned, to support the modern Court's activism was to claim for the justices "an institutionalized role as perpetrator[s] of limited coups d'etat. . . . The man who prefers results to processes has no reason to say that the Court is more legitimate than any other institution. If the Court will not listen, why not argue the case to some other group, say the Joint Chiefs of Staff, a body with rather better means for implementing its decisions" (1971:2–3, 6).

Bork's understanding of constitutional adjudication was ultimately rooted in his ethical relativism and his deep skepticism about constitutional rights. He insisted that "[w]here constitutional materials do not clearly specify the value to be preferred, there is no principled way to prefer any claimed human value to any other," and he argued that "[e]very clash between a minority claiming freedom and a majority claiming power to regulate involves a choice between the gratifications of the two groups. When the Constitution has not spoken, the Court will be able to find no scale, other than its own value preferences, upon which to weigh the respective claims to pleasure" (1971:8–9). Restating this argument some years later, he would continue to insist that "the judge who looks outside the historic Constitution always looks inside himself and nowhere else." On this reading, advocates of nonoriginalist constitutional interpretation "merely state a preference for rule by talented and benevolent autocrats over the self-government of ordinary folk. Whatever one thinks of that preference, and it seems to me morally repugnant, it is not our system of government, and those who advocate it propose a quiet revolution, made by judges" (1990:242, 252).

In light of this approach, Bork was sharply critical of much of modern constitutional doctrine. For example, while Justice Harlan had characterized the issue in *Griswold* as one of fundamental constitutional principle, Bork thought it concerned nothing more than "a husband and wife [who] assert that they wish to have sexual relations without fear of unwanted children [and a] law [that] impairs their sexual gratifications." In this light, he argued that the case could not be distinguished from a suit by an electric utility over a pollution regulation, and in either case, "the only course for a principled Court [wa]s to let the majority have its way." Acknowledging that his approach would imply that "broad areas of constitutional law ought to be reformulated," he rejected most of the modern Court's substantive due process and equal protection jurisprudence and much of its First Amendment law as well (1971:9–12, 18–20; see also Bork 1990:65–66).

While Bork's article put constitutional originalism squarely on the agenda of academic constitutional scholarship, it was his contemporary Raoul Berger who developed its implications most fully. By 1974, Berger had already published books examining the original understanding of judicial review (1969), impeachment (1973), and executive privilege (1974), and in 1977 he turned his attention to the Fourteenth Amendment. Building on Bickel and Charles Fairman, Berger conducted his own exhaustive review of the Reconstruction debates and concluded that the modern Court had dramatically rewritten the Fourteenth Amendment. He complained that "the Justices, who are virtually unaccountable, irremovable, and irreversible, have taken over from the people control of their own destiny, an awesome exercise of power," and he urged them to refrain from amending the Constitution by judicial fiat. In Berger's view, "[t]he Constitution represents fundamental choices that have been made by the people, and the task of the Courts is to effectuate them, not to construct new rights. When the judiciary substitutes its own value choices for those of the people it subverts the Constitution by usurpation of power." [68]

In making these arguments, Berger repeatedly insisted that "[t]he task here undertaken is that of an historian, to attempt accurately and faithfully to assemble the facts; that effort constitutes its own justification." [69] His work, however, was quite plainly a polemical response to Warren Court liberalism. He explicitly framed his study as an investigation of whether the Warren Court's constitutional revisions were authorized, and he noted in particular that he hoped to settle the Fourteenth Amendment controversies over desegregation, reapportionment, and incorporation of the Bill of Rights. His principal conclusion was that the modern Court "has flouted the will of the framers and substituted an interpretation in flat contradiction of the original design: to leave suffrage, segregation, and other matters to State governance. It has done this under cover of the so-called 'majestic generalities' of the Amendment . . . without taking into account the limited aims those terms were meant to express."[70] Berger's volume began and ended with a series of sharp denunciations of Warren Court activism, and he devoted roughly equal portions of the book to his examination of the Reconstruction Congress and to his critique of modern constitutional law. Like a number of subsequent conservative critiques of the Court, moreover, Berger's argument sometimes bordered on the apocalyptic. His final denunciation of judicial activism in the book's conclusion was peppered with allusions to Hitler, Stalin, and the Inquisition, along with the unsubstantiated insistence that American democracy itself would soon crumble if the Court did not change its ways (1997: 459–61). Whether or not Berger was aware of it, the agenda of constitutional scholarship during the 1970s — no matter how backward-looking its focus — was shaped by the contemporary, and intensely political, conflicts over the legitimacy of the Warren Court.

In short, originalism reemerged as a politically significant constitutional vision in the 1970s primarily because it was a convenient rhetorical device for buttressing preexisting conservative demands for judicial deference. Ever since the Court began adopting an expansive, evolutionary conception of Fourteenth Amendment liberty and equality, conservatives have argued that the Reconstruction Republicans did not intend to abolish segregation, guarantee suffrage, prohibit anti-abortion laws, or protect a right to sexual privacy. In other words, they have advanced an originalist argument for adopting a posture of judicial restraint.[71] Following the lead of Bork and Berger, a generation of originalist scholars has emphasized the peculiar security of a written Constitution, downplaying or dismissing the competing natural law traditions in American constitutional development, all in an effort to persuade the modern Court to exercise its rights-protecting power more sparingly.[72]

Once the originalist approach emerged, however, conservatives realized that it had the added advantage of supporting their critique of "government by judiciary" without abandoning judicial power altogether. All justices and constitutional scholars allow for some exceptions to the principle of judicial deference, and the originalist approach provides a relatively coherent set of rules for identifying those exceptions. Even Bork, for example, agreed that when the government clearly violated a provision of the constitutional text as originally understood — say, by enacting a content-based restriction on political speech — the Court should strike it down, and this argument allowed him to maintain that he was not abandoning constitutional rights altogether. Similarly, in working to recover the original constitutional principles of federalism and property rights, Rehnquist was beginning to articulate an alternative to Warren Court liberalism that did not render the Court irrelevant.

As conservatives stood poised to consolidate their control in the 1980s, then, it should have been clear that the Court would not become more restrained, but would instead start to draw the line between activism and restraint in a very different place. Most scholars did not recognize this possibility, however, and as the newly elected President Reagan set out to reshape the Court, constitutional conservatism was marked by a sharp, but still unacknowledged, tension. Conservatives continued to denounce liberal activism as undemocratic and hence illegitimate, but in a variety of constitutional contexts, they had now articulated clear demands for the active exercise of judicial power on behalf of conservative principles. Had conservatives not made this latter move, their increasing power in the federal courts would have made it ever more clear that they were enforcing a Constitution that was almost entirely statist and anti-rights. Since they themselves recognized that this was not a plausible vision of the late-twentieth-century constitutional order, they uncovered and built upon those constitutional traditions that could support their own conservative version of modern judicial power. As a result, contemporary judicial conservatism is characterized by two competing strains, with separate historical roots: the long-standing critique of judicial power and the more recent New Right critique of liberalism.

CHAPTER FIVE

THE REAGAN COURT
AND THE CONSERVATIVE ASCENDANCE
1980–1994

The Republican Party's post-1968 electoral successes put conservatives in a position to reshape the Constitution, but during the 1970s it was not altogether clear what form that reshaping would take. As their electoral victories continued in the 1980s, conservative political discourse on the Court was still dominated by criticism of the Warren Court's illegitimate activism, a critique increasingly expressed in the language of constitutional originalism, as conservatives fully took the turn toward history that Robert Bork and Raoul Berger had begun. In 1980, liberal constitutional scholar Paul Brest coined the term "originalism," describing (and criticizing) what was now a clearly defined scholarly movement, and five years later Reagan's attorney general, Edwin Meese, delivered a series of widely noted public addresses announcing that "[i]t has been and will continue to be the policy of this administration to press for a jurisprudence of original intention" (Brest 1980; Meese 1986:464; see Kalman 1996:72–77).

At the same time, the dawning recognition that rights-based constitutionalism was here to stay led some conservatives to abandon the quest for restraint and to develop instead their own conservative justifications for judicial power. In other words, some conservatives were well on their way to demanding that the newer, more conservative, Court exercise its power to enforce a newer, more conservative, Constitution. The conjuncture of the Court's successful institutionalization of judicial activism and the post-1968 conservative turn in American politics led conservatives to recognize that judicial power could be exercised on behalf of conservative goals. The New

Right critique of liberalism provided a number of such goals, most of which could be captured under the rubric "limited government," and these emergent constitutional principles led Justice William Rehnquist and his colleagues to exercise their newfound power in a number of contexts, despite their long-standing commitment to restraint. In short, faced with the opportunity to put their power to use, judicial conservatives were reluctant to adopt a posture of across-the-board deference. When Reagan elevated Rehnquist to chief justice in 1986, most scholars assumed that the conservative Court would abandon liberal activism and replace it with restraint, just as they had expected when Rehnquist first joined the bench in 1972. By the early 1990s, it seemed more likely that the conservative justices would abandon liberal activism not for restraint but instead for their own conservative activism. As it happened, however, neither of these alternatives came to pass. Instead, the justices with the deciding votes endorsed the newer conservative activism, but in a move that produced a sharp conflict with their conservative colleagues, they continued to reaffirm much of the Court's liberal activism as well.

Reagan's Judicial Politics

After four years of solid Democratic control in Washington, the Republicans recaptured both the presidency and the Senate in 1980. Launching a broad assault on the Democratic order that had its roots in the New Deal, Reagan waged a campaign to reshape the Court and the Constitution that was even more concerted than Nixon's had been. As Bruce Ackerman has noted, the Republican presidential coalition attempted to challenge the New Deal order by using Roosevelt's own model of presidential leadership in constitutional change. Rather than making a serious effort to amend the Constitution, the Reagan administration sought to achieve the same ends by appointing justices "who were able and willing to write transformative opinions that might consolidate a newly ascendant constitutional order" (1998:389–94). Nixon had pledged to appoint justices who shared his strict constructionist approach to the Constitution, and Reagan and his legal advisers carried this effort even further, systematically vetting judicial candidates on a series of ideological grounds (Silverstein 1994; Yalof 1999). In addition, the Reagan administration went much further than its predecessors in using the litigation resources of the federal Justice Department to transform the Constitution in a conservative direction, and it was supported in this effort by an emergent

set of conservative public interest litigation organizations. These appointment and litigation efforts have been the key mechanisms by which the partisan and constitutional orders are linked, but while they have proven robust
enough for conservatives to transform the law in some areas, they have had
only a limited impact in others.[1]

Since Democrat Jimmy Carter had served four years without an opportunity to fill a Supreme Court vacancy, Reagan came into office in 1980 with the
chance to continue the string of consecutive Republican appointments. With
the Senate now in Republican hands, moreover, Reagan faced relatively few
political constraints in naming a successor for Justice Potter Stewart in 1981.
Nonetheless, he did not immediately prioritize the goal of conservative constitutional change, as he followed his campaign pledge to nominate the
Court's first female justice by naming Sandra Day O'Connor, a state judge
and former legislative leader from Arizona. Reagan's selection of O'Connor
angered many of his conservative supporters, particularly because her legislative record showed signs of moderation on the abortion issue. Reagan did
elicit an indication that she was personally opposed to abortion, and he was
impressed with her solid conservative record on law and order issues, but it
is clear that he was downplaying such substantive considerations for the time
being (Yalof 1999:133–42).

After O'Connor's appointment, Reagan and his advisers were determined
to nominate conservative judges who were willing and able to transform the
law, but they did not have another opportunity until Chief Justice Warren
Burger's retirement in 1986. In the meantime, they sought to advance their
constitutional agenda through other avenues. Beginning in 1985, Meese publicly committed the administration to originalism, noting that "[i]n the cases
we file and those we join as amicus, we will endeavor to resurrect the original
meaning of constitutional provisions and statutes as the only reliable guide
for judgment." Affirming the administration's view "that only the sense in
which the Constitution was accepted and ratified by the nation . . . provide[s]
a solid foundation for adjudication," Meese insisted that "[a]ny other standard suffers the defect of pouring new meaning into old words, thus creating
new powers and new rights totally at odds with the logic of our Constitution
and its commitment to the rule of law." In his now-familiar view, he observed
that "[t]he power to declare acts of Congress and laws of the states null and
void is truly awesome. This power must be used when the Constitution
clearly speaks. It should not be used when the Constitution does not." Most
ambitiously, relying on Lincoln's response to the *Dred Scott* decision, Meese

rejected the doctrine of judicial supremacy, announcing that the administration would not be bound by wrongheaded judicial interpretations of the Constitution (1986:464–66; 1990:19; 1987:981–87). This challenge to judicial authority prompted a widespread critical response, but Meese continued to defend the Reagan agenda as necessary to promote "the integrity of the Constitution and its preservation as the supreme law of the land." [2]

Had it not been for scholars like Bork and Berger, Meese would have had a much smaller arsenal available when he led the Reagan administration's efforts at constitutional change. His critique of the Court in the mid-1980s, for instance, was significantly different from that which Nixon had advanced in the late 1960s. While Nixon had issued a vague call for "strict construction" along with his demand for judicial deference to the majority will, Meese was able to marshal a much more fully articulated "jurisprudence of original intention."

Meese's speeches also revealed some of the emerging tensions in the conservative approach. Like most advocates of originalism, his main concern usually seemed to be curbing judicial power, as when he quoted Justice Frankfurter's argument that "there is not under our Constitution a judicial remedy for every political mischief, for every undesirable exercise of legislative power" (Meese 1990:20). But while his addresses are best remembered for their denunciation of liberal activist decisions like *Roe v. Wade* as inconsistent with original meaning, Meese also called for the active judicial enforcement of constitutional principles of federalism. Such activism might well be consistent with his originalism, but if conservatives started discovering other constitutional principles that called for the active exercise of judicial power, they would soon find themselves in serious tension with their own long-standing commitment to restraint.

When Burger retired in 1986, with the GOP holding a six-seat edge in the Senate, Reagan's legal advisors reviewed his potential replacements under much more stringent selection criteria than they had used in nominating O'Connor. Emphasizing the candidates' substantive visions of the Constitution and the judicial role in a number of specific areas, these criteria were more detailed than anything that presidents had generally used in the past, and they reflected the key tensions at the heart of the evolving conservative vision of the Court. On the one hand, they called for prospective nominees to exhibit a commitment to restraint in the form of a "refusal to create new constitutional rights for the individual"; a strong posture of "deference to states in their sphere" and to federal agencies in theirs; a "disposition towards crim-

inal law as a system for determining guilt or innocence"; and a "respect for traditional values" that would presumably lead to deference to majoritarian morality. On the other hand, they called for a "disposition towards 'less government rather than more'"; a "recognition that the federal government is one
of enumerated powers"; an "appreciation for the role of the free market in
our society"; and a "commitment to strict principles of 'nondiscrimination'"
(by which they meant a color-blind aversion to affirmative action policies) —
any one of which could justify the active use of judicial power to constrain
the liberal state within constitutional limits (Yalof 1999:143–44). When conservatives had not been fully in control of the Court, they did not need to resolve these tensions. But with Reagan's elevation of Rehnquist to chief justice
and nomination of Antonin Scalia, a prominent conservative on the D.C.
Circuit, to fill Rehnquist's seat, conservative control of the Court seemed assured. If Rehnquist and Scalia were to lead a new conservative majority on
the Court, as Reagan hoped, the tensions were sure to rise to the surface.

As I have noted, the Reagan administration supplemented its judicial appointment strategy with a variety of parallel efforts to enact the New Right
constitutional vision into law. Charles Fried, solicitor general from 1985 to
1989, later recalled that the administration's campaign for "a more confident
society and a less intrusive government . . . was fought on two fronts. First,
tax reduction was supposed to starve politicians of the resources with which
they would regulate the economy, pursue their favorite projects, redistribute
wealth, and reward clients who kept them in office. The other front was the
legal front. . . . That battle was fought in the courts, which had for years been
complicit in the aggrandizement of government." Looking back on his four-
year tenure as solicitor general, Fried recalled that "[t]he tenets of the Reagan
Revolution were clear: courts should be more disciplined, less adventurous
and political in interpreting the law, especially the law of the Constitution;
the President must be allowed a strong hand in governing the nation and
providing leadership; justice and racial equality could be — and so should
be — achieved without twisting legal principles, and without distorting the
system of opportunity and reward for merit on which the morale of a free-
enterprise system depends" (1991:15–18).

That these multiple constitutional goals were inconsistent with each other
did not prevent the Reagan administration from acting on them, particularly
by means of constitutional litigation. As Lincoln Caplan has reported, Fried's
predecessor, Rex Lee, "encountered what he called 'enormous pressure' to
forsake his commitment to . . . the traditional restrained practices of the SG's

office, and to campaign for the Administration's agenda in the Supreme Court." When he resigned from office in 1985, Lee complained that "[t]here has been this notion that my job is to press the Administration's policies at every turn and announce true conservative principles through the pages of my briefs. It is not. I'm the Solicitor General, not the Pamphleteer General" (Caplan 1987:79, 107). In particular, Lee had resisted pressure to call for the Court to overturn *Roe v. Wade,* and Fried was widely believed to have received his own appointment in return for his willingness to do so. Fried has denied ever making such a commitment, but it is worth noting that as deputy solicitor general, he became acting solicitor general upon Lee's May 1985 resignation, and shortly thereafter, the Court agreed to hear a challenge to Pennsylvania's abortion regulations in *Thornburgh v. American College of Obstetricians and Gynecologists.* In July, Fried filed an *amicus* brief urging that *Roe* be overturned, and in August, Reagan announced Fried's nomination as solicitor general (Caplan 1987:149–50; Fried 1991:30–35).

Overturning *Roe* had become the dominant goal of constitutional conservatives because it linked the long-standing conservative critique of judicial power with the more recent New Right critique of liberalism. Reagan himself had often emphasized that "the issue of abortion must be resolved by our democratic process" and that Congress should "make its voice heard against abortion on demand and . . . restore legal protection for the unborn" (*quoted in* Whittington 2001a:384). In his *Thornburgh* brief, Fried argued that "[t]he textual, historical and doctrinal basis of [*Roe*] . . . is so far flawed that this Court should overrule it and return the law to the condition in which it was before that case was decided." He acknowledged that "the words of general constitutional provisions[ ] do not interpret themselves," but insisted that "the further afield interpretation travels from its point of departure in the text, the greater the danger that constitutional adjudication will be like a picnic to which the framers bring the words and the judges the meaning. Constitutional interpretation retains the fullest measure of legitimacy when it is disciplined by fidelity to the framers' intention as revealed by history, or, failing sufficient help from history, by the interpretive tradition of the legal community." Regarding the modern Court's interpretation of the Due Process Clause, he acknowledged that "[i]t is late in the day to argue that this provision should be limited to its apparent textual meaning," but urged the Court to avoid the "temptations" to which it had succumbed during "one of the most troubled and demoralizing episodes in our constitutional history."[3]

This was not the first time that conservatives had compared *Roe* to *Lochner v. New York,* as Fried was drawing heavily on the dissenting opinions of Justices Rehnquist and Byron White in the abortion cases. He continued by insisting that "the conviction held by some that free access to abortion is a fundamental expression of individual freedom . . . does not constitute constitutional argument":

> It is at best an intuition based in controversial moral and social theories of the good life and of an individual's situation in society, theories "which a large part of the country does not entertain." And when controversial but seemingly self-evident convictions are translated directly into constitutional doctrine, we risk repeating the whole lamentable story surrounding *Lochner* for which Justice Holmes composed the epitaph at its birth: "[The Constitution] is made for people of fundamentally differing views, and the accident of our finding certain opinions natural and familiar or novel and even shocking ought not to conclude our judgment upon the question whether statutes embodying them conflict with the Constitution of the United States."

After reviewing Holmes's call for judicial restraint, Fried endorsed Justice Hugo Black's theory of incorporation, which "was plainly intended to have the function of reining in such judicial extravagance and reanchoring the interpretation of [the Due Process] Clause in the constitutional text — though somewhat downstream of its historical starting point." In this light, he urged the Court to "anchor" its due process inquiry in the historical practices of the states at the time the Fourteenth Amendment was adopted, and he concluded by noting that "when constitutional law, which is above ordinary politics, seeks to settle disputes of value and vision which are the stuff of politics, both law and politics are more not less subject to the kind of intense pressures which have characterized the abortion debate since *Roe v. Wade.*"[4]

Fried's brief synthesized a decade of conservative constitutional argument, but the Court rejected it by a 5-4 vote, a defeat that reinforced the conservative preoccupation with judicial appointment and cemented the abortion issue as the dominant consideration in the administration's appointment decisions. In an interview the previous year, Meese had emphasized that in appointing federal judges, the administration was looking for people who, in addition to integrity, competence, and judicial temperament, also "have the proper judicial philosophy and approach to the bench, which precludes judicial activism, or substituting the courts for the legislature. In other words, we want judges who are interpreters of the law, not makers of new law." In response to a question on the relationship between judicial appointments and the abortion issue, he had characterized *Roe v. Wade* as a "usurpation of the legislative authority" and had acknowledged that a potential judge's views on the issue "might be indicative of the way in which that judge would generally approach the whole subject of judicial activism" (Wiley and Bodine 1985:44). The Court's 5-4 split in *Thornburgh* made clear that Justice Lewis Powell's vote was essential to the survival of *Roe,* and so the announcement of his retirement in 1987 sparked widespread attention to the nomination process for his successor. Seizing the opportunity to entrench his influence on the Court, Reagan nominated Robert Bork, who was willing and able to join Rehnquist and Scalia in transforming the Constitution.

In the fall of 1987, however, the Senate rejected Bork's nomination by the largest margin in history, in large part because of his skepticism toward privacy and abortion rights. In his opening statement at the confirmation hearings, Bork had declared that a "judge's authority derives entirely from the fact that he is applying the law and not his personal values." In applying that law, Bork insisted that judges should "attempt[ ] to discern what those who made the law intended. . . . If a judge abandons intention as his guide, there is no law available to him and he begins to legislate a social agenda for the American people." Bork acknowledged that judges should enforce those constitutional limits that they legitimately find in the original Constitution, but he reiterated that they should leave all other policy debates to the American people and their elected representatives (Bork 1990:300). Despite a concerted effort, however, he dramatically failed to convince either the Senate or the nation. In particular, several senators explicitly and repeatedly questioned him regarding his claim that *Griswold v. Connecticut* and its progeny had been wrongly decided, and a number of constitutional scholars testified against him on these grounds as well. The report of the Senate Judiciary Committee, which devoted twenty pages to the subject of privacy and other "unenumerated rights," declared that "Judge Bork's position on the right to privacy exposes a fundamentally inappropriate conception of what the Constitution means. Judge Bork's failure to acknowledge the 'right to be let alone' illuminates his entire judicial philosophy. If implemented on the Supreme Court, that philosophy would place at risk the salutary developments that have already occurred under the aegis of that right and would truncate its further elaboration."[5]

In this light, many scholars have read Bork's defeat as a public rejection of his constitutional originalism in general, and of his criticism of *Griswold* and

Roe in particular (Levinson 1988:135; Michelman 1988:1533; Tribe and Dorff 1991:3). Though Bork himself has contested the characterization, most scholars have argued that the hearings represented a significant national debate on the proper role of the courts in our constitutional democracy. Ronald Dworkin, for instance, has pointed out that "Bork was . . . encouraged to explain and defend his views in as much detail, and with as much clarification, as he wished. The argument and discussion of the hearings were often of extremely high quality [and t]hose who watched the hearings on television and followed the reports of them in the press seemed fascinated, delighted to join an extended seminar on the Constitution in its bicentennial year." Dworkin concluded, then, that "Bork was defeated mainly because he challenged a style of interpreting the Constitution that has become part of the American political tradition, and that the public, much to his surprise, largely supports" (1996b:278, 287; see Bork 1990:267–349).

Following this dramatic defeat, Reagan was initially unwilling to retreat, and he quickly nominated Bork's protege Douglas Ginsburg to fill Powell's seat. When the Ginsburg nomination was also derailed, however, Reagan turned to Anthony Kennedy, a moderately conservative and politically acceptable federal judge from the Ninth Circuit. After three days of perfunctory hearings — during which Kennedy "distanc[ed] himself quite specifically from Bork in the areas of First Amendment law and privacy" (Yalof 1999:164) — the Senate confirmed him unanimously. Bork's defeat marked the second time since 1970 that a Democratic Senate had forced a Republican president to choose a more moderate nominee, and the lesson was not lost on Reagan's vice president and successor, George H. W. Bush.

When faced with Justice Brennan's retirement in 1990, with the Senate still in Democratic hands, President Bush was determined to avoid a costly confirmation battle. He was also determined, however, to appoint a solidly conservative justice, and so his selection of First Circuit judge David Souter was widely interpreted as an effort to find a "stealth nominee" — someone who was not a well-known conservative ideologue and indeed had left such a sparse public record as to make him difficult to oppose on ideological grounds, but who nonetheless would prove a reliable conservative voice on the Supreme Court. Throughout the confirmation debates, Bush sought to downplay the abortion issue, repeatedly emphasizing Souter's "fairness" and judicial temperament and insisting that he himself had no "litmus test" for Supreme Court nominations, but the Court's role in the abortion debate remained at the forefront of media coverage of the nomination, and Bush still insisted that he had "selected a person who will interpret the Constitution, and . . . not legislate from the Federal bench."[6] In his own testimony before the Senate Judiciary Committee, Souter followed Kennedy's strategy of assuring the Democratic senators that he was no Robert Bork. He generally succeeded in this regard, impressing the senators with his intellect and his moderate views, and he was confirmed without much opposition.[7]

The following year, Brennan's longtime liberal ally, Thurgood Marshall, also retired. After only one term on the Court, Souter's moderate streak was already apparent, and so Bush faced significant pressure to appoint a more reliable conservative this time around, but he also remained preoccupied with the issue of confirmability. For both of these reasons, he settled on D.C. Circuit judge Clarence Thomas. Thomas's conservative credentials were solid, but because he was African American, Bush hoped that liberal opposition would be muted. The confirmation battle did not go according to plan, as the nation became transfixed by televised hearings regarding allegations of sexual harassment brought by a former aide; but Thomas was eventually confirmed by a narrow 52-48 vote (Yalof 1999:192–96). When he took his seat on the bench in 1991, he represented the tenth consecutive Republican appointment to the Court (not counting Reagan's elevation of Rehnquist to chief justice). Eight of these ten justices were still on the bench, and Republican leaders had every reason to believe that their appointees would usher in a conservative revolution in the law.

Liberal Activism in the 1980s and Early 1990s

Initially, some evidence suggested that this is just what the Rehnquist Court would do. As tables 2.1 and 2.2 (pages 40 and 41) illustrate, for example, the Burger Court had declared local, state, and federal statutes unconstitutional just as often as its more liberal predecessor, but the early Rehnquist Court reduced this rate significantly. In other words, the long-standing conservative critique of judicial power appeared to be influencing the Court, leading some early observers to describe the Rehnquist Court as so devoted to restraint that it threatened to abandon its commitment to constitutionalism (Chemerinsky 1989). In short, as the Reagan appointees joined the Court, liberal activism was hanging by a thread.

In the due process liberty context, for example, Rehnquist had been tirelessly insisting for years that the Court should extend heightened protection only to those "fundamental" liberties that were either "deeply rooted in this

Nation's history and tradition" or "implicit in the concept of ordered liberty such that neither liberty nor justice would exist" without them. If the Reagan appointees would join him, then he was sure to write these standards into law. At the close of the Burger era, he was regularly joined by White, O'Connor, and the Chief, and while they had not yet succeeded in overturning *Roe*, they were having significant success in other doctrinal contexts. Just three weeks after the Court reaffirmed *Roe* in *Thornburgh*, for example, White wrote for the Court in *Bowers v. Hardwick*, upholding a Georgia statute criminalizing consensual sodomy and coming as close as he could to rejecting the long line of modern substantive due process decisions as illegitimate judge-made law.

White began by posing the issue as "whether the Federal Constitution confers a fundamental right upon homosexuals to engage in sodomy and hence invalidates the laws of the many States that still make such conduct illegal and have done so for a very long time. The case also calls for some judgment about the limits of the Court's role in carrying out its constitutional mandate." He insisted that when recognizing "rights that have little or no textual support in the constitutional language," the Court must carefully identify "the nature of the rights qualifying for heightened judicial protection." Reading the Court's precedents narrowly, he insisted that "none of the rights announced in [the previous] cases bears any resemblance to the claimed constitutional right of homosexuals to engage in acts of sodomy that is asserted in this case. No connection between family, marriage, or procreation on the one hand and homosexual activity on the other has been demonstrated." In this light, he refused to announce a new fundamental right to engage in homosexual sodomy because the asserted right was neither "implicit in the concept of ordered liberty" nor "deeply rooted in this Nation's history and tradition."[8] The fact that White spoke for a majority in *Bowers* signaled that, despite the abortion cases, the Court was increasingly turning toward a narrow historical inquiry as the proper means for delineating the scope of constitutional rights.

The difference between *Thornburgh* and *Bowers* was Justice Powell's deciding vote, a vote that was influenced both by the long-standing conservative critique of substantive due process jurisprudence and by his own (mistaken) belief that he had never met a homosexual. During the Court's deliberations, Powell initially voted to strike down the sodomy law, arguing at the justices' conference that it imposed a cruel and unusual punishment prohibited by the Eighth Amendment. Six days later, however, he announced that he had changed his vote, acknowledging that the Eighth Amendment issue had neither been raised by the parties nor addressed by the courts below. On the fundamental rights issue, he reminded the other justices of the views he had expressed at conference: "I did not agree that there is a substantive due process right to engage in conduct that for centuries has been recognized as deviant, and not in the best interest of preserving humanity. I may say generally, that I also hesitate to create another substantive due process right." During this same period, he confided to his clerks — one of whom was, unbeknownst to Powell, a gay man — that he had never met a homosexual, and in his brief concurring opinion released some months later, he noted that "for the reasons stated by the Court, I cannot say that conduct condemned for hundreds of years has now become a fundamental right."[9] White, Rehnquist, O'Connor and Burger essentially convinced Powell to sign on to their argument that the Court should refrain from interfering with democratic lawmaking in the absence of clear textual support in the Constitution. Powell never fully adopted this argument — he remained committed, at heart, to Justice Harlan's brand of cautious judicial exposition of constitutional liberty — but in the gay rights context, it persuaded him enough to cast the deciding vote in favor of White's opinion. Where, as here, the conservative critique of liberalism lined up with the conservative critique of activism, the greatest pressure existed for the curtailment of judicially enforceable constitutional rights.

Two weeks before the *Bowers* decision, Chief Justice Burger had announced his retirement, and Powell followed suit the following year. Their replacements would join the three remaining Nixon/Ford appointees and the one previous Reagan appointee, and they would soon be joined by Bush's two appointees as well. By 1991, the only remaining Democratic appointee would be Justice White, and he was one of the Court's strongest critics of *Roe*. If the Republican justices could stick together, they would have a controlling bloc in the abortion cases and elsewhere. Unfortunately for conservatives, however, internal disagreements emerged almost immediately.

When Scalia replaced Burger on the Court in 1986, he became the leading advocate of the conservative vision of originalism and restraint. Like Justice Black before him, Scalia was suspicious of open-ended constitutional doctrines such as "evolving standards of decency" or "the traditions and conscience of our people." Unlike Black, however, he acknowledged that the text alone was sometimes an inadequate source of constitutional meaning, and so he supplemented Black's approach with an emphasis on our nation's legal traditions. In other words, to reduce the risk of illegitimate judicial lawmaking, Scalia urged the Court to protect only those rights that either were explicitly guaranteed in the constitutional text or had traditionally been protected by our society. Dissenting in *Rutan v. Republican Party of Illinois*, for example, he insisted:

> The provisions of the Bill of Rights were designed to restrain transient majorities from impairing long-recognized personal liberties. They did not create by implication novel individual rights overturning accepted political norms. Thus, when a practice not expressly prohibited by the text of the Bill of Rights bears the endorsement of a long tradition of open, widespread, and unchallenged use that dates back to the beginning of the Republic, we have no proper basis for striking it down. . . . I know of no other way to formulate a constitutional jurisprudence that reflects, as it should, the principles adhered to, over time, by the American people, rather than those favored by the personal (and necessarily shifting) philosophical dispositions of a majority of this Court.[10]

None of these arguments were new, but Scalia was developing the conservative vision of judicial power more fully than anyone before.

As I have noted, conservative critics of *Brown v. Board of Education* and *Roe* had long insisted that the Fourteenth Amendment could not possibly prohibit school segregation or anti-abortion laws because such laws had been widely accepted in 1868 and for many decades thereafter. In the *Rutan* opinion just quoted, Scalia objected to the Court's invalidation of party-based patronage in state employment decisions because such patronage had existed, "without any thought that it could be unconstitutional, [since] the earliest days of the Republic." In a similar decision a few years later, he would reiterate that the practice of "rewarding one's allies [and] refusing to reward one's opponents . . . is an American political tradition as old as the Republic. . . . If that long and unbroken tradition of our people does not decide these cases," he wondered, "then what does? . . . What secret knowledge . . . is breathed into lawyers when they become Justices of this Court, that enables them to discern that a practice which the text of the Constitution does not clearly proscribe, and which our people have regarded as constitutional for 200 years, is in fact unconstitutional?"[11]

Similarly, in another First Amendment context, Scalia insisted that "a test for implementing the protections of the Establishment Clause that, if applied with consistency, would invalidate longstanding traditions cannot be a proper reading of the Clause." Dissenting from the Court's prohibition of organized prayer at public school graduation ceremonies in *Lee v. Weisman,* he provided a long list of historical examples to show that "[f]rom our Nation's origin, prayer has been a prominent part of governmental ceremonies and proclamations." In Scalia's view, it was a clear usurpation of popular authority for the Court to invalidate this broad tradition — not to mention the "more specific tradition of invocations and benedictions at public school graduation exercises" themselves.[12]

Moreover, Scalia's religious freedom opinions made clear that he was rejecting one of the core commitments of modern liberal constitutionalism: the judicial protection of relatively powerless minority groups against discrimination. In *Weisman,* he went so far as to complain that the Court was banishing from public school graduation ceremonies "the expression of gratitude to God that a majority of the community wishes to make." It is a great virtue, he argued, for "religious believers of various faiths [to] join[] in prayer together, to the God whom they all worship and seek," and it is "senseless" "[t]o deprive our society of that important unifying mechanism, in order to spare the nonbeliever what seems to me the minimal inconvenience of standing or even sitting in respectful nonparticipation."[13] Two years earlier, in *Employment Division, Department of Human Resources of Oregon v. Smith,* he had insisted that "[v]alues that are protected against government interference through enshrinement in the Bill of Rights are not thereby banished from the political process." He had acknowledged that "leaving [religious] accommodation to the political process will place at a relative disadvantage those religious practices that are not widely engaged in," but he insisted that this "unavoidable consequence of democratic government must be preferred to a system in which each conscience is a law unto itself or in which judges weigh the social importance of all laws against the centrality of all religious beliefs."[14] Building on Frankfurter, Harlan, and Black, Scalia advanced his "text and traditions" approach as a fundamental challenge to the *Carolene Products* vision of the Constitution and the judicial role. He agreed that the Court should actively protect those rights and liberties that are firmly rooted in our constitutional text and traditions, but insisted that it should defer to majoritarian preferences in all other circumstances, even when the majority appeared to be treating a minority unfairly.

If it had been up to Scalia alone, then, the Court would have quickly retreated from its long-standing protection of constitutional rights in the Warren Court tradition, but he was often unable to persuade his fellow conservatives to join him. In *Smith,* he wrote for a bare majority of the Court, but O'Connor wrote separately to narrow the reach of his holding, a practice for which she was already becoming known, and which would soon be very familiar to observers of the Court.[15] And in *Weisman,* Scalia was in dissent, abandoned altogether by O'Connor and Kennedy, who joined the Court's liberals to hold that "at a minimum, the Constitution guarantees that government may not coerce anyone to support or participate in religion or its exercise, or otherwise act in a way which establishes a [state] religion or religious faith, or tends to do so." Writing for the Court, Kennedy rejected Scalia's argument that so long as a challenged government action was neutral among religious sects — as in this case, the delivery of a non-sectarian prayer — it did not violate the Establishment Clause. Kennedy offered a number of hedges at the end of his opinion to avoid overstating his support for rights-based activism, but that support was nonetheless firm. Unlike Scalia, he insisted unambiguously that government coercion of religious activity was prohibited, even when it was neutral and nonsectarian, and he and O'Connor have adhered consistently to this holding ever since.[16]

A similar split emerged among the Reagan appointees in the context of substantive due process, and Scalia was again frustrated at his failure to garner a judicial majority. In *Michael H. v. Gerald D.,* for example, he announced the Court's judgment in a plurality opinion upholding an 1872 California statute that automatically granted paternity of a married woman's child to her husband. In doing so, he rejected the paternity claim of Michael H., the lover of Carole D., who was married to Gerald D. Despite conclusive paternity tests, as well as the acknowledgment of all the relevant parties that Michael, rather than Gerald, was the biological father of, and had established a parental relationship with, the child at issue, Scalia rejected Michael's parental rights claim because of "the absence of any constitutionally protected right to legal parentage on the part of an adulterous natural father in Michael's situation, as evidenced by long tradition." Brennan insisted in dissent that the relevant inquiry was "whether parenthood is an interest that historically has received our attention and protection," rather than whether there were identifiable "historical traditions specifically relating to the rights of an adulterous natural father," but Scalia responded in a footnote that the Court should "refer to the most specific level at which a relevant tradition protecting, or denying protection to, the asserted right can be identified." When the Court fails to "adopt the most specific tradition as [its] point of reference," Scalia insisted, it will be left with unguided and arbitrary judicial discretion, for "a rule of law that binds neither by text nor by any particular, identifiable tradition is no rule of law at all." [17]

Justice Scalia adopted the same approach the following year in *Cruzan v. Director, Missouri Department of Health*, the Court's first hearing of a claimed constitutional "right to die." Here, Rehnquist delivered the opinion for a five-justice majority, assuming for the sake of argument that the "Constitution would grant a competent person a constitutionally protected right to refuse lifesaving hydration and nutrition," but holding that the state was free to require clear and convincing evidence of an incompetent person's wishes before such treatment could be withdrawn. The dissenting liberal justices insisted that Missouri's refusal to allow Nancy Cruzan's family to withdraw her life-sustaining treatment violated her "fundamental right to be free of unwanted artificial nutrition and hydration." Scalia joined Rehnquist's holding, but wrote separately to complain that by even raising the possibility of a constitutionally protected right to refuse lifesaving treatment, Rehnquist was unnecessarily running the risk of confusing the states' effort to grapple with the "difficult, indeed agonizing, question[ ]" of the right to die, just "as successfully as [the Court has] confused the enterprise of legislating concerning abortion." Instead, Scalia urged the Court to "announce, clearly and promptly, that the federal courts have no business in this field; that American law has always accorded the State the power to prevent . . . suicide . . . and [that] the point at which the means necessary to preserve [life] become 'extraordinary' or 'inappropriate,' are neither set forth in the Constitution nor known to the nine Justices of this Court any better than they are known to nine people picked at random from the Kansas City telephone directory." [18]

Again, however, Scalia was unable to write any of these words into law. In *Michael H.*, O'Connor and Kennedy refused to join the key footnote in his opinion because it "sketche[d] a mode of historical analysis to be used when identifying liberty interests protected by the Due Process Clause . . . that may be somewhat inconsistent with our past decisions in this area. On occasion the Court has characterized relevant traditions protecting asserted rights at levels of generality that might not be 'the most specific level' available." While Scalia and Rehnquist applied a standard that would refuse to recognize a constitutional liberty to engage in any activity that the states had at some time prohibited, and while Brennan objected that the plurality was turning the Constitution into "a stagnant, archaic, hidebound document," O'Connor and Kennedy cast the deciding votes for an approach that fell somewhere in between.[19] Similarly, in *Cruzan*, O'Connor wrote separately to make clear "that a protected liberty interest in refusing unwanted medical treatment may be inferred from our prior decisions." While Rehnquist had simply assumed the existence of such a liberty for the sake of argument, and while Scalia had all but denied its existence, O'Connor explicitly affirmed that "our notions of liberty are inextricably entwined with our idea of physical freedom and self-determination" and that these notions include the liberty to refuse unwanted treatment.[20] In short, the controlling justices on the Rehnquist Court rejected Scalia's modified version of Black's textualist approach, and followed instead Harlan's conception of reasoned judgment.

In the late 1980s and early 1990s, the key focus of these debates remained the abortion issue. Here, as elsewhere, the initial impression that the Reagan appointees would join a united conservative opposition turned out to be wrong. On her appointment to the Court in 1981, Justice O'Connor had quickly joined her fellow conservatives in calling *Roe* into question, but she ultimately proved unwilling to overturn the landmark precedent. Dissenting in *Akron v. Akron Center for Reproductive Health,* she referred to Judge Learned Hand's "Platonic Guardians" line and insisted that "when we are concerned with extremely sensitive issues, such as the one involved here, the appropriate forum for their resolution in a democracy is the legislature." Picking up on a phrase that the Court had used in prior cases, and that Solicitor General Lee had adopted in his *amicus* brief, she then argued that even if the abortion right were constitutionally protected, the Court should strike down only those regulations that imposed an "undue burden" on the exercise of the right.[21] O'Connor developed this "undue burden" formulation in an effort to curtail the Court's protection of abortion rights, but she would later turn it into a compromise approach that saved *Roe* from reversal.

The Court came very close to overturning *Roe* in 1989, but O'Connor cast a crucial deciding vote preventing it from doing so. In *Webster v. Reproductive Health Services,* Missouri attorney general William Webster relied on *Bowers* in defending his state's abortion restrictions and urging the Court to abandon *Roe,* but in what would become classic O'Connor style, she argued in her concurring opinion that the regulations at issue should be upheld even under the Court's existing standards, and thus that "there is no necessity to accept the State's invitation to reexamine the constitutional validity of *Roe.* . . . When the constitutional invalidity of a State's abortion statute actually turns on the constitutional validity of *Roe,* there will be time enough to reexamine *Roe.* And to do so carefully." Much to her colleagues' annoyance, O'Connor's vote cost Rehnquist a judicial majority for his opinion urging the abandonment of *Roe*. While she forestalled such a decision for the time being, however, it remained unclear what she would do if presented with a proper vehicle. After all, she still allowed substantial state interference with abortion access, and Justice Harry Blackmun issued a bitter dissenting opinion forecasting *Roe's* imminent demise.[22] Over the next two years, President Bush replaced Brennan and Marshall with Souter and Thomas, leaving Blackmun and John Paul Stevens as the Court's only known supporters of abortion rights.

In 1992, however, even this Court refused to overturn *Roe*, and in a move that was completely unexpected, O'Connor, Kennedy, and Souter jointly drafted a plurality opinion that endorsed the substantive due process jurisprudence on which *Roe* rested. In their remarkable opinion in *Planned Parenthood of Southeastern Pennsylvania v. Casey*, they adopted and applied O'Connor's "undue burden" standard, upholding most of the state's abortion restrictions, but they also explicitly endorsed the broad fundamental rights jurisprudence of which *Roe* was the most controversial example. Noting that Black's textualism and Scalia's "text and traditions" approach were "tempting, as a means of curbing the discretion of federal judges," the plurality nonetheless rejected them both as inadequate to the task of defining constitutional liberty. Citing a long line of cases, but relying in particular on Harlan's 1961 dissenting opinion in *Poe v. Ullman*, O'Connor, Kennedy, and Souter held that the Due Process Clause provides constitutional protection for "all fundamental rights comprised within the term liberty."[23] They acknowledged that their alternative approach would require the exercise of judgment, but they insisted, again supported by Harlan, that this "does not mean we are free to invalidate state policy choices with which we disagree." Joined by Blackmun and Stevens to form a majority on these important points, they held:

> Our law affords constitutional protection to personal decisions relating to marriage, procreation, contraception, family relationships, child rearing, and education. . . . These matters, involving the most intimate and personal choices a person may make in a lifetime, choices central to personal dignity and autonomy, are central to the liberty protected by the Fourteenth Amendment. At the heart of liberty is the right to define one's own concept of existence, of meaning, of the universe, and of the mystery of human life. Beliefs about these matters could not define the attributes of personhood were they formed under compulsion of the State.[24]

This sweeping endorsement of an unwritten and evolving conception of constitutional liberty sparked outrage and ridicule from their conservative colleagues and from many conservative scholars and activists as well.

In dissent, Scalia and Rehnquist had no new arguments to offer, but they reiterated their old ones at some length, with Scalia putting the issue most plainly. He insisted that "the power of a woman to abort her unborn child" is not a constitutionally protected liberty "for the same reason . . . that bigamy is not constitutionally protected — because of two simple facts: (1) the Constitution says absolutely nothing about it, and (2) the longstanding traditions of American society have permitted it to be legally proscribed." In Scalia's view, "[t]he permissibility of abortion, and the limitations upon it, are to be resolved like most important questions in our democracy: by citizens trying to persuade one another and then voting." Responding directly to O'Connor, Kennedy, and Souter, he denounced the Court's "new mode of constitutional adjudication that relies not upon text and traditional practice to determine the law, but upon what the Court calls 'reasoned judgment,' which turns out to be nothing but philosophical predilection and moral intuition." Recalling Black's longtime critique of Frankfurter and Harlan, Scalia offered a point-by-point insistence that the plurality's abstract legal standards were essentially meaningless; but like Black before him, he was unable to persuade his fellow justices.[25]

Though the *Casey* holding had the practical effect of allowing more state regulation of abortion than had been permissible under *Roe,* anti-abortion conservatives understandably viewed it as a crushing defeat. As Ronald Dworkin noted a few years later, O'Connor, Kennedy, and Souter had chosen to reaffirm "a more general view of the nature of the Constitution which they had been appointed to help destroy" (1996b:117).[26] These three Reagan-Bush appointees flatly rejected Scalia's critique of liberal activism, announcing their intention to continue defending an evolving concept of constitutional liberty. In subsequent years, as I show in chapter 6, they made good on this intention.

Because the *Casey* decision was issued at the end of Souter's second term, and given that he had also joined O'Connor and Kennedy (along with Stevens and Blackmun) in *Lee v. Weisman* just five days earlier, some observers were prompted to remark on the surprising emergence of a controlling centrist bloc on the Court (Dworkin 1992; Simon 1995). Despite these early indications, however, Souter would ultimately become a relatively consistent member of the Court's liberal wing, agreeing with O'Connor and Kennedy less frequently over time.[27] As a result, the key question on the Rehnquist Court was fast shaping up to be whether O'Connor and Kennedy would join with Rehnquist, Scalia, and Thomas. When they did so, the conservatives had a solid five-justice majority. But when either O'Connor or Kennedy defected, that majority would disappear.

The line between these two groups of conservative justices, moreover, was significantly influenced by the continuing legacy of Justices Harlan and Black. Recall that Harlan consistently held that there was an undefined core of judicially enforceable due process liberty; that reasoned judgment was an indispensable element of constitutional adjudication; and that this judgment should be tempered by a healthy dose of history and self-restraint. Black rejected this balancing approach in favor of an absolutist conception of textually guaranteed rights and a firm refusal to extend or modify those rights. Again, both Black and Harlan were motivated by a sharp fear of arbitrary judicial power, but this fear led them to dramatically different places. In fact, Harlan's judicial restraint was explicitly tied to an evolutionary conception of the Constitution (at least in the due process context), and Black's textualism was explicitly tied to the activist enforcement of constitutional rights. As constitutional conservatives gained an increasing foothold in the federal judiciary, the tensions between these competing critiques of modern judicial power could not be submerged for much longer.

The abortion cases were the most widely noted constitutional conflict of the early Rehnquist years, but in a wide range of other contexts, the conservative justices were similarly trimming liberal activist precedents but failing to overturn them altogether. For example, Rehnquist had long campaigned to limit the Equal Protection Clause to matters of race, and in 1980, John Hart Ely observed that his campaign seemed to be succeeding (1980:148–49). In two gender equality decisions the following year, moreover, Rehnquist was able to convince first a four-justice plurality and then a six-justice majority to apply a very deferential standard of review. In *Michael M. v. Superior Court,* upholding a state statutory rape law that punished men but not women, he made "only a slight concession to the Court's customary use of an intermediate standard of review for classifications based on sex" (Davis 1989:50). Observing somewhat disingenuously that "the Court has had some difficulty in agreeing upon the proper approach and analysis in cases involving challenges to gender-based classifications," he granted only that the "cases have held that the traditional minimum rationality test takes on a somewhat 'sharper focus' when gender-based classifications are challenged."[28] And in *Rostker v. Gold-*

berg, Rehnquist purported to be upholding the male-only military draft under *Craig v. Boren*'s "intermediate scrutiny," but he applied that scrutiny in an
exceedingly deferential form.

Rehnquist's success in this context was fleeting, however, and within a
year, O'Connor had led the Court firmly back to the path of activism in defense of gender equality. Writing for a bare majority in *Mississippi University
for Women v. Hogan* — with the four Nixon appointees in dissent — O'Connor held that those "seeking to uphold a statute that classifies individuals on
the basis of their gender must carry the burden of showing an exceedingly
persuasive justification for the classification."[29] By 1994, when a six-justice
majority held that the Equal Protection Clause prohibited discrimination in
jury selection on the basis of gender, this principle was firmly entrenched on
the Court.[30]

In the racial equality context, Rehnquist wrote for the Court in a 1991 decision holding that the Oklahoma City school district was now "unitary" and
that the school board was thereby constitutionally free to return to a system
of neighborhood schools. Emphasizing "the important value[ ] of local control of public school[s]," he observed that "[f]rom the very first, federal supervision of local school systems was intended as a temporary measure to
remedy past discrimination."[31] The conservative majority extended this
holding the following year by approving the partial withdrawal of judicial supervision from a school district even though it had not yet been found to
have established a unitary system in all areas of school policy *(Freeman v.
Pitts)*. And a few years later, Rehnquist reiterated that court-ordered remedies should be limited in time and scope and should "directly address . . . the
constitutional violation itself."[32] The Court's increasingly narrow vision of
constitutional equality was reinforced in this context by its conclusion —
rooted in long-standing conservative canons of restraint — that the effort to
integrate the public schools had proved beyond the capacity of the federal
courts. In this view, once school authorities had stopped formally segregating
students on the basis of race, the constitutional violation had ceased, and federal court supervision should be ended.

Similarly, the Court tightened its holding from *Washington v. Davis* that
the equal protection clause prohibits only intentional discrimination. In subsequent cases, the Burger Court had held that statistical evidence of a racially
disparate impact may sometimes be used to support an inference of discriminatory purpose, but had made this burden progressively more difficult to
carry.[33] In other words, around the same time the Court was curtailing judi-

cial supervision of school desegregation, it was also requiring alleged victims of racial discrimination to prove that specific, identifiable, intentionally discriminatory acts were the cause of any existing racial disparities. In *McCleskey v. Kemp*, for example, a bare majority of the Rehnquist Court upheld Warren McCleskey's death sentence despite strong statistical evidence that Georgia's capital punishment law was being administered in a racially discriminatory fashion. Writing for the Court, Powell insisted that aggregate statistical evidence was of little probative value and that a criminal defendant must prove that his own conviction was influenced by purposeful racial discrimination. This holding reflected the conservative critique of judicial power, the conservative support for the death penalty, and also the conservative criticism of liberal egalitarianism that I have discussed at length.

Though it was a statutory rather than a constitutional case, the Court's 5-4 decision in *Wards Cove Packing Co. v. Atonio* is also noteworthy here. Holding that statistical evidence of extreme racial disparity in a workforce could not by itself make out a *prima facie* case of Title VII discrimination, the Court rejected a civil rights claim against an Alaska cannery that, in Justice Stevens's dissenting view, bore "an unsettling resemblance to aspects of a plantation economy." As the dissenting justices recognized, the Court's holding that plaintiffs must "demonstrate that the disparity they complain of is the result of one or more of the employment practices that they are attacking . . . , specifically showing that each challenged practice has a significantly disparate impact on employment opportunities for whites and nonwhites," effectively reversed the *Griggs* standard's allocation of the burden of proof and, from their perspective, marked a substantial retreat by the Court.[34] As in the school desegregation cases, the conservatives' traditional commitment to judicial restraint was buttressed here by their newer critique of egalitarian social engineering.

Perhaps the Court's most significant conservative retrenchment came in the criminal procedure context, but even here, Justices O'Connor and Kennedy imposed some limits on their conservative colleagues, ensuring the continued survival of liberal activism. In *Maryland v. Craig*, for example, O'Connor wrote for a conservative majority in rejecting a criminal appeal resting on the Sixth Amendment's Confrontation Clause. In doing so, she upheld a state statute permitting a child witness who is alleged to be a victim of child abuse to testify via one-way closed-circuit television, but she limited the reach of the Court's holding by repeatedly emphasizing that the state must show in each individual case that such a procedure is necessary to protect the child witness from trauma. In the tradition of Justice Black, Scalia dissented on textualist grounds, complaining that the Court had seldom "failed so conspicuously to sustain a categorical guarantee of the Constitution against the tide of prevailing current opinion." He ended his opinion by "quot[ing] the document one last time (for it plainly says all that need be said): 'In *all* criminal prosecutions, the accused shall enjoy the right . . . to be confronted with the witnesses against him.'"[35]

Similarly, in the death penalty context, O'Connor delivered a Powell-like opinion announcing the Court's judgment in *Penry v. Lynaugh*. She agreed with four justices that the Eighth Amendment did not categorically prohibit the execution of the mentally retarded, but she agreed with the other four that it did require jury instructions regarding the mitigating effect of the defendant's mental retardation and history of childhood abuse. Four years later, in *Herrera v. Collins*, O'Connor and Scalia once again published dueling concurrences, pulling Rehnquist's opinion for the Court in opposite directions. Joined by Justice Thomas, Scalia insisted that a death row convict's assertion of actual innocence is not itself a constitutional claim, and that his death sentence should not be reviewed unless he asserts some constitutional defect in the procedures by which he was convicted and sentenced. Joined by Justice Kennedy, O'Connor disagreed, pointedly insisting that "the execution of a legally and factually innocent person would be a constitutionally intolerable event."[36] Though she joined her fellow conservatives in upholding the death sentence in this case, O'Connor forced Rehnquist to write the Court's opinion more narrowly than he otherwise would have.

Each of these decisions evinced the Court's trend toward greater deference and restraint in the area of criminal procedure. In the death penalty context in particular, the Court was leaving Justices Brennan and Marshall ever more isolated in dissent, although shortly after their retirements, Blackmun announced that he had come to agree with them. Dissenting from the Court's refusal to hear a death penalty appeal in *Callins v. Collins*, Blackmun dramatically announced that "[f]rom this day forward, I no longer shall tinker with the machinery of death." O'Connor and Kennedy would never go as far as Blackmun, but they would never go as far as Scalia in the other direction either. Scalia responded to Blackmun in *Callins* by observing that "[i]f the people conclude that . . . more brutal deaths may be deterred by capital punishment; indeed, if they merely conclude that justice requires such brutal deaths to be avenged by capital punishment; the creation of false, untextual and unhistorical contradictions within 'the Court's Eighth Amendment jurisprudence' should not prevent them."[37] Over the coming years, in contrast, O'Connor and Kennedy would continue the careful judicial monitoring of the death penalty's constitutionality in practice.

It was not yet fully clear, but the Court had left Justice Frankfurter's vision of broad judicial deference behind, in favor of an evolving but increasingly entrenched vision of rights-based constitutionalism. Moreover, the fact that the conservative call for restraint remained so often in dissent during the 1980s and early 1990s kept its internal tensions submerged. So long as constitutional conservatives were criticizing the Court's decisions, rather than seeking to enact their own positive vision into law, they could continue to lob a series of inconsistent critiques against modern judicial activism. The school desegregation and abortion decisions, for example, were wrong in the conservative mind both because they were judicially imposed and because they reflected illegitimate (and even immoral) liberal policy agendas. These two separate critiques would not always pull in the same direction, but conservatives continued to ignore that possibility for the time being.

The Rise of the New Right

While the conservative justices were arguing among themselves over how broadly to reject the Warren Court legacy, conservative activists were continuing to shift the national political climate to the right. By the 1980s, for example, evangelical Christians were playing a prominent role in the Republican Party's electoral successes. Jerry Falwell, one of the nation's leading "televangelists," founded the Moral Majority in 1979 and made a significant contribution to Reagan's successful campaign the following year by registering approximately 2 million new voters. By the end of Reagan's tenure, another of the Christian Right's leading national figures was making a respectable run for the Republican nomination for president: Pat Robertson garnered about a million votes in the 1988 primaries. The following year, Robertson and Ralph Reed founded the Christian Coalition, which along with Gary Bauer's Family Research Council, displaced the Moral Majority as the leading arm of the religious Right in the electoral and policy arenas (Diamond 1995:231, 244–50).

During this same period, a distinct group of traditionalist intellectuals emerged to develop more fully the religious critique of modern American culture that Falwell and Robertson were exploiting in the political arena. Conservative intellectuals like Richard John Neuhaus, William Bennett,

Hadley Arkes, and Robert Bork (after his retirement from the federal judiciary) complained that an amoral liberal culture was ruining the American
polity. Looking to Edmund Burke and Russell Kirk instead of Friedrich
Hayek, these traditionalists established their own institutions, separate from
but in alliance with those of the libertarians and neocons. Since its founding
in 1990, for example, the monthly opinion journal *First Things,* published by
the Institute on Religion and Public Life and edited by Neuhaus, has played a
role for religious conservatives similar to that played by *Commentary* and *The
Public Interest* for the neocons (Muncy 1997; Bork 1996a).[38] Drawing on conservative strains in both the Roman Catholic tradition and American fundamentalist Protestantism, these traditionalists have generally "maintain[ed]
that civilization requires moral constraints on the actions of individuals,"
and have thus differed from their more libertarian allies on a number of policy issues (Heineman 1997:1452).

   As I have noted, New Right activists brought their critique of liberalism to
bear on the law in part by appointing conservative judges, but also by litigat-
ing their newfound constitutional claims. And just as they were trying to persuade the Court to abandon its protection of a set of liberal constitutional
rights, Reagan administration lawyers were also trying to persuade it to actively enforce a newer set of conservative rights claims. Early in Reagan's first
term, for example, Attorney General William French Smith directed the solicitor general's office to support the religious freedom claims being advanced
by a conservative evangelical university in South Carolina. The Internal Revenue Service (IRS) had revoked Bob Jones University's tax exempt status on
the grounds that the school's prohibition of interracial dating among students violated federal civil rights policy. The university and the Reagan Justice Department challenged this action as a misreading of the federal tax
code, in the first instance, but also as a violation of the Free Exercise and Establishment Clauses. None of the justices were yet ready for this latter argument, as eight of them supported the IRS, with Rehnquist siding with Bob
Jones on the statutory grounds.[39]

   The *Bob Jones* case linked the emerging constitutional concerns of the religious Right with the ongoing New Right challenge to liberal civil rights orthodoxy. This latter concern was a key preoccupation of the Justice Department in the 1980s, as the Reagan administration sought to constitutionalize
the New Right critique of liberal egalitarianism by reading the Fourteenth
Amendment to protect white "victims" of affirmative action. As Solicitor
General Fried later recalled, the administration was "committed to ending

the drift to a quota society and to dismantling government-imposed racial preferences. The courts and especially the Supreme Court were where this battle was fought" (1991:90). Reagan's civil rights officials, particularly Assistant Attorney General William Bradford Reynolds, adhered to an extreme version of the color-blind principle, according to which race-conscious governmental action was never permitted, not even for remediation of proven discrimination (Reynolds 1984; see also Orfield 1996b).

Though Fried himself expressed some misgivings about this color-blind approach, he advanced it on the administration's behalf in his 1985 *amicus* brief in *Wygant v. Jackson Board of Education*. As I have suggested, this color-blind critique of affirmative action was part of a broader libertarian emphasis on limited government. The Reagan administration saw race-conscious policies as objectionable because they "dangerously aggrandize[ ] government. [They are] a threat to liberty and to the basic right of every person to be considered as a distinct individual and not in terms of the groups to which government says he belongs" (Fried 1991:90). Some years later, Fried recalled that the opposition to racial preferences had been motivated by a commitment to color-blindness, to be sure, but also by a reaction against "the sense that a new set of bureaucracies had sprung up with the power to order citizens about in new and intrusive ways. There was the ominous feeling — I know, because I shared it — that in enforcing racial preferences in private hiring practices, the proper distinction between public and private was being elided" (1999:52–53).

Spurred on by the Reagan administration's efforts, New Right activists established a variety of public interest law firms dedicated to advancing these conservative rights claims. In 1989, for example, Michael McDonald and Michael Greve, colleagues at the Washington Legal Foundation, founded the Center for Individual Rights (CIR), an organization dedicated to "reimpos[ing] constitutional limits on a meddlesome, interest-group-infested government."[40] Two years later, Clint Bolick and William "Chip" Mellor founded the Institute for Justice (IJ) with a similar mission:

Through strategic litigation, training, communications, and outreach, the Institute for Justice advances a rule of law under which individuals can control their own destinies as free and responsible members of society. We litigate to secure economic liberty, school choice, private property rights, freedom of speech, and other vital individual liberties, and to restore constitutional limits on the power of government. Through these activities we challenge the ideology of the welfare state and illustrate and extend the benefits of freedom to those whose full enjoyment of liberty is denied by government.

IJ's leaders and their allies set out to "sue the government when it stands in the way of people trying to earn an honest living, when it takes away individuals' property, when bureaucrats instead of parents dictate the education of children, and when government stifles." Moreover, "[t]he Institute's solutions to society's pressing concerns rest squarely on the merits of individual initiative, opportunity, and responsibility rather than on outcome-based, government-mandated solutions."[41]

More than any other development to date, the rise of these conservative public interest law firms highlighted the increasingly rights-based character of constitutional conservatism. After all, these organizations have explicitly modeled themselves on their liberal forerunners, noting, for example, that "[o]nce people turned first to the ACLU whenever government violated their rights. No longer. As that group has fought in recent years to create a right to welfare, to preserve racial preferences, and to prop up the pillars of the welfare state, people have increasingly sought a principled alternative that will protect individual rights rather than expand government. That alternative is the Institute for Justice."[42] Hoping to advance their vision of limited government, and recognizing that conservatives were now largely in control of the federal judiciary, these legal activists seized the opportunity to pressure the courts to use their power for conservative ends.

CIR would become best known for its anti–affirmative action lawsuits, but it would file a range of other rights-based conservative legal claims as well. For example, the organization has supported a variety of First Amendment claims, many of them successful, against anti-discrimination laws, sexual harassment policies, university speech codes, and policies denying government resources or equal treatment to religious organizations. It has also challenged a number of federal statutes for violating the constitutional structure of federalism.[43] IJ has supported all of these efforts and has also undertaken what it calls a "systematic campaign to restore the forgotten civil right: economic liberty."[44] In each of these contexts, conservative lawyers have regularly called on the federal courts to actively enforce constitutional limits on the democratically accountable branches of government.

Just as the NAACP had relied on, and also encouraged, an emerging body of pro–civil rights scholarship in the 1940s and 1950s, CIR's and IJ's litigation efforts in the 1990s were aided by a growing body of libertarian constitutional scholarship. Most notably, University of Chicago law professor Richard Epstein argued in a series of influential books and articles that the entire post–New Deal welfare-regulatory state should be struck down as a violation of both the federalism-based limits on national power and the constitutional provisions protecting property rights. In a 1987 *Virginia Law Review* article, he insisted that "the expansive construction of the [commerce] clause accepted by the New Deal Supreme Court is wrong, and clearly so," and he urged the courts to return to the nineteenth-century view that national regulatory authority did not extend to manufacturing, labor relations, or terms and conditions of employment. He objected to the size and scope of the modern state on the grounds of fidelity to the original Constitution, but also on substantive libertarian grounds. In this same article, for example, Epstein insisted that "[m]arkets are not just a good in themselves. They are powerful instruments for human happiness and well-being. . . . When viewed from this perspective, the Wagner Act, the Fair Labor Standards Act, and the Agricultural Marketing Act appear to be long-standing social disasters" (1987: 1388, 1453–55). Elsewhere, Epstein urged the judicial revitalization of the Contract Clause and the judicial invalidation of anti-discrimination laws, but most influential was his 1985 book on the Takings Clause (1984; 1992; 1985). In this latter book, he urged the Court to strike down "many of the heralded reforms and institutions of the twentieth century: zoning, rent control, workers' compensation laws, transfer payments [such as unemployment compensation and Social Security, and] progressive taxation," complaining that "[u]nder the present law the institution of private property places scant limitation upon the size and direction of the government activities that are characteristic of the modern welfare state" (1985:x).

In all of these works, Epstein acknowledged that his position would invalidate a wide range of state and federal legislation and that he was advocating a high degree of judicial intervention, but he insisted that if his arguments were correct, then "[t]he New Deal *is* inconsistent with the principles of limited government and with the constitutional provisions designed to secure that end." Even when acknowledging that the public's reliance on long-standing policies might caution against the wholesale judicial invalidation of the New Deal, he continued to urge the courts to strike down the Wagner Act and the Fair Labor Standards Act (FLSA), granting only that the enormous system of transfer payments provided by Social Security may be difficult or impossible to eliminate (1985:281, 324–29). He granted that the courts must sometimes decide to maintain "past errors that ha[d] become embedded in the legal system," but he insisted nonetheless that they should face the "powerful tension between the legacy of the past fifty years and the original constitutional understanding" (1987:1455).

In sum, Epstein relied on originalist conceptions of federalism and property rights to buttress a strong case for judicial activism, making clear that if the courts took the call for a return to original foundations seriously, then a substantial degree of judicial intervention would be required. His insistence that the courts should take that call seriously, precisely in order to rein in the modern welfare-regulatory state, significantly influenced a generation of conservative litigators, whose efforts in turn influenced the Court. Particularly in the interstate commerce and Takings Clause contexts, many of Epstein's arguments would be adopted by the Rehnquist Court in the 1990s, though the Court would never go as far as Epstein urged.

What was most striking about these conservative efforts, both intellectual and practical, was the significant degree to which they were in tension with the long-standing conservative commitment to restraint. Consider, for example, CIR senior counsel Terrence Pell's call for conservatives to "make copious use of the courts in their efforts to rein in an increasingly out of control bureaucratic state." In an effort to solicit conservative foundation money for CIR, Pell noted that while "the Ford and Rockefeller Foundations [had once] used the courts to push through broad programs of social reform, now it is conservative activists who are mounting high-profile cases to further policy objectives that could not be secured readily through more representative branches of government" (1998:28). Regardless of its merits, this agenda clearly sat uncomfortably with the traditional conservative critique of judicial power. While conservative judges, political activists, and constitutional scholars had long criticized the federal courts for striking down democratically enacted statutes and for usurping legislative and executive functions, many of these same conservatives were now urging the courts to supplant the regulatory policies adopted by elected legislators.

To the extent that constitutional conservatives recognized this tension, they generally sought to alleviate it in one of two ways. Some, like Epstein, forthrightly rejected the value of judicial deference, on the grounds of either fidelity to the original Constitution or the irrationality of legislative outcomes. Epstein's work was part of a larger scholarly movement among legal academics known as "law and economics," devoted to creating a legal system that optimally promotes the economic norm of "wealth maximization."

Many of these scholars — including the movement's founder, Richard Posner — rejected Epstein's originalism, but they all urged active judicial intervention to thwart legislative and administrative interference with the market.[45] During this same period, the emerging branch of social science research known as "rational choice" or "public choice" began to influence legal scholarship, and this work also tended to undermine the conservative case for judicial deference. Building on the path-breaking arguments of economists like Kenneth Arrow, Anthony Downs, James Buchanan, Ronald Coase, Douglass North, and Mancur Olson, a number of political scientists began insisting that virtually all political behavior could be modeled and predicted on the assumption that political outcomes were the product of actors seeking to maximize their preferences. In other words, political scientists brought the methods and assumptions of economics to bear on the study of individual decisionmaking in political settings (see generally Farber and Frickey 1991; Aldrich 1994).

Once they began applying these assumptions to the behavior of legislators, a large and distinguished group of political scientists came to the conclusion that legislation reflects not the public good but the private interests of the most powerful groups in society. Even if those private interests were not dominant, these scholars have argued, legislation could not reflect the majority will because legislative outcomes were dramatically influenced by voting procedures, agenda sequences, and the like. As Laura Kalman notes, public choice scholarship "painted a grim picture of a legislative process where the public interest was irrelevant, dominated by special interests and pre-existing preferences, and characterized by incoherent outcomes." In light of the irrationality of the legislative process, it was an open question why judges "should assume they could discern the will of the majority in legislatures, or why they would want to honor it if they could" (1996:81–82).

While some constitutional conservatives abandoned any pretense of judicial deference, others sought to deny the existence of any tension by fudging the meaning of judicial restraint and insisting that "properly understood, conservative litigation is fundamentally different from the sort of judicial activism long favored by liberal interest groups." For example, Pell insisted that CIR's efforts were consistent with the principle of restraint because the organization was only asking the courts to defend "individual rights against intrusive or overbearing governmental activity" and not "to undertake programs of social reform." He argued that CIR would only ask the courts "to set the permissible limits of governmental activity," and not ask them "to tell other branches of government how to exercise their power within those limits." Thus, in the affirmative action context, Pell noted that "[t]he salient feature of these lawsuits is their unremitting focus on the heavy-handed and entirely bureaucratic use of race by public institutions. Conservatives did not use these cases to extend the welfare state into new areas of American life, but to eliminate a clearly illegal extension of existing bureaucratic structure over the lives of ordinary Americans" (1998:28–30).

This argument, however, relied on a misleading conflation of judicial restraint and limited government. As I have noted, if judicial restraint means anything in the context of the long conservative critique of the Warren Court and its legacy, it must mean that the unelected judiciary is supposed to play a smaller role in settling divisive political conflicts. Thus, Pell cannot be right when he claims that "[s]o long as conservative public-interest litigators use the courts to reduce rather than increase the power of bureaucratic forces over American life, they will not be guilty of the sort of judicial activism long favored by their liberal counterparts" (1998:30). Whether they are seeking to expand or contract the welfare-regulatory state, if litigators are calling for decisionmaking by unelected judges, then it is judicial activism that they are promoting.

Conservative Activism in the 1980s and Early 1990s

In the affirmative action context, conservatives built on their partial success in *Bakke* by urging the Court to enforce the color-blind principle even more actively. For example, they challenged a number of local, state, and federal "set-aside" policies requiring a certain percentage of government contracting funds to go to minority-owned businesses. In *Fullilove v. Klutznick,* the Court upheld the 10 percent set-aside required by the federal Public Works Employment Act, applying a somewhat hazy degree of scrutiny, but clearly "reject[ing] the contention that in the remedial context the Congress must act in a wholly 'color-blind' fashion." In his lengthy plurality opinion, Burger repeatedly emphasized the need for "appropriate deference to the Congress, a co-equal branch charged by the Constitution with the power to 'provide for the . . . general Welfare . . .' and 'to enforce, by appropriate legislation,' the equal protection guarantees of the Fourteenth Amendment."[46] Justice Powell wrote separately to clarify, as he had held in *Bakke,* that race-conscious affirmative action policies were subject to strict scrutiny, but that they might nonetheless be upheld if they were narrowly tailored to serve some compelling government interest. Granting Congress significantly more deference than he had granted the University of California, he joined the Court in upholding the policy here.

Six years later, in *Wygant,* Powell continued to lead a badly fractured Court in reaffirming that race-conscious policies may sometimes be constitutionally legitimate, though here he struck down the policy at issue. In *Wygant,* Charles Fried argued for the Reagan administration that the Court should follow the "principle of full and complete equality of all persons under the law" that had been established in *Brown v. Board of Education.* Citing Nathan Glazer's *Affirmative Discrimination,* he observed that the United States is composed of a diverse set of racial and ethnic groups, rather than any single monolithic majority and minority, and he complained that the lower courts had "casual[ly] . . . wav[ed] aside . . . the fundamental Fourteenth Amendment principle of equal treatment for all persons regardless of race and of our republic's basic moral vision of the unity of all mankind." In support of this moral vision, Fried cited the Declaration of Independence, the first Justice Harlan's *Plessy* dissent, and the long line of Warren Court civil rights decisions, arguing that "the principle that . . . has unified the many minorities that make up our population" is the principle of color-blind equality before the law. In light of this principle, Fried insisted that race-conscious affirmative action programs "must satisfy the same constitutional standards as other forms of state-sponsored racial and ethnic discrimination."[47] At the urging of the Reagan administration, then, the Court struck down an employment policy that had been adopted by a democratically elected local school board. No one in the administration or on the Court acknowledged that such a decision was in tension with the long-standing conservative commitment to restraint.

In short, Powell's color-blind conception of the Fourteenth Amendment was buttressed by the anti-egalitarian litigation efforts of the Reagan administration, efforts that would prove even more influential in the coming years. Powell was firmly committed to the principle of color-blind equality, but he continued to balance that principle with the conservative commitment to restraint. As a result, the Court continued to uphold some affirmative action policies while raising serious questions about their constitutionality and striking down those that seemed to go too far.[48] After Powell's retirement in 1987, O'Connor stepped into his shoes as the swing voter on affirmative action, and she followed him in trying to balance the conservative commitments to color-blindness and judicial deference.[49]

Writing for the Court in *Richmond v. J. A. Croson Co.*, O'Connor held that
state and local affirmative action policies would be subject to the same strict
level of judicial scrutiny as other racial classifications in the law. In doing so,
she relied heavily on Powell's *Bakke* opinion, quoting his insistence that "the
guarantee of equal protection cannot mean one thing when applied to one
individual and something else when applied to a person of another color."
Like Powell, she questioned the one-way street aspect of the *Carolene Products* approach, insisting that "the standard of review under the Equal Protection Clause is not dependent on the race of those burdened or benefitted by
a particular classification." And like Powell, she insisted that the color-blind
principle is necessary to avoid a system of racial spoils in governmental decisionmaking.[50] Also like Powell, however, O'Connor refused to deduce from
these principles a per se prohibition on affirmative action, indicating that she
would uphold some race-conscious policies that served particularly important public purposes. She only identified one such purpose in *Croson* — that
of remedying past discrimination — and even here she followed Alexander
Bickel and Philip Kurland in holding that such race-conscious remedial measures could only be justified by "careful, specific findings of discrimination,"
and not by "[g]eneralized historical assertion about conditions somewhere
in the United States some time in the past."[51] Still, she pointedly insisted
that there may be other public purposes compelling enough to justify race-
conscious policies, sparking an increasingly impatient response from Scalia.

Writing separately, Scalia objected to O'Connor's apparent belief that,
"despite the Fourteenth Amendment, state and local governments may in
some circumstances discriminate on the basis of race in order (in a broad
sense) 'to ameliorate the effects of past discrimination.'" In Scalia's view,
"only a social emergency arising to the level of imminent danger to life and
limb — for example, a prison race riot, requiring temporary segregation of
inmates — can justify an exception to the principle embodied in the Fourteenth Amendment that our Constitution is colorblind." This color-blind
principle was so important to Scalia because he saw its opposite — that is,
"the tendency . . . to classify and judge men and women on the basis of . . .
the color of their skin" — as the source of all racial inequality. Citing Bickel
for support, he insisted that "discrimination on the basis of race is illegal, immoral, unconstitutional, inherently wrong, and destructive of democratic society," regardless of whose ox is gored.[52]

These color-blind arguments were temporarily relegated to a dissenting
position the following term, as Brennan persuaded four other justices to up-

hold a federal affirmative action program designed to increase minority own-ership of broadcast licenses.[53] With that exception, however, *Croson* turned out to be the first in a series of decisions striking down race-conscious poli-cies at the federal, state, and local level. After Thomas replaced Marshall in 1991, a firm five-justice majority proved willing to engage in the extensive ju-dicial activism necessary to enforce its color-blind reading of the Fourteenth Amendment.

In *Shaw v. Reno (Shaw I)*, for example, the conservative justices made clear that they would follow their color-blind principles even into the "political thicket" of legislative apportionment. Following the 1990 census, several southern states used race-conscious measures to increase the number of elec-toral districts with a majority black (or majority Hispanic) population. In *Shaw I*, however, the conservative majority held that regardless of whether a districting scheme disadvantaged any particular group, the Court would rec-ognize an equal protection claim whenever "the State has used race as a basis for separating voters into districts." Writing for the Court, O'Connor noted that the litigants "did not claim that the . . . reapportionment plan uncon-stitutionally 'diluted' white voting strength. They did not even claim to be white. Rather, [their] complaint alleged that the deliberate segregation of vot-ers into separate districts on the basis of race violated their constitutional right to participate in a 'color-blind' electoral process." Like all racial clas-sifications, the Court held, such race-conscious districting plans "pose the risk of lasting harm to our society" because "[t]hey reinforce the belief, held by too many for too much of our history, that individuals should be judged by the color of their skin."[54]

Shaw I and its progeny marked a sharp departure from the settled conser-vative view regarding electoral districting. During the Warren years, as I have noted, Justices Frankfurter and Harlan repeatedly rejected the Court's forays into legislative apportionment as instances of illegitimate judicial lawmaking. And in 1977, when Burger insisted "that drawing of political boundary lines with the sole, explicit objective of reaching a predetermined racial result can-not ordinarily be squared with the Constitution," none of his fellow justices joined him in dissent.[55] As recently as 1986, the Court's conservative justices seemed still to adhere to Frankfurter's and Harlan's view that questions of leg-islative apportionment were not matters for judicial resolution.[56] As in the government contracting context, however, Scalia, Thomas, Kennedy, and Rehnquist appeared willing to actively enforce a color-blindness require-ment for legislative districting. O'Connor joined them in 1993, as she had in

1989, but it remained an open question how far she was willing to go in imposing this color-blind vision on a nation that was not ready for it.

Affirmative action was just one of several doctrinal areas in which constitutional conservatives were now calling on the federal courts to exercise their power more vigorously. In the Tenth Amendment context, for example, conservatives had been building on Rehnquist's opinion in *National League of Cities v. Usery,* urging the Court to prevent Congress from interfering with state sovereignty, though they did not have much success with this argument in the 1980s. In a separate concurring opinion in *National League of Cities,* Blackmun had expressed some trepidation at the potential scope of the majority's holding, and in 1983, his change of heart allowed Brennan to write for the Court in upholding the application of the Age Discrimination in Employment Act (ADEA) to state employees. Brennan sidestepped the Court's recent precedent by holding that the ADEA posed less of an intrusion on state sovereignty than did the FLSA, but in a separate opinion, Stevens insisted that *National League of Cities* was wrong and should be overturned.[57] Within two years, Blackmun had been fully persuaded, and he wrote for the Court in overruling *National League of Cities* and upholding the application of the FLSA to local government employees. In *Garcia v. San Antonio Metropolitan Transit Authority,* following Brennan's elaboration of Herbert Wechsler's "political safeguards" argument, Blackmun insisted that the primary constitutional mechanisms for guarding state sovereignty were political rather than judicial.

Now in dissent again, the conservative justices advanced several arguments for adhering to *National League of Cities,* with Rehnquist confidently predicting that the principle announced in the earlier case would "in time again command the support of a majority of this Court." In a separate opinion, O'Connor denounced the Court for substantially altering the Constitution's original structure of federalism, insisting that its refusal to enforce the Tenth Amendment amounted to an abdication of judicial responsibility. She noted that while "the Framers of our Constitution intended Congress to have sufficient power to address national problems," they also "envisioned a republic whose vitality was assured by the diffusion of power . . . between the Federal Government and the States." Given the development of a nationally integrated economy, O'Connor noted, these two concerns had come into conflict, but rather than retreating, the Court should attempt to "reconcile the Constitution's dual concerns for federalism and an effective commerce power."[58] Attorney General Meese echoed these originalist arguments before the year was out, publicly complaining that the *Garcia* Court had "displayed . . . an inaccurate reading of the text of the Constitution and a disregard for the Framers' intention that state and local governments be a buffer against the centralizing tendencies of the national leviathan." Insisting "that there is a proper constitutional sphere for state governance under our scheme of limited, popular government," Meese called for the Court to abandon *Garcia* and to renew its earlier willingness to strike down congressional statutes that interfered with state sovereignty. In other words, in support of their view of federalism as "one of the most basic principles of our Constitution," Reagan administration officials were willing to call for the active judicial enforcement of constitutional limits on congressional authority.[59]

This sense of fidelity to the original Constitution was clearly one of the chief motivating factors in the Court's emerging brand of conservative activism, but it did not appear to be the only one. For one thing, the conservative justices were heeding the Reagan administration's call in a number of other contexts with much more tenuous originalist support. In the affirmative action cases, for example, the conservative justices had made virtually no effort to connect their color-blind reading of the Fourteenth Amendment to the original understanding of the text. Not in *Bakke* or *Fullilove* or *Wygant* or *Croson* or *Shaw I* did they provide any evidence that the Reconstruction Republicans who drafted and adopted the Fourteenth Amendment thought they were outlawing all racial classifications in the law. Even in the federalism context, moreover, where the conservative justices were clearly concerned with what they saw as an illegitimate departure from the original Constitution, they were influenced by some distinctly modern concerns as well.

In his own dissenting opinion in *Garcia,* for example, Powell emphasized not the original Constitution but the contemporary operation of the federal legislative process. He noted that "[f]ederal legislation is drafted primarily by the staffs of the congressional committees" and that "[t]he administration and enforcement of federal laws and regulations necessarily are largely in the hands of staff and civil service employees [who] may have little or no knowledge of the States and localities that will be affected by the statutes and regulations for which they are responsible." Though most of these public servants "are conscientious and faithful to their duties," Powell insisted, these "members of the immense federal bureaucracy are not elected, know less about the services traditionally rendered by States and localities, and are inevitably less responsive to recipients of such services, than are state legislatures, city councils, boards of supervisors, and state and local commissions, boards, and agencies. It is at these state and local levels — not in Washington as the Court so mistakenly thinks — that 'democratic self-government' is best exemplified."[60] Powell's concern for political accountability, reflecting the increasingly prominent public choice account of congressional lawmaking, would continue to influence conservative federalism arguments in the years to come. Whether or not it was an accurate assessment of the national legislative process, this account stood in sharp tension with the long-standing conservative demand for judicial deference to elected legislatures.

When the conservative justices returned to these questions a few years later, they picked up on both the originalist and the political accountability arguments from the *Garcia* dissents. Writing for the Court in *New York v. United States*, O'Connor relied on the Tenth Amendment in striking down a federal statute that had all but required states to form interstate compacts for the regional disposal of radioactive waste. Again emphasizing the original Constitution, she noted that the case "implicate[d] one of our Nation's newest problems of public policy and perhaps our oldest question of constitutional law." She acknowledged that Congress had substantial power to "encourage" the states to provide for the disposal of radioactive waste, but she insisted that the basic constitutional structure of federalism would not survive if Congress were allowed simply to "commandeer" the state legislatures, compelling them to adopt particular laws. In addition to being unfaithful to the original constitutional structure, O'Connor argued, such federal commandeering of state institutions would dilute the lines of political accountability, making it more difficult for citizens to punish their elected officials for adopting policies with which they disagreed.[61]

During this same period, Rehnquist also tried to revive a pre–New Deal conception of the Commerce Clause, according to which congressional regulatory authority extended only to activity that was both economic in character and national in scope.[62] Though he had limited success at first, the Court under his leadership would eventually revive the Commerce Clause, the Tenth and Eleventh Amendments, and §5 of the Fourteenth Amendment as judicially enforceable limits on congressional power. As in the affirmative action context, this federalism revival was facilitated in part by the constitutional litigation of the Reagan administration and conservative public interest litigators, who brought a steady stream of challenges to federal regulatory authority, providing the Court with ample opportunities to reassert these constitutional limits.

A roughly similar pattern characterized the Court's approach to the Constitution's other chief structural division of power: the separation of legislative and executive authority within the federal government. Prior to the New Deal, the Court had generally held that Congress could not constitutionally delegate its legislative power to the executive branch, but when Rehnquist joined the bench, it had not struck down a federal statute on these "nondelegation" grounds since 1935. Undeterred, conservatives began urging the revival of the nondelegation doctrine as part of a broader strategy of enforcing a strict conception of the separation of powers, which would have the effect of hampering the effective exercise of federal regulatory authority.[63] In separate opinions in 1980 and 1981, Rehnquist heeded this call, and as Fried has noted, the Reagan administration emphasized these arguments in its litigation efforts as well, insisting that "the authority and responsibility of the President should be clear and unitary."[64]

Though Rehnquist and the Reagan administration helped get things started, Justice Scalia emerged as the unquestioned conservative leader on separation of powers concerns.[65] In Scalia's view, the original Constitution drew a sharp line between legislative and executive authority, a line that had been blurred by the modern administrative state and that the Court should once again actively enforce. He developed this constitutional argument before joining the Court, while serving as assistant attorney general in the Ford administration, then as a scholar in residence at the American Enterprise Institute, and then as a federal appellate judge on the D.C. Circuit. In each of these capacities, he called for the revival of the nondelegation doctrine and insisted that innovative lawmaking procedures such as the "legislative veto" were unconstitutional. As in the federalism context, if carried to their logical conclusion, such arguments would call into question the constitutionality of much of the modern welfare-regulatory state — in this case, a long list of independent regulatory agencies to whom Congress had delegated lawmaking authority. Despite these implications, the Burger Court indicated that it would actively enforce these constitutional principles, following Scalia's lead in decisions like *INS v. Chadha* and *Bowsher v. Synar* (Brisbin 1997:18–51).

As in the Tenth Amendment cases, some of the conservative justices seemed untroubled by the fact that the Court was interfering with widely used legislative and administrative practices, but others would express some concern. By the late 1980s, when Scalia urged the Court to invalidate the federal statutes creating the Office of the Independent Counsel and the U.S. Sentencing Commission, none of his colleagues were willing to join him. Dissenting in the independent counsel case, he emphasized the simple command of the original Constitution that "the executive power shall be vested in a President of the United States," insisting that Congress had no authority to divest the president of his complete control over the government's prosecutorial authority. He reiterated his strict approach in the sentencing commission case the following year, but he was again rebuffed by his colleagues, who adopted a flexible, pragmatic, and evolutionary conception of the separation of powers, relegating Scalia's call for active judicial intervention to a lonely dissent.[66]

Scalia also sought to lead his conservative colleagues in the property rights context, following the path marked out by Richard Epstein and his fellow libertarian scholars by reinvigorating the Takings Clause as a limit on state and local regulatory authority. As in a number of other doctrinal contexts, Rehnquist's dissenting opinions in the 1970s had laid important groundwork here as well. Rejecting the modern "double standard," under which economic liberties had received less judicial protection than so-called preferred freedoms, the Rehnquist Court declared a renewed judicial commitment to constitutional property rights, particularly by prohibiting uncompensated "regulatory takings." As with the Commerce Clause and the nondelegation doctrine, the Court had essentially abandoned its regulatory takings jurisprudence after the New Deal. But in both *Nollan v. California Coastal Commission* and *Lucas v. South Carolina Coastal Council,* Scalia wrote for the Court in reviving these constitutional limits. In *Nollan,* he held that a California zoning commission could not constitutionally require, as a condition of a building permit, that a homeowner transfer to the public an easement across his beachfront property. In *Lucas,* he held that South Carolina's Beachfront Management Act, designed to halt erosion by prohibiting development along parts of the coastline, could not be applied to prohibit a property owner "from erecting any permanent habitable structures" on two beachfront residential lots unless the state compensated him for this complete economic loss. Two years later, in *Dolan v. City of Tigard,* Scalia joined Rehnquist's opinion holding that the Takings Clause prohibited a local government from requiring, again as a condition of a building permit, that a business owner dedicate a portion of her property for flood control and traffic improvements.

As in the federalism context, the dissenting liberal justices called attention to the potentially extraordinary implications of judicial efforts to enforce this doctrine in the context of the modern regulatory state, noting that zoning measures such as the one at issue in *Dolan* were "a species of business regu-

lation that heretofore warranted a strong presumption of constitutional validity." To this, Rehnquist replied that "simply denominating a governmental
measure as a 'business regulation' does not immunize it from constitutional
challenge on the grounds that it violates a provision of the Bill of Rights. . . .
We see no reason why the Takings Clause of the Fifth Amendment, as much
a part of the Bill of Rights as the First Amendment or Fourth Amendment,
should be relegated to the status of a poor relation in these comparable circumstances." [67] Elevating the Takings Clause to the same constitutional level
as the freedom of speech, the Rehnquist Court proved increasingly willing to
exercise its power in defense of constitutional property rights.

In a wide range of doctrinal contexts, then, the conservative justices of the
Rehnquist Court actively enforced constitutional limits on government
power. As this conservative activism was getting under way, the key unanswered question was how far the conservative justices would be willing to
carry it. Though two Democratic appointees had joined the Court in the early
1990s — the first since 1967 — the conservative justices had nonetheless consolidated their judicial majority, and as the twentieth century came to a close,
they would face both greater pressure and greater opportunity to expand
their influence on constitutional law.

Following the southern strategy, Republicans controlled the presidency
for all but four years from 1969 to 1992, when they lost it to Democrat Bill
Clinton. The Democrats' hegemony in Washington was brief, however, as the
Republicans recaptured both houses of Congress two years later. The GOP
had controlled the Senate intermittently since 1980, but had not had a governing majority in the House since the Eisenhower years. Running on a national platform dubbed the "Contract with America," seventy-three Republican freshman joined the lower chamber in January of 1995, committed to
scaling back the size and scope of the national welfare-regulatory state,
among other priorities. With the political winds blowing rightward, Clinton
sought reelection in 1996 in part by adopting significant elements of this conservative agenda, famously declaring in his State of the Union Address that
year that "the era of big government is over." While Clinton was quite successful in practicing what Stephen Skowronek (1993) has called "the politics
of preemption," the Democratic Party's fortunes declined even further after
his two terms in office. The GOP recaptured the presidency in 2000, giving it
control of all three branches in Washington. Moreover, the party that dominated national politics at the dawn of the twenty-first century was a far cry
from the liberal, northeastern Republicanism of Eisenhower and Rockefeller,

as it was now led by southern and western conservatives like Newt Gingrich, Tom DeLay, and George W. Bush.

If they needed it, the judicial conservatives of the Rehnquist Court now had ample reassurance that the political branches would support their conservative constitutional decisions. With no votes to spare, however, if any of the conservative justices abandoned their coalition, the reach of the constitutional revolution would be limited. In the Court's liberal activist decisions, O'Connor and Kennedy had already shown a reluctance to join their colleagues in jettisoning the landmark protections of individual liberty and minority rights that they had inherited. And in the conservative activist decisions, O'Connor had already provoked impatience from her conservative colleagues by limiting the reach of their holdings on a number of occasions. So far, these limits had not amounted to much — to many observers, they appeared more rhetorical than real — but if she began to take them seriously, then that side of the conservative revolution would be significantly limited as well.

PART III

THE REHNQUIST COURT
AND THE SPLINTERING OF
JUDICIAL CONSERVATISM
1994–2003

CHAPTER SIX

ACTIVISM AND RESTRAINT
ON THE REHNQUIST COURT

In the midst of a broader conservative ascendance in national politics, Justices William Rehnquist, Antonin Scalia, Clarence Thomas, Sandra Day O'Connor, and Anthony Kennedy consolidated their control of the U.S. Supreme Court. Having done so, they were presented with a golden opportunity to shape constitutional development. Constrained by the inherited traditions of constitutional discourse, the justices had three broad options from which to choose. First, they could attempt to maintain a consistent commitment to judicial restraint by exercising substantial deference to the elected branches across the board. Second, they could abandon the protection of liberal constitutional rights associated with the Warren Court tradition, and articulate a new set of conservative rights claims that they were willing to defend instead. None of the justices chose the first path, but Scalia, Thomas, and Rehnquist have, broadly speaking, opted for the second. Table 6.1 illustrates how this second approach is the mirror image of that taken by the Court's four most liberal justices. As the table also illustrates, O'Connor and Kennedy have chosen a third option, joining their conservative colleagues to promote the new conservative activism in defense of limited government, while continuing to support the older liberal activism as well.

Consider, for example, the landmark cases on gay rights and affirmative action decided at the end of the Court's 2002 term: *Lawrence v. Texas,* involving a liberal, rights-based challenge to the state's criminal sodomy statute, and *Gratz v. Bollinger* and *Grutter v. Bollinger,* involving a conservative, rights-based challenge to the University of Michigan's race-conscious admissions policies. None of the justices urged the Court to exercise restraint in

TABLE 6.1 *Support for Liberal and Conservative Activism on the Rehnquist Court*

Support for Conservative Activism?	Support for Liberal Activism?	
	Yes	No
Yes	O'Connor, Kennedy	Scalia, Thomas, Rehnquist
No	Stevens, Souter, Ginsburg, Breyer	—

both contexts. Though conservatives currently control the Court, Justice Felix Frankfurter's doctrine of judicial deference has no surviving heirs.[1] Most of the justices voted to exercise judicial review in either the liberal rights case or the conservative rights cases, but not both. Only O'Connor, Kennedy, and Stephen Breyer voted to exercise judicial review in both the gay rights and affirmative action contexts, and Kennedy was the only one to do so in all three cases. Notably, while O'Connor supported the Court's liberal activism in the sodomy case and its conservative activism in the affirmative action cases, she sought to hedge that activism in both contexts. She voted to strike down Texas's sodomy statute, but wrote separately to limit the reach of the Court's rationale. And she voted to strike down Michigan's affirmative action policy for undergraduate admissions in *Gratz*, but also voted to uphold Michigan's more flexible affirmative action policy for law school admissions in *Grutter*.

In case after case, O'Connor has supported judicial activism in defense of both liberal and conservative ends, but has tempered that activism by deciding cases on narrow grounds, refusing to issue any broad principles or rules. Though less frequent, and less widely noted, Kennedy has sometimes adopted a similar posture as well. After all, having endorsed the active judicial enforcement of both liberal and conservative rights claims, the only way for them to maintain any meaningful commitment to restraint has been to limit the reach of such activism at the margins. Thus, in some doctrinal contexts, O'Connor and Kennedy have joined their more liberal colleagues to preserve liberal activism (e.g., by striking down anti-abortion laws), while also setting some limits on that activism (e.g., by allowing a greater degree of state regulation in the form of waiting periods, informed consent, and the like). In other contexts, they join their more conservative colleagues to build conservative activism (e.g., by striking down federal statutes that exceed Congress's enumerated powers), while again setting some limits (e.g., by insisting that they will not ratchet congressional authority all the way back to its pre–New Deal scope).

O'Connor's and Kennedy's vision of the judicial role is fundamentally different from that of their conservative colleagues. Scalia, Thomas, and Rehnquist have drawn a sharp, categorical distinction between those contexts in which the original constitutional text declares limits that the courts should actively enforce, on the one hand, and those contexts in which the text is "silent" and hence calls for restraint, on the other. In the Court's liberal activist decisions on abortion, gay rights, and the like, these three conservatives have generally offered sharp dissents, denouncing the Court for illegitimately revising the Constitution to include these expansive new rights claims. In the conservative activist decisions, however, they have made the Court's most sweeping calls for judicial intervention — calling for an absolute principle of color-blindness or for a revival of dual federalism that would invalidate much of the post–New Deal regulatory state.

O'Connor's and Kennedy's vision has been the decisive one. The justices of the later Rehnquist Court have served a full ten consecutive terms together, which has provided ample opportunity to develop stable coalitions. Since the beginning of the 1994 term, when Breyer joined the Court, most high-profile constitutional conflicts pitted Scalia, Thomas, and Rehnquist, on the one hand, against David Souter, John Paul Stevens, Ruth Bader Ginsburg, and Breyer, on the other, leaving O'Connor and Kennedy with the deciding votes. During their first nine terms together, for example, these nine justices decided 155 cases by a 5-4 vote. In seventy-three of these cases, O'Connor and Kennedy joined their three fellow conservatives to form a conservative majority, but in thirty-six of them, either O'Connor or Kennedy defected, joining Stevens, Souter, Ginsburg, and Breyer to form a liberal majority.[2] In sum, in about half of the closely divided cases on the later Rehnquist Court, O'Connor and Kennedy joined their conservative colleagues to form the solid conservative majority that has been the Court's public image. But in almost a quarter of such cases, either O'Connor or Kennedy abandoned their fellow conservatives to form a liberal majority. Since there have also been a number of landmark decisions in which both O'Connor and Kennedy defected, creating a six-justice liberal majority, these numbers actually understate their decisive role.

O'Connor and Kennedy have almost always been in the Court's majority, as table 6.2 makes clear. Kennedy was the justice most likely to be in the

TABLE 6.2 *Frequency in Majority during Late Rehnquist Era**

Term/ Justice	Rehnquist	Stevens	O'Connor	Scalia	Kennedy	Souter	Thomas	Ginsberg	Breyer
1994	84.1	71.6	85.4	81.5	92.7	80.5	74.4	85.2	85.9
1995	86.5	72.2	90.5	82.4	93.2	89.2	82.2	83.8	83.8
1996	87.5	71.3	88.6	80.0	93.8	85.0	81.3	80.0	78.8
1997	89.0	76.9	90.0	76.9	94.5	83.5	82.4	82.4	84.6
1998	83.1	71.4	90.8	83.1	88.3	83.1	81.8	77.9	78.9
1999	87.7	63.0	94.5	80.8	87.7	73.6	84.9	68.5	75.3
2000	81.3	71.6	89.0	76.0	90.7	82.4	77.3	77.3	74.3
2001	82.7	69.3	86.1	71.6	88.0	74.7	77.3	77.3	81.1
Totals	85.3	71.1	89.3	79.0	91.2	81.6	80.2	79.2	80.5

Source: Original U.S. Supreme Court Database, with orally argued citation as unit of analysis.

*Percentage of formally decided full opinion cases in which each justice voted with the Court's majority.

majority during six of the eight terms from 1994 to 2001, and during his entire tenure on the Court, he has been in the majority in a remarkable 91.3 percent of the cases. O'Connor has almost always been second to Kennedy in this regard, and in the 1998 and 1999 terms, she surpassed him.

These patterns have not always held up. Neither of Clinton's two appointees have joined their fellow liberals in every case. Souter has sometimes abandoned his fellow liberals as well, unwilling to "develop a new and distinct body of constitutional law" that would disrupt "two centuries of uninterrupted (and largely unchallenged) state and federal practice."[3] Rehnquist has sometimes abandoned his fellow conservatives, for largely the same reason; he is more fully committed than Scalia and Thomas to judicial deference.[4] Hence, O'Connor and Kennedy are not the only justices who sometimes cast a decisive vote, and they are not the only justices who sometimes use their decisive votes to limit the reach of the Court's holding.[5]

Still, the general pattern is plain to see: O'Connor and Kennedy have voted to intervene in political conflicts in case after case, while simultaneously insisting that their activism will only go so far, and these votes and opinions control the Rehnquist Court. Since their votes are so often decisive, moreover, it is O'Connor's and Kennedy's vision of the judicial role — their particular effort to reconcile the long-standing conservative commitment to restraint and the New Right commitment to limited government — that explains the extraordinary activism of the Rehnquist Court. As I suggested earlier, the terms "activism" and "restraint" have not always been used with precision, but in at least three different respects, it makes sense to characterize the later Rehnquist Court as the most activist in American history.

First, beginning with the 1994 term, when the conservative majority started to come into its own, the Court struck down federal statutes more frequently than at any previous time in its history. The raw numbers presented in table 2.1 are merely illustrative, but since the Court had never before struck down so many provisions of federal law in such a short period, they do suggest that the contemporary Court has had an unusually skeptical attitude toward Congress. As table 6.3 makes clear, some of these federal statutes have been obscure or insignificant, but many have been prominent and widely supported.

Second, and relatedly, this Court has regularly declared its own authority in an overconfident tone, as its leading justices are committed to a strong conception of judicial supremacy. In a series of cases beginning with *City of Boerne v. Flores*, the justices have firmly reminded the coordinate branches

TABLE 6.3 *Federal Statutes Ruled Unconstitutional by the Supreme Court, In Whole or in Part, 1994–2002 Terms*

Federal Statute	Decision Striking Statute Down	Constitutional Basis
Federal Alcohol Administration Act (1935)	*Rubin v. Coors Brewing Co.*	First Amendment (commercial speech)
Ethics Reform Act (1989)	*United States v. National Treasury Employees Union*	First Amendment
Gun Free School Zones Act (1990)	*United States v. Lopez*	Federalism (Commerce Clause)
Securities Exchange Act (1934)	*Plaut v. Spendthrift Farm, Inc.*	Separation of powers
26 U.S.C. § 4371 (provision of Internal Revenue Code)	*United States v. IBM Corp.*	Export Clause (Article I, §9)
Federal Election Campaign Act (1971)	*Colorado Republican Campaign Comm. v. FEC*	First Amendment (campaign finance regulation)
Indian Gaming Regulatory Act (1988)	*Seminole Tribe of Florida v. Florida*	Federalism (state sovereign immunity)
Cable Television Consumer Protection and Competition Act (1992)	*Denver Area Educ. Tel. Consortium v. FCC*	First Amendment (commercial speech)
Indian Land Consolidation Act (1983)	*Babbitt v. Youpee*	Takings Clause
Religious Freedom Restoration Act (1993)	*City of Boerne v. Flores*	Federalism (Fourteenth Amendment, §5)
Communications Decency Act (1996)	*Reno v. ACLU*	First Amendment

Brady Handgun Violence Prevention Act (1993)	*Printz v. United States*	Federalism (Tenth Amendment)
Harbor Maintenance Tax (1986)	*United States v. United States Shoe Corp.*	Export Clause (Article I, §9)
Copyright Act (1976)	*Feltner v. Columbia Pictures Television*	Right to jury trial (Seventh Amendment)
Coal Industry Retiree Health Benefit Act (1992)	*Eastern Enterprises v. Apfel*	Takings Clause
Line Item Veto Act (1996)	*Clinton v. City of New York*	Separation of powers (Presentment Clause)
Criminal law authorizing forfeiture of any property involved in illegal currency smuggling	*United States v. Bajakajian*	Excessive Fines Clause
Section 316 of Communications Act of 1934 (prohibition of advertising for casino gambling)	*Greater New Orleans Broadcasting Association v. United States*	First Amendment (commercial speech)
Patent and Plant Variety Remedy Classification Act (1992)	*Florida Prepaid Postsecondary Educ. Exp. Bd. v. College Savings Bank*	Federalism (state sovereign immunity)

(continued)

TABLE 6.3 (*Continued*)

Federal Statute	Decision Striking Statute Down	Constitutional Basis
Trademark Remedy Clarification Act (1992)	*College Savings Bank v. Florida Prepaid Postsecondary Educ. Exp. Bd.*	Federalism (state sovereign immunity)
Fair Labor Standards Act Amendments of 1974	*Alden v. Maine*	Federalism (state sovereign immunity)
Age Discrimination in Employment Act (as amended, 1974)	*Kimel v. Florida Board of Regents*	Federalism (state sovereign immunity)
Violence against Women Act (1994)	*United States v. Morrison*	Federalism (Commerce Clause and Fourteenth Amendment, §5)
Telecommunications Act of 1996 (cable indecency provisions)	*United States v. Playboy Entertainment Group*	First Amendment
Omnibus Crime Control and Safe Streets Act of 1968 (provision purporting to overrule *Miranda v. Arizona*)	*Dickerson v. United States*	Fifth Amendment right against self-incrimination
Americans with Disabilities Act (1990)	*University of Alabama v. Garrett*	Federalism (state sovereign immunity)
Social Security Amendments of 1983 (requiring all federal judges to enter into the Social Security program)	*United States v. Hatter*	Compensation Clause (Article III, §2)

Legal Services Corporation Act (1974)	*Legal Services Corp. v. Velazquez*	First Amendment
Omnibus Crime Control and Safe Streets Act of 1968 (provision prohibiting the disclosure of illegally intercepted wire, electronic, and oral communications)	*Bartnicki v. Vopper*	First Amendment
Mushroom Promotion, Research, and Consumer Information Act (1990)	*United States v. United Foods*	First Amendment (commercial speech)
Child Pornography Prevention Act of 1996	*Ashcroft v. Free Speech Coalition*	First Amendment
Food and Drug Administration Modernization Act of 1997 (regulation of drug advertising)	*Thompson v. Western States Medical Center*	First Amendment (commercial speech)

that they will not be allowed to second-guess the Court's reading of the Constitution.

Third, and perhaps most notably, the later Rehnquist Court recognizes no "political thickets" in which it is unwilling to exercise its power. *Bush v. Gore* is the best example here, but the current Court has also been willing to impose constitutional limits on national, state, and local legislative authority in a wide variety of contexts. As tables 6.3 and 6.4 indicate, some of the Court's decisions have been familiar examples of liberal judicial activism in defense of civil rights or civil liberties, but many others have been examples of the newer conservative activism. In other words, the Court has been actively enforcing liberal conceptions of gay rights, gender equality, abortion rights, and the like, while also actively defending the right of religious groups to have equal access to state resources, the right of private organizations to choose their own members without interference from state antidiscrimination laws, and the right to live in an electoral district free from race-conscious gerrymandering. Again, O'Connor and Kennedy have cast the deciding votes in virtually all of these cases.

Even in those contexts in which the Court has been most restrained, Justices O'Connor and Kennedy have not carried that restraint as far as their conservative colleagues would like. Compared to its immediate predecessors, for example, the Rehnquist Court has invalidated state and local statutes much less frequently, as table 2.2 made clear. It has also become less likely to issue holdings that are broadly legislative in character, on the order of *Roe* or *Miranda*. And it has become less willing to "usurp" executive power by allowing courts to administer public institutions themselves. When these three concerns overlap, the Court has been much less likely to exercise its own authority. In the school desegregation context, for example, the conservative majority has held that it was "beyond the authority and beyond the practical ability of the federal courts to try to counteract the[ ] kinds of continuous and massive demographic shifts" that were causing the resegregation of public schools.[6] Concurring in *Missouri v. Jenkins,* as the Court put a halt to an extensive, eighteen-year effort by a federal district court to integrate the Kansas City schools, Thomas cited Donald Horowitz's *The Courts and Social Policy* and complained that too many judges had "directed or managed the reconstruction of entire institutions and bureaucracies, with little regard for the inherent limitations on their authority."[7] This conservative suspicion of institutional-reform litigation has extended beyond the schools context as well. The year after *Jenkins,* the Court decided *Lewis v. Casey,* rejecting a class

TABLE 6.4 *State and Local Statutes Ruled Unconstitutional by the Supreme Court, in Whole or in Part, 1994–2002 Terms*

State or Local Statute	Decision Striking Statute Down	Constitutional Basis
Illinois Consumer Fraud Act	*American Airlines v. Wolens*	Federal preemption
Ohio's prohibition on the distribution of anonymous campaign literature	*McIntyre v. Ohio Elections Commission*	First Amendment
Amendment to Arkansas Constitution providing for term limits for members of Congress	*U.S. Term Limits v. Thornton*	Qualifications Clause (Article I)
Oklahoma's motor fuels excise tax, as applied to retail stores on tribal land	*Oklahoma Tax Commission v. Chickasaw Nation*	Article I
Massachusetts' civil rights statute prohibiting discrimination on the basis of sexual orientation	*Hurley v. Irish-American Gay Group*	First Amendment (freedom of speech and association)
Georgia's congressional districting plan	*Miller v. Johnson*	Equal Protection Clause
North Carolina corporate tax provision	*Fulton Corp. v. Faulkner*	Dormant Commerce Clause
Florida statute prohibiting banks from dealing in insurance	*Barnett Bank v. Nelson*	Federal preemption
State statutory prohibition of advertising of alcoholic beverages	*44 Liquormart, Inc. v. Rhode Island*	First Amendment (commercial speech)

(continued)

TABLE 6.4 (*Continued*)

State or Local Statute	Decision Striking Statute Down	Constitutional Basis
Colorado constitutional amendment prohibiting all state and local government efforts to outlaw discrimination against gays and lesbians	*Romer v. Evans*	Equal Protection Clause (gay rights)
Montana regulation of the use of arbitration in contracts	*Doctor's Associates, Inc. v. Casarotto*	Federal preemption
North Carolina congressional districting plan	*Shaw v. Hunt*	Equal Protection Clause
Texas congressional districting plan	*Bush v. Vera*	Equal Protection Clause
Virginia Military Institute's exclusion of women	*United States v. Virginia*	Equal Protection Clause (gender equality)
Mississippi statute conditioning appeals from trial court decrees terminating parental rights on the affected parent's ability to pay court costs	*M.L.B. v. S.L.J.*	Equal Protection and Due Process Clauses
Florida statute canceling early release credits awarded to prisoners	*Lynce v. Mathis*	Ex Post Facto clause

Georgia statute requiring drug tests for all candidates for state office	*Chandler v. Miller*	Fourth Amendment
Maine property tax law	*Camps Newfound/Owatonna v. Town of Harrison*	Dormant Commerce Clause
Louisiana "open primary" for congressional elections	*Foster v. Love*	Federal preemption
Provision of state tax code discriminating against nonresidents	*Lunding v. New York Tax Appeals Tribunal*	Privileges and Immunities Clause (Article I, §2)
Iowa statute authorizing full police search of a car when issuing a traffic citation	*Knowles v. Iowa*	Fourth Amendment
Colorado regulations requiring initiative petition circulators to be registered voters	*Buckley v. American Constitutional Law Foundation*	First Amendment
Alabama's franchise tax law	*South Central Bell Tel. Co. v. Alabama*	Commerce Clause
California durational residency statute limiting new residents' welfare benefits	*Saenz v. Roe*	Equal Protection and Privileges or Immunities Clauses (constitutional right to interstate travel)
Chicago's Gang Congregation Ordinance	*Chicago v. Morales*	Due Process Clause
"Native Hawaiian" requirement to vote for Office of Hawaiian Affairs	*Rice v. Cayetano*	Fifteenth Amendment

(continued)

TABLE 6.4 (*Continued*)

State or Local Statute	Decision Striking Statute Down	Constitutional Basis
Washington regulations governing oil tanker operations	*United States v. Locke*	Federal preemption
Texas law eliminating requirement that the testimony of a youthful sexual assault victim be corroborated	*Carnell v. Texas*	Ex Post Facto Clause
Washington "grandparents' rights" visitation statute	*Troxel v. Granville*	Substantive due process
State "blanket primary" law	*California Democratic Party v. Jones*	Freedom of association
Sentencing provisions of state hate crimes law	*Apprendi v. New Jersey*	Due Process Clause
Nebraska's "partial birth abortion" statute	*Stenberg v. Carhart*	Substantive due process
New Jersey civil rights statute prohibiting discrimination on the basis of sexual orientation	*Boy Scouts v. Dale*	Freedom of association
Massachusetts statute barring state entities from contracting with	*Crosby v. National Foreign Trade Council*	Federal preemption

companies doing business with Burma (1996)		
Missouri constitutional amendment, requiring that ballots for congressional candidates who did not support congressional term limits be marked with distinctive phrase	Cook v. Gralike	Elections Clause (Article I, §4, cl. 1)
Washington statute providing that designation of spouse as beneficiary of nonprobate asset was revoked automatically upon divorce	Egelhoff v. Egelhoff	Federal preemption
School board policy providing that school premises were not to be used by any individual or organization for religious purposes	Good News Club v. Milford Central School	First Amendment (freedom of speech and free exercise of religion)
Massachusetts regulations governing the advertising and sale of cigarettes, smokeless tobacco, and cigars	Lorillard Tobacco v. Reilly	First Amendment (commercial speech)
Local ordinance restricting door-to-door canvassing	Watchtower Bible and Tract Society of New York v. Stratton	First Amendment

(continued)

TABLE 6.4 (*Continued*)

State or Local Statute	Decision Striking Statute Down	Constitutional Basis
California statute requiring insurance companies to disclose information about policies in effect during Holocaust era	*American Insurance Association v. Garamendi*	Federal preemption
Texas criminal sodomy statute	*Lawrence v. Texas*	Substantive due process
California statute permitting prosecution for sex-related child abuse after statute of limitations has expired	*Stogner v. California*	Ex Post Facto Clause
Virginia cross-burning statute	*Virginia v. Black*	First Amendment

action challenge alleging that the Arizona Department of Corrections was providing inadequate legal research facilities and thereby depriving inmates of their right of access to the courts. Thomas again wrote separately to articulate his own sweeping denunciation of the remedial authority of the modern courts.

Thus, in a certain kind of case — one that involves a federal constitutional challenge that, if accepted, would require extensive judicial supervision of state and local institutions — the Rehnquist Court has been reluctant to exercise its power. Even in contexts such as this one, however, it has been O'Connor and Kennedy who have set the limits of the Court's restraint, and they have refused to go as far as their conservative colleagues would like. In both *Jenkins* and *Lewis v. Casey,* Thomas wrote the neoconservative critique of judicial capacity into the U.S. Reports, but none of his colleagues were willing to join him.[8] With the supportive votes of O'Connor and Kennedy, the conservative justices carried the day for judicial restraint in each of these cases, but they were unable to garner majority support for their sweeping denunciations of judicial power.

The Vitality of Liberal Activism

Even in the school desegregation and prisoners' rights cases, then, the Rehnquist Court has not read its own power as narrowly as conservatives have urged, and in a wide range of other cases, either O'Connor or Kennedy (or sometimes both) have gone even further in abandoning their conservative colleagues. Joining with the Court's more liberal justices in case after case, they have reaffirmed and even extended the landmark liberal precedents of the Warren and early Burger years. Over the dissents of one or more of their fellow conservatives, Justices O'Connor and Kennedy joined the Court in reaffirming *Shapiro v. Thompson, Miranda v. Arizona,* the Warren Court's landmark school prayer decisions, the Fourth Amendment exclusionary rule established in *Mapp v. Ohio,* the constitutional guarantee of gender equality first announced by the early Burger Court, and the lodestar of modern liberal activism, *Roe v. Wade.* In the gay rights context, the deciding votes of O'Connor and Kennedy have initiated a potentially expansive new regime of judicially enforceable liberty and equality.

None of these developments were inevitable. The Court issued its surprising reaffirmation of *Roe* in 1992, but it still appeared quite reluctant to extend the realm of unenumerated rights any further. In *Washington v. Glucksberg,* for example, the Court took up the question of physician-assisted suicide, unanimously rejecting a claim of a broad constitutional "right to die." Writing for the Court, Rehnquist followed Justice White's approach in *Bowers v. Hardwick,* framing the question as whether due process liberty "includes a right to commit suicide which itself includes a right to assistance in doing so." Examining the relevant history, Rehnquist found "a consistent and almost universal tradition that has long rejected the asserted right, and continues explicitly to reject it today. . . . To hold for respondents, we would have to reverse centuries of legal doctrine and practice, and strike down the considered policy choice of almost every State." Applying a deferential mode of rationality review, he upheld the statute at issue, noting that the Court was thereby allowing the ongoing "debate about the morality, legality, and practicality of physician assisted suicide . . . to continue, as it should in a democratic society."[9] As I have noted, the modern Court's expansive and evolutionary conception of due process liberty had been a prime target for conservative critique. In Scalia's 1995 Tanner Lectures at Princeton University, for example, he characterized the doctrine of substantive due process as "the departure [from constitutional text] that has enabled judges to do more freewheeling lawmaking than any other" (1997:24). In case after case, Justices Scalia, Thomas, and Rehnquist had followed Hugo Black in denouncing substantive due process as illegitimate judge-made law, and the Court's unanimous decision in *Glucksberg* seemed to suggest that the aspirations of liberal constitutionalism had been severely chastened (Tushnet 1999b:89–90, 2003). The Court's liberal justices joined its conservatives in exercising restraint, and the decision was supported by both the Clinton administration and some leading liberal constitutional scholars.[10] The longstanding conservative critique of judicial power appeared to have made significant inroads into the modern constitutional order.

While their decision in *Glucksberg* was unanimous, however, the justices remained closely divided on the proper scope of judicially enforceable constitutional liberty. Rehnquist wrote for the Court, but fully five justices wrote separately to limit the reach of his holding. Souter relied on Justice Harlan for a broad defense of substantive due process, and O'Connor made clear that the Court's holding should not be taken as a final decision on the question of assisted suicide. As Cass Sunstein noted, O'Connor and the four liberals agreed "that there [wa]s no general right to suicide, assisted or otherwise, [but] left open the possibility that under special circumstances, people might have a right to physician-assisted suicide after all. In other words, the Court left the most fundamental questions undecided. Far from being odd or anomalous, this is the current Court's usual approach" (1999:ix). O'Connor and Souter's distinctive elaboration of Harlan's approach prevented Scalia, Thomas, and Rehnquist from succeeding in their abandonment of judicially enforceable liberty under the Due Process Clause.

In short, when *Glucksberg* was decided in 1997, it remained unclear whose opinion most accurately reflected the Court's view. The debate between Rehnquist and Souter closely replicated the earlier debate between Scalia and William Brennan — and before that, between Black and Harlan — and despite the unanimous holding, the debate remained unresolved. This debate continued in subsequent cases, with Souter serving as the leader of the Court's chastened liberal wing, and O'Connor and Kennedy casting the deciding votes and hence marking the limits of the Court's continued liberal activism. In *Sacramento v. Lewis,* the Court again unanimously rejected a due process claim, but Souter again made clear that Harlan's "reasoned judgment" approach was alive and well. Holding that the Sacramento police did not violate Phillip Lewis's Fourteenth Amendment right to life when he was killed in a car accident during a police chase, Souter observed that "[o]nly a purpose to cause harm unrelated to the legitimate object of arrest will satisfy the element of arbitrary conduct shocking to the conscience, necessary for a due process violation." Scalia and Thomas objected sharply to the Court's revival of Frankfurter's "shocks the conscience" test, and O'Connor and Kennedy wrote separately to express some skepticism of their own, but they were nonetheless willing to join Souter's opinion for the Court.[11] The following year, Scalia, Thomas, and Rehnquist objected to the Court's decision in *Chicago v. Morales,* which relied on due process grounds to invalidate a local ordinance authorizing police officers to order any group of individuals loitering in a public place to disperse if there was reason to believe that someone in the group was a gang member. In the view of Scalia, Thomas, and Rehnquist, the ordinance was perfectly constitutional because the constitutional text includes no "right to loiter" and because the states had a lengthy tradition of regulating loitering. As in so many other cases, however, O'Connor and Kennedy were unpersuaded. They each concurred in the Court's judgment, but wrote separately to clarify the limited reach of the Court's holding.

In 2000, O'Connor wrote the plurality opinion and cast the deciding vote in a case striking down Washington's "grandparent visitation" statute as a violation of the unenumerated "fundamental right of parents to make decisions concerning the care, custody, and control of their children." In doing so, she ignored Scalia's objection that "[j]udicial vindication of 'parental rights' under a Constitution that does not even mention them" would inevitably lead the Court to "usher[ ] in a new regime of judicially prescribed, and federally prescribed, family law." In classic O'Connor style, she split the difference between her colleagues' competing approaches, vacating the state Supreme Court's broad endorsement of parental rights and ruling that the statute had, in fact, been unconstitutionally applied in this case, but leaving for another day the question whether the statute was unconstitutional per se. She characterized parental rights as "perhaps the oldest of the fundamental liberty interests recognized by this Court," but she also noted that the Court could for now leave the question of "the precise scope" of those rights unanswered.[12]

When the Court struck down Nebraska's "partial birth abortion" law in *Stenberg v. Carhart,* that same year, O'Connor's vote was again decisive, and she again wrote separately to clarify the reach of the Court's holding. While the four liberal justices authored a broad reaffirmation of *Casey,* and while Kennedy joined the three anti-*Roe* conservatives in arguing that the statute did not unduly burden the abortion right, O'Connor split the difference. She joined the liberals in striking down the statute at issue, but noted that a number of states had adopted similar laws that were narrower than Nebraska's and that might well be constitutionally valid. In sum, in a long list of cases, O'Connor (and sometimes Kennedy) staked out a moderate position that would continue to protect fundamental personal liberties under the Due Process Clause, while remaining sensitive to the long-standing conservative concern with judicial lawmaking. They struck this balance not by marking off certain categories of law and policy that the courts would not enter, but by moving cautiously whenever they expanded judicially enforceable rights to a new context.

In hindsight, it is clear that the period from *Bowers* to *Glucksberg* marked the low point in the Court's protection of unenumerated liberties. The decades-long abortion battle had chastened even the Court's liberal justices, all of whom became reluctant to create "new" constitutional rights under the Due Process Clause. In this context, Scalia might well have led the Court in abandoning substantive due process altogether had it not been for O'Connor and Kennedy. Just six years after the *Glucksberg* decision, the two centrist justices would join the Court's liberals in overturning *Bowers,* with Kennedy offering a sweeping judicial declaration of constitutional liberty.

Writing for the Court in *Lawrence v. Texas,* Kennedy ignored *Glucksberg* altogether, building instead on a long line of earlier decisions, particularly *Casey,* in holding that gays and lesbians "are entitled to respect for their private lives." As in *Bowers,* the *Lawrence* case involved two gay men arrested for committing consensual sodomy in one of their own homes, but in sharp contrast to its earlier ruling, the Court held here that "[t]he State cannot demean their existence or control their destiny by making their private sexual conduct a crime. Their right to liberty under the Due Process Clause gives them the full right to engage in their conduct without intervention of the government." Reiterating his support for an evolutionary conception of the Constitution, Kennedy noted that when looking to our nation's history and traditions to give meaning to constitutional liberty, the Court should weigh recent traditions more heavily than ancient ones.[13]

Because Kennedy wrote for a judicial majority even without her vote, O'Connor was unable to limit the reach of the Court's holding. Still, she concurred in the judgment without joining his opinion, writing separately to indicate her own more narrow grounds for decision. Kennedy's holding had the effect of invalidating the criminal sodomy laws of thirteen states, but O'Connor addressed only those four that singled out same-sex sodomy for disparate treatment.[14] Relying on the Equal Protection rather than the Due Process Clause, O'Connor insisted that "the State cannot single out one identifiable class of citizens for punishment that does not apply to everyone else, with moral disapproval as the only asserted state interest for the law."[15]

While Kennedy's opinion for the Court in *Lawrence* relied heavily on *Casey,* O'Connor's concurring opinion built on another liberal precedent for which she and Kennedy had been responsible. In *Romer v. Evans,* they had joined the four liberal justices to strike down an anti-gay rights initiative in Colorado. Writing for the Court, Kennedy had relied on a line of decisions holding that "if the constitutional conception of 'equal protection of the laws' means anything, it must at the very least mean that a bare congressional desire to harm a politically unpopular group cannot constitute a *legitimate* governmental interest."[16] In these cases, the Court had built on Justice Stone's skepticism of legislative decisions that appeared to be motivated solely by prejudice against an unpopular minority, holding that such legislation was invalid even under the Court's lowest level of scrutiny. As Kennedy put it, the Colorado initiative at issue in *Romer* failed even this minimal scrutiny because such laws "raise[d] the inevitable inference that the disadvantage im-

posed is born of animosity toward the class of persons affected." The anti-gay
rights provision, he insisted, adopted "a classification of persons undertaken
for its own sake, something the Equal Protection Clause does not permit. . . .
A State cannot so deem a class of persons a stranger to its laws." [17]

Kennedy's *Romer* opinion was a cautious one, but he seemed to recognize
that the federal courts must protect minority groups that have faced prejudice and discrimination from majoritarian tyranny, and that gays and lesbians are such a group. He did not explicitly apply heightened scrutiny, but
he also did not preclude such scrutiny in the future, and his application of the
rational basis test revealed a similar concern for protecting gays and lesbians
from at least the most overt forms of state-sponsored discrimination.[18] Thus,
while Kennedy was careful to limit the holding's reach, it remains a striking
instance of liberal activism by the Rehnquist Court. As Louis Seidman has
noted, the *Romer* decision revealed "the radical possibilities offered by a
brand of constitutionalism that even the cautious and conservative Justices
who currently populate th[e] Court are unwilling to repudiate" (1996:73).

Unlike their fellow conservative justices, O'Connor and Kennedy continue to believe that the protection of relatively powerless minority groups
against majoritarian discrimination is one of the Court's most important duties. Just a month after *Romer,* they both joined Ginsburg's opinion striking
down the Virginia Military Institute's male-only admissions policy and insisting that states must demonstrate an "exceedingly persuasive justification"
for any gender-based classifications in the law. Writing for the Court in
United States v. Virginia, Ginsburg granted that "[s]ex classifications may be
used to compensate women for particular economic disabilities [they have]
suffered, . . . [but] may not be used, as they once were, . . . to create or per-
petuate the legal, social, and economic inferiority of women." As Kennedy
had suggested in *Romer,* moreover, Ginsburg indicated that the list of classifications subject to strict judicial scrutiny might well expand over time.[19]

As in *Casey,* the betrayal of his conservative colleagues in *Romer, United
States v. Virginia,* and *Lawrence* led Scalia to publish particularly angry dissenting opinions. In *Romer* and the VMI case, he denounced the majority for
applying some unacknowledged form of heightened scrutiny, called into
question the entire architecture of modern equal protection doctrine, and
criticized the Court for thwarting the democratic will. Joined by Rehnquist
and Thomas in his *Romer* dissent, Scalia accused the Court of applying
heightened scrutiny without admitting it, and insisted that under the *Caro-*

lene Products approach — which he carefully avoided endorsing — gays and lesbians did not warrant such heightened judicial protection. He argued that gays and lesbians were not in fact politically powerless, but actually a powerful special interest group, and that anti-gay animus was not in fact illegitimate prejudice, but rather legitimate disapproval of immoral behavior.[20] Similarly, Scalia pointed out that Ginsburg's requirement of an "exceedingly persuasive justification" for VMI's gender discrimination appeared to represent a tightening of the intermediate scrutiny that the Court had generally applied to such policies in the past. He complained that this unacknowledged adoption of strict scrutiny was particularly unwarranted "because it is perfectly clear that, if the question of the applicable standard of review for sex-based classifications were to be regarded as an appropriate subject for reconsideration, the stronger argument would be not for elevating the standard to strict scrutiny, but for reducing it to rational basis review." In support of this argument, Scalia insisted that "rational-basis review of sex-based classifications would be much more in accord with the genesis of heightened standards of judicial review" — again, the *Carolene Products* footnote — because women "constitute a majority of the electorate" and have achieved "a long list of legislation" demonstrating their political power. As in *Romer*, he appealed to the *Carolene Products* approach without explicitly endorsing it, and he argued that it did not justify the extension of heightened scrutiny to laws that discriminated on grounds other than race.[21]

From Scalia's perspective, the Court's modern equal protection doctrine seemed to authorize the unelected justices "to evaluate everything under the sun by applying one of three tests: 'rational basis' scrutiny, intermediate scrutiny, or strict scrutiny." He complained that "[t]hese tests [were] no more scientific than their names suggest, and [that] a further element of randomness [was] added by the fact that it is largely up to us which test will be applied in each case." Insisting that the modern Court had used such doctrinal tests as a vehicle for revising the Constitution, he objected that "whatever abstract tests we may choose to devise, they cannot supersede — and indeed ought to be crafted *so as to reflect*— those constant and unbroken national traditions that embody the people's understanding of ambiguous constitutional texts."[22] Following Justice Black, Scalia emphasized that the meaning of the written Constitution was fixed at its origin and that the formal amendment process is the sole legitimate method of constitutional change. In response to the claim that this historical approach would quickly produce an outmoded

Constitution, he insisted that the framers recognized the need for change and that they provided for it in Article V:

> The virtue of a democratic system . . . is that it readily enables the people, over time, to be persuaded that what they took for granted is not so, and to change their laws accordingly. That system is destroyed if the smug assurances of each age are removed from the democratic process and written into the Constitution. So to counterbalance the Court's criticism of our ancestors, let me say a word in their praise: they left us free to change. The same cannot be said of this most illiberal Court, which has embarked on a course of inscribing one after another of the current preferences of the society (and in some cases only the counter majoritarian preferences of the society's law trained elite) into our Basic Law.[23]

In light of his fixed vision of the Constitution, Scalia denounced both 1996 equal protection decisions as exercises of illegitimate government by judiciary. In the VMI case he observed that "[s]ince it is entirely clear that the Constitution of the United States — the old one — takes no sides in this educational debate, I dissent," and in *Romer* he complained that his colleagues were engaged in "acts, not of judicial judgment, but of political will." He insisted that "[t]his Court has no business imposing upon all Americans the resolution favored by the elite class from which the Members of this institution are selected."[24]

Scalia echoed all of these arguments in the substantive due process context in *Lawrence*. As in the equal protection cases, he read the Court's precedents narrowly, insisting that they did not authorize the invalidation of the sodomy laws of thirteen states, but even more fundamentally, he called those precedents themselves into question. Because Kennedy's decision in *Lawrence* relied so heavily on *Casey*, Scalia saw fit to reiterate his opposition to that holding, reserving particular scorn for the *Casey* plurality's "sweet-mystery-of-life passage."[25] Referencing *Lochner v. New York*, he proceeded to call into question the jurisprudence of substantive due process more generally, and to defend the Court's restrained approach in *Bowers* as "utterly unassailable." Deriding Kennedy's argument, he concluded by noting that "[i]t is indeed true that 'later generations can see that laws once thought necessary and proper in fact serve only to oppress'; and when that happens, later generations can repeal those laws. But it is the premise of our system that those judgments are to be made by the people, and not imposed by a governing caste that knows best." Reiterating a complaint he had expressed in *Romer*,

Scalia insisted that the Court's holding was "the product of a law-profession culture[ ] that has largely signed on to the so-called homosexual agenda, by which I mean the agenda promoted by some homosexual activists directed at eliminating the moral opprobrium that has traditionally attached to homosexual conduct."[26]

While Scalia is well known for his acerbic opinions, his rhetoric in these cases was particularly overwrought. His critique of society's liberal "law-trained elite" reflects a long-standing conservative device, but as Richard Brisbin has observed, "the frankness of Scalia's language seems atypical [for judges, and] appears more like the rhetoric of the militant political activist. Indeed, Scalia's opinions often ring with phrases like those spoken by the politicians and pundits of the recently revived conservative movement" (1997:ix). In *Romer*, Scalia characterized Kennedy's arguments as "ridiculous," "novel," and "extravagant," and objected that they have "no foundation in American constitutional law, and barely pretend[ ] to." He insisted that the Court was relying on a principle that "the world has never heard of" and complained that "our constitutional jurisprudence has achieved terminal silliness."[27] As Seidman has noted, Scalia's *Romer* dissent combined three traditional elements of "Warren Court bashing," only one of which has typically been found in the justices' written opinions: "Harlan's disgust with the supposed lack of technical competence of his colleagues and dismay at their failure to appreciate the limits of their role, . . . the sarcastic and condescending laments of the 'scholastic mandarins' who criticized the Court in the law reviews, and the angry, spasmodic responses to the Court's perceived assault on conventional mores voiced in tabloid editorials and on highway billboards" (1996:69).

Scalia emphasized his critique of government by judiciary throughout these dissenting opinions, but the Court's activism, by itself, cannot explain the stridency of his rhetoric or the depth of his anger. He objected to these decisions so strongly because his colleagues were (in his view) imposing their own predilections on the American people, but also because those predilections were themselves substantively objectionable (again, in his view). After all, as I suggested in chapter 5 and explore more fully below, there are a number of constitutional contexts in which Scalia is willing to exercise judicial power quite actively. In this light, his objection to the *Romer* and *Lawrence* decisions must be based at least in part on the substantive content of the Court's constitutional vision, and not solely on the fact that the unelected justices were thwarting the popular will.

Justice Scalia's dissenting rhetoric in the 1990s was sharper than that of previous generations for another reason as well. By this point, he had fully expected to lead the Court in abandoning liberal activism, and his rhetoric evinced anger at unexpected defeat. Despite his most ardent efforts in *Romer, United States v. Virginia,* and *Lawrence,* the Court has preserved a robust conception of judicially enforceable fundamental rights. In the area of gender equality, even Rehnquist came to acknowledge that a meaningful standard of review must be applied to state-sponsored discrimination, concurring in the judgment in the VMI case. In the gay rights context, Rehnquist has continued to join Scalia and Thomas in dissent, but they have been unable to derail the Court's steady expansion of constitutional liberty and equality. The Rehnquist Court has certainly been more cautious than its predecessors in protecting unenumerated rights, granting as much room as possible for democratic majorities to legislate around the edges of those rights, but Scalia and his conservative colleagues have simply failed in their effort to displace such protection altogether. The abortion and gay rights decisions are the most notable examples, but they are part of a more general pattern in which the current conservative Court has continued to exercise judicial power to protect constitutional rights and liberties that are decidedly in the tradition of Warren Court liberalism.

Justices O'Connor and Kennedy have not always abandoned their conservative colleagues, but even when they have voted together, they have often refused to go as far as Scalia and Thomas would like. In the criminal procedure context, for example, the five conservative justices have regularly chipped away at the landmark precedents of the Warren Court, but even here — in cases involving Fourth Amendment limits on police searches, Fifth and Sixth Amendment limits on trial procedures, and Eighth Amendment limits on criminal punishment — the Court has refused to abandon these judicially enforceable constitutional rights altogether. When the five conservative justices have united in rejecting a constitutional challenge to state criminal procedures, O'Connor has often written separately to limit the reach of the Court's holding. And she and Kennedy have often used their decisive swing votes to search, case-by-case, for deprivations of constitutionally protected liberty that have gone too far.

In the immigration rights context, for example, O'Connor joined the four liberal justices in *Zadvydas v. Davis* to hold that the indefinite detention of immigrants subject to deportation would raise serious constitutional questions. Kennedy joined the conservative dissenters in *Zadvydas,* but just three days earlier, he had joined the four liberals to hold that a statute entirely precluding judicial review of deportation orders would be constitutionally questionable. As in *Zadvydas,* the liberal justices avoided the constitutional issue in *INS v. St. Cyr* by narrowly construing the relevant statute, a resort to the "passive virtues" that may well have been necessary to garner O'Connor and Kennedy's fifth votes. In *Demore v. Hyung Joon Kim,* both O'Connor and Kennedy voted with the conservatives, holding that Congress was constitutionally free to require the temporary detention of a deportable alien even in the absence of a "determination that he posed either a danger to society or a flight risk." Even here, however, Kennedy (and Rehnquist) limited the reach of the conservative decision by refusing to join O'Connor, Scalia, and Thomas in holding that Congress had deprived the federal courts of jurisdiction to review such detention decisions altogether.[28] Similarly, in a variety of Fourth and Fifth Amendment cases, the Rehnquist Court's conservative majority has granted state authorities greater leeway to conduct searches and encourage confessions, but O'Connor and Kennedy have still drawn some lines.[29]

Scalia and Thomas have also urged greater deference in the Eighth Amendment context, insisting that the provision places no requirement of proportionality on criminal punishments. In their view, for example, a state's "three strikes and you're out" law would face no constitutional barrier even if it had the effect of imposing life imprisonment as a punishment for relatively minor crimes. In two 2003 decisions from California, their conservative colleagues joined them to uphold the sentences under review, but they refused to jettison the proportionality requirement altogether. As is her wont, O'Connor reserved the right to invalidate a criminal sentence in some future case if she found it unconstitutionally disproportionate.[30] In another Eighth Amendment context, Scalia and Thomas insisted that the ban on cruel and unusual punishments applied only to the act of sentencing itself and not to the conditions of confinement once a sentence has been imposed, but O'Connor and Kennedy disagreed, holding that needlessly abusive prison conditions were sometimes unconstitutionally cruel and unusual. In *Hope v. Pelzer,* for example, O'Connor and Kennedy joined a six-justice liberal majority to hold that Alabama prison guards had violated the Eighth Amendment by handcuffing a prisoner to a "hitching post" located well above his head, and leaving him there for seven hours in the hot sun with little drinking water and no bathroom breaks. Thomas had complained for several years that the Court was turning the Eighth Amendment into a "National Code of

Prison Regulation," but he never persuaded anyone besides Scalia or Rehnquist to join him, and sometimes not even them.[31]

In the Court's death penalty cases, Justice O'Connor has again generally supported the conservative doctrine of restraint while indicating that her deference to majoritarian deprivations of rights has some limits. In *Atkins v. Virginia,* she wrote for the Court in holding that the nation's evolving standards of decency now prohibited the execution of the mentally retarded, thus overturning her own opinion for the Court in *Penry v. Lynaugh* thirteen years earlier. Joined by Kennedy and the four liberal justices, she held in *Atkins* that such executions were categorically prohibited by the Eighth Amendment after all. Just four months after drawing this line at the execution of the mentally retarded, she and Kennedy refused to draw the same line at the execution of juveniles, but the following year, they were back with the liberals in *Wiggins v. Smith,* throwing out a death sentence on the grounds of ineffective assistance of counsel.[32] In short, the line that O'Connor and Kennedy have drawn between constitutionally legitimate and illegitimate death sentences stands as the law of the land.

In addition to criminal procedure, the conservatives have also led the Court in adopting a more restrained posture in the Establishment Clause context. Here again, O'Connor and Kennedy have set the limits of the Court's newfound deference. As I noted in chapter 5, they have continued to join their liberal colleagues in holding that the First Amendment prohibits state-sanctioned prayer in the public schools. Similarly, they voted in 1994 to hold that the State of New York could not constitutionally create a special school district just for members of a Satmar Hasidic sect in the village of Kiryas Joel. While they joined most of Justice Souter's opinion for the Court, however, they each wrote separately to note that New York's problem had been caused in part by the Court's own case law, which had unduly restricted state and local governments from accommodating religion by providing special education services within private sectarian schools. They each suggested, in particular, that the Court's decision in *Aguilar v. Felton* should be reconsidered, a suggestion that Scalia, Thomas, and Rehnquist echoed in dissent.[33]

With five justices having announced their willingness to overturn *Aguilar,* the original parties to that case filed an unusual procedural motion, under Federal Rule of Civil Procedure 60(b), persuading the Court to rehear the case and reach the opposite result in *Agostini v. Felton.* In the earlier case, the Court had held that the state could not send public school teachers into parochial schools to provide remedial education. It was this holding that had led the state instead to create a wholly separate public school district for Kiryas Joel. In *Agostini*, O'Connor wrote for a five-justice majority in holding that New York was free to provide remedial education in the parochial schools after all. Moving away from the high wall of separation that the Warren and Burger Courts had built, the five conservative justices announced that they would allow a much greater degree of legislative accommodation of religion.

Agostini was one of a number of cases in which Souter led the liberals in holding that the Establishment Clause prohibits government aid to religious schools that might be divertible to sectarian activities; Thomas led the conservative members of the Court in holding that such aid is permissible as long as it "is offered on a neutral basis and the aid is secular in content," even if it is diverted to religious purposes; and O'Connor split the difference, arguing that the Establishment Clause prohibits government aid that is actually diverted (not merely potentially divertible) to sectarian activities, even if it is provided on a neutral basis.[34] Three years after *Agostini*, for example, the Court upheld a related policy under which public school districts received federal funds to provide computer equipment and other instructional materials to both public and private schools, again overturning a precedent to reach this judgment. Writing for a four-justice plurality in *Mitchell v. Helms*, Thomas emphasized the policy's neutrality among religious sects and the prominent role of private choice in directing the money to particular schools, apparently crafting his Establishment Clause standards with the looming issue of school vouchers in mind. Souter continued to emphasize the flat ban on subsidization of religion as a central element of the Establishment Clause, and so it was clear that he would strike down a vouchers policy despite its evenhandedness. But it was also clear that O'Connor again would have the deciding vote.

In *Mitchell*, O'Connor voted with Thomas but refused to join his opinion. Two years later, in *Zelman v. Simmons-Harris*, she joined her four conservative colleagues in upholding a school vouchers policy from Ohio in which the vast majority of participating schools were religious institutions. In doing so, however, she once again wrote separately to clarify the limited reach of the holding, insisting that the Court was departing from its Establishment Clause precedents only marginally, if at all. On her reading of those precedents, when a government program "distributes aid to beneficiaries, rather than directly to service providers," it does not violate the Establishment Clause so long as the "beneficiaries . . . have a genuine choice among religious and nonreligious organizations when determining the organization to which they will direct that aid." And on her reading of the record in *Zelman,* "the Cleveland voucher program afford[ed] parents of eligible children genuine nonreligious options" and hence was constitutionally permissible.[35]

Despite their agreement in the vouchers case, the five conservative justices do not represent a unified bloc in the Establishment Clause context any more than elsewhere, as O'Connor and Kennedy have supported a stronger principle of separation than their conservative colleagues. By reaching liberal results in *Lee v. Weisman, Kiryas Joel,* and *Santa Fe Independent School District v. Doe,* they have relegated the demands of Rehnquist, Scalia, and Thomas for judicial deference to a series of angry dissents. Moreover, O'Connor's fact-focused, case-by-case decisionmaking approach is the antithesis of Scalia's penchant for categorical line drawing. Concurring in *Kiryas Joel,* for example, she called into question the doctrinal test that the Court had developed in *Lemon v. Kurtzman,* acknowledging that "[i]t is always appealing to look for a single test, a Grand Unified Theory that would resolve all the cases that may arise under a particular Clause," but insisting that "the same constitutional principle may operate very differently in different contexts." As with any other complex constitutional question, she noted, there were many factors relevant to the Establishment Clause inquiry, and they were likely to be present in different degrees in different cases. In this light, O'Connor insisted that "setting forth a unitary test for a broad set of cases may sometimes do more harm than good." Scalia agreed that the *Lemon* test should be abandoned, but pointedly noted that "[u]nlike Justice O'Connor, . . . I would not replace *Lemon* with nothing, and let the case law 'evolve' into a series of situation-specific rules . . . unconstrained by any 'rigid influence.' . . . To replace *Lemon* with nothing is simply to announce that we are now so bold that we no longer feel the need even to pretend that our haphazard course of Establishment Clause decisions is governed by any principle. The foremost principle I would apply is fidelity to the longstanding traditions of our people, which surely provide the diversity of treatment that Justice O'Connor seeks, but do not leave us to our own devices."[36] Like many of her scholarly critics, Scalia has rejected O'Connor's case-by-case approach as arbitrary and unprincipled.

Thus, even in those contexts in which the Rehnquist Court has been most successful in curtailing liberal activism, the conservative justices have been internally divided. In the religious establishment cases, as in the equal protection and due process contexts, Scalia, Thomas, and Rehnquist have urged sweeping doctrinal revisions in originalism's name, but they have at best had only partial success. Most importantly, the limits of that success have been defined not by their own views, but by those of Justices O'Connor and Kennedy. The constitutional line between government funding for parochial school tuition (a permissible accommodation of religion) and state-sponsored prayer in the public schools (a prohibited establishment of religion) is not one that Scalia, Thomas, and Rehnquist have drawn, as they would defer to elected majorities in both instances. But O'Connor and Kennedy have disagreed, and as I have sought to make clear in this and other contexts, their views are decisive on the current Court.

O'Connor and Kennedy frequently have cast deciding votes to support liberal activism and often, though less frequently, have cast deciding votes to support conservative restraint. In both sets of cases, they have used their votes to mark the limits of the Court's holding, often announcing such limits in a separate opinion that ties the holding to the facts of the particular case and simultaneously suggests a number of hypothetical cases that might come out differently. Among the cases I have discussed so far in this chapter, either O'Connor or Kennedy has done so in *Missouri v. Jenkins, Glucksberg, Sacramento v. Lewis, Chicago v. Morales, Stenberg, Lawrence, Demore v. Hyung Joon Kim, Kiryas Joel, Mitchell,* and *Zelman.* As I indicated in chapter 5, there are a number of pre-1994 examples of such behavior as well. When they actually vote against their conservative colleagues in a landmark case — as in *Lawrence,* for example — it is clear that the conservative majority is divided. Even when they vote together, however, O'Connor's and Kennedy's separate, limiting opinions have important practical effects. Their fellow conservative justices clearly have treated such doctrinal limits seriously, often writing separate opinions of their own to pull the Court's holding in the opposite direction. In case after case, moreover, the opinions by O'Connor and Kennedy have served to inform both the lower courts and the elected legislatures of the limited reach of the Court's holdings and to signal that the Court itself might revisit the issue in the future.[37]

In a wide variety of doctrinal contexts, these two Reagan appointees have cast deciding votes in favor of preserving key tenets of modern liberal constitutionalism. Following Justice Harlan, they have reaffirmed that the judicial role includes the common law elaboration of constitutional liberty, and they have extended this approach into the equal protection context as well. Again following Harlan, however, they have sought to cabin and constrain this judicial elaboration with a healthy dose of history and self-restraint. While

Casey has sewn abortion rights safely into the constitutional fabric for the foreseeable future, for example, the current Court has allowed the states greater leeway to regulate abortion access. And while the Court is now willing to extend constitutional equality to protect gays and lesbians in at least some contexts, there is little chance that it will revive the broad substantive guarantee of racial equality toward which the Warren and early Burger Courts had reached. Again, the conservative justices have indeed put significant limits on a number of the broad constitutional rights guarantees that they inherited, but in light of the stated aims of the conservative critics of the Warren Court, these limits have been imposed only at the margins. From the perspective of pro-life activists, the surprising fact is not that the Rehnquist Court narrowed the scope of constitutionally protected abortion rights, but that it nonetheless reaffirmed *Roe's* central holding. If one of the conservatives' goals has been to put a stop to such judicial decisions protecting liberal rights claims, then they have clearly failed.

The Flowering of Conservative Activism

When constitutional conservatives have sought to build upon, rather than disavow, the rights-protecting function of modern constitutionalism, they have been much more successful. As I have been arguing at some length, modern conservatives have tried to curtail the liberal activism they inherited from the Warren Court, while simultaneously seeking to develop a distinctive new conservative activism of their own. They have been more successful at this latter task because Justices O'Connor and Kennedy have generally proven more willing to create new rights than to abandon old ones. Again, however, Justices Scalia and Thomas have not been able to push this activism as far as they would like because O'Connor and Kennedy have regularly prevented the Court from adopting their colleagues' sweeping, categorical principles.

O'Connor and Kennedy do not always agree with each other. They each emphasize particular areas in which they are concerned with the Court's overreaching. But since both of their votes are essential to the conservative majority on the Court, they each have the ability to set the limits of conservative activism in a particular context. In the Court's affirmative action cases, for example, Kennedy has fully joined the color-blind activism advanced by Scalia, Thomas, and Rehnquist, but O'Connor has not. The same has been true in some of the conservative free speech and free exercise decisions; but in the federalism and property rights contexts, it has more often been Kennedy who has tempered the Court's conservative activism with a dose of caution.

Once having consolidated their judicial majority in the mid-1990s, the conservative justices quickly moved to strike down those state and federal policies that violated their vision of constitutionally limited government. In the affirmative action context, Scalia and Thomas led the way, consistently maintaining that the Fourteenth Amendment imposed a strict regime of color-blind law. When the Court scrutinized a federal minority business set aside policy in *Adarand Constructors, Inc. v. Pena,* for example, Scalia reiterated that "government can never have a 'compelling interest' in discriminating on the basis of race in order to 'make up' for past racial discrimination in the opposite direction." In his view, there should be "no such thing as either a creditor or a debtor race" because "[t]hat concept is alien to the Constitution's focus upon the individual, and its rejection of dispositions based on race." As he had argued six years earlier in *Richmond v. Croson,* he insisted that "[t]o pursue the concept of racial entitlement — even for the most admirable and benign of purposes — is to reinforce and preserve for future mischief the way of thinking that produced race slavery, race privilege and race hatred. In the eyes of government, we are just one race here. It is American." [38]

If possible, Thomas's rejection of liberal egalitarianism swept even more broadly than Scalia's. As I have noted, he is singularly hostile to judicially imposed egalitarian reforms of public institutions like schools and prisons. In *Lewis v. Casey,* he alone called into question the landmark Warren Court precedents of *Griffin v. Illinois* and *Douglas v. California* — describing them as "rooted in largely obsolete theories of equal protection" [39] — and in *Missouri v. Jenkins,* he alone insisted that *Brown v. Board of Education* did not outlaw all racially imbalanced schools, but merely prohibited explicit racial classifications in the law. "At the heart of . . . the Equal Protection Clause," Thomas argued in *Jenkins,* "lies the principle that the government must treat citizens as individuals, and not as members of racial, ethnic, or religious groups. It is for this reason that we must subject all racial classifications to the strictest of scrutiny." [40] Like Scalia, Thomas wrote separately in *Adarand,* insisting that "[a]s far as the Constitution is concerned, it is irrelevant whether a government's racial classifications are drawn by those who wish to oppress a race or by those who have a sincere desire to help those thought to be disadvantaged." [41]

Scalia and Thomas have pressed this point most persistently, but Justices Rehnquist and Kennedy have not been far behind. Kennedy had first made his color-blind views known in an apocalyptic dissenting opinion in *Metro Broadcasting v. FCC,* invoking Jim Crow segregation, South African apartheid, and Nazi citizenship law to express his opinion of the affirmative action program at issue.[42] Writing for the Court five years later in *Miller v. Johnson,* he cited *Bakke, Croson,* and *Adarand* for the proposition that the "central mandate" of the Equal Protection Clause is "racial neutrality in governmental decisionmaking," and he insisted that "[t]his rule obtains with equal force regardless of the race of those burdened or benefitted by a particular classification." Holding that "the Government must treat citizens as individuals, not as simply components of a racial, religious, sexual, or national class," he invalidated a race-conscious districting scheme from Georgia.[43]

In this last case, the conservative justices were building on their holding in *Shaw v. Reno (Shaw I),* following their color-blind principles into the political thicket of legislative districting. They sometimes tried to reconcile these decisions with their commitment to restraint by arguing that the Court itself had originally been responsible for the unconstitutional gerrymandering that it was now called upon to strike down.[44] Even if this claim were persuasive, however, the Court was still overturning decisions made in the first instance by democratically accountable state legislatures and governors, along with the federal Justice Department, in an arena that was once considered altogether beyond the ambit of judicial competence. Following the logic of the Rehnquist Court's holdings, federal judges in at least one case went so far as to throw out the results of democratic elections.[45] In a role reversal from the Warren Court years, the dissenting liberal justices in these cases denounced the conservative majority for interfering with the operation of the political branches, complaining that the Court was shifting "responsibility for setting district boundaries from the state legislatures, which are invested with front line authority by Article I, to the courts, and truly to this Court, which is left to superintend the drawing of every legislative district in the land."[46] In the affirmative action context, such arguments for judicial deference fully persuaded the Court's liberals, and even more importantly, gave pause to Justice O'Connor.

Alone among her conservative colleagues, O'Connor regularly expressed some concern with the Court's sweeping interventions in this context. She cast a number of deciding votes to strike down affirmative action policies, but as in the Court's liberal activist decisions, she often limited the reach of the

Court's holdings by suggesting other circumstances under which such policies might survive constitutional scrutiny. Writing for the Court in *Adarand*, O'Connor extended *Croson* and overruled *Metro Broadcasting* by holding that strict scrutiny should apply to race-conscious policies at the federal as well as state levels, but she pointedly insisted that such scrutiny would not always be fatal and that some race-conscious plans might still be upheld. Exercising the "passive virtues," she would not even let the Court issue a final decision on the particular dispute, which she reversed and remanded without an explicit declaration of unconstitutionality.

Similarly, in the racial gerrymandering decisions, Justice O'Connor joined her conservative colleagues to hold that government should generally not consider race when drawing electoral districts, but stopped short of Scalia and Thomas's insistence that such racial gerrymandering was always invalid. In O'Connor's decisive view, race should not be the predominant factor in districting decisions, but it may be considered in an effort to achieve some particularly important state interests. She has frequently written for the Court in these cases, relegating the views of Scalia and Thomas to concurring opinions. In *Bush v. Vera*, she took the unusual step of writing both the Court's plurality opinion and a separate concurring opinion in the same case, with the concurring opinion an effort to clarify the limited reach of the main opinion. And in *Easley v. Cromartie,* when the boundaries of North Carolina's Twelfth Congressional District came back to the Court for the fourth time, O'Connor voted with the four liberals to uphold them, despite what the other four conservatives characterized as a persistent pattern of race-conscious districting.[47] Her deciding vote had led the Court into this "political thicket" eight years earlier, in *Shaw I,* and it was now her deciding vote that marked the limits of this field of conservative activism. As Tinsley Yarbrough (2002) has noted, this story remains unfinished, but it seems likely that state legislatures will continue to take race into account when drawing electoral districts. If they do so, it will be the result of O'Connor's deciding vote.

Even more dramatically, public universities continue to employee race-conscious admissions policies because O'Connor has decided that they may do so. Each time O'Connor cast a deciding vote to strike down a race-conscious policy, she insisted that such policies might be legitimate under certain circumstances, implicitly calling attention to the momentous question that the Court had not revisited since *Bakke:* whether the race-conscious admissions policies in use at hundreds of colleges and universities throughout the country are constitutionally permissible. Throughout the 1990s, the Center for Individual Rights (CIR) had been waging a coordinated, nation-wide litigation campaign against such policies, persuading the Fifth Circuit to hold that the University of Texas Law School was unconstitutionally dis-criminating against white applicants, and filing similar suits against the Uni-versities of Washington and Michigan.[48] Successfully orchestrating a conflict among the federal circuits, CIR finally persuaded the High Court to revisit the issue during its 2002 term.

In two landmark decisions involving the University of Michigan, O'Con-nor thwarted the conservative litigators (and her conservative colleagues) by adhering to Justice Powell's compromise in *Bakke*. She voted with the four conservative justices (and Justice Breyer) to strike down Michigan's under-graduate admissions policy, which weighed applicants on a numerical scale and automatically awarded a twenty-point bonus to all underrepresented mi-norities, but she voted with the four liberal justices to uphold Michigan's law school admissions policy, which gave a more flexible boost to such minori-ties in the course of individualized consideration of every applicant. In doing so, she garnered a judicial majority for Powell's long-contested endorsement of race-conscious measures to promote educational diversity, thus entrench-ing his analysis into constitutional law for the foreseeable future.

Justice O'Connor refused to join her conservative colleagues in invalidat-ing the law school policy because, like Powell, she was convinced that the courts should balance the principle of color-blind equality with appropriate deference to university officials on matters of educational policy. Citing Pow-ell's opinions in *Bakke* and *Board of Curators of the University of Missouri* v. *Horowitz*, along with Justice Stevens's opinion in *Regents of the University of Michigan v. Ewing*, O'Connor noted that her holding in *Grutter* was "in keeping with [the Court's] tradition of giving a degree of deference to a uni-versity's academic decisions, within constitutionally prescribed limits." Re-markably, given the Rehnquist Court's willingness to enforce its vision of color-blind law in earlier cases, she held that "[t]he Law School's educational judgment that [student body] diversity is essential to its educational mis-sion is one to which we defer." This deference was not without limits, and O'Connor undertook an independent review of the university's evidence for the educational benefits of diversity; but that review was much more defer-ential than the one that CIR was urging. Quoting Powell, she insisted that "'good faith' on the part of a university [should be] 'presumed' absent 'a showing to the contrary.'" This deference was justified for O'Connor because, like Powell, she was convinced that "[n]ot every decision influenced by race is equally objectionable."[49]

This point marked a fundamental disagreement with her fellow conservatives, who had long insisted that "that there is a moral [and] constitutional equivalence between laws designed to subjugate a race and those that distribute benefits on the basis of race in order to foster some current notion of equality."[50] Continuing to insist on the strict judicial enforcement of color-blind law, Justices Scalia and Thomas rejected O'Connor's holding that educational diversity was a compelling state interest, while Rehnquist and Kennedy emphasized that neither of the University of Michigan's admissions policies was narrowly tailored to promote that interest. All four of these conservative justices expressed considerable skepticism toward the educational officials responsible for adopting and administering the policies, complaining that "the ostensibly flexible nature of the Law School's admissions program that the Court finds appealing appears to be, in practice, a carefully managed program designed to ensure proportionate representation of applicants from selected minority groups." They were particularly incensed by "the unprecedented deference the Court gives to the Law School, an approach inconsistent with the very concept of 'strict scrutiny.'"[51]

The Rehnquist Court's affirmative action decisions have been part of a broader pattern in which the five conservative justices have endorsed the active judicial enforcement of conservative constitutional principles, only to have either O'Connor or Kennedy frustrate their conservative colleagues by limiting the reach of this activism. In their effort to constitutionalize the critique of the modern welfare-regulatory state, for example, the conservative justices have turned to several preexisting strains in constitutional discourse that lend support to their commitments — most importantly, the Constitution's federalism-based limits on national legislative power. As I have noted in chapter 4 and 5, Rehnquist was fleetingly successful during the Burger years in persuading the Court to revive long-discarded constitutional limits on congressional power. When the Court reversed course, overturning *National League of Cities v. Usery* in *Garcia v. San Antonio Metropolitan Transit Authority,* Rehnquist predicted that his approach would one day again prevail, and he subsequently led the Court in ensuring that this prediction proved correct. In a series of widely noted decisions under his leadership, the Court has revived pre–New Deal constitutional arguments, and crafted some new ones as well, in order to strike down a variety of federal statutes as illegitimate infringements on state authority. Again, however, despite the sweeping calls for judicial enforcement of limited government sounded by Scalia, Thomas, and Rehnquist, O'Connor and Kennedy have been unwilling to go so far. They have joined their conservative colleagues to form a reliable five-justice majority in the recent federalism decisions, but they have often stopped short of endorsing the sweeping conservative activism that their colleagues have demanded.

This "federalism revolution," as it has sometimes been called, began in earnest with *United States v. Lopez,* when the Court struck down a federal statute on Commerce Clause grounds for the first time since the New Deal. Following a long line of modern cases, the Clinton administration had defended the Gun-Free School Zones Act by arguing that the Interstate Commerce Clause grants Congress the power to regulate even intrastate activities, so long as they "substantially affect" interstate commerce, and that the possession of guns in public schools clearly does so. In support of its argument, the administration garnered evidence that "violent crime reduces the willingness of individuals to travel to areas within the country that are perceived to be unsafe" and that "[a] handicapped educational process [caused by the presence of guns in schools] will result in a less productive citizenry." Writing for the Court, Rehnquist rejected these arguments because they did not appear to have any limits: "Under the theories that the Government presents . . . , it is difficult to perceive any limitation on federal power, even in areas such as criminal law enforcement or education where States historically have been sovereign." Surveying the modern precedents, Rehnquist acknowledged that the Court had upheld a variety of congressional regulations of local economic activity, so long as that activity "substantially affected interstate commerce." The most notorious of these precedents, for conservatives, was *Wickard v. Filburn,* the 1942 decision upholding the federal regulation of wheat grown for home consumption. Rehnquist insisted, however, that the object of the congressional regulation must itself be "economic activity," and in his view, the Gun-Free School Zones Act was clearly "a criminal statute that by its terms has nothing to do with 'commerce' or any sort of economic enterprise, however broadly one might define those terms." Though the prior cases had given great deference to congressional action, and though the broad language in those opinions had suggested the possibility of even further expansion, Rehnquist drew the line here, declining to proceed any further.[52]

The Court extended this holding five years later in *United States v. Morrison,* striking down the civil damages provision of the 1994 Violence against

Women Act. In this statute, declaring that all "persons within the United States shall have the right to be free from crimes of violence motivated by gender," Congress had provided a federal civil remedy for victims of such violence, along with a number of other efforts at prevention and deterrence. Again assigning the Court's opinion to himself, Chief Justice Rehnquist held that while gender-motivated crimes of violence may well substantially affect interstate commerce, they are not themselves economic activities, and hence are not subject to congressional regulation under the Commerce Clause. He reiterated that this determination was to be made by the Court rather than Congress itself, and he noted that to accept Congress's findings here would be to abandon the careful enumeration of national powers and hence to "obliterate the Constitution's distinction between national and local authority." For Rehnquist, "[t]he regulation and punishment of intrastate violence" was a classic "example of the police power, which the Founders denied the National Government and reposed in the States."[53]

In addition to its authority over interstate commerce, Congress also invoked its power, granted by §5 of the Fourteenth Amendment, "to enforce, by appropriate legislation, the provisions" of that amendment. Since those provisions include the sweeping Due Process and Equal Protection Clauses, this congressional power has sometimes been read quite broadly, but the Rehnquist Court had been construing it more narrowly for several years. In *City of Boerne v. Flores,* the Court had overturned a Warren-era precedent to hold that when enforcing the requirements of due process and equal protection, Congress cannot interpret those principles in its own right, but must follow the Court's reading of them. Ignoring the broad, bipartisan support for the Religious Freedom Restoration Act in both houses of Congress, the Court had invalidated the statute as an illegitimate congressional attempt to expand the scope of the Fourteenth Amendment's implicit guarantee of religious liberty beyond that which the Court itself had recognized. In short, the Court was insisting that like the commerce power, the limits of this congressional power were a matter for judicial determination. Reiterating this argument in *Morrison,* Rehnquist held that because private gender-motivated violence did not (in the Court's view) violate the Equal Protection Clause, Congress could not outlaw such violence on the grounds that it was "enforcing" that clause.

Throughout these cases, the conservative justices have evinced an interest in reviving pre–New Deal conceptions of the nature and scope of Congress's enumerated powers. Since doing so would potentially call into question

much of the federal legislation of the last half of the twentieth century, however, most of them have proceeded cautiously. In two additional sets of cases,
they have also sought to develop expansive interpretations of the Tenth and
Eleventh Amendments as independent limits on federal legislative power. In
other words, while the Court has put some constraints on Congress's enumerated powers at the margins, it has also held that even when Congress is legitimately exercising those powers — by regulating interstate commerce, for
example — the Tenth Amendment prohibits it from "commandeering" the
institutions of state government and the Eleventh Amendment prohibits it
from subjecting state governments to lawsuits against their will. In all of these
cases, the conservative justices have called attention to the fact that the federal government has exceeded the constitutional limits on its authority without clearly specifying how broadly those limits should be (re)imposed.

   In the Tenth Amendment context, the Court had first held in *New York v.
United States* that Congress could not constitutionally compel the state legislatures to pass laws that assist federal regulatory efforts, and it subsequently
held that Congress could not commandeer the state and local executive
branches to assist in such efforts either. Writing for the Court in *Printz v.
United States,* Justice Scalia struck down a provision of the 1993 Brady Bill
that required state and local law enforcement officials to conduct background
checks on prospective handgun purchasers. Two county law enforcement officers argued that the Tenth Amendment prohibited Congress from requiring them to carry out federal laws, and the five conservative justices agreed.
Just the year before, the conservative majority had begun its effort to revive
the concept of state sovereign immunity as yet another constitutional limit
on federal regulatory authority. In *Seminole Tribe of Florida v. Florida,* Rehnquist held that Congress's powers under Article I, such as the commerce
power, do not include the authority to subject states to federal suit at the
hands of private individuals. He relied on a Fuller Court precedent, *Hans v.
Louisiana,* for the propositions that "each State is a sovereign entity in our
federal system; . . . that it is inherent in the nature of sovereignty not to be
amenable to the suit of an individual without its consent[; and] that federal
jurisdiction over suits against unconsenting States was not contemplated by
the Constitution when establishing the judicial power of the United States."[54]
While the federal courts had long held that the states were immune from suit
unless Congress expressly revoked that immunity, the Rehnquist Court went
further by limiting Congress's power to do so.

   The Court's Eleventh Amendment arguments have been closely intertwined with its narrow reading of Congress's power to enforce the Fourteenth Amendment. In *Seminole Tribe,* the Court suggested that unlike Congress's Article I powers, its §5 power did include the authority to abrogate the states' immunity from suit. As I have noted, however, the Court held the following year in *City of Boerne* that when acting under this Fourteenth Amendment power, Congress is limited by the Court's interpretation of the Due Process and Equal Protection Clauses. Taken together, the sovereign immunity and §5 holdings significantly narrowed Congress's authority in the civil rights field by "jeopardiz[ing] many federal statutes that purport to govern the states in their capacity as employers, as market participants, and as service providers" (Sherry 1999:23). When the Court held in 1999 that Congress could not subject the states to suits for patent infringement, the political implications of this doctrine were obscured, but the following year, the Court began extending this immunity to the civil rights issues at the heart of the Fourteenth Amendment.[55]

In a series of decisions in 2000 and 2001, the conservative majority reaffirmed that Congress may abrogate the states' sovereign immunity when necessary to enforce the Fourteenth Amendment, but held that when Congress sought to do so in the Violence against Women Act, the Age Discrimination in Employment Act, and the Americans with Disabilities Act, it had exceeded its §5 authority. Because neither private acts of gender motivated violence nor public discrimination on the basis of age or disability violated the Due Process or Equal Protection Clauses, as interpreted by the Court, Congress was not free to outlaw such practices in the name of enforcing the Fourteenth Amendment.[56]

As in the affirmative action cases, the extent of judicial activism implied by the Court's federalism revival has given pause to the Court's more pragmatic conservatives, leading them to hedge on just how far they are willing to carry this revival. In *Lopez,* for example, Kennedy agreed with his conservative colleagues that the Constitution's structural division of governmental power provided a vital protection of individual liberty that the post–New Deal Court had been neglecting to defend, but he also noted that "[t]he history of the judicial struggle to interpret the Commerce Clause during the transition from the economic system the Founders knew to the single, national market still emergent in our own era counsels great restraint before the Court determines that the Clause is insufficient to support an exercise of national power. That history gives me some pause about today's decision, but I join the Court's opinion with these observations on what I consider to be its necessary though limited holding." Joined by O'Connor, Justice Kennedy went on to insist that the modern precedents that expanded congressional power — such as the decisions upholding the 1964 Civil Rights Act — "are not called in question by our decision today," thus making clear that regardless of the apparent implications of Rehnquist's opinion for the Court, only three justices were willing to call for a full-scale revival of pre–New Deal principles of federalism.[57]

Just as Kennedy sought to hedge the Court's holding in *Lopez*, Justice O'Connor sought to do so in *Printz*. Writing separately, she emphasized that while "[o]ur precedent and our Nation's historical practices support the Court's holding today," Congress retained a number of legitimate means at its disposal for furthering the purposes of the Brady Act.[58] Her hesitation here was rooted in her fear that the Court's approach could threaten a vast and disruptive expansion of the judicial role in enforcing limits on congressional power. She and Kennedy rejected a strict adherence to original meaning in the federalism context because, as Kennedy noted in *Lopez*, "the Court as an institution and the legal system as a whole have an immense stake in the stability of our Commerce Clause jurisprudence as it has evolved to this point. . . . That fundamental restraint on our power forecloses us from reverting to an understanding of commerce that would serve only an 18th-century economy, dependent then upon production and trading practices that had changed but little over the preceding centuries; it also mandates against returning to the time when congressional authority to regulate undoubted commercial activities was limited by a judicial determination that those matters had an insufficient connection to an interstate system."[59] When O'Connor and Kennedy have written separately to limit the Court's holdings in this way, Justice Thomas has often written separately to pull the Court in the opposite direction. In both *Lopez* and *Printz*, for example, he published concurring opinions urging the Court to enforce the original constitutional structure of federalism even more boldly.

In the sovereign immunity context, O'Connor and Kennedy have consistently joined the conservative majority, often writing for the Court themselves, but have again suggested some limits to this new line of activism. In *Idaho v. Coeur d'Alene Tribe of Idaho*, Kennedy announced the Court's judgment, narrowing the scope of an important exception to sovereign immunity that the Court had recognized for almost ninety years, but O'Connor wrote separately to indicate that that exception should be preserved in full.[60] Two years later, Kennedy again wrote for the Court, this time in *Alden v. Maine,* holding that "[i]n light of history, practice, precedent, and the structure of the Constitution, . . . the States retain immunity from private suit in their own courts, an immunity beyond the congressional power to abrogate by Article I legislation." The states would possess such immunity even without the Eleventh Amendment, he insisted, because it "is a fundamental aspect of the sovereignty which the States enjoyed before the ratification of the Constitution, and which they retain today . . . except as altered by the plan of the Convention or certain constitutional Amendments." On Kennedy's reading, members of the founding generation considered immunity from private suits central to sovereign "dignity" and would never even have suggested that the Constitution might strip the states of this immunity. Kennedy insisted that this view was the only one consistent with "the structure of the Constitution" and "the essential principles of federalism," and he concluded that "Congress has vast power but not all power." [61]

The following year, O'Connor wrote for the Court in extending sovereign immunity still further in *Kimel v. Florida Board of Regents,* and the year after that, she and Kennedy joined Rehnquist's opinion for the Court in *Board of Trustees of the University of Alabama v. Garrett.* They wrote separately in the latter case, going out of their way to describe the Americans with Disabilities Act as "a milestone on the path to a more decent, tolerant, progressive society," but despite this sentiment, they agreed with their fellow conservatives that the act exceeded congressional authority. Because Congress had failed to demonstrate that the states had been violating the Fourteenth Amendment in their treatment of people with disabilities, it had no grounds to regulate the states' actions in the guise of "enforcing" that amendment. [62]

Like their conservative colleagues, O'Connor and Kennedy are skeptical of Congress's capacity to respect the constitutional limitations of its own power, but unlike those justices, they recognize that if the Court is going to provide those limits for Congress, it had better do so cautiously. Their separate opinion in *Garrett* was a typical one for them — brief and opaque, apparently designed to limit the reach of the Court's holding, but failing to make clear where those limits lie — the kind of opinion that has led some observers to describe O'Connor's and Kennedy's frequent hedges as more rhetorical than real. As in the affirmative action context, however — and as with their separate opinions in the Court's liberal activist decisions as well — these hedges have imposed meaningful limits on the Court's activism.

In *Nevada Department of Human Resources v. Hibbs,* for example, the Court upheld the Family and Medical Leave Act against a sovereign immunity challenge. With the Bush administration and a slew of former congressmen urging the Court to uphold the statute, O'Connor and even Rehnquist backed down. Similarly, while a majority of the current justices disagree with *Garcia's* narrow reading of the Tenth Amendment, the Court declined the opportunity to overrule that precedent in *Reno v. Condon.* Distinguishing *New York* and *Printz,* Rehnquist upheld the Drivers Privacy Protection Act, which prohibits the states from selling personal information obtained through drivers license records to private companies for use in telemarketing. He held that since the federal statute only regulated the activities of the state governments as part of a broader, general regulation of interstate commerce — private companies were also prohibited from selling such information — it did not violate the Tenth Amendment. Three years later, when California urged the Court to extend the doctrine of sovereign immunity to the courts of sister states in *Franchise Tax Board v. Hyatt*— that is, to hold that the government of one state cannot be sued in the courts of another state — the Court rejected this invitation as well. In doing so, the Court reaffirmed *Nevada v. Hall,* with no complaint from Rehnquist (who had dissented in the earlier case), and even relied in part on *Garcia.*

Both *Condon* and *Hyatt* were unanimous decisions, with even Justices Scalia and Thomas recognizing the limits of judicially enforceable principles of federalism.[63] More often, however, these conservative justices have pushed their new brand of activism as far as O'Connor and Kennedy would allow. For just one final example, consider Kennedy's deciding vote in *U.S. Term Limits v. Thornton.* While Rehnquist, O'Connor, and Scalia joined Thomas's dissenting opinion, Kennedy refused to do so, joining the liberal justices to support national power against state interference. O'Connor and Kennedy's caution has sometimes actually reversed the Court's decision, as in *Hibbs* or *Thornton,* but more often has required their fellow conservatives to draft the majority opinion more narrowly. For example, while Thomas's concurring opinion in *Lopez* called for the wholesale abandonment of modern precedents, Rehnquist's majority opinion claimed simply to be applying those precedents and concluding that the possession of guns in schools did not "substantially affect" interstate commerce. Rehnquist may well share Thomas's vision of federalism, but he was forced to temper his opinion for the Court because two members of his five-justice majority were unwilling to go so far.

In sum, the five conservative justices of the later Rehnquist Court agree that the constitutional structure of federalism is an essential means of preserving constitutional liberty, but O'Connor and Kennedy (and sometimes even Rehnquist) remain troubled by the extraordinary degree of judicial activism that would be required to enforce that original understanding in the context of the modern welfare-regulatory state. As a result, they have prevented the Court from adopting the sweeping version of the federalism revival outlined most clearly by Justice Thomas. It is for this reason that, as many scholars have noted, "the Court's federalism decisions have more struck an ideological blow for limited federal government than truly put a significant damper on federal regulatory power" (Balkin and Levinson 2001:1058).

In the separation of powers context, the Court has again shown an interest in reviving pre–New Deal constitutional limits on congressional lawmaking, but has stopped short in the face of the widespread invalidations of modern legislation that would ensue. In *Clinton v. City of New York,* for example, the Court struck down the 1996 Line Item Veto Act as an unconstitutional departure from the lawmaking procedures of Article I. Kennedy joined Rehnquist, Thomas, Stevens, Souter, and Ginsburg in an unusual majority voting alignment, and he wrote separately to emphasize the importance of active judicial supervision of the line between legislative and executive power in the federal government. Nonetheless, Kennedy joined his colleagues three years later in *Whitman v. American Trucking Associations,* recognizing that the full-scale judicial revival of the original constitutional design would threaten too great a disruption of the modern state, and thus rejecting a nondelegation challenge to the Clean Air Act. Writing for the Court in this latter case, Justice Scalia upheld the act's directive to the Environmental Protection Agency (EPA) to set "ambient air quality standards the attainment and maintenance of which . . . are requisite to protect the public health," acknowledging that Congress had provided adequate guidelines to constrain the authority it was granting to the executive branch, but making clear that he was willing to draw a constitutional line if necessary.[64]

The same pattern has been repeated in the property rights cases, with Scalia, Thomas, and Rehnquist continuing their effort to revive constitutional limits on government regulatory authority, and Kennedy and O'Connor preventing them from pushing this revival too far. In *Lucas v. South Carolina Coastal Council,* when Scalia wrote for the Court in requiring compensation for a "regulatory taking" imposed by an environmental land-use

regulation, Kennedy had concurred only in the judgment, writing separately
to suggest that Scalia's analysis limited state regulatory authority too severely.
In *Eastern Enterprises v. Apfel,* Kennedy again concurred only in the judgment, this time depriving O'Connor of a judicial majority for her opinion.
He agreed that the regulatory statute at issue was unconstitutional, but he
fully rejected O'Connor's reading of the Takings Clause, going so far as to
complain that calling "this sort of governmental action a taking . . . is both
imprecise and, with all due respect, unwise." He acknowledged that the Coal
Industree Retiree Health Benefit Act had imposed "a staggering financial
burden" on Eastern Enterprises — perhaps "as great [as] if the Government
had appropriated one of Eastern's plants" — but argued that "the mechanism
by which the Government injures Eastern is so unlike the act of taking specific property that it is incongruous to call the Coal Act a taking, even as that
concept has been expanded by the regulatory takings principle."[65]

While Kennedy has usually been the Court's moderating force in the property rights context, O'Connor has sometimes played this role as well. In yet
another dispute over environmental regulations and land use in 2001, Kennedy held for the Court that the fact that a regulation had been on the books
before Anthony Palazzolo acquired a parcel of waterfront property did not
foreclose him from pursuing a regulatory takings claim against that regulation. Having clarified the constitutional rule, however, Kennedy refused to
say whether a taking had actually occurred in this case, remanding that question to the lower courts and prompting O'Connor and Scalia to issue dueling concurrences on how those courts should proceed. O'Connor's opinion
was a typically fact-specific one, and it prompted a typically impatient reply
from Scalia.[66] Similarly, O'Connor joined Rehnquist's opinion for a bare
conservative majority in *Phillips v. Washington Legal Foundation,* but then
voted with the liberal justices five years later in *Brown v. Legal Foundation of
Washington* to limit the holding's reach. Because of O'Connor's and Kennedy's votes, the Court has revived a long-dormant notion of judicially enforceable property rights. But also because of their votes, the Court has declined to endorse the expansive vision of such rights that many conservatives
have been urging.

The Takings Clause is not the only constitutional provision providing protection to property rights, but it is the one that the Rehnquist Court's
conservatives have most often emphasized. Given the legacy of *Lochner v.
New York,* they have generally avoided relying on the Due Process Clause, but

Rehnquist has shown some interest in reviving the Contract Clause, as has Thomas in the Excessive Fines Clause and the Ex Post Facto Clause. In *United States v. Bajakajian,* Thomas joined the four liberal justices to hold that the Excessive Fines Clause prohibited criminal forfeitures of personal property if they were "grossly disproportional to the gravity of a defendant's offense," and in *Eastern Enterprises v. Apfel,* he called into question a two-hundred-year-old precedent holding that the Ex Post Facto Clause prohibited only retroactive criminal punishments, suggesting that it may apply to retroactive civil fines as well.[67] In this last case, needless to say, he wrote only for himself.

Most notably, the conservative justices have put the First Amendment to similar use as a limit on government regulatory authority. For example, the conservative justices have had substantial success in extending First Amendment protection to commercial advertising. The Court's voting lineup has been a bit unusual in this context, as Stevens and Souter have sometimes joined the conservatives in defending free speech and Rehnquist has sometimes joined the liberals in urging deference to government regulatory authority. Nonetheless, the Court has been steadily heightening its protection of speech in this context, and it has been led by the conservative justices in doing so. The Burger Court had first extended constitutional protection to "commercial speech" in 1976, overturning a New Deal precedent to do so, but it had balanced this concern against the substantial state interest in protecting consumers from false, deceptive, and misleading advertising.[68] As the conservative justices consolidated their control during the Rehnquist years, Scalia, Thomas, and Kennedy began to complain that this balancing approach provided inadequate protection to free speech, with Thomas in particular urging full First Amendment protection for commercial advertising.

In *Rubin v. Coors Brewing Co., 44 Liquormart, Inc. v. Rhode Island, Greater New Orleans Broadcasting Association v. United States, Lorillard Tobacco Co. v. Reilly,* and *Thompson v. Western States Medical Center,* the Court struck down state or federal regulations of advertising for alcohol, tobacco, prescription drugs, and gambling. The frequency of such decisions suggested that this was an area of newfound concern, but while Thomas urged the Court to strike down virtually all content-based regulations in this field, O'Connor advocated a careful, fact-specific, doctrinal approach, upholding some regulations and striking down others. Though she and Rehnquist have sometimes defected from their fellow conservative justices in this context, the free speech arguments have usually persuaded Stevens and Souter, giving Kennedy, Scalia, and Thomas a consistent judicial majority on this issue since 1995.[69]

Doctrinally, these cases have emphasized the First Amendment guarantee of free speech, but from another perspective they reflect the Court's revival of constitutional limits on economic regulation — what we might think of as "the Lochnerization of the First Amendment."[70] In *United States v. United Foods,* for example, Kennedy wrote for the Court in striking down an agricultural regulation that required mushroom producers to contribute to a fund supporting mushroom advertising, prompting Justices Breyer and Ginsburg to complain in dissent that the Court was unduly scrutinizing "this common example of government intervention in the marketplace." The Clinton appointees raised the specter of *Lochner* — insisting that like the Due Process Clause, "the First Amendment [does not] seek[ ] to limit the Government's economic regulatory choices in this way" — but this specter no longer haunts the Rehnquist Court.[71]

The commercial speech cases have been part of a broader effort by the conservative justices to develop a distinctive conservative vision of the freedom of speech. Since this liberty was so obviously an important principle in the original Constitution (as amended by the Bill of Rights), the conservatives have challenged the free speech jurisprudence of their liberal predecessors not by urging judicial deference to democratically enacted censorship, but instead by transforming the contexts in which the freedom of speech applies. The Rehnquist Court's vision of the freedom of speech is not a partisan vision — the Court defends the right of liberals as well as conservatives to speak their mind — but it is clearly a conservative vision, as the Court has defended this freedom primarily in those contexts in which liberal legislators have sought to infringe upon it.

In the area of campaign finance regulation, for example, Justices Scalia and Thomas have repeatedly insisted that legislative efforts to limit campaign spending violate the First Amendment. This area of law is governed by the Court's landmark decision in *Buckley v. Valeo,* which held that since spending money was essential for making one's voice heard, campaign expenditures were constitutionally protected under the First Amendment. Reviewing Congress's post-Watergate amendments to the Federal Election Campaign Act under strict scrutiny, the *Buckley* Court upheld the act's limits on campaign contributions as a valid effort to police political corruption, but it struck down the limits on campaign expenditures, as applied to both campaign organizations themselves and other individuals or groups, acting independently. In support of this latter holding, the Court noted that "the concept that government may restrict the speech of some elements of our society in order to enhance the relative voice of others is wholly foreign to the First Amendment."[72]

As the amount of money involved in our nation's political campaigns and elections ballooned, the *Buckley* precedent was extensively criticized by constitutional scholars, but the justices of the Rehnquist Court remained sharply divided over what to do about it. In a series of cases beginning in the mid-1990s, Stevens and Ginsburg insisted that both contributions and expenditures could be limited, and hence that half of *Buckley*'s holding should be overturned, while Scalia, Thomas, Rehnquist, and Kennedy insisted that neither could be limited, and hence that the other half of *Buckley*'s holding should be overturned. O'Connor prevented her fellow conservatives from garnering a judicial majority, and Kennedy sometimes stopped short of Scalia, Thomas, and Rehnquist's sweeping activism as well. In *Colorado Republican Federal Campaign Committee v. FEC,* for example, Kennedy joined Scalia and Rehnquist in insisting that the government could not constitutionally restrict political party expenditures on behalf of a candidate, even if they were coordinated with the candidate's campaign. When this case returned to the Court five years later, O'Connor joined the four liberal justices in rejecting Kennedy's argument, holding that a party's coordinated expenditures, unlike its truly independent ones, could be restricted.[73]

Kennedy's view had also been relegated to a dissenting position the previous year in *Nixon v. Shrink Missouri Government PAC,* as the Court upheld contribution limits much lower than those at issue in *Buckley.* In dissent, Kennedy agreed with Thomas and Scalia that Missouri's contribution limits did "not come even close to passing any serious scrutiny," but he was nonetheless determined to leave some room for continued democratic deliberation. He was convinced that "serious constitutional questions" confronted any legislative effort to regulate expenditures and contributions, but he did not want to "foreclose [such efforts] at the outset."[74] Still, Kennedy and his fellow conservatives were largely on the same page, leaving O'Connor with the deciding vote, and in this regard, the *Colorado Republican* and *Shrink Missouri* decisions were a preview of the Court's monumental ruling in *McConnell v. FEC.* O'Connor joined the four liberals to uphold the most significant provisions of the 2002 Bipartisan Campaign Reform Act (known popularly as the "McCain–Feingold Bill"), Congress's most extensive effort at campaign finance regulation in thirty years.

In sum, Justice Kennedy has joined his fellow conservatives in enforcing a set of libertarian-inspired limits on campaign regulations, but has expressed some hesitation about unduly constraining Congress's ability to respond to this important national problem. Because Justice O'Connor has expressed even greater hesitation, the Court's conservative activism has usually remained in dissent. When she and Kennedy have both joined their conservative colleagues, they have authorized the active judicial supervision of state and federal regulations of electoral campaigns. In *Republican Party of Minnesota v. White*, for example, they both joined Scalia's opinion for a bare conservative majority, applying strict scrutiny and striking down a Minnesota canon of judicial conduct that restricted electioneering by candidates for judicial office.

As I explained previously, libertarian conservatives coming to power in the 1970s and 1980s quickly demanded judicial activism in defense of limited government, while their partners in the New Right — the religious conservatives — continued to counsel judicial deference to majoritarian morality. Once these evangelical conservatives recognized the potential of rights-based activism themselves, they too began to bring a number of innovative rights arguments to the Rehnquist Court's attention. Like their libertarian allies, the religious Right established a number of organizations committed to advancing such arguments and, like their libertarian allies, they mobilized the First Amendment to new ends. In *Rosenberger v. University of Virginia* and *Good News Club v. Milford Central School*, for example, the five conservative justices answered the call of the American Center for Law and Justice (ACLJ), the Christian Legal Society, Focus on the Family, and the Family Research Council, relying on both the Free Exercise and Free Speech Clauses in striking down policies excluding religious organizations from public resources that facilitated speech.[75]

In *Rosenberger,* the Court held that a public university could not constitutionally exclude a student-run religious newspaper from generally available funding for student activities, and in *Good News Club,* it held that a public school district could not exclude religious organizations from access to generally available school facilities. In each case, the conservative majority held that such exclusionary policies amounted to impermissible viewpoint discrimination against religious speech. As the dissenting liberal justices pointed out, these cases also implicated the First Amendment's Establishment Clause, since the Court was (in their view) allowing the provision of direct government support for religious proselytizing. For the five conservatives on the bench, this concern was outweighed by the religious organizations' rights to free speech and equal treatment. In Justice Thomas's view, in particular, legislative practices that excluded religious groups from generally available government aid were "born of bigotry," and hence prohibited by both the Free Speech and Free Exercise Clauses.[76]

Just as O'Connor and Kennedy have supported, while also hedging, the Court's continued liberal activism under the Establishment Clause, they similarly have supported but also hedged its newfound conservative activism under the Free Exercise and Free Speech Clauses. In *Rosenberger,* for example, O'Connor tried to balance Kennedy's principle of government neutrality toward religion and Souter's prohibition on state funding of religious activities. Both she and Kennedy also invited a broader constitutional challenge to the widespread use by public universities of compulsory student fees to fund a variety of student-run organizations. But when a group of evangelical students at the University of Wisconsin answered this invitation a few years later, Kennedy wrote for the Court in refusing to extend this line of conservative activism any further.[77]

The fact that all three of these cases arose out of educational institutions linked the free speech arguments even more closely to New Right conservatism, a central theme of which has been that our nation's schools are dominated by liberal elites bent on imposing their views, stifling conservative dissent, and silencing the voice of the religious. As in the affirmative action and property rights contexts, moreover, the conservative litigants who have initiated these cases have experienced them as a struggle for civil rights, constitutional liberty, and nondiscrimination. To reiterate, the conservative position in these cases is a rights-protecting position, and the conservative justices of the Rehnquist Court have generally been sympathetic to it. If it were once possible to describe constitutional debates as a battle between liberal advocates of rights and conservative advocates of judicial restraint, that is no longer the case. Consider the Court's decision in *Boy Scouts of America v. Dale,* which was widely described in the national media as a judicial defeat for the cause of gay and lesbian rights. That description is accurate, but it is equally accurate to describe it as a judicial victory for the right of private organizations to choose their own members. In his opinion for the Court's bare conservative majority, after all, Chief Justice Rehnquist held that New Jersey's public accommodations law, applied so as to require the Boy Scouts of America to accept gay members, violated the organization's freedom of expressive association.[78]

Liberal and Conservative Activism on the Rehnquist Court

The Rehnquist Court's First Amendment decisions have been emblematic of its constitutional jurisprudence more generally. Justice Kennedy has been the Court's strongest supporter of free speech, wherever it leads, and he has also been the Court's most activist justice across the board, willing to exercise judicial power quite regularly in defense of both liberal and conservative rights claims. As table 6.5 shows, Justices Scalia and Thomas have voted most often to strike down federal statutes on constitutional grounds, but they have been closely followed by Rehnquist, Kennedy, and O'Connor. Justice Stevens has voted most often to strike down state and local statutes, but he too has been closely followed by Kennedy and O'Connor. In total, Kennedy has exercised judicial review most often, with O'Connor close behind. As I suggested in chapter 2, merely counting the cases in which the Court exercises judicial review does not provide a comprehensive picture of the breadth of judicial power. As Mark Graber (2000) has noted, there are a number of significant ways to exercise judicial power without voting to declare a statute unconstitutional, and for that matter, there are a number of cases declaring statutes unconstitutional that do not represent particularly significant exercises of judicial power.[79] Still, these data on the frequency of support for judicial review are illustrative, and they are borne out by a careful reading of the particular cases. For example, when the Court reviews criminal judgments imposing the forfeiture of property or civil judgments imposing punitive damages, it does not call into question the constitutionality of any statutes; however, Kennedy has exhibited a singular lack of deference to decisions by state and local judge and juries in each of these contexts.[80]

In the free speech context, as elsewhere, Kennedy's activism has sometimes pulled the Court in a conservative direction, sometimes in a liberal direction, and sometimes in a direction harder to characterize. I have detailed his conservative free speech holdings at some length, but he also cast the deciding vote in the Court's 1989 flag-burning decision, and he has been more protective of speech than his fellow conservatives in the pornography context as well.[81] When the Court struck down the Communications Decency Act in *Reno v. ACLU*, Kennedy joined Stevens's opinion for the Court in full, while

TABLE 6.5 *Support for Judicial Review on the Late Rehnquist Court**

Justice	Federal	State and Local	Total
Kennedy	22	29	51
O'Connor	21	29	50
Scalia	25	23	48
Thomas	25	23	48
Souter	17	28	45
Stevens	12	31	43
Rehnquist	22	19	41
Breyer	14	27	41
Ginsburg	14	25	39

Source: Justice-Centered Rehnquist Court Database.
*Number of cases in which each justice voted to strike down federal, state, and local statutes on constitutional grounds during the 1994–2000 terms.

O'Connor wrote separately, joined by Rehnquist, in an effort to narrow the free speech holding. Five years later, when the Court struck down the Child Pornography Prevention Act, Kennedy wrote for the Court's liberal majority, while the other four conservative justices sought to narrow the holding, urging greater deference to the congressional interest in regulating pornography on the Internet.[82] In the hate speech context, six justices held in *Virginia v. Black* that the First Amendment permitted government to single out cross burning as a particularly valueless form of expression, while four justices held that the Virginia statute at issue was nonetheless unconstitutional, because it failed to require prosecutors to prove that the act of burning had been intended as a threat. O'Connor, of course, was in both groups, insisting in her classic style that a properly drafted cross-burning law would be constitutionally legitimate, but that this one had not met her standards. Kennedy wrote for the only three justices who insisted that all cross-burning laws were unconstitutional, regardless of how carefully they had been drafted, because they singled out a particular form of expression for punishment on the basis of its content.

Again, Justice Kennedy's free speech activism is representative of his vision of judicial power. As Jeffrey Segal and Harold Spaeth have shown, he is the only justice who is more likely than not to strike down statutes supported by

liberals and more likely than not to strike down statutes supported by conservatives, though Justice O'Connor again comes very close as well.[83] Given
his regular support for enforcing constitutional limits on both state and federal government, in support of both liberal and conservative ends, Kennedy
is the Court's most activist justice. O'Connor is close behind, though she has
been even more likely than Kennedy to hedge the Court's activist holdings.
Since these two justices carry the deciding votes, the constitutional jurisprudence of the Rehnquist Court is a rights-protecting jurisprudence, and the
Rehnquist Court is an activist Court.

In a wide range of doctrinal contexts, the conservative justices of the
Rehnquist Court have imposed politically significant constitutional limits on
the elected institutions of government, particularly Congress. In the areas of
campaign finance, affirmative action, civil rights regulation, religious accommodation, environmental regulation, and tobacco advertising, the Court has
inserted itself into divisive political conflicts and attempted to resolve them.
If this pattern was not yet clear by 2000, then *Bush v. Gore* made it so. As if
deciding the outcome of the nation's presidential election were not evidence
enough, the decision also had the effect of overturning the laws of thirty-
seven states (which like Florida, used a ballot-counting standard emphasizing the intent of the voter), laws that had long existed and long been unchallenged, on behalf of a dubious interpretation of the original Constitution.
The Rehnquist Court has developed a distinctive conservative jurisprudence
for the new century, and this jurisprudence is a far cry from the judicial abnegation once practiced by Oliver Wendell Holmes, Learned Hand, and Felix Frankfurter. As Tushnet has noted, the justices no longer even agonize
over the legitimacy of judicial review when they strike down a federal statute
(1999b:82–85; 2003:214–15).

O'Connor and Kennedy have cast the deciding votes for this new conservative activism in case after case, but their own jurisprudence has served
in two distinct ways to defend the Court against the charges of politiciza-
tion that have arisen in response. First, as I have noted at some length, they
have tempered the reach of the new conservative activism. A number of
scholars have rightly emphasized that this activism has not amounted to a
revolutionary break with the New Deal/Great Society constitutional order,
but this is only because O'Connor and Kennedy have not allowed their conservative colleagues to carry it as far as they would like (Tushnet 2003:33–35).
If O'Connor's fellow conservatives had had their way in *Grutter,* the Court
would have foreclosed all race-conscious affirmative action policies nation-

wide, tossing the institution into a political maelstrom. Second, O'Connor and Kennedy have combined their support for conservative activism with a firm commitment to liberal activism as well. So long as the Court keeps issuing decisions like *Lawrence v. Texas,* liberals and Democrats will not abandon their long-standing support for the institution.

• • •

Although the public face of the Rehnquist Court has been that of a five-justice conservative majority, these justices have proven every bit as divided as were Harlan and Black during the Warren years. As I have noted, moreover, the lines of division are similar. Scalia and Thomas have built on Black's legacy in an effort to construct a comprehensive originalist case for restraint, while O'Connor and Kennedy have looked instead to Harlan. Following Harlan's common law method, they have preserved a broad vision of due process liberty, and unlike Harlan, they have extended this activism to the equal protection context as well. Since they have also supplemented Harlan's approach with a distinctive brand of conservative activism built on the New Right critique of liberalism, O'Connor and Kennedy have extended their own power substantially farther than Harlan himself would have tolerated. Put another way, Justices O'Connor and Kennedy have followed a version of Harlan's "reasoned judgment," but unlike their predecessor, they have placed no areas of law and policy off limits to judicial action.

CHAPTER SEVEN

LAW AND POLITICS
ON THE REHNQUIST COURT

The burden of the last chapter was to trace the striking pattern of liberal and conservative activism on the late Rehnquist Court. The burden of this one is to explain why and how such a pattern came about. In the seventeen years since William Rehnquist became chief justice, the leading scholarly descriptions of his Court have repeatedly changed in response to its latest decisions. Three years into Rehnquist's tenure, for example, Erwin Chemerinsky used the *Harvard Law Review*'s annual foreword to complain that the conservative Court was carrying the principle of judicial restraint so far as to threaten "a vanishing Constitution" (1989). Two years later, Dean Guido Calabresi of Yale Law School expressed this sentiment even more colorfully by publicly declaring, "I despise the current Supreme Court and find its aggressive, willful, statist behavior disgusting" (1991:7A). Just the following year, however, this same Court decided *Planned Parenthood v. Casey* and *Lee v. Weisman,* making clear that it was neither straightforwardly conservative nor restrained.

In the wake of these decisions, a variety of scholars began to emphasize the Rehnquist Court's surprising centrism. Ronald Dworkin's initial account of the *Casey* decision in the *New York Review of Books* was titled "The Center Holds," and James Simon published a book-length treatment under the same title a few years later (Dworkin 1992; Simon 1995). Bruce Ackerman had already been referring to the Reagan revolution as "a failed constitutional moment" before the *Casey* decision, but he soon incorporated the case into his updated account (1991:50–56; 1998:397–400). All of these treatments emphasized the crucial role played by Justices Sandra Day O'Connor, Anthony Kennedy, and David Souter in thwarting the conservative constitutional revolution, and these accounts seemed confirmed when the Court issued decisions like *Romer v. Evans* and *United States v. Virginia* in 1996. During this same period, in fact, some conservatives began denouncing the Rehnquist Court in exceedingly harsh terms, as they found liberal activism even harder to swallow when it was perpetrated by allegedly conservative justices.[1]

The Court was also issuing a variety of conservative decisions during the mid-1990s, but it was possible to characterize them as reflecting the same healthy moderation as the contemporaneous liberal decisions. When Cass Sunstein published his widely noted book on "judicial minimalism" in 1999, he praised the Rehnquist Court for its efforts to enforce important constitutional limits without unduly impinging on democratic processes. In doing so, he emphasized the Court's recent liberal decisions in *Romer* and the VMI case, and also its recent conservative decisions in *Washington v. Glucksberg* and *Adarand Constructors, Inc. v. Pena*. Drawing early attention to O'Connor's and Kennedy's penchant for issuing narrow holdings that left many things undecided, he praised this approach as a healthy effort to balance the principles of democracy and constitutionalism, and one reviewer noted at the time that "[i]t is rare that a work of constitutional theory so precisely expresses . . . the mood of a particular Supreme Court" (Rosen 1999:44).

No sooner had Sunstein's book appeared, however, did the Court's federalism revolution go into full swing, leading many scholars to emphasize (and complain about) the Court's excessive activism. Particularly after *Bush v. Gore,* the leading scholarly accounts emphasized that the activist conservative justices were ushering in a new conservative constitutional order (Balkin and Levinson 2001; Tushnet 2003). By 2003, even Sunstein was denouncing the Rehnquist Court's "illegitimate activism," complaining that the current Court's "most dramatic and important tendency" was its "willing[ness] to strike down congressional (and also state) enactments, not when the Constitution is clear, but when it is unclear and when reasonable people can disagree about what it means" (2003:27–29). The only real disagreement among these recent accounts has been how broadly to characterize the new conservative activism. Writing in the wake of *Bush v. Gore,* and emphasizing *Board of Trustees of the University of Alabama v. Garrett* as well, Jack Balkin and Sanford Levinson advanced a strong claim that the nation was witnessing a conservative constitutional revolution (Balkin and Levinson 2001; see also Colker and Brudney 2001). Mark Tushnet, in slight contrast, published a book-length treatment characterizing the "new constitutional order" as conservative, but not revolutionary. While he acknowledged that further expansion was possible, Tushnet insisted that "the Court has not made revolutionary moves or treated its own doctrine expansively. The doctrines the Court has articulated are, taken at face value, relatively modest in their impact on the New Deal–Great Society constitutional order" (2003:35).

All of these most recent accounts dismissed the Rehnquist Court's continued pattern of liberal decisions (in certain contexts) as either inconsequential or the product simply of *stare decisis*. The inadequacy of this minimization became apparent just as Tushnet's book was published, with the Court's decisions in *Grutter v. Bollinger* and *Lawrence v. Texas* in the summer of 2003. As of this writing, there has not yet been a full scholarly response to these decisions, but Levinson's initial reaction was instructive. In an article titled "Redefining the Center," published shortly after the two landmark liberal decisions, he attributed them to the Court's "reassessment of where the solid center of American opinion is now located." Though recent years had generally seen the conservatives prevail, "last week, the stars were aligned for a series of liberal decisions" (2003).

This review of recent scholarly assessments of the present Court has necessarily been brief, but the tension among the leading accounts is clear. It hardly seems likely that the justices who control the Rehnquist Court were restrained conservatives in 1989, centrists in 1992, activist conservatives in 1999, and then liberals in 2003. Rather than shifting our characterization of the Court from year to year, it seems worthwhile to take an analytic step back and attempt to make sense of the whole. To do so, some further reflections on the interaction of law and politics in constitutional development are necessary. After all, it might be the case that the Court's apparently shifting decisions are explained by the justices' sense of fidelity to our fundamental law, regardless of the political consequences. Alternatively, the complex pattern of liberal and conservative decisions might be attributable to the idiosyncratic political preferences of the Court's median justice, with her declarations of fidelity to law nothing more than misleading and self-serving rhetoric.

Law without Politics?

When pressed, no justices or Court scholars really believe that the Court's decisions are mechanically controlled by law, such that political influence is excluded altogether. Still, some constitutional conservatives continue to suggest that such a possibility is realistic and desirable. The Republican presidents who have been primarily responsible for staffing the Rehnquist Court,

for example, have often suggested that their judicial appointees would practice "strict constructionism" or judicial restraint or some other allegedly apolitical approach to constitutional adjudication. Similarly, advocates of originalism, both on and off the bench, sometimes insist that the chief benefit of
their approach is that it will remove politics from the Court's decisionmaking. Like Hugo Black before him, for example, Justice Antonin Scalia has
insisted that adhering to the original meaning of the text is the only way to
constrain arbitrary judicial discretion. When the justices abandon the constitutional text as their guide, in Scalia's and Black's view, they are left with
nothing but their own preferences. Thus, throughout his tenure, Scalia's
principal strategy for constraining judicial power has been to conduct constitutional interpretation through a process of categorical reasoning that permits as little judicial discretion as possible. He has acknowledged that the
original meaning of the Constitution is not the only place one might look to
find such categorical rules, but "when one does not have a solid textual anchor or an established social norm from which to derive the general rule, its
pronouncement appears uncomfortably like legislation" (1989:1184-85; see
also Bork 1990:242).

Scalia has gone further than Black in acknowledging that the Court's
judge-made legal rules are mutable and must sometimes be modified, but he
has insisted that the important question "is whether, *as mutated and modified*, they must *make sense*. The requirement that they do so is the only thing
that prevents this Court from being some sort of nine-headed Caesar, giving
thumbs-up or thumbs-down to whatever outcome, case by case, suits or offends its collective fancy."[2] In Scalia's view, "it displays more judicial restraint
to [base decisions on general rules] than to announce that, 'on balance,' we
think the law was violated here — leaving ourselves free to say in the next case
that, 'on balance,' it was not." Reflecting on his dissenting opinion in the
Court's 1988 decision upholding the independent counsel statute, he noted
that by announcing the general rule that all executive power is vested in the
president, he had provided a constraint for his own subsequent decisionmaking: "If the next case should have such different facts that my political or
policy preferences regarding the outcome are quite the opposite, I will be unable to indulge those preferences; I have committed myself to the governing
principle."[3] Chief Justice Rehnquist and Justice Clarence Thomas have not
agreed with Scalia on every particular, but they would all claim that the line
between the Court's liberal activist decisions (which they denounce as illegitimate) and its conservative activist decisions (which they enthusiastically

support) was drawn by the written Constitution itself and not by their own political preferences. Like Scalia, Thomas has urged his colleagues to adhere to the original understanding of the Constitution because such an approach would work "to reduce judicial discretion and to maintain judicial impartiality. [B]y tethering their analysis to the understanding of those who drafted and ratified the text, modern judges [would be] prevented from substituting their own preferences for the Constitution" (2001).

This effort to foreclose political influence from constitutional adjudication has not worked. The constitutional decisions of Scalia, Thomas, and Rehnquist have reflected a good-faith effort to develop a distinctive, post–Warren Court jurisprudence, but they certainly have not represented an apolitical derivation of the original Constitution. As Felix Frankfurter noted in response to Black many years ago, the rigid adherence to an unchanging text is more likely to foster the distortion of text and history than it is to constrain judicial discretion. The conservative justices may well believe that their duty is to enforce only the explicit provisions of the original Constitution, but the Rehnquist Court's conservative activism has in fact been rooted primarily in New Right constitutional commitments that have emerged over the past three decades. In other words, those constitutional conservatives who have insisted that the apparent tension between their activism and their demand for restraint is resolved by a set of disembodied legal categories have ignored the very clear political roots of their own constitutional ideas.

Consider the conservative majority's recent series of activist decisions. The conservative justices have made strong originalist arguments in support of some of these decisions, but even here, these arguments have not been readily separable from their very modern New Right critiques of the welfare state, liberal social engineering, and the like. In other contexts, they have made a plausible but hotly contested originalist case, mining U.S. legal history to support their reading of the Constitution, but facing trenchant challenges from those — most often Justice Souter — who have read that history differently. And in still others, they have made no originalist argument at all, because no plausible argument was available. Particularly where the Fourteenth Amendment is concerned, the conservative justices have often chosen simply to ignore the ongoing scholarly debates about its original meaning. With such inconsistent originalist support for their own activist decisions, it appears that some other motivating factor is at work.

In the equal protection context, Justices Scalia, Thomas, and Rehnquist have made almost no effort to provide historical support for their strict color-blind vision. If any of the voluminous research on the drafting and adoption of the Fourteenth Amendment supported this vision, one would expect them to have cited it, but they have instead contented themselves with the sweeping abstract assertion that race-conscious affirmative action policies are "at war with the principle of inherent equality that underlies and infuses our Constitution." In support of this assertion, advanced in his *Adarand* concurrence, Thomas cited the Declaration of Independence for the proposition that "all men are created equal."[4] Whatever this argument tells us, it does not have much to do with the original meaning of the Fourteenth Amendment, adopted some nine-two years after Jefferson wrote the Declaration. In *Richmond v. Croson,* in *Adarand,* in the University of Michigan cases (*Gratz* and *Grutter*), and in *Shaw v. Reno* and its progeny, Scalia, Thomas, and Rehnquist have provided no evidence of that original meaning.

Even after Justice Thurgood Marshall and a number of scholars pointed out that the same Reconstruction Congress that drafted the Fourteenth Amendment also adopted a variety of race-conscious remedial measures designed to benefit the former slaves, the conservative justices failed to respond with a historical argument of their own.[5] According to the approach professed by Justices Scalia, Thomas, and Rehnquist, it is legitimate for the Court to strike down recently enacted types of legislation that conflict with long-standing constitutional principles, but not to strike down long-standing legislation that appeared in the past to be consistent with constitutional principles. These historical lines, however, are very difficult to draw. From Marshall's perspective, the race-conscious admissions policies employed by public universities looked similar, in relevant respects, to the remedial legislation adopted by the Reconstruction Congress, but from Scalia, Thomas, and Rehnquist's angle, such policies look like products of the New Deal/Great Society welfare state. All of these arguments are contested, but since the conservative justices have failed to make a historical case of their own, it is difficult to give them the benefit of the doubt. The absence of any detailed historical argument to support their color-blind reading of the Equal Protection Clause raises suspicion that the conservatives are striking down democratically enacted affirmative action policies at least in part because of the New Right critique of liberal egalitarianism. In other words, their originalist approach is not actually providing the neutral bulwark against political judging that they claim as its chief benefit.

If the other examples of conservative activism on the Rehnquist Court fit the same pattern, then the impact of the New Right on the Supreme Court will be plain. In the federalism context, the conservative justices have provided much more in the way of historical evidence to support their activist holdings, but their efforts have been inconsistent even here. The historical arguments are once again contested, but it is clear that contemporary conservatives have been building on long-standing constitutional traditions regarding the limits of federal legislative authority. The Rehnquist Court's sharp distinction between the federal government's commerce authority and the states' police powers, for example, recalls the Progressive Era child labor cases, in which the Court held that Congress could not legitimately use its enumerated powers as a pretext for exercising a general police power. The New Deal Court overturned these decisions in the late 1930s and early 1940s, and while the Rehnquist Court has shown no interest in reviving the production/commerce distinction on which they rested, it has drawn an equally categorical line between federal and state authority.[6]

While Rehnquist has been the Court's most influential advocate of reviving such judicially enforceable limits on congressional power, Thomas has pushed these limits the farthest and has made the most extensive originalist case for doing so. Writing separately in *United States v. Lopez,* he complained about the modern Court's illegitimate revisions of the constitutional design and urged his colleagues "to temper our Commerce Clause jurisprudence in a manner that both makes sense of our more recent case law and is more faithful to the original understanding of that Clause." Even more strongly than Rehnquist, Thomas has objected to the post–New Deal doctrine of deference to congressional regulatory authority because it threatens to eviscerate the constitutional concept of enumerated powers as a means of achieving limited government. Thus, while Rehnquist merely applied the modern Court's "substantial effects" test a little more strictly in *Lopez,* Thomas urged the abandonment of this test as an illegitimate departure from the original constitutional design. In support of this historical claim, he offered a lengthy review of eighteenth-century definitions of "commerce," the ratification debates in the original states, and the Court's early case law on the commerce power.[7]

In addition to their specific concerns about the original meaning of particular clauses — evinced by Thomas's mining of eighteenth-century dictionaries — the conservative justices have repeatedly articulated a more general argument that the original constitutional structure of federalism is essential to the protection of constitutional rights. Writing for the Court in *Lopez,* for example, Rehnquist urged a return to "first principles," drawing on *The Federalist* and the Court's own precedents to suggest that "a healthy balance of power between the States and the Federal Government will reduce the risk of tyranny and abuse from either front."[8] In *Printz*, Scalia observed that the separation of the federal and state spheres of authority "is one of the Constitution's structural protections of liberty," relying on Madison's famous "double security" passage from *The Federalist* No. 51 in support, and in *Morrison*, Rehnquist reiterated that "[t]he constitutionally mandated balance of power between the States and the Federal Government was adopted by the Framers to ensure the protection of our fundamental liberties."[9]

In the federalism cases, then, the conservative justices of the Rehnquist Court do appear to have been influenced by a sense of fidelity to the original Constitution, but this fidelity has not prevented them from responding to more modern concerns as well. Most notably, shades of the neoconservative critique of the welfare-regulatory state and the public choice critique of congressional lawmaking can be found throughout their opinions. After all, the federal statutes that the conservative justices have been calling into question — the Gun-Free School Zones Act, the Violence against Women Act, the Americans with Disabilities Act, the Family and Medical Leave Act, and the like — are precisely the sort of statutes that libertarian conservatives have been criticizing for a generation. In the conservative mind, these statutes represent an overreaching federal government that is ignoring the constitutional limits of its authority in order to regulate the lives of individual property owners, consumers, business owners, and the like. As Suzanna Sherry has suggested, "[t]oo many statutes written with too little care have meant that the courts must resolve the ambiguities. And perhaps those careless congressional tentacles regulating more aspects of life with greater detail have contributed to the Court's hostility toward even justifiable congressional enactments. Perhaps Congress's eagerness to enact popular statutes without much concern about either their clarity or their constitutionality has increased the Court's mistrust of the federal legislature" (1999:23). Similarly, Shep Melnick (2003) has noted that one of the key themes in the Court's recent federalism opinions has been the preservation of political accountability, as the conservative justices simply do not trust Congress to act in the public interest.

In *New York v. United States*, for example, the Court noted that when elected officials at either the federal or state level choose to adopt and administer a regulatory regime, those officials will be accountable to the electorate, "[b]ut where the Federal Government directs the States to regulate, it may be state officials who will bear the brunt of public disapproval, while the federal officials who devised the regulatory program may remain insulated from the electoral ramifications of their decision."[10] The Court reiterated this complaint in *Printz,* noting that "[b]y forcing state governments to absorb the financial burden of implementing a federal regulatory program, Members of Congress can take credit for 'solving' problems without having to ask their constituents to pay for the solutions with higher federal taxes. And even when the States are not forced to absorb the costs of implementing a federal program, they are still put in the position of taking the blame for its burdensomeness and for its defects."[11] In other words, the conservative justices have been concerned with what they see as the pernicious consequences of the post–New Deal Court's deference to congressional lawmaking. This concern is clearly a modern one, not closely tethered to the historical Constitution.

As in other areas of the law, it is difficult to tease out the relative influence on the Court of these "legal" and "political" factors, the conventional description of which implies a greater degree of independence between them than actually exists. The modern conservative commitment to limited government has been shaped in part by long-standing constitutional traditions, present since the Founding, and the contemporary conservative reading of the Founding-era history has also been shaped in part by the New Right critique of the modern state. When the conservative justices criticized Congress in the case concerning the Family and Medical Leave Act (FMLA) for using §5 as a pretext for enacting "a substantive entitlement program of its own," their argument clearly reflected both a constitutionally rooted concern for limited government and a broad suspicion of the modern Congress.[12]

While these competing influences cannot be neatly separated, it is clear that the conservative commitment to originalism is not by itself an adequate explanation for the federalism revival. For one thing, the conservatives' Tenth Amendment holdings have been less closely tied to the original text than their Commerce Clause decisions, and their sovereign immunity and §5 arguments have appeared to depart even more blithely from original meaning. Writing for the Court in *Printz,* Justice Scalia acknowledged at the very outset that "there is no constitutional text speaking to this precise question, [and hence that] the answer . . . must be sought in historical understanding and practice, in the structure of the Constitution, and in the jurisprudence of this Court." Surveying the nation's historical practices, he found virtually no pre–twentieth century examples of congressional efforts to impress state executives into service, and he insisted that the relatively numerous modern examples were of "such recent vintage" that they did not amount to "a constitutional tradition that lends meaning to the text." Turning to the question of constitutional structure, Scalia emphasized the "dual sovereignty" that was implicit in the original Constitution and that was rendered explicit by the Tenth Amendment. This opinion was an unexceptional instance of Scalia's usual approach, but because the relevant text and traditions provided so little guidance here, a number of critics denounced the decision as a *Griswold*-like example of judicial lawmaking.[13]

Similarly, the sovereign immunity decisions have been rooted in the Eleventh Amendment, but the conservative justices have themselves acknowledged that they rest on a broader, nontextual conception of state immunity from suit. The text of the amendment prohibits the federal courts from entertaining suits by citizens of one state against the government of another state, but the Rehnquist Court has extended this doctrine beyond that textual limitation in three distinct ways. In *Alden v. Maine,* the Court held that sovereign immunity applies in the states' own courts as well as in federal courts, and the following year, in *Kimel v. Florida Board of Regents,* it held that sovereign immunity applies to federal suits brought by a state's own citizens, as well as suits brought by citizens of other states. Two years after that, in *Federal Maritime Commission v. South Carolina State Ports Authority,* the Court held that while the Eleventh Amendment limits only the "Judicial power of the United States," the broader concept of state sovereign immunity extends to federal administrative proceedings as well.

Writing for the Court in this last case, Justice Thomas acknowledged that the text appeared inapplicable and that "the relevant history d[id] not provide direct guidance," but he reiterated that "the sovereign immunity enjoyed by the States extends beyond the literal text of the Eleventh Amendment." Given the dearth of his ordinarily preferred textual and historical evidence, Thomas appealed to the overall structural design of the Constitution, in which States were accorded "the dignity that is consistent with their status as sovereign entities," and he speculated that "if the Framers thought it an impermissible affront to a State's dignity to be required to answer the complaints of private parties in federal courts, we cannot imagine that they would have found it acceptable to compel a State to do exactly the same thing before the administrative tribunal of an agency." For an originalist, this is pretty thin evidence for justifying the Court's exercise of the power of judicial review. It certainly marked a departure from the doctrine that the Court should defer to the political branches when neither the constitutional text nor our legal traditions clearly prohibits the law or policy in question. After

all, while Thomas insisted here that the Court should defend the unenumerated "dignity and respect" due to state governments as sovereign entities, he
has objected whenever the Court defends the unenumerated dignity and respect due to individual persons.[14]

The Court's reading of §5 of the Fourteenth Amendment has also been
vulnerable on originalist grounds. As I have already acknowledged, the details of Reconstruction history are a matter of intense historical debate, but
it is fairly clear that the congressional Republicans who drafted and adopted
the Fourteenth Amendment intended Congress, and not the Court, to be
the primary enforcer of its broad rights guarantees. Justice Stephen Breyer
has pointed out that the amendment was "specifically designed as an expansion of federal power and an intrusion on state sovereignty"; hence, the
Rehnquist Court's "evidentiary demands, its non-deferential review, and its
failure to distinguish between judicial and legislative constitutional competencies [were] improperly invad[ing] a power that the Constitution as-
signs to Congress."[15] As in the affirmative action context, the conservative
justices have failed to confront this argument with historical evidence of their
own. To the extent that the Rehnquist Court's federalism revival has been
rooted in fidelity to original meaning, then, it has been a 1789 version of original meaning that minimizes the constitutional change wrought during Reconstruction.

Once again, the fact that some, but not all, of the conservative justices' federalism doctrines are firmly grounded in constitutional history raises the suspicion that the proximate cause and key motivation of the federalism revival
have lain elsewhere. This suspicion is furthered by the fact that the leading
academic advocates of this revival have been conservatives who are sharply
critical of the modern welfare-regulatory state (Epstein 1987). In the absence
of this hostility to government regulation, it is difficult to imagine the Court
reviving nineteenth-century visions of the proper scope of federal power.
Moreover, where the narrow vision of federal power cuts against other conservative values, the conservative justices have sometimes departed from
their usual approach. In *United States v. Oakland Cannabis Buyers' Cooperative,* for example, the five conservative justices read congressional authority
to regulate illicit drugs quite broadly, preventing California from allowing
the medicinal use of marijuana and prompting the dissenting liberal justices
to complain that the Court was unnecessarily hampering state regulatory ex-
perimentation.[16] Similarly, in *Crosby v. National Foreign Trade Council,* the
conservative justices (and indeed the whole Court) read the federal govern-

ment's authority over foreign affairs as broad and exclusive, disallowing the states from seeking to promote human rights in Burma.[17]

Still, in most contexts, the Rehnquist Court has read federal legislative authority more narrowly than at any time since the New Deal, and it has revived a variety of constitutional doctrines — not just those regarding federalism — that might serve to impose some limits on the modern state. Many of the Court's property rights and free speech decisions, for example, have reflected a similar concern, and again, only some of these decisions have been supported by any originalist argument at all. In the commercial speech cases, for example, Thomas has gone further than any other justice in contending that there is no "philosophical or historical basis for asserting that 'commercial' speech is of 'lower value' than 'noncommercial' speech," and hence that state and federal regulations of alcohol and tobacco advertising (among other things) are unconstitutional.[18] As Mark Graber has noted, however, Thomas has failed to offer any historical argument in support of this claim, perhaps because "no scholar claims that the persons responsible for the First Amendment intended to protect advertising" (2003:88).

Similarly, Justices Scalia, Thomas, and Rehnquist have advanced an aggressive claim that virtually all limits on campaign contributions or expenditures are unconstitutional. In support of this doctrine, they have appealed to the central purpose of the First Amendment, but they have not supplied any well-developed originalist arguments. Dissenting in *Austin v. Michigan State Chamber of Commerce,* for example, Scalia speculated about what Jefferson and Madison would have thought of a Michigan statute prohibiting corporations from using corporate treasury funds for independent election-related expenditures, but he offered no historical evidence to support those speculations. He did cite Tocqueville's *Democracy in America,* but that 1835 classic surely reveals very little about the original meaning of the First Amendment, adopted in 1791.[19] Dissenting ten years later in *Nixon v. Shrink Missouri Government PAC,* Thomas objected that while the modern Court "ha[d] extended First Amendment protection to a multitude of forms of 'speech,' such as making false defamatory statements, filing lawsuits, dancing nude, . . . burning flags," and the like, it was now refusing to protect political speech, "the primary object of First Amendment protection." Thomas cited Robert Bork's 1971 "neutral principles" article and quoted Madison on the importance of "the equal freedom . . . of examining and discussing the[ ] merits and demerits of . . . candidates" for public office, but once again, he offered no detailed historical argument.[20]

The property rights decisions have been more firmly rooted in original meaning, but have quite obviously reflected New Right political demands as well. In *Phillips v. Washington Legal Foundation* and *Brown v. Legal Foundation of Washington,* the Washington Legal Foundation persuaded the Court to closely scrutinize a widely used method for financing indigent legal aid. Justice O'Connor ultimately prevented the Court from invalidating the method, but the episode clearly reflected a conservative effort to mobilize the Takings Clause on behalf of contemporary political goals. More generally, the Court's takings jurisprudence has reflected a broad conservative campaign to limit the government's authority to regulate private property in the name of environmental protection, historical preservation, and the like.

If the spectrum of constitutional principles that Scalia, Thomas, and Rehnquist are willing to actively enforce is actually drawn from their reading of the original Constitution, then it is remarkable how closely it resembles the New Right policy agenda of the late twentieth century. The originalist approach was ostensibly designed to remove politics from constitutional adjudication, but that is not what has actually happened in practice. As I have noted again and again, much of the new conservative activism has been rooted in long-standing constitutional traditions, particularly those regarding federalism and limited government, and it would not be surprising if some of these traditions overlapped with the conservative critique of modern liberalism. It would be surprising, however, if the 1787 Constitution included virtually all of the significant elements of this critique. The litany of conservative activism that I have described bears such a close resemblance to the New Right political agenda that it is difficult to avoid the conclusion that the conservatives sometimes bend the original Constitution to promote conservative ends. As Graber has noted, originalism as actually practiced is not politically neutral and does not prevent the conservative justices from reaching decisions that are consistent with their preferences (2003:87–90; see also Levinson 1996).

Scalia, Thomas, and Rehnquist's activism does not always support conservative ends, but it certainly does so most of the time, and the broad pattern of their votes and opinions can be more fully explained by reference to the New Right vision of limited government than by reference to the original Constitution. While these three justices have repeatedly urged the Court to refuse to protect allegedly fundamental rights that (in their view) cannot be found in either the constitutional text or our nation's legal traditions, they have themselves joined a number of decisions that can only be characterized as activist defenses of novel conservative rights claims. The free speech rights of commercial advertisers have only a tenuous connection to the original meaning of the constitutional text, as does the right to live in an electoral district free from race-conscious gerrymandering. The conservative justices' federalism and property rights arguments are more firmly rooted in the original Constitution, but there are some exceptions even in these areas. In short, modern conservative activism is rooted in contemporary constitutional commitments that have not primarily been motivated by a sense of fidelity to the original meaning of the constitutional text.

Bush v. Gore is the best example here. Scalia, Thomas, and Rehnquist's justification for stopping the Florida recounts was rooted in a reading of the original constitutional text — Article II, §1 — but it is impossible to credit this argument as the true motivating force behind their decision. The widespread description of the case as conservative activism run amok seems indisputable.[21] Richard Posner, one of the decision's most prominent *defenders*, has noted forthrightly that "*Bush v. Gore* is an activist decision. . . . The Court thrust itself boldly into the center of a political struggle. . . . The three most conservative Justices dusted off a forgotten provision of the Constitution . . . and gave it a meaning very likely unintended by the Constitution's framers, whom conservative lawyers and judges tend to venerate to the point of idolatry" (2001:217–18). Prior to November 2000, virtually all legal scholars and judges would have described presidential vote-counting as an area of law entrusted to other institutions of government for the resolution of any conflicts — state courts, executives, and legislatures, in the first instance, and Congress for the ultimate decision.[22] Again, if it were not clear before, the *Bush v. Gore* decision suggests that the proximate cause of the recent revival of conservative judicial activism lies with the post-1968 conservative shift in American politics.

Put another way, the conservative justices' chief motivation has been their hostility toward modern liberalism rather than a particular vision of judicial power. Consider, for example, the conservative position in two prominent gay rights cases. In *Romer v. Evans,* religious conservatives sought to use democratic procedures to get rid of antidiscrimination laws that they opposed. They were successful at the polls, and their allies on the Court urged deference to this democratic outcome. But in *Boy Scouts v. Dale,* these same conservatives used the courts themselves to impose limits on democratically enacted antidiscrimination laws. The vision of constitutional equality advanced by Justices Scalia, Thomas, and Rehnquist is rooted in the New Right critique

of egalitarianism and liberal "social engineering" that emerged during the
1970s. In the face of legislative infringements on gay rights, this critique of liberalism has led them to exercise judicial restraint and to denounce the Court
for "imposing upon all Americans the resolution favored by the elite class
from which the Members of this institution are selected."[23] In the face of legislative efforts to defend minority rights, however, this same vision has led to
their endorsing the active exercise of judicial power in an effort to prevent
such policies of social engineering.

If the constitutional logic of these opinions is a coherent one (and I think
that it is), it is a logic regarding the denunciation of liberal egalitarianism, not
the denunciation of government by judiciary. When considered together
with the Court's recent decisions limiting congressional authority to regulate
discrimination against the old and the disabled, to accommodate the practices of religious minorities, to stop violence against women, and the like, the
anti-egalitarian pattern is even more striking (see Rubenfeld 2002). Scalia,
Thomas, and Rehnquist insist that they support judicial activism when, and
only when, the original Constitution calls for it, but such disembodied legal
considerations alone cannot explain the actual pattern of their decisions.

As I noted in chapter 6, Justices O'Connor and Kennedy have adopted a
much less categorical approach to constitutional adjudication, one that more
forthrightly acknowledges the necessity and difficulty of judicial efforts to
balance competing values. Like their colleagues' originalism, their emphasis
on "reasoned judgment" reflects a relatively coherent set of legal principles,
but not one that forecloses political choice.

Politics without Law?

In light of the striking emergence of conservative activism on the Rehnquist
Court, it is not surprising that some scholars have attributed the Court's decisions solely to the justices' own policy preferences. A long line of political
scientists has tried to debunk an overly legalistic understanding of the Court
by means of statistical analyses that explain judicial behavior without reference to legal considerations at all, and the Court's recent conservative decisions have reinforced this overtly political account. The leading academic advocates of this approach, Jeffrey Segal and Harold Spaeth, have described the
Rehnquist Court as their "most persuasive ally," noting that *Bush v. Gore* and
the sovereign immunity decisions had significantly strengthened their case
for the "attitudinal model" of judicial decisionmaking (2003:31).

While the statistical analysis of Supreme Court decisions has generally been confined to academic political science departments, the perception that the justices pursue their own preferred results has reached more broadly, and again, this perception has been reinforced by the apparent conservative abandonment of restraint. Jeffrey Rosen, for example, has regularly criticized Rehnquist Court activism in pieces written for a general audience, and he has pointedly insisted that this activism reveals conservative legal principles as a sham. Complaining that "Scalia has an uncanny ability to reach the result that happens to coincide with his own preferences in case after case," Rosen has insisted that while "[e]xtreme deference to the traditional practices of democratic majorities is a plausible vision of the judicial role," it is not one to which Scalia consistently adheres. On Rosen's reading, "Scalia chooses among mutually inconsistent interpretive principles . . . in order to reach results that he finds politically congenial" (1997b:28). Noting in 1995 that the conservative justices had "plunged into the political thicket [of affirmative action] without worrying about the political consequences," Rosen sought to remind them that the Court "is supposed to be a body of principle, not politics, committed to interpreting the law, not making it. . . . For those . . . who have been sympathetic to the conservative rhetoric of judicial restraint, strict constructionism and devotion to the original understanding of the Constitution, it's hard not to read the race decisions without feeling embarrassed and foolish and slightly duped, [because these] cases reveal the conservative judicial project to be unprincipled at its core" (1995:19; see also Rosen 1996a; 2000c).

Similarly, Segal and Spaeth have long insisted that legal principles such as originalism and judicial restraint are nothing more than rhetorical covers for the justices' own predilections. Relying on their analysis of judicial votes from the beginning of the Warren era through the end of the Supreme Court's 1989 term, they argued that "the mere fact that justices may wrap themselves in the mantle of restraint does not mean that they actually practice what they preach. Indeed, even the most nodding acquaintance with the real world ought to make such a posture suspect." On their reading, "[w]ith the single exception of Rehnquist," every justice who served during this period "appear[ed] to use restraint . . . as a means to rationalize, support, and justify their substantive policy concerns. If they support a policy, . . . restraint serves as a useful cloak to conceal the nakedness of a barefaced statement of substantive preferences." And even Rehnquist, who does "appear[ ] reluctant to declare actions unconstitutional, . . . does not extend [that reluctance] to constitutional issues on which the government generally takes a liberal position, such as affirmative action . . . and the taking of property" (1993:300, 326–27; see also Spaeth and Teger 1982). Updating this argument some years later, Segal and Spaeth demonstrated that the liberal justices of the Rehnquist Court were more likely to strike down conservative statutes and the conservative justices were more likely to strike down liberal statutes (2002:412–16).

In a similar vein, political scientists Glenn Phelps and John Gates set out to examine whether justices actually adhere to the interpretive theory of originalism by means of a content analysis of all of Rehnquist's and Brennan's opinions from 1973 to 1982. They found that Rehnquist was not much more likely to appeal to historical or textual justifications than was Brennan, and concluded by questioning whether "we [can] take seriously the claim of *any* Justice that he or she reached a particular outcome by the command of the law rather than by the predilection of their [sic] politics."[24]

These accounts of judicial behavior are sometimes referred to as "instrumentalist" because they suggest that the law is simply an instrument for judges to use as they see fit. On this reading, the law exerts little or no independent influence on what judges do. One implication of my research is that in making this suggestion, scholarly advocates of the attitudinal model have relied on an unacceptably thin rendering of conservative legal ideas. As part of their effort to test whether the justices are influenced by law, these scholars have tended to operationalize constitutional conservatism in terms of one easily coded principle, such as "The Court should defer to legislative decisions," or "The Constitution should be interpreted in accord with its original meaning." Needless to say, they have found that conservative justices do not always adhere to these principles as stated, and they have concluded that the justices use jurisprudential principles such as "judicial restraint" or "originalism" simply to cloak their own policy preferences. The problem with these arguments is that no past or current justice has claimed that the Court should always defer to the decisions of democratically elected legislatures. Neither has any justice held that the original intentions of the framers are the only legitimate source of constitutional meaning (or, for that matter, that those intentions are wholly irrelevant to constitutional meaning). Since real-world constitutional philosophies are more complex, and tend to be composed of multiple, competing principles, it is necessary to provide a much fuller account of these ideas before dismissing them as irrelevant.

Put another way, these extralegal accounts of judicial behavior have overstated the coherence of the conservative constitutional vision in an effort to show that the conservative members of the bench abandon that vision whenever it is convenient to do so. Constitutional conservatives have long advocated judicial restraint, but they have long advocated limited government as well, and these principles sometimes pull in opposite directions. The fact that modern constitutional conservatism is composed of multiple competing principles should not be surprising. In that respect, it is no different from the post–New Deal liberal constitutional vision that it has sought to displace — or, indeed, from any effort to articulate a broad vision of the constitutional order. And since the conservative principle of judicial restraint exists in tension with other conservative constitutional principles, Segal and Spaeth are wrong to assume that if a justice's proclaimed adherence to restraint is genuine, then its use "will be even-handed [and] it will apply across the policy-making board" (1993:305).

So while these scholars have demonstrated that liberal justices are more likely to engage in liberal activism and that conservative justices are more likely to engage in conservative activism, such a pattern does not necessarily imply that judicial decisions are unconstrained by law. As I have noted at some length, the conservative justices' chief motivation can easily be characterized as hostility to modern liberalism, but a chief motivation is not the same as a sole motivation, and these justices have not in fact sought to read each and every one of their own political preferences into the Constitution. While conservative constitutional scholars have sometimes advocated the full abandonment of restraint in pursuit of conservative constitutional ideals, none of the conservative justices have felt free to go so far. Thomas has gone the furthest, but even he stops short of the views of, say, Richard Epstein. Segal and Spaeth's own data show that O'Connor, Kennedy, Scalia, and Thomas each upholds at least 20 percent of the liberal statutes for which a viable constitutional challenge reaches the Court. Rehnquist, for his part, upholds 60 percent of those statutes, more than Ginsburg, Souter, or Stevens. Meanwhile, O'Connor and Kennedy each votes to strike down at least 47 percent of the conservative statutes under similar circumstances, and Scalia and Thomas each strikes down at least one-third of those conservative statutes as well (2002:416). These patterns simply cannot be explained by reference to the justices' policy preferences alone.

The most difficult hurdle for these overtly political accounts of the Rehnquist Court has been the Court's continued support for liberal activism. Perhaps most notably, *Romer* and *Lawrence* stand together as a remarkable declaration of support for gay rights by the conservative Court. Kennedy's opinion in *Romer* was cautious, but it clearly recognized that the federal courts must protect minority groups that have faced prejudice and discrimination from majoritarian tyranny, and that gays and lesbians are such a group. In a gay rights case, just ten years after *Bowers v. Hardwick*, a justice appointed by Ronald Reagan declared for the Court that "[a] State cannot so deem a class of persons a stranger to its laws." [25] Just seven years later, this same conservative justice went even further, holding that the *Bowers* "precedent demeans the lives of homosexual persons," that it "was not correct when it was decided, and . . . is not correct today," and that gays and lesbians "are entitled to respect for their private lives." The great Republican statesmen who drafted the Fourteenth Amendment in the wake of the Civil War, Kennedy noted, knew that "later generations can see that laws once thought necessary and proper in fact serve only to oppress." O'Connor joined Kennedy's opinion in *Romer* and wrote separately in *Lawrence* to make clear that "moral disapproval" of gays and lesbians, "like a bare desire to harm the group, is an interest insufficient to satisfy" the Court's constitutional scrutiny.[26] Together, these decisions show that two members of the conservative majority were willing to cast deciding votes for constitutional arguments in support of gay rights, and even to write sweeping opinions endorsing such arguments. There was nothing inevitable about this development, and there is no evidence to suggest that it can be explained solely as a result of O'Connor's and Kennedy's preexisting political preferences.

The response by Justices O'Connor and Kennedy to conservative rights claims is also difficult to explain without reference to law. As I have noted at some length, these swing justices have regularly and repeatedly frustrated their conservative colleagues by limiting the reach of their conservative decisions. Scholars have sometimes read O'Connor's careful, fact-specific opinions in these cases as mere rhetoric, designed to distract attention from her unambiguous conservative activism. But the limits that she articulates do in fact have concrete legal and policy effects, as decisions like *Easley v. Cromartie*, *Grutter v. Bollinger*, and *Nevada Department of Human Resources v. Hibbs* make clear.

Throughout the affirmative action and racial gerrymandering cases, for example, O'Connor endorsed the color-blind reading of the Equal Protection Clause, but alone among the conservative majority, she has been unwilling to enforce that reading without reservation. It is not that she is less committed to color-blind equality than her colleagues; it is just that her vision of the judicial role tempers her willingness to enforce that commitment. Like her fellow conservatives, she has repeatedly insisted that "[c]lassifications of citizens solely on the basis of race are by their very nature odious to a free people whose institutions are founded upon the doctrine of equality. They threaten to stigmatize individuals by reason of their membership in a racial group and to incite racial hostility." [27] Unlike these colleagues, however, she has been troubled by the extensive activism that would be necessary to enforce such a principle in a political context in which bipartisan legislative majorities continue to endorse, or at least fail to repeal, race-conscious affirmative action policies. O'Connor is herself quite suspicious of such policies, as her opinions over more than two decades have made clear, but she still voted to hand conservatives a stinging defeat in *Grutter.*

O'Connor's decision to limit the reach of conservative activism in this case cannot be explained solely by reference to her own, perhaps moderate, views on affirmative action. This explanation cannot be adequate because O'Connor (and sometimes Kennedy) have adopted an identical approach in many different areas of the law. In the federalism context, for example, they have limited the reach of the Court's activism, not because they object to its goals, but because they insist on leaving room for continued democratic deliberation. Like their conservative colleagues, O'Connor and Kennedy support the Court's efforts to revive long-standing constitutional principles of federalism that would (as they see it) impose some much-needed limits on the modern liberal state. Like Scalia, Thomas, and Rehnquist, they are sharply suspicious of congressional lawmaking, complaining with some regularity about that body's irresponsible efforts to curry public favor and satisfy powerful special interests. In short, they share the same basic substantive concerns as their conservative colleagues.[28] Despite these concerns, they have hedged the federalism revolution, allowing it to proceed only so far and no farther. As Shep Melnick (2003) has suggested, this caution may reflect a prudent decision not to attack the legislative heart of the New Deal or the civil rights revolution, but it is a sort of prudence that cuts across multiple areas of constitutional doctrine. In other words, the frequent hedging on the parts of O'Connor and Kennedy reflects a particular vision of the judicial role, a jurisprudential stance rather than, or in addition to, a moderate politics.

In the religious freedom context, O'Connor has again sought to limit the reach of the Court's conservative activism. Concurring in *Rosenberger v. University of Virginia,* she provided one of her most explicit discussions of her preference for careful, case-by-case line drawing, noting that when "two bedrock principles" are in conflict, as with the doctrine of neutrality toward religion and the prohibition of public funding for religion in this case, "neither can provide the definitive answer. . . . Resolution instead depends on the hard task of judging — sifting through the details and determining whether the challenged program offends the Establishment Clause. Such judgment requires courts to draw lines, sometimes quite fine, based on the particular facts of each case." In her characteristic move, she insisted that "[t]he nature of the dispute does not admit of categorical answers, nor should any be inferred from the Court's decision today." As always, since her fifth vote was necessary to the Court's holding, this limiting construction carried great weight. She voted with her fellow conservatives, but made clear that she might not follow them as far as they wanted to go.[29]

O'Connor is no less persuaded than Justices Scalia and Thomas of the virtues of government neutrality toward religion, just as she is no less persuaded of the virtues of color-blindness or property rights or limited government. However, she has consistently sought to reconcile these principles with her continued suspicion of "government by judiciary." The fact that she and Kennedy have so often voted to strike down democratically enacted statutes, while at the same time circumscribing the reach of their holdings, suggests a general concern on their part that cuts across areas of constitutional doctrine. Rather than insisting that O'Connor believes in federalism, but less so than Rehnquist; that she believes in color-blind equality, but less so than Scalia; that she believes in free speech for religious speakers, but less so than Thomas, I have tried to describe her own justifications for these decisions. These justifications suggest that she has acted on the basis of a general approach regarding the limited legitimacy and capacity of the unelected judiciary. O'Connor and Kennedy have not operationalized this principle of restraint in the way to which we are most accustomed, but they nonetheless take this principle quite seriously. They see their fundamental duty as enforcing constitutional limits on our democratic government, but they are reluctant to authorize sweeping judicial disruptions of majoritarian politics. As a result, they seek to move cautiously, "one case at a time," as Cass Sunstein (1999) has so nicely put it.

To explain the jurisprudence of O'Connor and Kennedy, and hence that of the Rehnquist Court itself, we need to look at their visions of the judicial role as well as their political ideologies. Those accounts that suggest that O'Connor and Kennedy are simply "less conservative" than some of their colleagues are not so much wrong as incomplete. After all, from one angle, O'Connor and Kennedy clearly are less conservative than Scalia, Thomas, and Rehnquist. They are moderate conservatives, or "country club Republicans," critical of modern liberalism but hostile to the social conservatism of the religious Right (Tushnet 1998). As some scholars have noted, these swing justices are only on the Court because, like Stevens and Souter, the Republican presidents who appointed them faced significant political constraints that prevented them from selecting a Robert Bork. Thus, when Segal and Spaeth coded the justices' political values on a scale from −1.00 (extremely conservative) to 1.00 (extremely liberal), and listed O'Connor and Kennedy with higher values than Scalia, Thomas, and Rehnquist, they certainly captured an important part of the decisionmaking dynamics on the Rehnquist Court.[30]

Still, from a different angle, it is clear that the lines dividing the conservative justices have as much to do with their competing visions of the judicial role as with the degree of their conservatism. All of the justices seek to balance constitutional liberty and democratic governance, but these two groups of conservatives have sought to do so in distinctly different ways. After all, if O'Connor and Kennedy are simply moderates, rather than liberals or conservatives, they could just as easily have decided to reject both liberal and conservative rights claims, following Frankfurter's path of judicial restraint. In *Gratz* and *Lawrence,* such moderate conservatism could have led them to uphold Michigan's affirmative action policy (at the undergraduate college) and Texas's sodomy law. Why, instead, did they strike down both policies, coming to support rights-based activism across the board?

Scholarly efforts to explain such decisions without reference to law tend to remain too vaguely specified to account for the actual pattern of judicial decisions. Referring to O'Connor and Kennedy as "moderate," for example, tells us little about the actual content of their constitutional ideas. It cannot tell us why they disagree with Stevens and Souter so often. Or why they have written very conservative opinions in a wide range of constitutional cases. Or, for that matter, why they have written very liberal opinions in a different set of cases. As with the purely legalistic accounts, then, the purely political explanations cannot explain the mixed pattern of conservative influence on the law. They cannot explain why the conservative Court has continued to defend liberal conceptions of constitutional rights, as well as the newer conservative conceptions. Nor can they explain why O'Connor and Kennedy have so often limited the reach of the conservative activist decisions that they themselves have supported. If the justices are motivated solely by their own political preferences, then neither of these developments makes any sense.

The Rehnquist Court's pattern of judicial activism certainly cannot be explained as the product of the justices' politically neutral application of the law, and this recognition has understandably led some observers to look for an explanation outside the law altogether. Some justices, in some cases, do appear to have ignored or manipulated the law in an effort to promote their own, extralegal preferences. But most justices, in most cases, make a sincere effort to follow the law as they see it. The way that Scalia and Thomas see it is, not surprisingly, tinged by conservative ideology (to put it mildly). But their vision of the law cannot be reduced to a laundry list of GOP priorities. The *Bush v. Gore* decision may well have been motivated by partisan concerns, but if so, it was an exceptional rather than representative case. Even this decision, moreover, reflected a broader conservative vision of the judicial role that has characterized the Rehnquist Court's constitutional decisions more generally. If constitutional conservatives had not developed an expansive vision of judicial power, in which the Court is duty-bound to enforce (conservative) constitutional limits on an unprincipled Congress, it would have been much more difficult for the conservative justices to intervene in the 2000 presidential election.

Timing, Conjuncture, and the Path of the Law

In sum, the existing accounts of judicial decisionmaking on the Rehnquist Court are unpersuasive. Modern conservatives have not simply been following the dictates of an unambiguous constitutional text. Nor have they merely been manipulating constitutional ideas to suit their own ends. We cannot understand the options that the justices of the Rehnquist Court have faced, or the choices that they have made, by reference to either legal or political factors in isolation. The failure of these approaches suggests a more general point: that it may not be particularly useful to characterize "legal" and "political" factors as separate and distinct influences on the Court. In the context of constitutional adjudication, the legal ideas and political interests that shape judicial behavior are mutually constitutive. Justice Scalia's emphasis on text and legal traditions is not politically neutral and is not the one true way to interpret the Constitution, but it does constrain his decisionmaking, leading him to be particularly concerned with certain sorts of rights violations and particularly unconcerned with others.[31] Similarly, Justice O'Connor's case-by-case evaluation of state and federal legislation in light of constitutional principle — simultaneously activist and cautious — is not unrelated to her own pragmatic conservatism, but neither is it reducible to a set of moderate positions on the various legislative proposals of the day. The important divisions on the current Court are those that I described in chapter 6, and these divisions are simply not captured by an account of the justices' idiosyncratic preferences on a host of particular policy issues.

My alternative account, which should by now be clear, is that judicial decisionmaking and constitutional development can only be explained by reference to the justices' efforts to grapple with, make sense of, and sometimes modify, the multiple jurisprudential traditions that they have inherited. To explain why the current justices have viewed some inherited traditions as fixed, but others as ripe for alteration or abandonment, I have emphasized the ongoing interaction between the logic of partisan political order, on the one hand, and the institutionalized pattern of ideas associated with constitutional interpretation, on the other. The conjuncture of these relatively autonomous processes both constrains the justices' available alternatives (in any given context) and constitutes the preferences that they seek to promote. The justices have significant discretion in shaping constitutional law, but all of their available paths are formed by institutionally embedded legal categories. For members of the Supreme Court, as for other office holders, it remains clear that "[w]hether institutional rules are applied or resisted, juxtaposed or transformed, they shape and direct the actions of both institutional incumbents and those who seek their control" (Orren and Skowronek 1996:139).

Legal and political influences on the Court are mutually constitutive. The justices' ostensibly political preferences have themselves been constituted in part by legal ideas, and those legal ideas, in turn, have been derived in large part from ongoing debates in the broader political system. None of the contemporary conservative constitutional arguments have been made from whole cloth. In the absence of constitutional traditions regarding the limited powers of the national government, Chief Justice Rehnquist and his conservative colleagues would have had no legal resources with which to advance their call for strict limits on congressional regulatory authority. But the mere presence of such a tradition cannot explain its contemporary revival by the Court. There are other long-standing constitutional traditions, after all, that the conservatives have not revived. In other words, their arguments about the original meaning of the constitutional text and the defects of the modern welfare-regulatory state are not readily separable.

This account calls into question the conventional narrative in which conservatives falsely professed to believe in judicial restraint until they themselves took control of the Court, at which time they dramatically changed their tune. Rosen spoke for many Court watchers when he complained about "the unselfconscious hypocrisy with which [today's conservative judicial activists] are abandoning the judicial philosophies on which they have staked their careers" (2000c:21). But as I have shown at some length, the contradictions in contemporary judicial conservatism, if contradictions they be, have been present in Rehnquist's jurisprudence from the beginning. It is simply not the case that the Court's recent revival of judicial activism in the federalism context (to which Rosen was referring) emerged *ex nihilo*. Rehnquist himself had been advocating just such a revival since the mid-1970s. The relevant question, then, is not why the conservatives suddenly abandoned restraint when they took control of the federal judiciary, but why Rehnquist and his fellow conservatives have considered their long-standing constitutional vision a coherent and consistent one. Put another way, the question is not why conservatives have abandoned a long-held principle to achieve a preferred result, but how they have reconciled two long-standing principles that are in tension.

Again, conservative activism did not emerge simply because the words of the original constitutional text commanded it, but neither did it come from out of the blue, with post-1994 conservative justices discovering their newfound majority and suddenly deciding to put it to political use. Rather, conservative activism evolved over time, as justices increasingly opposed to 1960s liberalism joined the bench. It is certainly possible to characterize these conservative shifts in the law as nakedly political efforts to bend the Constitution to conservative ends, but it is more accurate to describe them as the product of fundamental debates over what the law is. These debates are very much politicized, but they still consist (for the most part) of good faith efforts by judges to interpret and apply our fundamental law as best they can. To understand these inherently politicized legal debates, we need to trace the interplay of relatively autonomous legal ideas and ongoing cycles of political pressure and partisan change.

The conjuncture of these separate processes periodically presents the justices of the Supreme Court with crucial opportunities to shape the direction of constitutional law. In the wake of the New Deal, the justices of the Hughes and Stone Courts faced one such juncture. As Martin Shapiro has observed, these justices faced two alternatives once they had taken control of the Court: "One was to dismantle the fortifications. The other was to rebuild and shift to new targets. After all, why destroy a weapon of political warfare that so much blood had been shed to capture? One New Deal faction, the judicial modesty school, opted for dismantling. The other invented the preferred position doctrine — singling out certain claims relating to speech, voting, and the criminal process for special judicial solicitude." Shapiro characterizes this choice in strictly partisan terms, insisting that the preferred position doctrine was invented "to explain why it was virtue to use the fort to protect Democrats when it had been vice to use it to protect Republicans" (1983:220), but this is surely not the whole story. The conflict among Harlan Stone, Hugo Black, and Felix Frankfurter was a jurisprudential debate rather than, or at least more than, a partisan conflict. After all, the post–New Deal Court extended the constitutional rights "relating to speech, voting, and the criminal process" to all individuals, regardless of their partisan identification, and these jurisprudential foundations shaped constitutional development for decades to come.[32] Frankfurter marked out a path of judicial abnegation, but he ultimately failed to persuade his colleagues to follow him. Stone and Black, each in their own way, urged the Court down the path of rights-based activism, and this choice was eventually consolidated during the Warren years.

The conservative justices of the Rehnquist Court have faced another crucial opportunity, but as in all such instances, their options have been shaped by the inherited traditions of constitutional discourse. As Graber has noted, "the strategic and policy choices justices make are largely but not fully constrained by the legal arguments that can plausibly be made at a given time" (1999:30). Scalia, Thomas, and Rehnquist's strategy has generally been to appeal to historical evidence of original meaning where that seems to help, and to rely on the allegedly plain meaning of the text in other circumstances. In every line of doctrine in which they have actively sought to enforce limits on government power, they have built on preexisting (though often contested) constitutional traditions. It is undeniable, for instance, that there is a long tradition, dating to the Founding, regarding the importance of property rights. Thus, the Court's New Right constitutional commitments have been rooted in broader political developments, but the extent to which they have come to be reflected in constitutional discourse has turned on the ability of conservatives to marshal plausible constitutional arguments in their support. Where a given conservative policy preference would require bending the Constitution until it breaks, the conservative justices have not done so.

Given their position at the center of the Court, O'Connor and Kennedy have made the most consequential choices among the available paths. To understand the simultaneous revival of conservative activism and survival of liberal activism, we need to understand their deciding votes. It is their vision of the judicial role that explains why the Rehnquist Court has dramatically transformed constitutional law in a conservative direction in some areas, while reaffirming and even expanding landmark liberal precedents in others. Justices Scalia and Thomas have urged a much broader conservative revolution in the law, but their jurisprudential vision has simply not been controlling on the Rehnquist Court. Consider, for example, the cases I discussed at greatest length in chapters 5 and 6. In *Casey, Lawrence, Romer, United States v. Virginia,* and *Lee v. Weisman,* Scalia's and Thomas's arguments were in dissent. In *Michael H. v. Gerald D.,* Scalia managed to garner a majority vote for his preferred result, but not for his opinion, and so he wrote for a plurality. In *Cruzan, Croson, Adarand, Missouri v. Jenkins, Lopez, Morrison, Printz,* and *Whitman v. American Trucking Associations,* Scalia and Thomas (once he had joined the Court) voted with the majority, but one or both of them wrote separately to complain that the Court was not going far enough. Only where Rehnquist, O'Connor, and Kennedy have joined them have they been able to write their conservative vision into law, and even then, they have been able to go only so far as their conservative colleagues would allow.

These divisions on the current Court have been widely noted, but they have not been well understood. The conservative justices have competing substantive visions of the Constitution, with varying degrees of support for libertarian principles of limited government and varying degrees of opposition to modern liberal egalitarianism. These sorts of political ideas, broadly understood, explain the Rehnquist Court's jurisprudence more fully than the justices' particular policy preferences on affirmative action, gay rights, and the like. But even these ideas do not tell the whole story, as the conservative justices have largely agreed on these substantive principles. Their key lines of disagreement have reflected not different levels of support for limited government, but instead competing conceptions of the judicial role.

All five of the conservative justices have balanced the substantive constitutional principles that they hope to actively enforce with a continuing commitment to restraint, but they have struck this balance in two distinct ways. Scalia, Thomas, and Rehnquist have drawn a categorical distinction between those contexts in which the Constitution speaks (and hence calls for judicial enforcement) and those in which it is silent (and hence calls for no judicial action at all). In general, the latter category has included liberal rights claims in the Warren Court tradition, while the former has included the newer conservative rights claims.

In contrast, O'Connor and Kennedy have been willing to actively enforce both liberal and conservative rights claims, but O'Connor has almost always tempered the reach of that activism at the margins (and Kennedy has sometimes done so as well). They have modeled their own jurisprudence on Justice Harlan's "reasoned judgment," by which they mean an active defense of constitutional liberty and equality (with those principles understood as relatively flexible and evolving), tempered by a healthy dose of history and self-restraint. In doing so, O'Connor and Kennedy see themselves as extending a long common law tradition of case-by-case adjudication. While Scalia and Thomas operationalize judicial restraint as a sweeping posture of deference, to be exercised within a particular category of cases, O'Connor and Kennedy treat restraint as a call for caution and circumspection in all cases. Judicial restraint, so defined, is something that O'Connor and Kennedy clearly take quite seriously. Otherwise, the Court would be declaring both anti-abortion laws and affirmative action laws unequivocally unconstitutional, neither of which it has done. It is not, however, the usual sense in which conservatives have demanded restraint. O'Connor and Kennedy seek to proceed more slowly and incrementally than Scalia and Thomas in virtually all cases, but there are essentially no cases in which they exercise any significant deference to the elected branches. They are very much willing to strike down democratically enacted laws that conflict with their understanding of the Constitution, but when they do so, they hedge the decision, limiting it to its particular facts and refraining from issuing any clear principles of broad applicability.

None of the five conservatives, it is worth reiterating, have adopted a posture of pure judicial deference in the Frankfurter mold. They might well have done so, but by the time they came to the bench, the very mission of an independent Supreme Court had come to be identified — in the minds of ordinary citizens and of the justices themselves — with the enforcement of rights-based limits on political action. For the justices to abandon this role would be to call into question the very justification for their office. Absent some unforeseen shock to our constitutional order, the Court will not return to this restrained vision. Most of the justices themselves recognize this point, which explains why they have chosen one of two alternative paths instead. Even Rehnquist, the Court's most consistent advocate of restraint, has rejected this option, joining his conservative colleagues to support most of the new conservative activism and occasionally supporting some liberal activist precedents as well.

I am not arguing, as some have, that the Court will never adopt a posture of deference as its guiding principle for judicial action, since new judicial majorities will always seek to use their newfound power for their own ends (Silverstein and Ginsburg 1987; Lasser 1988). In fact, as I noted in chapters 1 and 2, Frankfurter came very close to persuading the Court to do just that. The decisions of the Burger and Rehnquist Courts have created what we might think of as a "policy feedback" effect, with the Court's protection of conservative rights claims fostering the development of organized conservative interests committed to defending judicially enforceable rights, and with those interests, in turn, demanding ever more active judicial protection.[33] While this is a useful explanation of post-1968 constitutional development, there is nothing necessary or inevitable about it, and in a different time and place, things would have turned out differently.

Throughout this book, I have emphasized that the particular sequence by which competing principles become embedded in constitutional discourse often has a significant effect on subsequent developments. Modern rights-based constitutionalism was institutionalized on the Court prior to the conservative shift in national politics. This sequence led constitutional conservatives to be relatively more successful where they built upon, rather than disavowed, the rights-protecting function of modern constitutionalism. This differential pattern of success has in turn created a powerful incentive for conservatives to develop their own rights-based constitutional vision, a process that has rendered it ever harder for them to articulate a coherent general case for judicial restraint. Thus, over time, the legal terrain has changed the very preferences (or "attitudes") of the conservatives themselves, leading to the displacement of judicial restraint by a relatively new, rights-based conservatism.

Put another way, the pattern of modern constitutional development has been shaped in large part by certain secular historical trends that are difficult to reverse, particularly the growth of judicial power, the post–New Deal abandonment of original foundations, and the "rights revolution" of the late twentieth century.[34] Modern conservatives have advocated judicial restraint in a constitutional system increasingly characterized by widely accepted practices of judicial activism, and they have advocated originalism in a system increasingly distant from its original roots. In a broad range of doctrinal areas, contemporary conservatives have picked up on those constitutional traditions that could support their own conservative rights-based arguments. Had they not done so, but merely continued to object to the liberal version of rights-based judicial activism, they would have been enforcing a Constitution that was almost entirely statist and anti-rights. While such a minimalist constitutional vision is conceivable, it is beyond the acceptable bounds of contemporary constitutional discourse. Since constitutional conservatives cannot plausibly argue for a Constitution that does not protect rights at all, they have built on our constitutional traditions of federalism and limited government to stake out a new judicial role that is compatible with modern conservatism.

• • •

The Rehnquist Court has developed a distinctive, post–Warren Court jurisprudence, the most significant feature of which is an utter lack of deference to Congress. Whether pursuing the original Constitution's structural division of government powers, a libertarian curb on economic regulation, or the protection of relatively powerless minority groups, the current Court brooks no disagreement from the coordinate branches of the federal government. The primary goals of this book have been to describe the content of this distinctive jurisprudence and to offer an historical explanation of how it came to be. As Holmes noted more than a century ago, however, the historical study of the law is important not because we must always adhere to preexisting legal rules. Rather, "it is the first step toward an enlightened scepticism [sic], that is, toward a deliberate reconsideration of the worth of those rules" (1897:22).[35] If the constitutional jurisprudence of the Rehnquist Court is failing to serve the needs of the modern American polity, then that jurisprudence can and should be abandoned.

CONCLUSION

MODERN CONSERVATISM
AND JUDICIAL POWER

Sandra Day O'Connor has played such a decisive role since 1994 that this Supreme Court more truly belongs to her than to the chief justice. And the most significant feature of constitutional development on the "O'Connor Court" has been the success on the part of conservatives in expanding judicial power and exercising that power on behalf of conservative ends. This Court's expansive vision of judicial power was clear before December 12, 2000, but *Bush v. Gore* brought it into sharp relief. Rights-based judicial activism has become so firmly entrenched in the American polity that the Court was able to settle a narrowly divided national election without provoking any serious threat to its own power. In fact, while some scholars (and some dissenting justices) speculated that the decision might amount to a "self-inflicted wound," it has paradoxically had the effect of increasing national support for judicial power. The public's overall support for the Supreme Court has remained relatively steady in the wake of *Bush v. Gore,* but the aggregate numbers mask a dramatic increase in support among Republicans. For example, from June 2000 to mid-December 2000 (right after the decision), the percentage of Gallop Poll respondents who had either "a great deal" or "quite a lot" of confidence in the Supreme Court rose slightly, from 47 percent to 49 percent. By June 2001, it had risen to 50 percent. Among Republicans, however, this degree of confidence jumped from 48 to 67 percent, and then settled back down to 62 percent. During the same period, Democratic support dropped from 44 to 40 percent, but then rebounded to 46 percent.[1]

In sum, liberal and Democratic support for the Court took a temporary hit from *Bush v. Gore,* but it quickly rebounded and is likely to remain strong over the long term, in large part because Justices O'Connor and Anthony

Kennedy have preserved so much of the Warren Court legacy. The election decision has been roundly criticized, but most contemporary American liberals remain firmly committed to a vigorous independent judiciary as an important bulwark of liberty. All *Bush v. Gore* appears to have done is to solidify the commitment of contemporary conservatives to this same principle, thus making even less likely the development of an influential political constituency for curbing the Court. Just as the Marshall Court expanded federal judicial power in the early years of the nineteenth century by issuing decisions that "swelled (or at least did not diminish) the ranks of influential politicians who favored that power" (Graber 1999:39), so too with the O'Connor Court in the early years of the twenty-first. The current Court's continued willingness to exercise its power on behalf of liberal as well as conservative ends has tended to reinforce support for judicial power among political elites.

The nation's ever-firmer commitment to rights-based activism, in turn, has undermined the continued conservative calls for judicial restraint in contexts such as abortion and gay rights. Put another way, the conservatives' abandonment of restraint has enabled them to influence the law in a number of areas, but has unintentionally constrained their influence in others. By turning away from the path of Felix Frankfurter's, conservatives were able to revive the federalism-based limits on congressional power, but had they continued along that path, their long-standing demands for judicial deference in the abortion and gay rights contexts might have proven more successful. Instead, the dramatic rise of conservative activism has weakened the rhetorical force of judicial restraint arguments throughout constitutional discourse, thus facilitating the Court's liberal decisions in such cases as *Planned Parenthood v. Casey, Romer v. Evans,* and *Lawrence v. Texas.* The current Court is the most activist in American history, and the justices with the swing votes have been willing to engage in this activism to serve a variety of constitutional ends. O'Connor's and Kennedy's decisions to extend meaningful scrutiny to laws that restrict reproductive rights or discriminate against gays and lesbians would have proven much more difficult had judicial restraint survived as the principal ideal of constitutional conservatism.

It has not so survived, and we cannot understand the current Court if we continue to insist that it has. A number of scholars had noted the rise of conservative activism before *Bush v. Gore,* and this observation has been even more widespread in that decision's wake (Seidman 1996; Rosen 2000c; Posner 2001; Balkin and Levinson 2001). Still, other scholars have continued to deny or understate the extent of this activism, particularly by minimizing the scope of the federalism revolution (Silverstein 2003; Whittington 2003; Rossum 2003; Tushnet 2003). I hope this book has made clear that while the reach of the O'Connor Court's activism is a matter for continuing debate, there is no realistic sense in which this Court can be described as a tribunal committed to restraint. Supreme Court justices appointed by Republican presidents have been no more restrained than those appointed by Democrats. They exercise judicial review just as frequently, and they are no more reluctant to enter political thickets.

Contemporary judicial conservatism is a rights-based conservatism. When the conservative justices have asserted their own power, they have generally justified such assertions on either originalist or rights-protecting grounds. In *Bush v. Gore*, for example, the per curiam opinion relied on a new and potentially sweeping equal protection claim, while William Rehnquist's concurring opinion emphasized the original text of Article II. These two sorts of justifications have often overlapped, with the conservative justices mobilizing originalist arguments on behalf of conservative rights claims. Even in the federalism cases, which have primarily implicated arguments of constitutional structure, the conservatives have still defended their decisions in part on rights-protecting grounds. And even when their principal goal has been to thwart congressional efforts to expand legal rights guarantees, the conservative justices have relied on rights-protecting doctrines in doing so. So while many of the Court's conservative activist holdings can be described as efforts to limit rights granted by other institutions — the federalism-based limits on congressional civil rights statutes, the freedom-of-association limits on state civil rights statutes, the color-blind limits on affirmative action policies, the free-speech limits on sexual harassment laws, and so forth — these have still been (in the conservative mind) rights-protecting decisions. They have generally been initiated by aggrieved rights-bearers (such as rejected white university applicants), have generally been supported by rights-based organizations (such as the Center for Individual Rights), and have generally been defended by the conservative justices in the language of constitutional rights.

We cannot evaluate the O'Connor Court's jurisprudence if we do not have an accurate picture of it. There are a number of grounds on which contemporary constitutional conservatism might be defended, but judicial restraint is not one of them. The conservative justices continue to speak in the language of Frankfurterian self-restraint, but since none of them actually advocates a posture of across-the-board deference, this language has become more misleading than helpful. As advanced by conservatives, both on and off the Court, the demand for restraint is often couched as a shrill denunciation of their opponents for usurping the popular will, and in this form, the argument is particularly unconducive to constitutional dialogue. As I have noted at some length, Antonin Scalia has become notorious for such shrill denunciations, and they are in fact a defining feature of contemporary conservatism.

One particularly extreme example was a 1996 symposium entitled "The End of Democracy? The Judicial Usurpation of Politics," in which the editors of *First Things* raised the possibility that "[t]he government of the United States of America no longer governs by the consent of the governed. With respect to the American people, the judiciary has in effect declared that the most important questions about how we ought to order our life together are outside the purview of 'things of their knowledge.'" The editors proceeded to observe that "[t]he question here explored, in full awareness of its far-reaching consequences, is whether we have reached or are reaching the point where conscientious citizens can no longer give moral assent to the existing regime." Citing Jefferson's description of the right of revolution in the Declaration of Independence, they issued an apparent call for armed resistance to the illegitimate American "regime." This call spurred Walter Berns and Gertrude Himmelfarb to resign publicly from the journal's editorial advisory board, and even led Robert Bork to distance himself from the symposium, while holding fast to the views expressed in his own article therein. These views had included the claim that "a majority of Justices have decided to rule us without any warrant in law" and that "this tendency of courts . . . is the inevitable result of our written Constitution and the power of judicial review."[2]

While Bork may be unwilling to go along with the call for armed revolution, he has been more responsible than anyone else for casting the debate over judicial power in such apocalyptic terms. In his 1996 book, titled *Slouching toward Gomorrah: Modern Liberalism and American Decline,* he declared that "[c]ontrary to the plan of the American government, the Supreme Court has usurped the powers of the people and their elected representatives. . . . Congress and the President check and balance one another, but neither of them can stop the Court's adventures in making and enforcing left-wing policy" (1996a:109). Such allegations of judicial tyranny have been around for a long time, but contemporary conservatives have made them sharper and more widespread than ever. When Nixon nominated Lewis Powell and Rehnquist in 1971, for example, he criticized some of the Court's decisions, but still praised the institution and counseled caution in denouncing it (Dean

2001:257–58). There were other Court critics who went further than Nixon at the time, but it is much more common today to hear conservatives suggesting that American democracy is on the verge of collapse as a result of judicial activism. The disappointment at unexpected defeats, combined with the widespread use of the religious imagery of sin and redemption, has produced the rhetorical excesses that characterize so much contemporary conservative commentary on the Court. While some scholars may dismiss such arguments as mere rhetoric, the rhetoric has its influence, and the influence is numbing.

These regular denunciations of judicial power are misleading at best and profoundly destructive of constitutional politics at worst. They preempt a more productive conversation about constitutional meaning, distracting our attention from the actual locus of constitutional conflict. While we still tend to associate judicial restraint arguments with conservatives, the O'Connor Court's liberal justices have taken to responding to the rise of conservative activism by quoting Alexander Bickel, Louis Brandeis, and Harlan Stone on the merits of restraint. Their rhetoric is usually more tempered, but such arguments are just as misleading in their hands as in Scalia's or Bork's. In *Bush v. Gore*, for example, Stephen Breyer looked to Bickel in noting that "[t]hose who caution judicial restraint in resolving political disputes have described the quintessential case for that restraint as [one] . . . marked, among other things, by the 'strangeness of the issue,' its 'intractability to principled resolution,' its 'sheer momentousness, . . . which tends to unbalance judicial judgment,' and 'the inner vulnerability, the self-doubt of an institution which is electorally irresponsible and has no earth to draw strength from.' Those characteristics mark this case." Quoting Stone and then Brandeis, Breyer continued: "I fear that in order to bring this agonizingly long election process to a definitive conclusion, we have not adequately attended to that necessary 'check upon our own exercise of power,' 'our own sense of self-restraint.' Justice Brandeis once said of the Court, 'The most important thing we do is not doing.' What it does today, the Court should have left undone."[3]

Breyer is in fact one of the current Court's most deferential justices, but as Richard Epstein (2000) has noted, it is disingenuous for either liberals or conservatives to claim "that judicial restraint is the hallmark of sound judicial construction" because no judges any longer believe it. Louis Seidman observed as early as 1996 that "the real dispute in modern constitutional law is not between advocates of activism and restraint, but between advocates of liberal and conservative activism." He noted even then that there was no "significant difference between 'liberal' and 'conservative' Justices with regard to the frequency with which they support 'activist' results. Both liberals and conservatives can regularly be found arguing for activism and for restraint in various contexts" (1996:87–88). All of the justices see the Constitution as a charter of fundamental principles which it is the Court's painful duty to enforce whenever the elected branches attempt to violate them. The real disagreement between liberals and conservatives is over what those principles are.

Put another way, while constitutional conservatives continue to emphasize the long-standing critique of "government by judiciary," their primary concern is more often with liberalism than with judicial power. The conservatives who have criticized the Court most sharply in the past decade — Scalia, Bork, and their allies — have been concerned with abortion and euthanasia and gay rights, not judicial activism itself (Whittington 1998b). Around the same time as the *First Things* symposium, for example, presidential candidate Pat Buchanan used a Heritage Foundation address to denounce "judicial dictatorship" and "the gross usurpation of power by federal courts," insisting that "in America today, the power that stands astride this country like a colossus is not the power of the majority; it is not the power of the governed; it is the power of the judiciary. The Supreme Court, not the majority, decides what is right or wrong in America." While Buchanan denounced judicial power as undemocratic and hence illegitimate per se, he seemed particularly interested in demonstrating that "[w]e get one kind of society when decisions are made by the majority [and that w]e get another kind when decisions are made by judges." In other words, his concern was with the political direction of modern judicial activism, not with activism itself. He argued that since the mid-1960s, "the Court has been in the vanguard of an intellectual elite that believes that the prevailing social order of middle-class America is deeply flawed, unjust, and irrational," and he described "the beneficiaries of the Court's protection [as m]embers of various minorities including criminals, atheists, homosexuals, flag burners, illegal immigrants (including terrorists), convicts, and pornographers" (1996:1–5). It is the "culture wars," rather than a concern for democracy, that motivates many of the sharpest conservative attacks on judicial power.[4]

Moreover, the overall effect of these constant critiques of judicial power — particularly when combined with the ongoing active exercise of that power by liberal and conservative justices alike — has been to normalize the impression that the justices are simply seeking to write their own views into the Constitution. Bork and the advocates of the "attitudinal model," for instance, are united in their critique of every Supreme Court justice since John Marshall as dishonest, deceitful, and motivated only by a pursuit of his own preferred policy outcomes (Bork 1996b, 1990; Segal and Spaeth 1993:74–124). This link between the critique of judicial activism, on the one hand, and instrumental accounts of judicial decisionmaking, on the other, is not a new one. In his 1964 *Harvard Law Review* foreword, Philip Kurland ended his long denunciation of Warren Court activism by noting that the political scientists may well be right that the quantitative measurement of judicial results is more important than the Court's rationalizing legal fictions (1964:175). A few years earlier, political scientist Sidney Ulmer began his article on "Supreme Court Behavior and Civil Rights" (1960) by quoting one of Frankfurter's many denunciations of his colleagues for result-oriented decisionmaking, and then provided statistical evidence to suggest that this was in fact what Frankfurter's colleagues had been doing.

It remains true today that opponents of judicial decisions tend to denounce them as result-oriented, that such denunciations tend to operate as self-fulfilling prophecies, and that such prophecies may have the effect of undermining judicial authority.[5] Since constitutional conservatives have made such attacks on judicial power ubiquitous, but have not actually succeeded in curtailing the exercise of judicial activism, we now have a system of federal courts that are as activist as ever, but whose legitimacy is perpetually under attack. Assessing the impact of such attacks is beyond the scope of this study, but they have the potential to undermine judicial authority in our constitutional democracy. After all, if the nine unelected members of the Supreme Court are simply imposing their personal preferences on the nation as a whole, then there is of course no justification whatsoever for the power of judicial review, let alone the active employment of that power.[6] Though rejected by most contemporary conservatives, Bork's and Buchanan's recent proposals to abolish or severely limit judicial review by constitutional amendment made the potential implications of the conservative critique of judicial power particularly clear.[7]

But if the exercise of judicial power is at least sometimes desirable or necessary in a constitutional democracy — as most political elites and all Supreme Court justices agree — then constantly undermining the authority on which this power rests may prove unwise. The critique of modern judicial power may remain strategically and rhetorically useful for those who are participating in constitutional debates, but it continues to impose substantial costs on constitutional discourse as a whole.

Perhaps most importantly, the continued use of judicial restraint rhetoric by conservatives renders it difficult for the American public to express its views on the Rehnquist Court's distinctive constitutional jurisprudence. The post-1968 electorate has certainly played a role in enacting this new constitutional order — by handing repeated victories at the polls to the Republican Party — but it has not had the chance to vote on it directly because Republican candidates continue to campaign on a platform of judicial restraint. With some regularity, the O'Connor Court has been invalidating provisions of recently enacted, and widely popular, federal statutes such as the Violence against Women Act, the Religious Freedom Restoration Act, the Age Discrimination in Employment Act, and the Americans with Disabilities Act, but "[i]nstead of debating the merits of [this] Court, [our presidential candidates] are still debating the merits of the Warren Court" (Rosen 2000b). The Court's recent federalism decisions, of course, are intended to reflect constitutional principle, regardless of the popular will. Nonetheless, the normal operation of the judicial appointment process has provided the public with periodic opportunities to transform the Court by electing the presidents and senators who staff it. If no Republican politicians are willing to support the O'Connor Court's decisions on the campaign trail, however, then the public is denied this opportunity.[8]

Were the American people to have such an opportunity, it would then be important to evaluate the available alternatives from which they might choose. The constitutional vision of the current Court may or may not represent a wise and just elaboration of our legal traditions, and that is a conversation well worth having. This conversation has too often been hindered by our continued association of constitutional conservatism with judicial restraint, but if I have succeeded in wresting that rhetoric away from contemporary conservatives, then we can turn to the more productive task of evaluating the Court's distinctive rights-based conservatism. As Jack Balkin and Sanford Levinson have noted, it is the justices' "contending visions [of the American constitutional order], rather than judicial craft, that should be at the heart" of our constitutional debates (2001:1094; see also Chemerinsky 1989).

At first glance, the conservative justices appear to have a narrow but controlling judicial majority, even discounting the Republican-appointed, but surprisingly liberal, John Paul Stevens and David Souter. On closer inspection, however, Scalia's and Clarence Thomas's sharp rejection of liberal activism has most often been expressed in dissenting opinions, because O'Connor and Kennedy have regularly refused to join it. And their sweeping endorsement of conservative activism has most often been expressed in concurring opinions, because O'Connor and Kennedy have joined it but have been unwilling to go quite as far as Scalia and Thomas would like. The limits of the Court's activism — in both liberal and conservative directions — are determined by O'Connor's and Kennedy's constitutional vision, and so it is this vision that we should evaluate when we evaluate the Rehnquist Court.

Among constitutional scholars, Cass Sunstein has offered the best defense of the approach taken by O'Connor and Kennedy, characterizing it as a principled commitment to "judicial minimalism." By "minimalism," Sunstein means something very similar to what Bickel used to call the "passive virtues" — deciding cases on narrow grounds, leaving many things undecided, issuing provisional decisions, and the like — all of which are valuable, in Bickel's and Sunstein's view, because they will allegedly reduce the power of the unelected courts relative to the rest of the political system.[9] As exemplars of this approach on the O'Connor Court, Sunstein points to many of the same decisions that I have emphasized. Whether exercising activism or restraint, he insists, the O'Connor Court has properly "avoid[ed] broad rules and . . . proceed[ed] in a way that complements and does not displace democratic processes" (1999:261). Whether the Court has upheld a democratically enacted policy against constitutional challenge (as in *Washington v. Glucksberg* or *Grutter v. Bollinger*) or has struck down such a policy (as in *Romer* or *Adarand Constructors, Inc. v. Pena*), it has generally sought to frame its decisions as narrowly as possible.

Sunstein's defense of the O'Connor Court is not fully persuasive, however, especially if it is taken to suggest a relatively narrow vision of the judicial role. Sunstein himself is ambivalent on this point, but as Mark Tushnet has noted, judicial minimalism paradoxically maximizes judicial power. The one-case-at-a-time approach, like Frankfurter's and Harlan's old balancing approaches, provides no clear standards to guide future decisions, and hence leaves the justices themselves free to decide each case as they see fit (Tushnet 2003:140). It is for this reason that Hugo Black was so critical of Frankfurter's approach, and that Scalia remains so critical of O'Connor's. In Black's and Scalia's eyes, this case-by-case jurisprudence represents an abandonment of the principled character of the rule of law.

After all, O'Connor and Kennedy, the Court's most minimalist justices, have also been the most activist. On affirmative action they are more mini-malist than Scalia, and on abortion they are more minimalist than Harry Blackmun, but the end result is that they have supported both liberal and conservative activism in case after case. For this reason, they have voted to ex-ercise the power of judicial review more frequently than anyone else on the current Court. At bottom, the term "minimalist" seems a curious appellation for a Court that struck down thirty federal statutes in seven years. O'Connor and Kennedy seek to proceed more slowly and incrementally than Scalia and Thomas in virtually all cases, but there are essentially no cases in which they exercise any significant deference to the elected branches. They are perfectly willing to strike down democratically enacted laws that conflict with their understanding of the Constitution. It is just that when they do so, they hedge the decision, limiting it to its particular facts and refraining from issuing any clear principles of broad applicability.

The most notorious instance of this tendency was *Bush v. Gore*. Refusing to join their fellow conservative justices in relying on an originalist reading of Article II of the Constitution, O'Connor and Kennedy reached the same re-sult on different grounds, halting the ongoing ballot recounts as a violation of equal protection. They recognized the potentially sweeping impact of this holding on the nation's electoral system, however, and so they declared that "[o]ur consideration is limited to the present circumstances, for the problem of equal protection in election processes generally presents many complexi-ties."[10] As Sunstein himself has noted, "the Court's effort to cabin the reach of its decision seemed ad hoc and unprincipled — a common risk with min-imalism" (Sunstein 2001:212), and as this example makes clear, O'Connor's and Kennedy's cautious, case-by-case approach has produced a Court that is playing an ever-broader role in our political system (see Tushnet 2003: 138–41).

O'Connor and Kennedy have authored some of the Court's most sweep-ing declarations of judicial supremacy. In their plurality opinion in *Casey*, they insisted that one reason not to overturn *Roe v. Wade* was that doing so would damage the Court's legitimacy. In support of this argument, they claimed that the American people's aspiration "to live according to the rule of law . . . is not readily separable from their understanding of the Court in-vested with the authority to decide their constitutional cases and speak before all others for their constitutional ideals."[11] Similarly, when Congress re-sponded to the Court's decision in *Employment Division v. Smith* by seeking to enact a broader constitutional guarantee of religious liberty than that which the Court itself had recognized, O'Connor and Kennedy forcefully reaffirmed the Court's role as the supreme and final interpreter of the Constitution. Writing for the Court in *City of Boerne v. Flores,* Kennedy followed Harlan's dissenting opinion in *Katzenbach v. Morgan,* insisting that Congress's power to enforce the provisions of the Fourteenth Amendment was limited to enforcing those provisions as they had been interpreted by the Court. In Kennedy's words, the Fourteenth Amendment and the Bill of Rights "set forth self executing prohibitions on governmental action, and this Court has had primary authority to interpret those prohibitions. . . . The power to interpret the Constitution in a case or controversy remains in the Judiciary." Kennedy insisted that "[l]egislation which alters the meaning of the Free Exercise Clause cannot be said to be enforcing the Clause. [Otherwise,] what Congress would be enforcing would no longer be, in any meaningful sense, the 'provisions of [the Constitution].'" This argument might also be said to apply to *judicial* interpretations that alter the meaning of the Free Exercise Clause, but in the view of Justices O'Connor and Kennedy, it is the Court, and only the Court, that has the authority to declare (and hence to alter) the Constitution's meaning.[12] Together with the Court's other recent decisions limiting Congress's authority to expand our federal civil rights laws, the *Boerne* case represented as sweeping an assertion of judicial supremacy as the Court has ever made.

With these decisions in mind, some observers have criticized O'Connor and Kennedy for their willingness, even eagerness, to substitute their own visions of the good for those of the people's elected representatives. Calling attention to the Court's "skeptical examination of Congress's fact-finding processes" in *Board of Trustees of the University of Alabama v. Garrett,* for example, Tushnet noted that the Rehnquist "Court regards Congress not as a partner but as something of a recalcitrant subordinate whose actions have to be looked at with great care" (2003:51). Even more pointedly, Jeffrey Rosen has sarcastically described O'Connor as "a majority of one," complaining that on "almost any of the most divisive questions of American life, . . . O'Connor either has decided it or is about to decide it on our behalf" (2001b). The justices in control of the current Court decide each case anew, and like Frankfurter before them, they have an inflated perception of their own capacity to do so. O'Connor and Kennedy extend their own power much further than Frankfurter's, moreover, because they have preserved no areas of law or policy that are immune from judicial resolution. In *Bush v. Gore,* after all, they went so far as to settle the outcome of a presidential election, by a single judicial vote, over the sharp dissenting argument that they were trampling the democratic process. Frankfurter and Harlan were firm supporters of judicial supremacy, but only within its proper sphere, and they continually sought to remind their fellow justices to steer clear of political thickets such as this one. O'Connor and Kennedy hope to bring judicial principle to bear on all political conflicts, but Frankfurter would have joined Breyer in noting the much greater likelihood that such decisions will bring politics to bear on the judicial process.[13]

The best justification for the Court's decision in *Bush v. Gore* was a broadly pragmatic concern with avoiding the national crisis that would result if the election had been thrown to Congress. The conservative justices did not mention this "reason of state" justification in their opinions, but several of them alluded to it in public comments after December 2000, and federal judge Richard Posner subsequently developed it at some length (Rosen 2001a; Posner 2001). As Rosen notes, *Bush v. Gore* was foreshadowed by the *Casey* plurality's declaration that they "had to save the country from legislative battles that would only polarize and divide Americans" (2001a). O'Connor and Kennedy might not put it this explicitly, but they appear to have shared Posner's judgment regarding the 2000 election controversy that "Congress is not a competent forum for resolving such disputes." In Posner's view, the Court rightly sought "to keep Congress out of the picture, so far as that is possible to do. It is a large, unwieldy, undisciplined body (actually two bodies), unsuited in its structure, personnel, and procedures to legal dispute resolution" (2001:145, 250). This justification is clearly inconsistent with the original meaning of the Constitution, but it reflects the current justices' expansive vision of the Court's role and capacity, and their extreme skepticism of Congress.

Many scholars have described *Bush v. Gore* as *sui generis,* with the conservative justices departing from their usual constitutional principles to reach a partisan decision because the stakes were so high.[14] This characterization makes some sense — the case was, after all, literally unprecedented — but if my account of the O'Connor Court's jurisprudence is persuasive, then these scholars are missing the most significant implications of the decision. If *Bush v. Gore* merits criticism, it is because it reflected an imperious vision of the judicial role that has characterized the current Court more generally, and not solely because it was a partisan decision in a particular case.[15] Put another way, *Bush v. Gore* is the best example of two separate characteristics of Justice O'Connor's jurisprudence: not just the "ticket good for this train only" quality of avoiding principles susceptible of consistent application, but also her hostility to Congress. Reviewing O'Connor's role in particular, Rosen has noted that "the opinion displayed a fear of Congress as a partisan body not to be trusted with important political and constitutional decisions. It exalted the power of the only institution that the court trusts to identify illegal discrimination in America — namely, itself" (2001b:32). When we evaluate the contemporary Court, it is this vision of judicial power that we should be evaluating.

· · ·

Whether you view the approach of O'Connor and Kennedy as unprincipled, case-by-case balancing, ungoverned by rules and standards — or instead as a pragmatic effort to defend constitutional liberty and equality while avoiding sweeping judicial limits on legislative power — will depend on your assessment of the likely alternatives. Rosen is not wrong when he complains that O'Connor "views the Court in general, and herself in particular, as the proper forum to decide every political and constitutional question in the land" (2001b). But if O'Connor had not marked out this distinctive vision of the judicial role — or if President Reagan had advanced some other hypothetical nominee in her stead — she probably would not have exercised Frankfurterian deference across the board (which would be Rosen's preference), and she certainly would not have joined the liberals in enforcing a Warren Court Constitution (which would be my own). Rather, she and the Court would most likely have adopted Scalia's categorical vision of sweeping deference toward government abuses of rights in the Warren Court tradition and sweeping activism in defense of a newer set of conservative rights. That Court would not have been a better one.

NOTES

Introduction

1. Tushnet (1996b:66) describes this "country-club Republicanism" as "an ideology that joins protection of the interests of the relatively well-to-do with a modest sense of noblesse oblige with respect to those disadvantaged by the economic system." See Shapiro 1983.

2. Tushnet 2003:1. Political scientist David Plotke (1996:1) has used the term "political order" in a similar fashion, referring to "a durable mode of organizing and exercising political power at the national level, with distinct institutions, policies, and discourses."

3. When I refer to modern judicial conservatism, or modern constitutional conservatism, I mean to suggest a complex and influential jurisprudential tradition, not a collection of conservative policy priorities or partisan identifications. I refer to this vision as "conservative" because it has been shaped in large part by conservative understandings of law and politics, but my interest is in exploring a particular body of constitutional thought, rather than in identifying a particular set of constitutional scholars and judges as politically conservative. In fact, many of those whose ideas have played an important role in the development of this constitutional discourse have themselves been political liberals — for example, justices like Frankfurter and Black, and constitutional scholars like Bickel and Herbert Wechsler.

4. Scalia and Thomas might also describe an activist Court as one whose opinions bear a certain legislative quality, as in cases like *Miranda* and *Roe,* or whose decisions display an excessive willingness to administer public institutions such as schools and prisons. I explore these alternative characterizations of activism and restraint in the chapters that follow.

5. In so using the terms "activism" and "restraint," I follow a recent suggestion of Cass Sunstein's: "Some people label a decision 'activist' when they think that the court has departed from the correct approach to the Constitution," but the term can also be used in a "purely descriptive" sense, in which "a decision that is activist in not necessarily wrong." In this latter sense, "a court might be described as activist if it strikes down the actions of other branches of government," but since everyone thinks that the Court should sometimes do so, "a court that is activist, in this sense, might be something to celebrate" (2003:27).

6. As political scientist Keith Whittington has observed, "judges are likely to be generally sympathetic with the basic assumptions and commitments of an enduring political order," but they "are not immediately accountable to electoral and political interests and are less responsive [than elected institutions] to transitory political pressures. . . . The institutional role and norms of the judiciary further insulate the courts from parti-

san pressures. Judges are supposed to worry about the law, and the individuals selected to be judges are socialized into taking that role seriously. The particular procedures of the courts reinforce that orientation, putting lawyers, texts and precedents in the foreground of judicial operations" (1998a:24).

7. In this light, my work relies on a "constitutive," rather than an "instrumental," conception of law. Those of us who understand legal ideas in constitutive terms insist that they are not merely resources to be used at will by legal actors, but that they play a substantial role in shaping — or constituting — the very identities and interests of those actors. See generally McCann 1996.

Chapter One

1. Stone was originally appointed to the Court by Republican president Calvin Coolidge in 1925, but was elevated to chief justice by FDR in 1941. Black was FDR's first Court appointee, in 1937, and Frankfurter was his third, in 1939.

2. President Franklin D. Roosevelt, Radio Address of March 9, 1937, Senate Report No. 711, 75th Cong., 1st Sess., pp. 41–44, *reprinted in* Murphy, Fleming, and Barber 1995:320–21.

3. 198 U.S. 45, 75–76 (1905).

4. *Adkins v. Children's Hospital*, 261 U.S. 525, 570 (1923). Similarly, dissenting in *Meyer v. Nebraska*, 262 U.S. 390, 412 (1923), Holmes observed: "I think I appreciate the objection to the law but it appears to me to present a question upon which men reasonably might differ and therefore I am unable to say that the Constitution of the U.S. prevents the experiment being tried."

5. 281 U.S. 586, 595 (1930).

6. 252 U.S. 416, 433 (1920).

7. *Gompers v. United States*, 233 U.S. 604, 610 (1914).

8. 297 U.S. 288, 346–48 (1936).

9. *United States v. Butler*, 297 U.S. 1, 78–79, 87 (1936).

10. 300 U.S. 379, 402–4 (1937). Sutherland began this opinion by explicitly rejecting Thayer's argument for judicial restraint, which had so influenced Holmes.

11. *Home Building and Loan Association v. Blaisdell*, 290 U.S. 398, 448–49, 451–53 (1934).

12. Id. at 442–43, 407, 415. The Marshall quotes are from *McCulloch v. Maryland*.

13. This claim is supported by the bulk of contemporary constitutional scholarship on the New Deal. Bruce Ackerman (1998:383), for example, has argued that "America's modern Constitution was created during the Roosevelt Administration through processes unknown to Article Five." See also Gillman 1993; Nedelsky 1990. And even Barry Cushman (1998), whose important recent work makes clear that the New Deal Court did not sever all prior doctrinal roots, agrees that that Court enacted a "constitutional revolution."

14. Note Frankfurter's observation in his 1936 lectures on the Commerce Clause that "one of the greatest duties of a judge [is] the duty not to enlarge his authority. That the

Court is not the maker of policy but is concerned solely with questions of ultimate power, is a tenet to which all Justices have subscribed. But the extent to which they have translated faith into works probably marks the deepest cleavage among the men who have sat on the Supreme Bench" (1937:80–81). After a decade on the bench himself, he reiterated that the "only safeguard against crossing the line between adjudication and legislation is an alert recognition of the necessity not to cross it and instinctive, as well as trained, reluctance to do so" (1947:55).

15. Frankfurter's dissenting opinion in *West Virginia State Board of Education v. Barnette,* discussed below, included a full three-page excerpt from Thayer's article.

16. 298 U.S. 238, 290–91 (1936). See also *Schechter Poultry Corporation v. United States,* in which the Court struck down the 1933 National Industrial Recovery Act, which authorized the executive branch to establish codes of fair competition in various industries, including maximum hours and minimum wages, prohibitions of child labor, and guarantees of the right to organize unions; and *United States v. Butler,* in which the Court struck down the 1933 Agricultural Adjustment Act, designed to stabilize production in agriculture by assuring farmers that their products would be sold at a fair price.

17. *NLRB v. Jones and Laughlin Steel Corporation,* 301 U.S. 1, 37 (1937).

18. 310 U.S. 586, 604 (1940).

19. Frankfurter's memo to Stone, dated May 27, 1940, is reprinted in Murphy, Fleming, and Barber 1995:1167–68. See also Simon 1989:106–14.

20. 299 U.S. 353, 364–65 (1937).

21. 302 U.S. 319, 323, 325–38 (1937).

22. 314 U.S. 160, 174 (1941).

23. 316 U.S. 535, 541 (1942).

24. 323 U.S. 214, 216 (1944).

25. As Gillman notes, "[t]he traditional mechanism by which the Constitution sought to protect this broader field of liberty . . . might have been made obsolete by the exigencies of industrialization, but for Stone this meant that courts should devise a more modern mechanism, not that courts should abandon their longstanding tradition of preserving individual liberty against an overreaching government" (1994a:647).

26. 316 U.S. 535, 544 (1942).

27. The corporation had argued that the legislative findings — which characterized "filled milk" as injurious to health and as a fraud upon the public — were wrong, but Stone insisted that the courts were not authorized to second-guess those findings: "Even in the absence of such aids the existence of facts supporting the legislative judgment is to be presumed, for regulatory legislation affecting ordinary commercial transactions is not to be pronounced unconstitutional unless in the light of the facts made known or generally assumed it is of such a character as to preclude the assumption that it rests upon some rational basis within the knowledge and experience of the legislators" (304 U.S. 144, 152 (1938)).

28. Id. at 152–53 n. 4. On this second point, see Stone's opinion for the Court in *South Carolina v. Barnwell Brothers,* 303 U.S. 177, 184 n. 2 (1938).

29. 304 U.S. 144, 152–53 n. 4 (1938).

30. 310 U.S. 586, 604, 599, 605–7 (1940).

31. 319 U.S. 624, 638 (1943).

32. Id. at 641.

33. 328 U.S. 549, 553–56 (1946). Only seven justices heard the case, with Reed and Burton joining Frankfurter's opinion; Douglas and Murphy joined Black's dissent, which urged the Court to decide the merits; and Rutledge provided the deciding vote against addressing the merits, but refused to endorse Frankfurter's broad political questions doctrine. On Frankfurter's political questions jurisprudence, note also his opinion in *Coleman v. Miller,* 307 U.S. 433, 460–70 (1939).

34. 319 U.S. 624, 646–48 (1943).

35. *Opelika,* 316 U.S. 584, 608, 623–24 (1942); *Barnette,* 319 U.S. 624, 643–44 (1943).

36. 314 U.S. 252, 265 (1941).

37. *Chambers v. Florida,* 309 U.S. 227, 235 n. 8 (1940).

38. *Adamson,* 332 U.S. 46, 54 (1947).

39. Id. at 73–75.

40. Id. at 46, 69, 91, 75.

41. See, for example, *Malinsky v. New York,* 324 U.S. 401 (1945).

42. *Adamson,* 332 U.S. 46, 67–68 (1947).

43. Id. at 63–64.

44. By Fred Shapiro's count, Fairman's 1949 piece was the nineteenth most cited law review article from 1947 to 1985 (Shapiro 1985:1550).

45. Another similarity between Fairman's and Berger's historical work is their repeated use of "derogatory hints and comments which gave the impression that the framers of the amendment, and Bingham in particular, were not very bright; that they held the strangest ideas about the Constitution; knew little about it, or about the decisions of the Supreme Court under it; . . . and that it was not to be expected anything intelligible could come from their hands" (Crosskey 1954:11). Such derogatory comments about the framers of the Fourteenth Amendment were consistent with the predominant historiography of Reconstruction in 1949, but have since been rejected by the leading historians of the era (Foner 1988).

46. *Adamson,* 332 U.S. 46, 89 (1947).

Chapter Two

1. Simply counting the cases in which the Court exercises judicial review cannot provide a complete picture of the scope of judicial power, particularly because, as Mark Graber has noted, the Court "has numerous techniques for limiting government power that do not require declaring a statute unconstitutional" (2000:29). Nonetheless, the raw numbers are illustrative of broad patterns of activism and restraint throughout the Court's history.

2. *Lee Optical,* 348 U.S. 483, 477–78 (1955).

3. 336 U.S. 77, 90–92 (1949).

4. Frankfurter's opinion here built directly on an unsigned editorial he had written more than twenty-five years earlier entitled "Can the Supreme Court Guarantee Toleration?" (1925). His answer, of course, was no. Paraphrasing his editorial, he observed in *Dennis* that "[c]ivil liberties draw at best only limited strength from legal guarantees. Preoccupation by our people with the constitutionality, instead of with the wisdom, of legislation or of executive action is preoccupation with a false value. . . . The ultimate reliance for the deepest needs of civilization must be found outside their vindication in courts of law." 341 U.S. 494, 496, 525, 555–56 (1951). See Bickel 1970:29–30.

5. 341 U.S. 494, 526, 539 (1951). For other examples of Frankfurter's restrained approach in the First Amendment context, see *Terminiello v. Chicago* and *Feiner v. New York*. For another example of his deference to Congress, see *American Communications Association v. Douds*.

6. 356 U.S. 86, 104–5, 119–120, 128 (1958).

7. 367 U.S. 497, 503–4 (1961).

8. 352 U.S. 567, 590–91 (1957). Note also Frankfurter's opinions in *Joint Anti-Fascist Refugee Committee v. McGrath* and *Youngstown Sheet and Tube Co. v. Sawyer,* in which he supported judicial intervention, but only after a lengthy discussion of standing, justiciability, and the Court's other doctrines for avoiding decision.

9. *Knapp v. Schweitzer,* 357 U.S. 371, 375 (1958).

10. 338 U.S. 25, 27 (1949).

11. 359 U.S. 121, 124, 140–48 (1959).

12. 342 U.S. 165, 169, 172 (1952). Frankfurter may have borrowed this last phrase from Cardozo's observation in *Palko v. Connecticut* that the Due Process Clause prohibits state statutes that impose "a hardship so acute and shocking that our polity will not endure it." 302 U.S. 319, 328 (1937).

13. 354 U.S. 234, 266–67 (1957). Note also *Wieman v. Updegraff,* 344 U.S. 183, 196 (1952), in which Frankfurter held that the state could not require teachers to take an oath that they were not and had never been members of any subversive groups. Such a requirement would violate the freedom of association for anyone, but it was particularly objectionable for teachers, "the priests of our democracy."

14. *Kingsley Pictures Corp. v. Regents of the University of the State of New York,* 360 U.S. 684, 696 (1959).

15. 328 U.S. 582, 594, 597 (1946). This case was just one of a number of examples in which Frankfurter sought to defend Fourth Amendment privacy even more actively than Douglas, the great civil libertarian (Kersch 2002:81–82).

16. See, e.g., *On Lee v. United States* and *Irvine v. California.*

17. 333 U.S. 203, 231 (1948).

18. *Zorach v. Clauson.*

19. *McGowan v. Maryland,* 366 U.S. 420, 461 (1961).

20. See *Lane v. Wilson; Smith v. Allwright; Shelley v. Kraemer;* and *Sipuel v. Board of Regents of the University of Oklahoma.*

21. *Terry v. Adams.*

22. 347 U.S. 497, 499–500 (1954).

23. 347 U.S. 483, 489 (1954).

24. Id. at 489–92.

25. *Congressional Record* 102:4460; *Race Relations Law Reporter* 1:435 (1956).

26. The South Carolina and Alabama resolutions were both enacted in February 1956. See *Race Relations Law Reporter* 1:437 (1956). Virginia later sponsored a seven-hundred-page study of the Reconstruction history that "would enable 'judges, lawyers, teachers, and students' to determine for themselves whether decisions such as that in *Brown v. Board* 'comport with the reconstruction amendments as originally understood and intended'" (Berns 1987:216–17). On the southern reaction to *Brown*, see generally Powe (2000:57–74).

27. Around the same time, Jackson described Fairman's article and a companion piece by Stanley Morrison as "the most comprehensive and objective studies of the origin and adoption of the Fourteenth Amendment." *Beauharnais v. Illinois*, 343 U.S. 250, 294 (1952).

28. Hand had defended a constrained vision of judicial power at least since 1908, when he lambasted the Court's *Lochner* decision in the *Harvard Law Review*. During his long tenure on the bench, he voted only three times to invalidate a statute on constitutional grounds — none of them involving the Bill of Rights — and he later expressed regret for even these instances (Gunther 1994:118–23). He did author a widely noted pro-free speech opinion during World War I, but even in that case, *Masses Publishing Co. v. Patten*, he did not actually strike down the statute at issue.

29. In the Holmes Lectures, Hand endorsed Hughes's account of constitutional change in *Home Building and Loan Association v. Blaisdell* and noted that it is "impossible to fabricate how the 'Framers' would have answered the problems that arise in a modern society had they been reared in the civilization that has produced those problems. We should indeed have to be sorcerers to conjure up how they would have responded" (1958:34–35). See also *Reiss v. National Quotation Bureau*, 276 Fed. 717, 719 (S.D.N.Y. 1921), in which he insisted that the Constitution does not "embalm[ ] inflexibly the habits of 1789." See generally Gunther 1994:319–20.

30. During the 1950s, at least, the very purpose of the *Harvard Law Review* forewords seemed to be to criticize the Court's poor craftsmanship. This was a principal theme of Harold Jaffe's inaugural foreword in 1951, as well as Ernest Brown's in 1958, Hart's in 1959, and Erwin Griswold's in 1960. See also Bickel and Wellington 1957. See generally Tushnet and Lynch 1994–95; White 1978b.

31. Following Frankfurter's argument in *Dick v. New York Life Insurance Co.*, Hart complained that "[t]o call upon judges to vote on complex and often highly controversial issues after only a couple of hours, more or less, of private study of briefs and record is to invite votes which are influenced more strongly by general predilections in the area of law than they are by lawyerlike examination of the precise issues presented for decision." If the justices spent more time on each case, "it seems unlikely that the voting records of the Justices would lend themselves quite as readily as they do to neat pigeon-

holing in the charts of professors of political science . . . who believe that you can lump together votes in all civil-liberties cases, in all anti-trust cases, in all employment-injury cases, and the like, and find out how a Justice thinks" (1959:124–25).

32. In 1994, William Eskridge and Philip Frickey edited and published Hart and Sacks's volume in a form substantially similar to the 1958 tentative edition. All cites below are to this 1994 edition.

33. Hart and Wechsler were, in fact, active collaborators during this period. See Hart and Wechsler 1953.

34. Bickel (1986:16, 18, 24). All cites in the text are to the 1986 reprint edition of *The Least Dangerous Branch,* which was first published in 1962.

35. Bickel (1986:24–27). Bickel's argument here recalled Frankfurter's *Barnette* dissent, which had insisted that "[o]ur system is built on the faith that men set apart for this special function, freed from the influences of immediacy and from the deflections of worldly ambition, will become able to take a view of longer range than the period of responsibility entrusted to Congress and legislatures." 319 U.S. 624, 665 (1943).

36. Bickel (1986:239). Here, Bickel built explicitly on Frankfurter's observation in *Sweezy* that judicial judgment "must rest on fundamental presuppositions rooted in history to which widespread acceptance may fairly be attributed." 354 U.S. 234, 267 (1957).

37. Kahn (1994:82, 73). For his reliance on Truman and Dahl, see Bickel 1986:17–23. See also Purcell 1973:260–66.

38. The fact that the justices and scholars had such divergent visions of law, democracy, and justice helps explain why the scholarly critiques were sometimes advanced with such sharp rhetoric, a tendency of which Hart's foreword was the best (or worst) example (Tushnet and Lynch 1994–95:491). It is also a tendency that some conservative critics of the Court have continued to this day. See, e.g., Bork 1996a; 1996h; Muncy 1997.

Chapter Three

1. As Howard Gillman (1997:192) has shown, the roots of the originalist approach in fact reach all the way back to the founding, as "there was a consensus in [early] court opinions and legal treatises that judges were obligated to interpret the Constitution on the basis of the original meaning of constitutional provisions." It was only after the emergence of a competing evolutionary approach in the mid-twentieth century, however, that advocates of originalism were forced to fully articulate and defend its major premises.

2. *Lucas v. Forty-fourth General Assembly of Colorado.*

3. *Jacobellis v. Ohio; A Quantity of Copies of Books v. Kansas.*

4. *Griffin v. County School Board; Bell v. Maryland.*

5. *Schneider v. Rusk; Aptheker v. Secretary of State.* For a useful survey (and acerbic critique) of the Court's 1963 term, see Kurland 1964.

6. The phrase "democracy of rights" is Stephen Griffin's, and as he suggests, the Court was certainly not leading the nation towards this new democratic vision by itself (2002). As Charles Epp (1998) has shown in a persuasive comparative study of rights revolutions,

the American one was the product, first and foremost, of the rights-based activism and litigation of civil rights advocates. I take up Epp's argument more fully below; for the moment, I mean only to suggest that with respect to the relationship among governmental institutions during the 1960s, it was the Court that was pushing the hardest for the expansion of rights.

7. The double jeopardy case was *Benton v. Maryland*. See generally Powe (2000: 412–15).

8. 391 U.S. 145, 174 (1968).

9. 367 U.S. 497, 542–43 (1961).

10. Id. at 548, 551–52.

11. Among the many opinions that have cited Harlan's argument in *Poe* are the plurality opinion in *Planned Parenthood v. Casey*, 505 U.S. 833, 848–50 (1992); Justice Powell's opinions for the Court in *Akron v. Akron Center for Reproductive Health*, 462 U.S. 416, 427 (1983), and *Moore v. East Cleveland*, 431 U.S. 494, 501–2 (1977); and Justice Stewart's concurring opinion in *Roe*, 410 U.S. 113, 169 (1973). See Dworkin 1996a:44–45.

12. 381 U.S. 479, 482, 484, 499–500 (1965).

13. Id. at 528.

14. 372 U.S. 726, 730–32 (1963).

15. 381 U.S. 479, 507, 510–12, 522–27 (1965).

16. *Rochin*, 342 U.S. 165, 175–77 (1952).

17. 389 U.S. 347, 372–73 (1967). See also *Berger v. New York*.

18. The Court that decided *Winship* in 1970 was no longer led by Earl Warren, but because my concern here is describing Harlan and Black's dissenting critiques of the Warren Court, rather than focusing on the Warren Court as such, I refer in this chapter to a number of cases from their last years on the Court, just after the Warren era had ended.

19. 397 U.S. 358, 369–72, 377, 381–82 (1970). Earlier that same year, Black had complained in *Goldberg v. Kelly*, 397 U.S. 254, 276 n. 6 (1970), that the Court's "search for the 'collective conscience of mankind,' . . . [was] only a euphemism for an individual's judgment. Judges are as human as anyone and as likely as others to see the world through their own eyes and find the 'collective conscience' remarkably similar to their own."

20. *Wesberry v. Sanders*, 376 U.S. 1, 48 (1964).

21. *Shapiro v. Thompson*, 394 U.S. 618, 677 (1969).

22. The Douglas quote is from *Boddie v. Connecticut*, 401 U.S. 371, 384–85 (1971). For Black's views on the matter, see his dissenting opinions in *Boddie*, *Griswold*, and *Harper v. Virginia State Board of Elections*.

23. 369 U.S. 186, 301–2 (1962).

24. Id. at 332–34, 339–40.

25. 372 U.S. 368, 381, 384, 388–90 (1963).

26. 369 U.S. 186, 332–33 (1962).

27. 376 U.S. 1, 14 (1964). Harlan pointed out that the Court's decision "impugns the

validity of the election of 398 Representatives from 37 States, leaving a 'constitutional' House of 37 members now sitting" (id. at 21–22).

28. Id. at 14, 31, 41–42.

29. 372 U.S. 368, 381 (1963).

30. 377 U.S. 533, 568 (1964).

31. *Wesberry,* 376 U.S. 1, 42, 48 (1964).

32. *Reynolds,* 377 U.S. 533, 568, 566 (1964).

33. Harlan noted further that six of the ten reconstructed states had constitutions with similar provisions, making it improbable that the Reconstruction Congress — which exacted ratification of the Fourteenth Amendment as the price of readmission for these states — considered such provisions to be in conflict with the amendment's Equal Protection Clause. Following a practice that Black had pioneered, he added an appendix containing further evidence from the congressional history of the drafting and adoption of the Fourteenth Amendment. 377 U.S. 533, 594–95, 602–8, 625–32 (1964).

34. Id. at 608–10.

35. Justice Stewart supported some of the reapportionment decisions, but he generally agreed with Harlan's argument in this regard. Dissenting in *Lucas v. Forty-fourth General Assembly,* 377 U.S. 713, 746–48 (1964), for example, he insisted that "[t]he Court's draconian pronouncement, which makes unconstitutional the legislatures of most of the 50 States, finds no support in the words of the Constitution, in any prior decision of this Court, or in the 175-year political history of our Federal Union. With all respect, I am convinced these decisions mark a long step backward into that unhappy era when a majority of the members of this Court were thought by many to have convinced themselves and each other that the demands of the Constitution were to be measured not by what it says, but by their own notions of wise political theory." For helpful accounts of the reapportionment cases, see Powe 2000:241–55 and Brandwein 1999:156–84, the latter of which provides a careful elaboration of Frankfurter's and Harlan's historical arguments.

36. For an example of historical scholarship supporting Warren Court activism, see William Van Alstyne's rejection, after a thorough independent review, of Harlan's reading of Reconstruction history in *Reynolds.* Paralleling Bickel's account of segregation, Van Alstyne (1965) insisted that the legislative history of the Fourteenth Amendment did not preclude the Court's decision in *Reynolds.* In an attempt to respond to Van Alstyne's historical account (and to buttress Harlan's), Raoul Berger (1977) launched his extensive historical research on the Reconstruction Congress, which I take up more fully in chapter 4.

37. Because the scholars were following the Court's lead, almost all of this work focused on the original understanding of the Fourteenth Amendment, rather than the 1787 Constitution or the Bill of Rights. Berger did publish an exhaustive examination of the framers' original understanding of judicial review in 1969, but he too would soon turn his attention to the Reconstruction amendments, going far beyond Kelly in denouncing the Warren Court's historical arguments in this regard.

38. 400 U.S. 112, 154 (1970). Since the Court agreed with Harlan with respect to state and local elections, Congress was in fact forced to offer a constitutional amendment on this point, which was ratified as the Twenty-sixth Amendment in 1971.

39. Id. at 200–3.

40. The quotation is from Harlan's dissent in *Oregon v. Mitchell*, id. at 203.

41. *Adamson*, 332 U.S. 46, 91 (1947).

42. 383 U.S. 663, 669 (1966).

43. 351 U.S. 12, 34–39 (1956).

44. 372 U.S. 353, 361–62 (1963).

45. 383 U.S. 663, 681–84, 677–78 (1966).

46. 372 U.S. 353, 361–62 (1963).

47. *Harper,* 383 U.S. 663, 686 (1966).

48. In dissent, Black reiterated that neither clause is an "appropriate . . . vehicle for the 'shock the conscience' test" because neither "justifies judges in trying to make our Constitution fit the times, or hold laws constitutional or not on the basis of a judge's sense of fairness." 401 U.S. 371, 374, 394 (1971). See also Black's dissenting opinion in *Hunter v. Erickson,* 393 U.S. 385, 396–97 (1969).

49. For other examples in which Harlan and Black agreed in dissent, leading the Court to rule more narrowly than it otherwise might have, see *Bell v. Maryland* and *Kramer v. Union Free School District No. 15.*

50. 397 U.S. 254, 262–65 (1970).

51. 394 U.S. 618, 658–62, 677 (1969).

52. 397 U.S. 254, 274–76 (1970).

53. See also Powe 2000:497.

54. Some of the Warren Court's contemporary supporters defended the Court on precisely these grounds (Cox 1968:15–16).

55. The congressional complaint was by Alabama representative George Andrews. See Powe 2000:187–90; Weaver 1967:258.

56. Wallace's 1964 campaign also laid important groundwork for the conservative re-alignment. As Taylor Branch notes, Wallace's successes that year built on his earlier refusal, as Alabama governor, to allow the racial integration of the flagship state university by literally "standing in the schoolhouse door" to block Kennedy's deputy attorney general Nicholas Katzenbach from entering the registration building: "His stand against Washington and do-gooder bureaucrats planted a conservative standard which, further rinsed of overtly racial content, came to dominate American politics for more than a generation" (1988:822).

57. Thurmond's speech is reprinted in the *Congressional Record,* S22304-5 (September 17, 1964).

58. In a March 1963, letter to Bickel, Frankfurter praised an article of Bickel's criticizing the Court and noted, "You law professors really should sharpen your pens, so that there is no mistaking as to what the trouble is and where the blame lies." Referring to his liberal activist opponents on the Court, he continued, "I can give you proof that if you

would speak out, you would get under their skins" (*quoted in* both Simon 1989:255 and Hirsch 1981:183). For a collection of Bickel's essays in *The New Republic,* see Bickel 1965.

59. For helpful discussions of Bickel's development in this regard, see Smith 1985:174–75 and Purcell 1976. Note also Robert Bork's observation that "[l]ater in his all-too-brief career [Bickel] came to doubt the capacity of the Supreme Court to manage principles of the sort his early work envisioned" (1990:193). While Bickel became increasingly critical as the Warren era progressed, Wechsler spoke less frequently and, when he did so, simply reiterated the measured criticism of his 1959 Holmes Lectures (Wechsler 1965).

60. Interestingly, in denouncing the reapportionment decisions, Bickel and his fellow scholars repeatedly condemned the Court's support for the principle of "one man, one vote," despite the fact that the justices consistently described this principle as "one person, one vote." Contrast Bickel 1970 and Kurland 1964 with the Court's opinions in *Gray v. Sanders* and *Reynolds.*

61. Kurland developed the institutional capacity argument even more fully than Bickel, insisting that the Court "cannot act until a problem is presented to it by way of an adversary proceeding in the form of a case or controversy"; that it "lacks machinery for gathering the wide range of facts and opinions that should inform the judgment of a prime policy maker"; that it lacks also any "means of supervising or enforcing the decrees that it promulgates"; that in any "contest between the president and the Court or between the Court and the Congress, the Court is not likely to enhance its power"; and that "[t]he Court's capacity to express whatever will it has is entirely dependent upon the support of public opinion" (1970b:196–201).

62. Note, for example, Bickel's offhand dismissal of "the sophistry of arguments that the supremacy of the judges is consistent with democratic theory so long as the judges enhance the democratic process rather than restricting it, which is supposedly what they do in First Amendment and apportionment cases" (1970:113).

Chapter Four

1. My account of the Fortas nomination is drawn from Kalman 1990:327–58; Silverstein 1994; Simon 1973; Powe 2000:465–75; Blum 1991:213–17; and Edsall and Edsall 1992:74–84.

2. "Toward Freedom from Fear" is reprinted in the *Congressional Record,* S12936–9 (May 13, 1968).

3. Nixon, "Toward Freedom from Fear," *Congressional Record,* S12937 (May 13, 1968).

4. This was not simply a matter of good luck, as the Nixon administration actively participated in the investigation that led to Fortas's resignation (Powe 2000:477–78; Kalman 1990:362–70).

5. "The President's Nationwide Address Announcing His Intention To Nominate Lewis F. Powell, Jr., and William H Rehnquist To Be Associate Justices," October 21, 1971, *Weekly Compilation of Presidential Documents* 7 (October 25, 1971):1431–32.

6. For an insider's account of Nixon's surprise, last-minute selection of Rehnquist, see Dean 2001.

7. See Rehnquist 1980 and his dissenting opinion in *Furman v. Georgia,* 408 U.S. 238, 468–70 (1972). See generally Maveety 1987 and Whittington 2003.

8. Rehnquist's first term, in 1971, was an incomplete one, as he joined the Court in the middle of the year and participated in only about half of the cases.

9. In two of those terms, Rehnquist tied with two other justices for the most solo dissenting opinions.

10. Mark Tushnet (1999b) has described these cases as an aborted effort to complete FDR's Second Bill of Rights, a foundation of the New Deal/Great Society constitutional order, while Ronald Kahn (1994) has argued that such claims overstate the Warren Court's commitment to egalitarianism.

11. *Wheeler v. Montgomery,* 397 U.S. 280, 282–83 (1970).

12. 397 U.S. 471, 484–85, 489–90 (1970).

13. 411 U.S. 1, 18–29, 33, 55 (1973). For a helpful discussion, see Kahn 1994:141–47.

14. The Warren Court had first expressed its impatience with southern resistance to school desegregation in *Cooper v. Aaron,* but not until the mid-1960s did it begin to demand that school officials integrate their schools at once. The key cases were *Griffin v. County School Board of Prince Edward County, Bradley v. School Board,* and especially *Green v. County School Board.*

15. This case, *Alexander v. Holmes County Board of Education,* marked the first time that the NAACP had been opposed by the Justice Department in a desegregation case at the high Court (Simon 1973:126–28; Wilkinson 1979:119–20, 216–18; Orfield 1996a: 9–13; Edsall and Edsall 1992:81–82).

16. *Swann v. Charlotte-Mecklenburg Board of Education,* 402 U.S. 1, 26, 16 (1971).

17. In the latter case, the Court observed that "[j]ust as the race of students must be considered in determining whether a constitutional violation has occurred, so also must race be considered in formulating a remedy." *North Carolina State Board of Education v. Swann,* 402 U.S. 43, 45 (1971).

18. 402 U.S. 1, 16, 23–26, 30–32 (1971). Four months after this decision, in denying a stay application in his capacity as Circuit Justice, Burger sought to emphasize the limiting statements in the *Swann* opinion, and took the unusual step of having his order mailed to federal judges throughout the country. *Winston-Salem/Forsyth County Board of Education v. Scott.* See Wilkinson 1979:149–50; Graglia 1976:140.

19. 407 U.S. 451, 466, 471, 482, 474, 477 (1972). See also *United States v. Scotland Neck City Board of Education.*

20. 413 U.S. 189, 238, 224 (1973). See generally Jeffries 1994:282–331.

21. Id. at 257–58; *Delaware State Board of Education v. Evans,* 446 U.S. 923, 927 (1980) (Rehnquist, J., dissenting from denial of *cert.*); *Columbus Board of Education v. Penick,* 443 U.S. 449, 513 (1979). See Davis 1989:58–60.

22. 433 U.S. 406, 413, 418 (1977).

23. When the *Dayton* case returned to the Court two years later, for example, Rehnquist and Powell were again in dissent, with Powell calling for "a thoughtful reexamination of the proper limits of the role of courts in confronting the intractable problems of public education in our complex society." He observed that the Court's holdings "seem[ed] remarkably insensitive to the now widely accepted view that a quarter of a century after *Brown I*, the federal judiciary should be limiting rather than expanding the extent to which courts are operating the public school systems of our country." See *Dayton Board of Education v. Brinkman (Dayton II)*. Powell's dissent appeared in a companion case, *Columbus Board of Education v. Penick*, 443 U.S. 449, 479–80, 487 (1979), but applied to the *Dayton* case as well.

24. 426 U.S. 229, 240, 248 (1976).

25. *McGautha v. California*, 402 U.S. 183, 207–8, 221 (1971).

26. *People v. Anderson*. Reagan is quoted in Simon 1973:271.

27. Chief Justice Burger also insisted that the Court was wrongly infringing on an area of legislative competence. 408 U.S. 238, 466, 470, 417–18, 432, 464–65, 403–5 (1972).

28. Id. at 419–20.

29. Id. at 410.

30. 428 U.S. 153, 179–80 (1976).

31. *Woodson v. North Carolina*.

32. *Loving v. Virginia*, 388 U.S. 1, 11 (1967).

33. *Stanley v. Georgia*, 394 U.S. 557, 566 (1969).

34. 405 U.S. 438, 453 (1972).

35. *Roe v. Wade*, 410 U.S. 113, 152–53 (1973). On Brennan's *Eisenstadt* opinion, see Woodward and Armstrong 1979:206.

36. *Roe*, 410 U.S. 113, 172–74 (1973).

37. As Stewart noted in his concurring opinion in *Roe*, the Court had "understandably d[one] its best to avoid reliance on" substantive due process in *Griswold*, since it had "purported to sound the death knell for the doctrine" just two years earlier in *Ferguson v. Skrupa*. But since the Connecticut statute did not violate any specific provision of the Constitution, "it was clear to me then, and it is equally clear to me now, that the *Griswold* decision can be rationally understood only as . . . one in a long line of pre-*Skrupa* cases decided under the doctrine of substantive due process, and I now accept it as such." 410 U.S. 113, 167–68 (1973).

38. 410 U.S. 179, 221–22 (1973).

39. 428 U.S. 52, 92–93 (1976).

40. *Eisenstadt*, 405 U.S. 438, 471–72, 467 (1972).

41. After dissenting in *Danforth*, Burger joined Powell's opinion reaffirming *Roe* in *Akron v. Akron Center for Reproductive Health*, but then dissented three years later in *Thornburgh v. American College of Obstetricians and Gynecologists*, urging the Court to reexamine *Roe*.

42. *Lindsey v. Normet*, 405 U.S. 56, 74 (1972); *Moore v. East Cleveland*.

43. 406 U.S. 164, 178–82 (1972). Harlan's dissenting opinion was in *Levy v. Louisiana.* See also Rehnquist's dissenting opinion in *New Jersey Welfare Rights Organization v. Cahill.*

44. 413 U.S. 634, 649–50, 656–57 (1973). See also Burger's dissenting opinion in the companion case of *In re Griffiths,* and Rehnquist's dissenting opinions in *Nyquist v. Mauclet* and *Toll v. Moreno.*

45. 430 U.S. 762, 777–80, 784 (1977).

46. *Frontiero v. Richardson,* 411 U.S. 677, 682 (1973); *Craig v. Boren,* 429 U.S. 190, 197 (1976).

47. *Craig,* 429 U.S. 190, 220–21 (1976). See also *Frontiero,* 411 U.S. 677, 691 (1973).

48. Dworkin's essay on "The Jurisprudence of Richard Nixon" first appeared in the *New York Review of Books* in 1972 and was later reprinted as "Constitutional Cases" in his widely influential book, *Taking Rights Seriously* (1978:147).

49. While most of the new libertarian activism was incorporated within the Republican Party, some activists instead joined the new Libertarian Party, founded in 1972.

50. See, e.g., Hayek's prefaces to the 1956 and 1976 editions of the book (1994:xxxiv–xxxv, xxiii–xxiv).

51. Regarding the community action programs, Moynihan observed, "This is the essential fact: The government did not know what it was doing" (1969:170). Similarly, the 1966 Coleman Report, a congressionally commissioned study on equality of educational opportunity, convinced him that federal education spending was a waste of money (Mosteller and Moynihan 1972; Moynihan 1969:194–95).

52. Horowitz's four case studies were recent legal conflicts regarding the Great Society's Model Cities program, public school funding equity, juvenile justice reform, and the Fourth Amendment exclusionary rule (1977).

53. *DeFunis v. Odegaard,* 507 P.2d 1169, 1178–85 (Wash. 1973).

54. 416 U.S. 312, 333–44 (1974). See also Douglas (1980:119–20).

55. Brief of the Anti-Defamation League of B'nai B'rith as Amicus Curiae, *DeFunis,* at 19–23, 31.

56. Kurland (1970a:674–76); Brief of the ADL of B'nai B'rith as Amicus Curiae, *Regents of the University of California v. Bakke,* at 11. Bickel had also expressed earlier support for affirmative action on the grounds of expediency, noting in *The Least Dangerous Branch* that the courts should exercise the passive virtues and uphold legislatively adopted racial quotas for the time being (1986:71–72).

57. 438 U.S. 265, 289–96 (1978). In *Affirmative Discrimination,* Glazer had also rejected any heightened judicial solicitude for relatively powerless minorities, arguing that almost all members of the so-called white majority were themselves members of specific ethnic or religious groups that had faced discrimination in the past: "We are indeed a nation of minorities; to enshrine some minorities as deserving of special benefits means not to defend minority rights against a discriminating majority but to favor some of these minorities over others" (1975b:200–1). Though Powell did not cite Glazer, he was clearly indebted to Glazer's argument, and also to Rehnquist's dissenting opinion in *Sug-*

arman v. Dougall, discussed earlier. Powell did cite a recent article by Richard Posner insisting that "the use of a racial characteristic to establish a presumption that the individual also possesses other, and socially relevant, characteristics, exemplifies, encourages, and legitimizes the mode of thought and behavior that underlies most prejudice and bigotry in modern America" (Posner 1974:12; see Bybee 2000:281–85).

58. In addition to *Keyes* and *Rodriguez,* discussed above, note also Powell's concurring opinion in *Frontiero.*

59. 435 U.S. 78, 96 n. 6 (1978).

60. 474 U.S. 214, 230 (1985).

61. *Fry v. United States,* 421 U.S. 542, 550, 559 (1975).

62. 426 U.S. 833, 845 (1976).

63. Id. at 857–58, 862–65. For examples of scholarly criticism, see Choper 1980; Barber 1976; Michelman 1977; Tribe 1977.

64. 440 U.S. 410, 432–33, 439 (1979).

65. The "regulatory takings" doctrine originated with Holmes's 1922 holding that "[t]he general rule . . . is, that while property may be regulated to a certain extent, if regulation goes too far it will be recognized as a taking." *Pennsylvania Coal Co. v. Mahon,* 260 U.S. 393, 415 (1922).

66. 438 U.S. 234, 241–42 (1978).

67. *Webster v. Reproductive Health Services,* 492 U.S. 490, 521 (1989).

68. Berger (1997:18, 314). The citations are to Berger's twentieth-anniversary reprint of *Government by Judiciary,* but all of the passages appeared in identical form in the original 1977 edition.

69. Berger also emphasized that his historical sources — the records of the Thirty-ninth Congress — were "free from the reproach often leveled at legislative history — that it is 'enigmatic.'" These records "are of a far more trustworthy character, being a stenographic transcription of what was said . . . from day to day by those engaged in framing the Amendment. It is a verbatim account of what occurred, recorded while it was happening, comparable to a news film of an event at the moment it was taking place and free from the possible distortion of accounts drawn from recollection or hearsay" (1997:6–9; see also Berger 1979:529–32).

70. On the incorporation, school segregation, and reapportionment questions, Berger endorsed the historical claims of Fairman, Bickel, and Harlan, respectively, insisting that the framers did not intend to incorporate the Bill of Rights, to abolish segregation, or to require equally apportioned state legislatures. He similarly rejected the doctrine of substantive due process, leading him to deride virtually all modern justices of the Supreme Court (1997:6–7, 458, 155–73, 132–45, 90–115).

71. Most originalist scholars have focused on Reconstruction-era history, but some have emphasized the original founding instead (McDowell 1988; Clinton 1989; Berns 1987).

72. For a representative example, note Earl Maltz's argument that when interpreting the Constitution, judges should always "be guided by the intent of the Framers," and

that when "dealing with ambiguous constitutional limitations such as the equal protection clause, the Framers are to be taken as intending to reach only those evils explicitly discussed in debate. Thus, the appropriate scope of judicial review is . . . extremely limited" (1983:811–12).

Chapter Five

1. For a helpful account of this sort of "partisan entrenchment" in the courts, see Balkin and Levinson 2001.

2. *Washington Post,* November 13, 1986, A21, col. 1. For examples of the critical response, see the ACLU's denunciation of his views as an "invitation to lawlessness." *New York Times,* October 24, 1986, A17, col. 1 (noting also the critical comments of American Bar Association president Eugene C. Thomas and Harvard law professor Laurence Tribe). See also Anthony Lewis, "Law or Power?" *New York Times,* October 27, 1986, A23, col. 1 (criticizing Meese's "calculated assault on the idea of law in this country"). Perhaps most notable was the fact that Meese's comments drew public responses from Justices Brennan and Stevens, marking the first time since the New Deal that members of the Court had "entered into debate with a senior figure from the Executive Branch" (Caplan 1987:121; see Brennan 1986; Stevens 1985).

3. Brief for United States as *Amicus Curiae* in Support of Appellants, *Thornburgh,* filed July 15, 1985.

4. Ibid.

5. Nomination of Robert H. Bork to be Associate Justice of the Supreme Court of the U.S., Report of the Senate Committee on the Judiciary, 100th Cong., 1st Sess., p. 36 (1987). For an excellent brief summary of these events, see Garrow 1994:668–72.

6. "Comments by President on His Choice of Justice," *New York Times,* July 24, 1990, A18, col. 1. See also Maltese 1998:130–31.

7. The votes were 13–1 in the Judiciary Committee and 90–9 in the full Senate. On the senators' positive impressions of Souter, see Ellen Goodman, "The Judge Who Speaks in Two Voices," *Boston Globe,* September 20, 1990, 23.

8. 478 U.S. 186, 190–95 (1986).

9. After his retirement from the Court, Powell confessed that his vote in *Bowers* was probably a mistake (Agneshwar 1990). His Memorandum to the Conference is reprinted in Schwartz 1996a:209, and his decisionmaking process is recounted in Jeffries 1994:511–30 and Garrow 1994:652–67. The passage from Powell's concurrence appears at 478 U.S. 186, 198 n. 2 (1986).

10. 497 U.S. 62, 95–96 (1990).

11. Id. at 104; *Board of County Commissioners, Wabaunsee County v. Umbehr,* 518 U.S. 668, 688–89 (1996).

12. 505 U.S. 577, 631, 633–35 (1992).

13. Id. at 646.

14. 494 U.S. 872, 890 (1990).

15. For an earlier example, also in the religious freedom context, see *Lynch v. Don-*

nelly. When Reagan administration officials briefly considered O'Connor as a possible replacement for Chief Justice Burger in 1986, conservatives were already complaining about her "troublesome propensity" to narrow the Court's conservative holdings by writing separately (Yalof 1999:145–49).

16. 505 U.S. 577, 587, 597–98 (1992). See also *Santa Fe Independent School District v. Doe.*

17. 491 U.S. 110, 121–29, 137–39 (1989).

18. 497 U.S. 261, 278–84, 302, 292–94 (1990).

19. 491 U.S. 110, 132, 141 (1989).

20. 497 U.S. 261, 287 (1990).

21. 462 U.S. 416, 465, 453 (1983). O'Connor's opinion was joined by White and Rehnquist. On the solicitor general's arguments, see Epstein and Kobylka 1992:238–47.

22. 492 U.S. 490, 525–26, 560 (1989). On the Court's decisionmaking process in *Webster,* see Schwartz 1996b:260–338; 1996a:12–64; Simon 1995:126–43; Garrow 1994: 673–80.

23. The plurality cited Black's opinion in *Adamson v. California* and Scalia's in *Michael H.* as examples of the arguments they were rejecting. In support of their alternative approach, they pointed to Frankfurter's opinion in *Rochin v. California* and a number of other precedents, but relied primarily on Harlan's argument in *Poe.* 505 U.S. 833, 847–50 (1992).

24. 505 U.S. 833, 849–51 (1992).

25. Id. at 979–84, 1000.

26. The extent to which the plurality endorsed the jurisprudence of *Roe,* as opposed to simply upholding it as binding precedent, remains a matter of some dispute. Since the opinion offered a lengthy argument for upholding *Roe* on the grounds of *stare decisis,* some scholars have read it as adhering to *Roe* without endorsing its correctness as an original matter (Tushnet 2003:91–92). Nonetheless, I follow Dworkin, Garrow 1997, Gillman 1994a:649–50, and Kahn 1994:255–59 in characterizing the plurality's holding more broadly. After all, O'Connor, Kennedy, and Souter explicitly noted the "correctness" of the Court's decisions in *Griswold* and *Eisenstadt v. Baird,* and they observed that these decisions "support the reasoning in *Roe* relating to the women's liberty." Even if *Roe* was in error, they noted, "that error would go only to the strength of the state interest in fetal protection, not to the recognition afforded by the Constitution to the woman's liberty. . . . The soundness of this prong of the *Roe* analysis is apparent from a consideration of the alternative. If indeed the woman's interest in deciding whether to bear and beget a child had not been recognized as in *Roe,* the State might as readily restrict a woman's right to choose to carry a pregnancy to term as to terminate it, to further asserted state interests in population control, or eugenics, for example. Yet *Roe* has been sensibly relied upon to counter any such suggestions." 505 U.S. 833, 852–53, 858–59 (1992).

27. During his first three terms on the Court, Souter's annual rates of agreement with O'Connor were 93.7 percent, 76.5 percent, and 76.7 percent; with Kennedy, they were

88.2 percent, 87.3 percent, and 82.5 percent. By the 1999, 2000, and 2001 terms, these rates had dropped to 68.1 percent, 74.6 percent, and 68.5 percent with O'Connor, and to 61.1 percent, 72.6 percent, and 62.7 percent with Kennedy. These data were obtained from Harold Spaeth's U.S. Supreme Court Judicial Database. For a more extensive analysis of Souter, see Keck 2003.

28. 450 U.S. 464, 468 (1981).

29. 458 U.S. 718, 724 (1982).

30. *J.E.B. v. Alabama ex rel. T.B.*

31. *Board of Education of Oklahoma City v. Dowell*, 498 U.S. 237, 244–48 (1991).

32. *Missouri v. Jenkins*, 515 U.S. 70, 88 (1995).

33. In *Arlington Heights v. Metropolitan Housing Development Corp.*, for example, the Court had indicated that the cases will be "rare" in which evidence of discriminatory impact alone is adequate to support an inference of discriminatory purpose; and in *Personnel Administrator of Massachusetts v. Feeney*, the Court had read *Davis* and *Arlington Heights* as endorsing "the settled rule that the Fourteenth Amendment guarantees equal laws, not equal results." 442 U.S. 256, 273 (1979).

34. 490 U.S. 642, 664, 657 (1989). Congress endorsed the dissenters' interpretation of the statute by passing the 1991 Civil Rights Act, which reversed the Court's decision in this and several other 1989 cases.

35. 497 U.S. 836, 860, 870 (1990) (emphasis added by Scalia).

36. 506 U.S. 390, 419 (1993).

37. 510 U.S. 1141, 1145, 1142–43 (1994).

38. William F. Buckley Jr.'s *National Review* has been the most influential publication that has explicitly sought to unite the various wings of the conservative movement (Buckley 1995).

39. For the Court's rejection of the religious freedom arguments, see *Bob Jones University v. United States*, 461 U.S. 574, 602–4 (1983). For a good account of the Reagan Justice Department's actions on the case, see Caplan 1987:51–64.

40. This statement is from a November 24, 1998 letter from Michael S. Greve to CIR supporters, in which he noted that "CIR has pursued this goal in the nation's courts with single-minded devotion for almost ten years." CIR's official publications regularly describe the organization's goal as seeking "the re-invigoration of meaningful constitutional constraints on government" (CIR, 1997–98 Annual Report). See generally Keck 2000.

41. These quotations are from the introductory statement and "Electronic Brochure" available on IJ's Web site at www.ij.org/index.shtml.

42. Ibid.

43. For a good summary, see "The Mission of CIR," available on-line at www.cir-usa.org/mission_new.html.

44. IJ's "Electronic Brochure," available on-line at www.ij.org/profile/index.html. This property rights campaign has been supported by the Washington Legal Foundation and a number of other conservative groups as well.

45. The founding work of this movement was Posner's *Economic Analysis of Law* (1972). See generally Posner 1990:353–92; Kalman 1996:77–82.

46. Burger also quoted Jackson and Brandeis on the merits of judicial restraint. 448 U.S. 448, 482, 472, 490–91 (1980).

47. Brief for the U.S. as *Amicus Curiae* Supporting Petitioners, *Wygant v. Jackson Board of Education,* June 25, 1985.

48. In addition to *Wygant,* see *Local 28 of the Sheet Metal Workers, Int'l Association v. EEOC; United States v. Paradise;* and *Johnson v. Transportation Agency.*

49. O'Connor's case-by-case activism in the affirmative action context was apparent even before 1987. Note, for example, her opinion concurring in part with the Court's holding in *Wygant.*

50. 488 U.S. 469, 493–94 (1989).

51. Compare the language I have quoted, from Bickel and Kurland's *amicus curiae* brief in *DeFunis,* at 22–23, with O'Connor's *Croson* opinion, at 498–506.

52. 488 U.S. 469, 520–21 (1989). See Bickel 1975:133. Scalia had objected just as strongly to Powell's efforts in *Bakke* two decades earlier, describing his landmark opinion "as an excellent compromise between two Committees of the American Bar Association on some insignificant legislative proposal," but complaining that it was "thoroughly unconvincing as an honest, hard-minded, reasoned analysis of an important provision of the Constitution" (Scalia 1979:148–49; see Brisbin 1997:30–31).

53. *Metro Broadcasting v. FCC.*

54. 509 U.S. 630, 681–82, 641–42, 657 (1993).

55. *United Jewish Organizations v. Carey,* 430 U.S. 144, 181 (1977).

56. In *Davis v. Bandemer,* O'Connor was joined by Burger and Rehnquist in insisting "that the partisan gerrymandering claims of major political parties raise a nonjusticiable political question that the judiciary should leave to the legislative branch as the Framers of the Constitution unquestionably intended." 478 U.S. 109, 144–45 (1986).

57. *EEOC v. Wyoming.*

58. 469 U.S. 528, 580, 584, 581 (1985).

59. Meese's comments were originally delivered as a speech to the American Bar Association in Washington, D.C., on July 9, 1985, and were later reprinted in the *South Texas Law Review* (1986:465–66, 458–60).

60. 469 U.S. 528, 556–57 (1985).

61. 505 U.S. 144, 149 (1992). O'Connor had foreshadowed this holding in a statutory decision the previous year, holding that the federal Age Discrimination in Employment Act did not prohibit the states from imposing mandatory retirement ages on their own judges. Reading the statute narrowly so as to avoid a constitutional difficulty, she noted that establishing judicial qualifications "is a decision of the most fundamental sort for a sovereign entity," and hence that the Tenth Amendment might well prohibit Congress from interfering with such decisions by the states. *Gregory v. Ashcroft,* 501 U.S. 452, 460 (1991). See Tushnet 2003:42–43.

62. See, for example, Rehnquist's dissenting opinion in *Hodel v. Virginia Surface Mining & Reclamation Association.*

63. As Daniel Farber and Philip Frickey have pointed out, public choice scholars have endorsed this revival of the nondelegation doctrine, because "[i]f Congress isn't allowed to delegate, there will be less legislation, so society [will be] better off" (1991:83).

64. *Industrial Union Department v. American Petroleum Institute; American Textile Manufacturers Institute v. Donovan;* Fried 1991:133.

65. In Scalia's own words, "[i]f there is anyone who, over the years, [has] had a greater interest in the subject of separation of powers [than I], he does not come readily to mind" (*quoted in* Smith 1993:39).

66. *Morrison v. Olson; Mistretta v. United States.*

67. 512 U.S. 374, 402–7, 392 (1994).

Chapter Six

1. As I noted in chapter 2, even Frankfurter did not adopt a posture of pure deference, but he came the closest of any modern justice.

2. The data from the 1994 through 2000 terms are from Edelman and Chen (2001), which I have updated through the end of the 2002 term.

3. *Atwater v. Lago Vista,* 532 U.S. 318, 353–54, 340 (2001). Thus, even though O'Connor wrote for the cause of liberal activism here, she did so in dissent.

4. As has been his penchant since joining the Court, Rehnquist remains willing to dissent alone, and when he does so, it is always to criticize his colleagues for their illegitimate activism. See, for example, *Chandler v. Miller* and *Watchtower Bible and Tract Society of New York v. Stratton.*

5. Consider, for example, *Board of Education of Pottawatomie County v. Earls,* in which Breyer cast the deciding vote to allow suspicionless drug testing of public school students participating in extracurricular activities, but wrote separately to express his understanding of the limited reach of the Court's holding.

6. *Freeman v. Pitts,* 503 U.S. 467, 495 (1992).

7. 515 U.S. 70, 126 (1995).

8. In *Jenkins,* O'Connor and Thomas published dueling concurrences, seeking to read the Court's holding more narrowly and broadly, respectively. See also *Freeman v. Pitts.*

9. 521 U.S. 702, 720, 723, 735 (1997).

10. See, for example, Sunstein 1999 and the Clinton administration's Brief for the U.S. as *Amicus Curiae* Supporting Petitioners in *Glucksberg.*

11. Concurring only in the judgment, Scalia complained that Souter's opinion was even worse than his *Glucksberg* opinion, having replaced the standard of "arbitrary impositions" and "purposeless restraints," which was bad enough (in Scalia's view), with "the ne plus ultra, the Napoleon Brandy, the Mahatma Gandhi, the Cellophane of subjectivity, th' ol' 'shocks-the-conscience' test." 523 U.S. 833, 836, 857–62 (1998).

12. *Troxel v. Granville*, 530 U.S. 57, 65–66, 92–93, 73 (2000).

13. 123 S. Ct. 2472, 2484, 2480 (2003).

14. The other nine states criminalized sodomy, and punished it equally, whether committed by people of the same or the opposite sex.

15. 123 S. Ct. 2472, 2487 (2003).

16. *Romer*, 517 U.S. 620, 634 (1996), quoting *U.S. Department of Agriculture v. Moreno*, 413 U.S. 528, 534 (1973). Along with *City of Cleburne v. Cleburne Living Center*, Sunstein has referred to these cases as "the *Moreno-Cleburne-Romer* trilogy" (1996:59–64).

17. 517 U.S. 620, 634–35 (1996).

18. Significantly, in enumerating the groups within the ambit of protection of anti-discrimination laws, Kennedy observed that "Colorado's state and local governments have not limited anti-discrimination laws to groups that have *so far* been given the protection of heightened equal protection scrutiny under our cases." Id. at 628–29 (emphasis added).

19. Ginsburg noted that "[t]he Court has *thus far* reserved most stringent judicial scrutiny for classifications based on race or national origin." 518 U.S. 515, 531–33 (1996) (emphasis added).

20. 517 U.S. 620, 652, 644–46 (1996). For a similar argument, see Bork 1996a:113–14.

21. 518 U.S. 515, 574–75 (1996).

22. 518 U.S. 515, 567–68 (1996).

23. Id. at 567.

24. 518 U.S. 515, 567 (1996); 517 U.S. 620, 653, 636 (1996).

25. That is, the plurality's observation that "[a]t the heart of liberty is the right to define one's own concept of existence, of meaning, of the universe, and of the mystery of human life." 123 S. Ct. 2472, 2489 (2003).

26. Id. at 2491–97.

27. 517 U.S. 620, 639, 652–53 (1996).

28. 123 S. Ct. 1708, 1713 (2003).

29. In the Fourth Amendment context, see *Ferguson v. Charleston*. In the Fifth Amendment context, see *Dickerson v. United States*, in which the Court reaffirmed *Miranda*, and *McKune v. Lile*.

30. See *Ewing v. California* and *Lockyer v. Andrade*. See also *Harmelin v. Michigan*. On a related question, Scalia has insisted that the Constitution places no proportionality requirement on punitive damages in civil lawsuits. See *Pacific Mutual Life Insurance Co. v. Haslip*, *BMW v. Gore*, and *State Farm Mutual Automobile Insurance Co. v. Campbell*.

31. The quote is from Thomas's opinion dissenting alone in *Farmer v. Brennan*, 511 U.S. 825, 859 (1994). Two years earlier, he had been joined only by Scalia in complaining that the Court had only recently deemed "the Cruel and Unusual Punishment Clause . . . to apply at all to deprivations that were not inflicted as part of the sentence for a crime." *Hudson v. McMillian*, 503 U.S. 1, 18 (1992). See Graber 2003:81–82.

32. The case involving the execution of juveniles was *In re Stanford*.

33. *Kiryas Joel Village School District v. Grumet.*

34. The quoted language is from O'Connor's summary of Thomas's holding in *Mitchell v. Helms,* 530 U.S. 793, 837 (2000).

35. *Mitchell,* 536 U.S. 639, 669, 676 (2002). As in so many other contexts, Rehnquist had laid the groundwork for these doctrinal changes in a series of earlier opinions. See, for example, *Committee for Public Education & Religious Liberty v. Nyquist* and *Mueller v. Allen.*

36. 512 U.S. 687, 718, 750–51 (1994).

37. In this regard, note the 2002 decision by federal District Judge Rakoff striking down the federal death penalty statute on the grounds that it posed an unconstitutional risk of executing the actually innocent. *United States v. Quinones* (2002).

38. 515 U.S. 200, 239 (1995).

39. 518 U.S. 343, 378 (1996).

40. 515 U.S. 70, 120–21 (1995).

41. 515 U.S. 200, 240 (1995).

42. 497 U.S. 547, 631–38 (1990).

43. 515 U.S. 900, 904, 911–12 (1995). See also Kennedy's opinion for the Court in *Rice v. Cayetano.*

44. Concurring in the judgment in *Holder v. Hall,* for example, Thomas noted that "[i]n response to judicial decisions and the promptings of the Justice Department, the States themselves, in an attempt to avoid costly and disruptive Voting Rights Act litigation, have begun to gerrymander electoral districts according to race. That practice now promises to embroil the courts in a lengthy process of attempting to undo, or at least to minimize, the damage wrought by the system we created." 512 U.S. 874, 905 (1994).

45. The Court's ruling in *Bush v. Vera* prompted a three-judge District Court panel to invalidate the results of primary elections in thirteen of Texas's thirty House districts in the midst of an election year and to order that new elections be held with judicially redrawn districts. *Vera v. Bush* (S.D. Tex. 1996).

46. Souter's dissenting opinion in *Bush v. Vera,* 517 U.S. 952, 1045–56 (1996). Note also Ginsburg's observation in *Miller,* 515 U.S. 900, 935–36 (1995), that "federalism and the slim judicial competence to draw district lines weigh heavily against judicial intervention in apportionment decisions; as a rule, the task should remain within the domain of state legislatures."

47. Though Breyer, rather than O'Connor, wrote for Court in this case, he peppered his opinion with quotations from her opinions in *Shaw I, Miller,* and *Bush v. Vera.*

48. *Hopwood v. Texas; Smith v. University of Washington Law School; Gratz v. Bollinger; Grutter v. Bollinger.*

49. *Grutter,* 123 S. Ct. 2325, 2338–39 (2003).

50. Thomas's concurring opinion in *Adarand,* 515 U.S. 200, 240 (1995).

51. The quoted passages are from Rehnquist and Thomas's dissenting opinions, respectively. Scalia and Kennedy joined Rehnquist's opinion and criticized O'Connor's deferential approach in their own opinions as well. 123 S. Ct. 2325, 2369, 2350 (2003).

52. 514 U.S. 549, 559–64, 567–68 (1995).

53. 529 U.S. 598, 605, 615–17 (2000). Rehnquist wrote for the Court again the following year in *Solid Waste Agency v. U.S. Army Corps of Engineers,* 531 U.S. 159, 162, 172 (2001), holding that the Clean Water Act's (CWA) regulation of "navigable waters" did not "confer federal authority over an abandoned sand and gravel pit in northern Illinois which provides habitat for migratory birds." He refused to defer to the Corps's interpretation of the statue as granting such jurisdiction, since by invoking "the outer limits of Congress' power," such an interpretation would raise a serious constitutional problem under the Commerce Clause.

54. 517 U.S. 44, 72, 54 (1996).

55. The patent infringement case was *Florida Prepaid Postsecondary Education Expense Board v. College Savings Bank.*

56. *Morrison; Kimel v. Florida Board of Regents; Board of Trustees of the University of Alabama v. Garrett.*

57. 514 U.S. 549, 568, 573–74 (1995).

58. 521 U.S. 898, 945 (1996).

59. 514 U.S. 549, 573–74 (1995).

60. The precedent was *Ex parte Young,* which held that despite the principle of state sovereign immunity, the federal courts do have jurisdiction over suits seeking prospective injunctive relief against state officials for ongoing violations of federal law.

61. 527 U.S. 706, 754, 713, 715, 748, 758 (1999).

62. 531 U.S. 356, 375–76 (2001).

63. See also *Lapides v. Board of Regents of the University System of Georgia,* in which a unanimous Court held that a state's act of removing a lawsuit to federal court constituted a waiver of its sovereign immunity.

64. In his characteristic fashion, Justice Thomas has been even more eager to draw such a constitutional line. In *Whitman,* he wrote separately to note his willingness, in some future case, "to address the question whether our delegation jurisprudence has strayed too far from our Founders' understanding of separation of powers." 531 U.S. 457, 465, 487 (2001).

65. 524 U.S. 498, 540, 542 (1998). As Tushnet has pointed out, moreover, while O'Connor joined the other three conservatives in striking down the statute on Takings Clause grounds, her opinion was so focused on the specific (and unusual) facts of the case that it did not substantially clarify the scope of the Court's takings jurisprudence (1999b:92–94; see also Tushnet 2003:60–61).

66. *Palazzolo v. Rhode Island.*

67. *Bajakajian,* 524 U.S. 321, 334 (1998). The precedent Thomas called into question in *Eastern Enterprises* was *Calder v. Bull.*

68. *Virginia State Board of Pharmacy v. Virginia Citizens Consumer Council.* See also *Central Hudson Gas & Electric Corporation v. Public Service Commission of New York.* For the New Deal Court's view, see *Valentine v. Chrestensen.*

69. In *44 Liquormart,* for example, Kennedy joined Stevens's opinion for the Court in

full, but O'Connor wrote separately in an effort to narrow the holding, while Scalia and Thomas wrote separately in an effort to broaden it. In *Lorillard,* O'Connor wrote for the Court, while Kennedy, Scalia, and Thomas all wrote separately to reach more broadly, and in *Thompson v. Western States,* Kennedy joined O'Connor's opinion for the Court, with only Thomas concurring separately to urge even greater speech protection.

70. I have borrowed the phrase from Morton Horwitz (1993:109), though he uses it somewhat differently than I do here.

71. 533 U.S. 405, 428 (2001). O'Connor joined most of Breyer's dissent as well, though not the portion that I have quoted in the text.

72. 424 U.S. 1, 48–49 (1976).

73. *FEC v. Colorado Republican Federal Campaign Committee.*

74. 528 U.S. 377, 409–10 (2000).

75. All four of these organizations filed *amicus* briefs in the *Good News* case, and the ACLJ and the Christian Legal Society did so in the *Rosenberger* case as well.

76. *Mitchell v. Helms,* 530 U.S. 793, 829 (2000).

77. In this case, *Board of Regents of the University of Wisconsin v. Southworth,* Kennedy rejected the students' claim that the First Amendment prohibited the university from compelling them to support the speech of groups advocating abortion rights, gay rights, and the like.

78. Similarly, conservative litigators have been developing a First Amendment argument against workplace sexual harassment laws, which have sometimes been interpreted to require certain restrictions on workplace speech. See, for example, *DeAngelis v. El Paso Municipal Police Officers' Association.* See generally Volokh 1997.

79. I would also caution that these data may convey a false sense of precision, since the identification of cases that have declared a statute unconstitutional is not always straightforward. Moreover, since I have relied on several different sources for such data in this book — principally the Congressional Research Service's analysis of the Constitution and the *U.S. Supreme Court Judicial Databases* maintained by political scientists Harold Spaeth and Sara Benesh — there are some inconsistencies across the various tables that I have presented. I use these multiple sources because they each have certain advantages. For example, the CRS analysis provides the most authoritative and comprehensive source for declarations of unconstitutionality — it is the only source I am aware of that covers the Court's entire history — while Benesh and Spaeth's *Justice-Centered Rehnquist Court Database* is the only source providing a count of all the cases in which a particular justice voted to strike down a statute, regardless of whether the Court majority voted to do so.

80. See, for example, Kennedy's dissenting opinion in *Bennis v. Michigan* and his opinion for the Court in *State Farm Mutual Automobile Insurance Co. v. Campbell.*

81. The flag-burning case was *Texas v. Johnson.*

82. In this case, *Ashcroft v. Free Speech Coalition,* O'Connor wrote one of her characteristic opinions, concurring in the judgment in part and dissenting in part, agreeing

with the Court's invalidation of one provision of the law but disagreeing with its invalidation of another. See also *Ashcroft v. ACLU,* 535 U.S. 564, 591 (2002), in which Kennedy concurred in the Court's rejection of a facial challenge to the Child Online Protection Act, but noted that "[t]here is a very real likelihood that the . . . Act . . . is overbroad and" hence unconstitutional. O'Connor expressed a similar concern, while the other three conservative members of the Court were again more deferential to Congress.

83. By Segal and Spaeth's count, there were 170 cases during the 1986–98 terms in which at least one justice voted to strike down a law as unconstitutional. Most of the justices were quite likely to support such declarations in either a liberal or conservative direction, but not both. Kennedy supported 68.8 percent of the opportunities for conservative activism and 57.0 percent of the opportunities for liberal activism. O'Connor's numbers were 77.5 percent and 47.7 percent, respectively (2002:412–16).

Chapter Seven

1. The most notable example was the 1996 symposium entitled "The End of Democracy? The Judicial Usurpation of Politics," in the monthly religious journal *First Things* (Muncy 1997).

2. *Dickerson v. United States,* 530 U.S. 428, 455 (2000).

3. Scalia 1989:1179–80. It may be worth emphasizing that Scalia's use of the term "judicial restraint" here is different from my own. His vote in the independent counsel case may have been "restrained" in a certain sense of the word, but it did not reflect the conventional conception of restraint as deference to democratic decisionmakers. He dissented alone in this case because his fellow justices were led by this more conventional conception to defer to the post-Watergate congressional judgment that high-ranking executive branch officials could not be adequately investigated by regular Justice Department attorneys.

4. 515 U.S. 200, 240 (1995).

5. Dissenting in *Regents of the University of California v. Bakke,* Marshall noted that one of the chief grounds of opposition to the 1866 Freedmen's Bureau Act had been that it "gave special benefits to Negroes," and that "[t]he bill's supporters defended it — not by rebutting the claim of special treatment — but by pointing to the need for such treatment." In this light, Marshall insisted, "it is inconceivable that the Fourteenth Amendment was intended to prohibit all race-conscious relief measures." 438 U.S. 265, 397–98 (1978). Marshall was relying here on historical research conducted by Eric Schnapper for the NAACP's *amicus curiae* brief, research subsequently published in the *Virginia Law Review* (Schnapper 1985). When other scholars replied by noting that while the Freedmen's Bureau Acts had been designed to provide benefits to the former slaves, they had done so in race neutral terms, still others responded in turn by uncovering a number of Reconstruction-era statutes that clearly included explicit racial classifications and that provided benefits to free blacks as well as former slaves (Siegel 1998; Rubenfeld 1997). In a separate, but related, historical debate, Andrew Kull (1992) noted that the

Thirty-ninth Congress explicitly rejected a draft constitutional amendment that would have imposed a strict rule of racial nondiscrimination, opting instead for the vaguer and less sweeping formulation of "equal protection of the laws."

6. The child labor cases were *Hammer v. Dagenhart* and *Bailey v. Drexel Furniture Co.*, and they were reversed in *United States v. Darby*, when Justice Stone wrote for a unanimous Court in upholding the 1938 Fair Labor Standards Act.

7. 514 U.S. 549, 584–85, 599–600 (1995). Note also Thomas's concurring opinions in *Printz v. United States* and *United States v. Morrison*, and his dissenting opinions in *U.S. Term Limits v. Thornton* and *Camps Newfound/Owatonna, Inc. v. Town of Harrison.*

8. 514 U.S. 549, 552 (1995). The quotation extolling "a healthy balance of power" is from O'Connor's opinion for the Court in *Gregory v. Ashcroft*, 501 U.S. 452, 458–59 (1991), which also reflects an extensive reading of *The Federalist.*

9. 521 U.S. 898, 921–22 (1997); 529 U.S. 598, 616 n. 7 (2000).

10. 505 U.S. 144, 168–69 (1992).

11. 521 U.S. 898, 930 (1997). See also *Alden v. Maine*, 527 U.S. 706, 750–51 (1999); *Nevada Department of Human Resources v. Hibbs*, 123 S. Ct. 1972, 1986 (2003).

12. The quotation is from Kennedy's dissenting opinion, joined by Scalia and Thomas, in *Hibbs*, 123 S. Ct. 1972, 1992–93 (2003).

13. 521 U.S. 898, 905, 918 (1997). Justice Stevens drew such a comparison when reading his dissent from the bench, and Jeffrey Rosen subsequently elaborated on it in the *New Republic* (1997a).

14. 535 U.S. 743, 754–55, 760, 769 (2002).

15. *Board of Trustees of the University of Alabama v. Garrett*, 531 U.S. 356, 388 (2001).

16. This case was a statutory decision, but the conservative justices evinced no concern with the constitutional limits on congressional authority that they had expressed elsewhere.

17. Three years later, Rehnquist, O'Connor, and Kennedy joined Souter's opinion advancing a similar argument for the Court in *American Insurance Association v. Garamendi*, disallowing the states from requiring insurance companies to compensate the families of Holocaust victims who had been policy holders. Breyer joined the majority as well, but in an unusual voting alignment, Scalia and Thomas joined Ginsburg and Stevens in dissent.

18. *44 Liquormart, Inc. v. Rhode Island*, 517 U.S. 484, 522 (1996). Scalia has voted with Thomas in all the commercial speech cases, but he refused to join the sweeping activism in *44 Liquormart*, noting that none of the parties or *amici* had provided much evidence of the relevant original intentions, nineteenth-century state legislative practices, or national legal traditions. See also *Rubin v. Coors Brewing Co.* and *Lorillard Tobacco Co. v. Reilly.*

19. 494 U.S. 652, 693–94 (1990).

20. 528 U.S. 377, 411–12 (2000). Thomas's other campaign finance opinions have not filled this gap. See, for example, *Colorado Republican Federal Campaign Committee v. FEC.*

21. For a representative example of such criticism, see Rosen 2000a.

22. For the most exhaustive and persuasive argument along these lines, see Gillman 2001.

23. *Romer,* 517 U.S. 620, 636 (1996).

24. Phelps and Gates proceeded to note their suspicion "that Justices invoke particular *interpretive* approaches only when those approaches converge with their *substantive* understanding of the Constitution." As their language in the above quotation makes clear, however, they seem to equate a justice's "substantive understanding of the Constitution" with the "predilection of [her] politics" (1991:593–96 [emphasis in original]; see also Phelps and Gates 1996; Howard and Segal 2002).

25. *Romer,* 517 U.S. 620, 635 (1996).

26. *Lawrence,* 123 S. Ct. 2472, 2482, 2484, 2486 (2003).

27. *Shaw v. Reno,* 509 U.S. 630, 647 (1993).

28. Note, for just two examples, O'Connor's characterization of the Age Discrimination in Employment Act as an "unwarranted response to a perhaps inconsequential problem" (*Kimel v. Florida Board of Regents,* 528 U.S. 62, 89 [2000]), and Kennedy's observation that the line item veto would serve the important purpose of "restrain[ing] persistent excessive spending" by the federal government (*Clinton v. City of New York,* 524 U.S. 417, 449–50 [1998]).

29. 515 U.S. 819, 847–52 (1995).

30. Segal and Spaeth (2002:322) coded the conservative justices' political values as follows: Scalia (-1.00), Rehnquist (-0.91), Thomas (-0.68), Kennedy (-0.27), and O'Connor (-0.17).

31. For a similar argument about originalism's constraining force in another context, see Gillman 1997.

32. As Kevin McMahon has noted, moreover, Shapiro's "analysis . . . fails to explain why the biggest losers before the Roosevelt Court were not only Republicans but the staunchly Democratic defenders of southern white supremacy as well" (2000:21).

33. As a number of scholars have noted in recent years, such policy feedback effects are a recurrent feature of political development (Pierson 1993; Orren and Skowronek 2002:741–47; Mettler 2002).

34. I borrow here from Stephen Skowronek (1993), who has described the process by which "political time"—the recurrent cycles of partisan conflict—overlaps and interacts with "secular time"—the persistent patterns of political development such as the growth of the modern state.

35. Gillman has made a similar point in the language of modern social science, insisting that for empirical research on the Supreme Court to have any significant consequences for society as a whole, "it would . . . be useful if [our] conceptual apparatus made it easier to link our research to important normative debates" (1999a:77).

Conclusion

1. Similarly, aggregate response to the question "Do you approve or disapprove of the way the Supreme Court is handling its job?" was quite steady from August/September

2000, to January 2001, and then to June 2001, with approval percentages of 62, 59, and 62 percent, respectively. Among Republicans, however, the approval skyrocketed from 60 to 80 percent, and then settled back down to 74 percent. Among Democrats, approval of the Court plummeted from 70 to 42 percent, before partially rebounding to 54 percent (Kritzer 2001; see also Levinson 2002:21–28).

2. Editors of *First Things* (1996:3–9); Bork (1996b:22–23). The symposium itself included a series of brief articles by Robert Bork, Robert George, Hadley Arkes, Russell Hittinger, and Charles Colson, all sharply criticizing recent Court decisions. The participants seemed particularly influenced by Scalia's series of apocalyptic dissenting opinions in the summer of 1996 — in *United States v. Virginia, Romer,* and *BMW v. Gore.* On the resulting controversy, see "Correspondence," *First Things* 69 (January 1997):2–7; "The End of Democracy? A Discussion Continued," id. at 19–28; and "The Supreme Court 1997: A Symposium," *First Things* (October 1997):20–37.

3. 531 U.S. 98, 157–58 (2000).

4. Jeffrey Rosen (1996b) noted at the time that Buchanan's speech was more concerned with liberalism than with judicial power, and Gertrude Himmelfarb (1997) and Keith Whittington (1998b) later made the same point with respect to the *First Things* symposium.

5. As Bruce Ackerman has noted, the legal realist view that "[t]here is no such thing as legal interpretation distinct from political preference" tends to operate as "a self-fulfilling prophecy . . . : the more lawyers and judges believe in realism, the more they vindicate its predictions by playing politics" (1998:418). See also Seidman and Tushnet 1996:35–48.

6. Bickel made a similar point forty years ago, noting that "[i]t was never altogether realistic to conclude that behind all judicial dialectic there was personal preference and personal power and nothing else. In any event, that is a reality, if it be true, on which we cannot allow the edifice of judicial review to be based, for if that is all judges do, then their authority over us is totally intolerable and totally irreconcilable with the theory and practice of political democracy" (1986:80). For a different view, see Peretti 1999.

7. Concluding "that judges cannot be trusted with a written constitution and an unlimited and uncheckable power of judicial review," Bork has proposed a constitutional amendment either abolishing judicial review altogether or making all court decisions subject to congressional overruling (1996b:16–17; 1996a:117–19). Similarly, Buchanan concluded his 1996 Heritage Foundation address by proposing limited judicial terms; voter recall and removal of federal judges; congressional restriction of jurisdiction; allowing "the nation [to] decide at the next election whether to uphold or reject any Court decision creating a new 'right' or overturning a state or federal law"; and "allow[ing] the states, without the approval of Congress, to amend the Constitution." See also Graglia 1997:64. These proposals, of course, closely resemble the pre–New Deal Court-curbing proposals advocated by Learned Hand and Felix Frankfurter.

8. I thank Mark Graber for significant help in articulating this point. As Ackerman has noted, the presidential strategy of changing the Constitution by means of "transfor-

mative judicial appointments" is an "evolving practice [that] has grave deficiencies as a method of democratic change. . . . Given the ease with which Senatorial confirmation battles can obscure the underlying issues, it is just too easy for randomly selected Presidents to revolutionize constitutional law without the kind of popular support required" to make such changes legitimate (1998:404–5). This problem has been exacerbated in recent decades, as the average length of service for Supreme Court justices has risen dramatically, rendering the Court's electoral connection both less regular and less predictable.

9. Sunstein 1999:259–63. For a helpful account of the relationship between Bickel's and Sunstein's jurisprudence, see Tushnet 2003:130–32.

10. 531 U.S. 98, 109 (2000).

11. 505 U.S. 833, 868 (1992).

12. O'Connor dissented from Kennedy's holding in *City of Boerne* because she rejected the Court's interpretation of the Free Exercise Clause and agreed with Congress's alternative interpretation, but she still insisted that "Congress lacks the ability independently to define or expand the scope of constitutional rights by statute. [W]hen it enacts legislation in furtherance of its delegated powers, Congress must make its judgments consistent with this Court's exposition of the Constitution and with the limits placed on its legislative authority by provisions such as the Fourteenth Amendment." 521 U.S. 507, 524, 519, 545–46 (1997). See also *Dickerson v. United States* (2000), in which the Court, citing *City of Boerne,* turned back a congressional effort to overrule *Miranda v. Arizona.*

13. Dissenting in *Bush v. Gore,* 531 U.S. 98, 157 (2000), Breyer sought to remind his fellow justices of the lesson to be drawn from the disputed presidential election of 1876: "For present purposes, the relevance of this history lies in the fact that the participation in the work of the electoral commission by five Justices . . . did not lend that process legitimacy. Nor did it assure the public that the process had worked fairly, guided by the law. Rather, it simply embroiled Members of the Court in partisan conflict, thereby undermining respect for the judicial process."

14. See, for example, Silverstein 2003 and Gillman 2001. Balkin and Levinson did note that *Bush v. Gore* shared one theme with the rest of the conservative revolution — hostility to Congress — but they still characterized the decision as largely exceptional (2001:1062).

15. See Kramer (2001:156–57) for a similar argument.

CASES CITED

Abington School District v. Schempp, 374 U.S. 203 (1963)
Adamson v. California, 332 U.S. 46 (1947)
Adarand Constructors, Inc. v. Pena, 515 U.S. 200 (1995)
Adkins v. Children's Hospital, 261 U.S. 525 (1923)
Agostini v. Felton, 521 U.S. 203 (1997)
Aguilar v. Felton, 473 U.S. 402 (1985)
Akron v. Akron Center for Reproductive Health, 462 U.S. 416 (1983)
Alexander v. Holmes County Board of Education, 396 U.S. 19 (1969)
Alden v. Maine, 527 U.S. 706 (1999)
Allied Structural Steel Co. v. Spannaus, 438 U.S. 234 (1978)
American Airlines v. Wolens, 513 U.S. 219 (1995)
American Communications Association v. Douds, 339 U.S. 382 (1950)
American Insurance Association v. Garamendi, 123 S. Ct. 2374 (2003)
American Textile Manufacturers Institute v. Donovan, 452 U.S. 490 (1981)
Apprendi v. New Jersey, 530 U.S. 466 (2000)
Aptheker v. Secretary of State, 378 U.S. 500 (1964)
Arlington Heights v. Metropolitan Housing Development Corp., 429 U.S. 252 (1977)
Ashcroft v. ACLU, 535 U.S. 564 (2002)
Ashcroft v. Free Speech Coalition, 535 U.S. 234 (2002)
Ashwander v. TVA, 297 U.S. 288 (1936)
Atkins v. Virginia, 536 U.S. 304 (2002)
Atwater v. Lago Vista, 532 U.S. 318 (2001)
Austin v. Michigan State Chamber of Commerce, 494 U.S. 652 (1990)

Babbitt v. Youpee, 519 U.S. 234 (1997)
Bailey v. Drexel Furniture Co., 259 U.S. 20 (1922)
Baker v. Carr, 369 U.S. 186 (1962)
Baldwin v. Missouri, 281 U.S. 586 (1930)
Barenblatt v. United States, 360 U.S. 109 (1959)
Barnett Bank v. Nelson, 517 U.S. 25 (1996)
Bartkus v. Illinois, 359 U.S. 121 (1959)
Bartnicki v. Vopper, 532 U.S. 514 (2001)
Beauharnais v. Illinois, 343 U.S. 250 (1952)
Bell v. Maryland, 378 U.S. 226 (1964)
Bennis v. Michigan, 516 U.S. 442 (1996)
Benton v. Maryland, 395 U.S. 784 (1969)
Berger v. New York, 388 U.S. 41 (1967)

Betts v. Brady, 316 U.S. 455 (1942)

BMW v. Gore, 517 U.S. 559 (1996)

Board of County Commissioners, Wabaunsee County v. Umbehr, 518 U.S. 668 (1996)

Board of Curators of the University of Missouri v. Horowitz, 435 U.S. 78 (1978)

Board of Education of Oklahoma City v. Dowell, 498 U.S. 237 (1991)

Board of Education of Pottawatomie County v. Earls, 536 U.S. 822 (2002)

Board of Regents of the University of Wisconsin v. Southworth, 529 U.S. 217 (2000)

Board of Trustees of the University of Alabama v. Garrett, 531 U.S. 356 (2001)

Bob Jones University v. United States, 461 U.S. 574 (1983)

Boddie v. Connecticut, 401 U.S. 371 (1971)

Bolling v. Sharpe, 347 U.S. 497 (1954)

Bowers v. Hardwick, 478 U.S. 186 (1986)

Bowsher v. Synar, 478 U.S. 714 (1986)

Boy Scouts of America v. Dale, 530 U.S. 640 (2000)

Bradley v. School Board, 382 U.S. 103 (1965)

Bridges v. California, 314 U.S. 252 (1941)

Brown v. Board of Education, 347 U.S. 483 (1954)

Brown v. Board of Education *(Brown II)*, 349 U.S. 294 (1955)

Brown v. Legal Foundation of Washington, 123 S. Ct. 1406 (2003)

Buckley v. American Constitutional Law Foundation, 525 U.S. 182 (1999)

Buckley v. Valeo, 424 U.S. 1 (1976)

Bush v. Gore, 531 U.S. 98 (2000)

Bush v. Vera, 517 U.S. 952 (1996)

California Democratic Party v. Jones, 530 U.S. 567 (2000)

Calder v. Bull, 3 U.S. 386 (1798)

Callins v. Collins, 510 U.S. 1141 (1994)

Camps Newfound/Owatonna v. Town of Harrison, 520 U.S. 564 (1997)

Carmell v. Texas, 529 U.S. 513 (2000)

Carter v. Carter Coal, 298 U.S. 238 (1936)

Carter v. West Feliciana Parish School Board, 396 U.S. 290 (1970)

Central Hudson Gas and Electric Corp. v. Public Service Commission, 447 U.S. 557
    (1980)

Chambers v. Florida, 309 U.S. 227 (1940)

Chandler v. Miller, 520 U.S. 305 (1997)

Chicago v. Morales, 527 U.S. 41 (1999)

City of Boerne v. Flores, Archbishop of San Antonio, 521 U.S. 507 (1997)

City of Cleburne v. Cleburne Living Center, 473 U.S. 432 (1985)

City of Rome v. United States, 446 U.S. 156 (1980)

Clinton v. City of New York, 524 U.S. 417 (1998)

Colegrove v. Green, 328 U.S. 549 (1946)

Coleman v. Miller, 307 U.S. 433 (1939)

College Savings Bank v. Florida Prepaid Postsecondary Education Expense Board, 527 U.S. 666 (1999)

Colorado Republican Federal Campaign Committee v. Federal Election Commission, 518 U.S. 604 (1996)

Columbus Board of Education v. Penick, 443 U.S. 449 (1979)

Committee for Public Education and Religious Liberty v. Nyquist, 413 U.S. 756 (1973)

Cook v. Gralike, 531 U.S. 510 (2001)

Cooper v. Aaron, 358 U.S. 1 (1958)

Craig v. Boren, 429 U.S. 190 (1976)

Crosby v. National Foreign Trade Council, 530 U.S. 363 (2000)

Cruzan v. Director, Missouri Department of Health, 497 U.S. 261 (1990)

Dandridge v. Williams , 397 U.S. 471 (1970)

Davis v. Bandemer, 478 U.S. 109 (1986)

Davis v. United States, 328 U.S. 582 (1946)

Dayton Board of Education v. Brinkman, 433 U.S. 406 (1977)

Dayton Board of Education v. Brinkman *(Dayton II),* 443 U.S. 526 (1979)

DeAngelis v. El Paso Municipal Police Officers' Association, 51 F.3d 591 (5th Cir. 1995)

DeFunis v. Odegaard, 507 P.2d 1169 (Wash. 1973), *vacated and remanded,* 416 U.S. 312 (1974)

DeJonge v. Oregon, 299 U.S. 353 (1937)

Delaware State Board of Education v. Evans, 446 U.S. 923 (1980)

Demore v. Hyung Joon Kim, 123 S. Ct. 1708 (2003)

Dennis v. United States, 341 U.S. 494 (1951)

Denver Area Educational Telecommunications Consortium v. FCC, 518 U.S. 727 (1996)

Dick v. New York Life Insurance Co., 359 U.S. 437 (1959)

Dickerson v. United States, 530 U.S. 428 (2000)

Doctor's Associates, Inc. v. Casarotto, 517 U.S. 681 (1996)

Doe v. Bolton, 410 U.S. 179 (1973)

Dolan v. City of Tigard, 512 U.S. 374 (1994)

Douglas v. California, 372 U.S. 353 (1963)

Dred Scott v. Sandford, 60 U.S. 393 (1857)

Duncan v. Louisiana, 391 U.S. 145 (1968)

Easley v. Cromartie, 532 U.S. 234 (2001)

Eastern Enterprises v. Apfel, 524 U.S. 498 (1998)

Edwards v. California, 314 U.S. 160 (1941)

Egelhoff v. Egelhoff, 532 U.S. 141 (2001)

Eisenstadt v. Baird, 405 U.S. 438 (1972)

Equal Employment Opportunity Commission v. Wyoming, 460 U.S. 226 (1983)

Employment Division, Department of Human Resources of Oregon v. Smith, 494 U.S. 872 (1990)

Engel v. Vitale, 370 U.S. 421 (1962)

Escobedo v. Illinois, 378 U.S. 478 (1964)

Everson v. Ewing Township, 330 U.S. 1 (1947)

Ewing v. California, 123 S. Ct. 1179 (2003)

Ex Parte Young, 209 U.S. 123 (1908)

Farmer v. Brennan, 511 U.S. 825 (1994)

FEC v. Colorado Republican Federal Campaign Committee, 533 U.S. 431 (2001)

Federal Maritime Commission v. South Carolina State Ports Authority, 535 U.S. 743 (2002)

Feiner v. New York, 340 U.S. 315 (1951)

Feltner v. Columbia Pictures Television, 523 U.S. 340 (1998)

Ferguson v. Charleston, 532 U.S. 67 (2001)

Ferguson v. Skrupa, 372 U.S. 726 (1963)

Florida Prepaid Postsecondary Education Expense Board v. College Savings Bank, 527 U.S. 627 (1999)

Foster v. Love, 522 U.S. 67 (1997)

44 Liquormart, Inc. v. Rhode Island, 517 U.S. 484 (1996)

Franchise Tax Board v. Hyatt, 123 S. Ct. 1683 (2003)

Freeman v. Pitts, 503 U.S. 467 (1992)

Frontiero v. Richardson, 411 U.S. 677 (1973)

Fry v. United States, 421 U.S. 542 (1975)

Fullilove v. Klutznick, 448 U.S. 448 (1980)

Fulton Corp. v. Faulkner, 516 U.S. 325 (1996)

Furman v. Georgia, 408 U.S. 238 (1972)

Garcia v. San Antonio Metropolitan Transit Authority, 469 U.S. 528 (1985)

Gideon v. Wainwright, 372 U.S. 335 (1963)

Goldberg v. Kelly, 397 U.S. 254 (1970)

Gompers v. United States, 233 U.S. 604 (1914)

Good News Club v. Milford Central School, 533 U.S. 98 (2001)

Gratz v. Bollinger, 122 F. Supp. 2d 811 (E.D. Mich. 2000), *aff'd in part and rev'd in part*, 123 S. Ct. 2411 (2003)

Gray v. Sanders, 372 U.S. 368 (1963)

Greater New Orleans Broadcasting Assoc., Inc. v. United States, 527 U.S. 173 (1999)

Green v. County School Board, 391 U.S. 430 (1968)

Gregg v. Georgia, 428 U.S. 153 (1976)

Gregory v. Ashcroft, 501 U.S. 452 (1991)

Griffin v. County School Board of Prince Edward County, 377 U.S. 218 (1964)

Griffin v. Illinois, 351 U.S. 12 (1956)

Griffiths, In re, 413 U.S. 717 (1973)

Griggs v. Duke Power Co., 401 U.S. 424 (1971)

Griswold v. Connecticut, 381 U.S. 479 (1965)

Grutter v. Bollinger, 288 F.3d 732 (6th Cir. 2002), *aff'd,* 123 S. Ct. 2325 (2003)

Hammer v. Dagenhart, 247 U.S. 251 (1918)

Hans v. Louisiana, 134 U.S. 1 (1890)

Harmelin v. Michigan, 501 U.S. 957 (1991)

Harper v. Virginia State Board of Elections, 383 U.S. 663 (1966)

Herrera v. Collins, 506 U.S. 390 (1993)

Hodel v. Virginia Surface Mining and Reclamation Association, 452 U.S. 264 (1981)

Holder v. Hall, 512 U.S. 874 (1994)

Home Building and Loan Association v. Blaisdell, 290 U.S. 398 (1934)

Hope v. Pelzer, 536 U.S. 730 (2002)

Hopwood v. Texas, 78 F.3d 932 (5th Cir. 1996), *cert. denied,* No. 95-1773 (July 1, 1996)

Hudson v. McMillian, 503 U.S. 1 (1992)

Hunter v. Erickson, 393 U.S. 385 (1969)

Hurley v. Irish-American Gay, Lesbian and Bisexual Group of Boston, 515 U.S. 557 (1995)

Idaho v. Coeur d'Alene Tribe of Idaho, 521 U.S. 261 (1997)

Immigration and Naturalization Service v. Chadha, 462 U.S. 919 (1983)

Immigration and Naturalization Service v. St. Cyr, 533 U.S. 289 (2001)

In re _____. *See* name of party

Industrial Union Department v. American Petroleum Institute, 448 U.S. 607 (1980)

Irvine v. California, 347 U.S. 128 (1954)

Jacobellis v. Ohio, 378 U.S. 184 (1964)

J.E.B. v. Alabama ex rel. T.B., 511 U.S. 127 (1994)

Johnson v. Transportation Agency, Santa Clara County, California, 480 U.S. 616 (1987)

Joint Anti-Fascist Refugee Committee v. McGrath, 341 U.S. 123 (1951)

Jones v. Opelika, 316 U.S. 584 (1942)

Katz v. United States, 389 U.S. 347 (1967)

Katzenbach v. Morgan, 384 U.S. 641 (1966)

Keyes v. School District No. 1, Denver, Colorado, 413 U.S. 189 (1973)

Kimel v. Florida Board of Regents, 528 U.S. 62 (2000)

Kingsley Pictures Corp. v. Regents of the University of the State of New York, 360 U.S. 684 (1959)

Kiryas Joel Village School District v. Grumet, 512 U.S. 687 (1994)

Knapp v. Schweitzer, 357 U.S. 371 (1958)

Knowles v. Iowa, 525 U.S. 113 (1998)

Korematsu v. United States, 323 U.S. 214 (1944)
Kovacs v. Cooper, 336 U.S. 77 (1949)
Kramer v. Union Free School District No. 15, 395 U.S. 621 (1969)

Lane v. Wilson, 307 U.S. 268 (1939)
Lapides v. Board of Regents of the University System of Georgia, 535 U.S. 613 (2002)
Lawrence v. Texas, 123 S. Ct. 2472 (2003)
Lee v. Weisman, 505 U.S. 577 (1992)
Legal Services Corp. v. Velazquez, 531 U.S. 533 (2001)
Lemon v. Kurtzman, 403 U.S. 602 (1971)
Levy v. Louisiana, 391 U.S. 68 (1968)
Lewis v. Casey, 518 U.S. 343 (1996)
Lincoln Federal Labor Union v. Northwestern Iron and Metal Co., 335 U.S. 525 (1949)
Lindsey v. Normet, 405 U.S. 56 (1972)
Local 28 of the Sheet Metal Workers, International Association v. EEOC, 478 U.S. 421 (1986)
Lochner v. New York, 198 U.S. 45 (1905)
Lockyer v. Andrade, 123 S. Ct. 1166 (2003)
Lorillard Tobacco Co. v. Reilly, 533 U.S. 525 (2001)
Loving v. Virginia, 388 U.S. 1 (1967)
Lucas v. Forty-fourth General Assembly of Colorado, 377 U.S. 713 (1964)
Lucas v. South Carolina Coastal Council, 505 U.S. 1003 (1992)
Lunding v. N.Y. Tax Appeals Tribunal, 522 U.S. 287 (1998)
Lynce v. Mathis, 519 U.S. 433 (1997)
Lynch v. Donnelly, 465 U.S. 668 (1984)

Malinsky v. New York, 324 U.S. 401 (1945)
Mapp v. Ohio, 367 U.S. 643 (1961)
Maryland v. Craig, 497 U.S. 836 (1990)
Masses Publishing Co. v. Patten, 244 F. 535 (D.C.N.Y. 1917)
McCleskey v. Kemp, 481 U.S. 279 (1987)
McCollum v. Board of Education, 333 U.S. 203 (1948)
McConnell v. Federal Elections Commission, 124 S. Ct. 619 (2003)
McCulloch v. Maryland, 17 U.S. 316 (1819)
McGautha v. California, 402 U.S. 183 (1971)
McGowan v. Maryland, 366 U.S. 420 (1961)
McIntyre v. Ohio Elections Commission, 514 U.S. 334 (1995)
McKune v. Lile, 536 U.S. 24 (2002)
McLaurin v. Oklahoma State Regents for Higher Education, 339 U.S. 637 (1950)
Metro Broadcasting v. FCC, 497 U.S. 547 (1990)
Meyer v. Nebraska, 262 U.S. 390 (1923)

Michael H. v. Gerald D., 491 U.S. 110 (1989)
Michael M. v. Superior Court, 450 U.S. 464 (1981)
Miller v. Johnson, 515 U.S. 900 (1995)
Milliken v. Bradley, 418 U.S. 717 (1974)
Minersville School District v. Gobitis, 310 U.S. 586 (1940)
Miranda v. Arizona, 384 U.S. 436 (1966)
Mississippi University for Women v. Hogan, 458 U.S. 718 (1982)
Missouri ex rel Gaines v. Canada, 305 U.S. 337 (1938)
Missouri v. Holland, 252 U.S. 416 (1920)
Missouri v. Jenkins, 515 U.S. 70 (1995)
Missouri v. Jenkins, 495 U.S. 33 (1990)
Mistretta v. United States, 488 U.S. 361 (1989)
Mitchell v. Helms, 530 U.S. 793 (2000)
M.L.B. v. S.L.J., 519 U.S. 102 (1996)
Moore v. East Cleveland, 431 U.S. 494 (1977)
Morrison v. Olson, 487 U.S. 654 (1988)
Mueller v. Allen, 463 U.S. 388 (1983)

National League of Cities v. Usery, 426 U.S. 833 (1976)
Nevada v. Hall, 440 U.S. 410 (1979)
Nevada Department of Human Resources v. Hibbs, 123 S. Ct. 1972 (2003)
New Jersey Welfare Rights Organization v. Cahill, 411 U.S. 619 (1973)
New York v. United States, 505 U.S. 144 (1992)
New York Times Co. v. Sullivan, 376 U.S. 254 (1964)
Nixon v. Shrink Missouri Government PAC, 528 U.S. 377 (2000)
NLRB v. Jones and Laughlin Steel Corp., 301 U.S. 1 (1937)
Nollan v. California Coastal Commission, 483 U.S. 825 (1987)
North Carolina State Board of Education v. Swann, 402 U.S. 43 (1971)
Nyquist v. Mauclet, 432 U.S. 1 (1977)

Oklahoma Tax Commission v. Chickasaw Nation, 515 U.S. 450 (1995)
Olmstead v. United States, 277 U.S. 438 (1928)
On Lee v. United States, 343 U.S. 747 (1952)
Oregon v. Mitchell, 400 U.S. 112 (1970)

Pacific Mutual Life Insurance Co. v. Haslip, 499 U.S. 1 (1991)
Palazzolo v. Rhode Island, 533 U.S. 606 (2001)
Palko v. State of Connecticut, 302 U.S. 319 (1937)
Pasadena Board of Education v. Spangler, 427 U.S. 424 (1976)
Penn Central Transportation Co. v. New York City, 438 U.S. 104 (1978)
Pennsylvania Coal Co. v. Mahon, 260 U.S. 393 (1922)

Penry v. Lynaugh, 492 U.S. 302 (1989)
People v. Anderson, 493 P.2d 850 (1972)
Personnel Administrator of Massachusetts v. Feeney, 442 U.S. 256 (1979)
Phillips v. Washington Legal Foundation, 524 U.S. 156 (1998)
Planned Parenthood of Missouri v. Danforth, 428 U.S. 52 (1976)
Planned Parenthood of Southeastern Pennsylvania v. Casey, 505 U.S. 833 (1992)
Plaut v. Spendthrift Farm, Inc., 514 U.S. 211 (1995)
Plessy v. Ferguson, 163 U.S. 537 (1896)
Poe v. Ullman, 367 U.S. 497 (1961)
Printz v. United States, 521 U.S. 898 (1997)

A Quantity of Copies of Books v. Kansas, 378 U.S. 205 (1964)

Railway Express Agency v. New York, 336 U.S. 106 (1949)
Regents of the University of California v. Bakke, 438 U.S. 265 (1978)
Regents of the University of Michigan v. Ewing, 474 U.S. 214 (1985)
Reiss v. National Quotation Bureau, 276 F. 717 (S.D.N.Y. 1921)
Reno v. Condon, 528 U.S. 141 (2000)
Reno v. ACLU, 521 U.S. 844 (1997)
Republican Party of Minnesota v. White, 536 U.S. 765 (2002)
Reynolds v. Sims, 377 U.S. 533 (1964)
Rice v. Cayetano, 528 U.S. 495 (2000)
Richmond v. J. A. Croson Co., 488 U.S. 469 (1989)
Rochin v. California, 342 U.S. 165 (1952)
Roe v. Wade, 410 U.S. 113 (1973)
Romer v. Evans, 517 U.S. 620 (1996)
Rosenberger v. University of Virginia, 515 U.S. 819 (1995)
Rostker v. Goldberg, 453 U.S. 57 (1981)
Rubin v. Coors Brewing Co., 514 U.S. 476 (1995)
Rutan v. Republican Party of Illinois, 497 U.S. 62 (1990)

Sacramento v. Lewis, 523 U.S. 833 (1998)
Saenz v. Roe, 526 U.S. 489 (1999)
San Antonio Independent School District v. Rodriguez, 411 U.S. 1 (1973)
Santa Fe Independent School District v. Doe, 530 U.S. 290 (2000)
Schechter Poultry Corp. v. United States, 295 U.S. 495 (1935)
Schneider v. Rusk, 377 U.S. 163 (1964)
Seminole Tribe of Florida v. Florida, 517 U.S. 44 (1996)
Service v. Dulles, 354 U.S. 363 (1957)
Shapiro v. Thompson, 394 U.S. 618 (1969)
Shaw v. Hunt, 517 U.S. 899 (1996)
Shaw v. Reno, 509 U.S. 630 (1993)

Shelley v. Kraemer, 334 U.S. 1 (1948)

Sipuel v. Board of Regents of the University of Oklahoma, 332 U.S. 631 (1948)

Skinner v. Oklahoma, 316 U.S. 535 (1942)

Smith v. Allwright, 321 U.S. 649 (1944)

Smith v. University of Washington Law School, 233 F.3d 1188 (9th Cir. 2000)

Solid Waste Agency v. U.S. Army Corps of Engineers, 531 U.S. 159 (2001)

South Carolina v. Barnwell Brothers, 303 U.S. 177 (1938)

South Central Bell Telephone Co. v. Alabama, 526 U.S. 160 (1999)

Stanford, In re, 133 S.Ct. 472 (2002)

Stanley v. Georgia, 394 U.S. 557 (1969)

State Farm Mutual Automobile Insurance Co. v. Campbell, 123 S. Ct. 1513 (2003)

Stenberg v. Carhart, 530 U.S. 914 (2000)

Stogner v. California, 123 S. Ct. 2446 (2003)

Sugarman v. Dougall, 413 U.S. 634 (1973)

Swann v. Charlotte-Mecklenburg Board of Education, 402 U.S. 1 (1971)

Sweatt v. Painter, 339 U.S. 629 (1950)

Sweezy v. New Hampshire, 354 U.S. 234 (1957)

Terminiello v. Chicago, 337 U.S. 1 (1949)

Terry v. Adams, 345 U.S. 461 (1953)

Texas v. Johnson, 491 U.S. 397 (1989)

Thompson v. Western States Medical Center, 535 U.S. 357 (2002)

Thornburgh v. American College of Obstetricians and Gynecologists, 476 U.S. 747 (1986)

Toll v. Moreno, 458 U.S. 1 (1982)

Trimble v. Gordon, 430 U.S. 762 (1977)

Trop v. Dulles, 356 U.S. 86 (1958)

Troxel v. Granville, 530 U.S. 57 (2000)

United Jewish Organizations v. Carey, 430 U.S. 144 (1977)

United States v. Bajakajian, 524 U.S. 321 (1998)

United States v. Butler, 297 U.S. 1 (1936)

United States v. Carolene Products, 304 U.S. 144 (1938)

United States v. Darby, 312 U.S. 100 (1941)

United States v. Hatter, 532 U.S. 557 (2001)

United States v. IBM Corp., 517 U.S. 843 (1996)

United States v. Locke, 529 U.S. 89 (2000)

United States v. Lopez, 514 U.S. 549 (1995)

United States v. Montgomery County, 395 U.S. 225 (1969)

United States v. Morrison, 529 U.S. 598 (2000)

United States v. National Treasury Employees Union, 513 U.S. 454 (1995)

United States v. Oakland Cannabis Buyers' Cooperative, 532 U.S. 483 (2001)

United States v. Paradise, 480 U.S. 149 (1987)

United States v. Playboy Entertainment Group, 529 U.S. 803 (2000)

United States v. Quinones, 2002 U.S. Dist. LEXIS 11631 (S.D.N.Y. 2002)

United States v. Scotland Neck City Board of Education, 407 U.S. 484 (1972)

United States v. United Auto Workers, 352 U.S. 567 (1957)

United States v. United Foods, Inc., 533 U.S. 405 (2001)

United States v. U.S. Shoe Corp., 523 U.S. 360 (1998)

United States v. Virginia, 518 U.S. 515 (1996)

United States Department of Agriculture v. Moreno, 413 U.S. 528 (1973)

U.S. Term Limits v. Thornton, 514 U.S. 779 (1995)

Valentine v. Chrestensen, 316 U.S. 52 (1942)

Vera v. Bush, 933 F. Supp. 1341 (S.D. Tex. 1996)

Virginia v. Black, 123 S. Ct. 1536 (2003)

Virginia State Board of Pharmacy v. Virginia Citizens Consumer Council, Inc., 425 U.S. 748 (1976)

Wards Cove Packing Co. v. Atonio, 490 U.S. 642 (1989)

Washington v. Davis, 426 U.S. 229 (1976)

Washington v. Glucksberg, 521 U.S. 702 (1997)

Watchtower Bible and Tract Society of New York v. Stratton, 536 U.S. 150 (2002)

Watkins v. United States, 354 U.S. 178 (1957)

Weber v. Aetna Casualty and Surety Co., 406 U.S. 164 (1972)

Webster v. Reproductive Health Services, 492 U.S. 490 (1989)

Wesberry v. Sanders, 376 U.S. 1 (1964)

West Coast Hotel Co. v. Parrish, 300 U.S. 379 (1937)

West Virginia State Board of Education v. Barnette, 319 U.S. 624 (1943)

Wheeler v. Montgomery, 397 U.S. 280 (1970)

Whitman v. American Trucking Associations, 531 U.S. 457 (2001)

Wickard v. Filburn, 317 U.S. 111 (1942)

Wieman v. Updegraff, 344 U.S. 183 (1952)

Wiggins v. Smith, 123 S. Ct. 2527 (2003)

Williamson v. Lee Optical, 348 U.S. 483 (1955)

Winship, In re, 397 U.S. 358 (1970)

Winston-Salem/Forsyth County Board of Education v. Scott, 404 U.S. 1221 (1971)

Wolf v. Colorado, 338 U.S. 25 (1949)

Woodson v. North Carolina, 428 U.S. 280 (1976)

Wright v. Council of City of Emporia, 407 U.S. 451 (1972)

Wygant v. Jackson Board of Education, 476 U.S. 267 (1986)

Yates v. United States, 354 U.S. 298 (1957)

Youngstown Sheet and Tube Co. v. Sawyer, 343 U.S. 579 (1952)

Zablocki v. Redhail, 434 U.S. 374 (1978)
Zadvydas v. Davis, 533 U.S. 678 (2001)
Zelman v. Simmons-Harris, 122 S. Ct. 2460 (2002)
Zorach v. Clauson, 343 U.S. 306 (1952)

REFERENCES

Abraham, E. Spencer, and Steven J. Eberhard. 1978. "Preface." *Harvard Journal of Law and Public Policy* 1 (Summer).

Ackerman, Bruce. 1998. *We the People.* Vol. 2, *Transformations.* Cambridge: Harvard University Press.

———. 1991. *We the People.* Vol. 1, *Foundations.* Cambridge: Harvard University Press.

Agneshwar, Anand. 1990. "Ex-Justice Says He May Have Been Wrong." *National Law Journal* (November 5): 3.

Aldrich, John. 1994. "Rational Choice Theory and the Study of American Politics." In *The Dynamics of American Politics: Approaches and Interpretations,* ed. Larry Dodd and Calvin Jillson, 208–33. Boulder: Westview.

Alexander, Michael. 2001. *Jazz Age Jews.* Princeton: Princeton University Press.

Amar, Akhil Reed. 1998. *The Bill of Rights: Creation and Reconstruction.* New Haven: Yale University Press.

Balkin, Jack M., and Sanford Levinson. 2001. "Understanding the Constitutional Revolution." *Virginia Law Review* 87 (October): 1045–1109.

Barber, Sotirios A. 1976. "*National League of Cities v. Usery:* New Meaning for the Tenth Amendment?" *Supreme Court Review* 1976:161–82.

Bell, Daniel. 1972. "On Meritocracy and Equality." *Public Interest* 29 (Fall): 29–68.

Berger, Raoul. 1997. *Government by Judiciary: The Transformation of the Fourteenth Amendment,* 2d ed. Indianapolis: Liberty Fund.

———. 1979. "The Scope of Judicial Review: An Ongoing Debate." *Hastings Constitutional Law Quarterly* 6:613–35.

———. 1977. *Government by Judiciary: The Transformation of the Fourteenth Amendment.* Cambridge: Harvard University Press.

———. 1974. *Executive Privilege: A Constitutional Myth.* Cambridge: Harvard University Press.

———. 1973. *Impeachment: The Constitutional Problems.* Cambridge: Harvard University Press.

———. 1969. *Congress v. The Supreme Court.* Cambridge: Harvard University Press.

Berlet, Chip, and Matthew N. Lyons. 2000. *Right-Wing Populism in America: Too Close for Comfort.* New York: Guilford Press.

Berns, Walter. 1987. *Taking the Constitution Seriously.* New York: Simon and Schuster.

Bickel, Alexander M. 1986. *The Least Dangerous Branch: The Supreme Court at the Bar of Politics,* 2d ed. New Haven: Yale University Press.

———. 1975. *The Morality of Consent.* New Haven: Yale University Press.

———. 1970. *The Supreme Court and the Idea of Progress.* New Haven: Yale University Press.

————. 1965. *Politics and the Warren Court.* New York: Harper and Row.

————. 1961. "Foreword: The Passive Virtues." *Harvard Law Review* 75:40–79.

————. 1960. "Mr. Justice Black: The Unobvious Meaning of Plain Words." *New Republic* 142(11) (March 14): 13–15.

————. 1958. "Judicial Restraint and the Bill of Rights." *New Republic* (May 12): 16.

————. 1955. "The Original Understanding and the Segregation Decision." *Harvard Law Review* 69(1) (November): 1–65.

Bickel, Alexander M., and Harry H. Wellington. 1957. "Legislative Purpose and the Judicial Process: The Lincoln Mills Case." *Harvard Law Review* 71(1) (November): 1–39.

Black, Hugo L. 1960. "The Bill of Rights." *New York University Law Review* 35 (April): 865–69.

Blasi, Vincent. 1983. *The Burger Court: The Counter-Revolution That Wasn't.* New Haven: Yale University Press.

Blum, John Morton. 1991. *Years of Discord: American Politics and Society, 1961–1974.* New York: Norton.

Bork, Robert H. 1996a. *Slouching toward Gomorrah: Modern Liberalism and American Decline.* New York: Regan Books.

————. 1996b. "Our Judicial Oligarchy." In *The End of Democracy? The Judicial Usurpation of Politics,* ed. Mitchell S. Muncy, 10–17. Dallas: Spence Publishing.

————. 1990. *The Tempting of America: The Political Seduction of the Law.* New York: Free Press.

————. 1971. "Neutral Principles and Some First Amendment Problems." *Indiana Law Journal* 47(1) (Fall): 1–35.

Branch, Taylor. 1998. *Pillar of Fire: American in the King Years, 1963–65.* New York: Simon and Schuster.

————. 1988. *Parting the Waters: America in the King Years, 1954–63.* New York: Simon and Schuster.

Brandwein, Pamela. 1999. *Reconstructing Reconstruction: The Supreme Court and the Production of Historical Truth.* Durham: Duke University Press.

Brennan, William J., Jr. 1986. "The Constitution of the United States: Contemporary Ratification." *South Texas Law Review* 27:433–45.

Brest, Paul. 1981. "The Fundamental Rights Controversy: The Essential Contradictions of Normative Constitutional Scholarship." *Yale Law Journal* 90:1063–1109.

————. 1980. "The Misconceived Quest for the Original Understanding." *Boston University Law Review* 60:204–38.

Brinkley, Alan. 1994. "Reagan's Revenge — As Invented by Howard Jarvis." *New York Times,* June 19, sec. 6, 36, col. 1.

Brisbin, Richard A., Jr. 1997. *Justice Antonin Scalia and the Conservative Revival.* Baltimore: Johns Hopkins University Press.

Brown, Ernest J. 1958. "Foreword: Process of Law." *Harvard Law Review* 72:77–95.

Buchanan, Patrick J. 1996. "Ending Judicial Dictatorship." Heritage Lecture No. 553. Delivered January 29, 1996, at the Heritage Foundation, Washington, D.C.

Buckley, William F., Jr. 1995. "Standing Athwart." *National Review,* December 11, 46–48.

Burger, Warren E. 1967. "Address at Ripon College." Reprinted in *U.S. News and World Report,* August 7, 70–73.

Bussiere, Elizabeth. 1999. "The Supreme Court and the Development of the Welfare State: Judicial Liberalism and the Problem of Welfare Rights." In *Supreme Court Decision-Making: New Institutionalist Approaches,* ed. Cornell W. Clayton and Howard Gillman, 155–74. Chicago: University of Chicago Press.

———. 1997. *(Dis)Entitling the Poor: The Warren Court, Welfare Rights, and the American Political Tradition.* University Park: Pennsylvania State University Press.

Bybee, Keith. 2000. "The Political Significance of Legal Ambiguity: The Case of Affirmative Action." *Law and Society Review* 34(2):263–90.

———. 1996. "One People, One Race? The Constitution, Color Blindness, and the Problem of Political Judgment." Presented at the 1996 annual meeting of the American Political Science Association, San Francisco, California, August 29–September 1.

Calabresi, Guido. 1991. "Thomas Wins This Liberal's Support." *St. Petersburg Times,* July 30, 7A.

Caplan, Lincoln. 1987. *The Tenth Justice: The Solicitor General and the Rule of Law.* New York: Vintage Books.

Chemerinsky, Erwin. 1989. "Foreword: The Vanishing Constitution." *Harvard Law Review* 103:43–104.

Choper, Jesse H. 1980. *Judicial Review and the National Political Process: A Functional Reconsideration of the Role of the Supreme Court.* Chicago: University of Chicago Press.

Clayton, Cornell W., and Howard Gillman, eds. 1999. *Supreme Court Decision-Making: New Institutionalist Approaches.* Chicago: University of Chicago Press.

Clinton, Robert Lowry. 1989. Marbury v. Madison *and Judicial Review.* Lawrence: University Press of Kansas.

Colker, Ruth, and James Brudney. 2001. "Dissing Congress." *Michigan Law Review* 100 (October): 80–144.

Cox, Archibald. 1968. *The Warren Court: Constitutional Decision as an Instrument of Reform.* Cambridge: Harvard University Press.

Crosskey, William W. 1954. "Charles Fairman, 'Legislative History,' and the Constitutional Limitations on State Authority." *University of Chicago Law Review* 22:1.

Curtis, Michael Kent. 1986. *No State Shall Abridge: The Fourteenth Amendment and the Bill of Rights.* Durham: Duke University Press.

Cushman, Barry. 1998. *Rethinking the New Deal Court: The Structure of a Constitutional Revolution.* New York: Oxford University Press.

Dahl, Robert A. 1957. "Decision-Making in a Democracy: The Supreme Court as a National Policy Maker." *Journal of Public Law* 6:279–95.

Davis, Sue. 1989. *Justice Rehnquist and the Constitution.* Princeton: Princeton University Press.

Dean, John W. 2001. *The Rehnquist Choice: The Untold Story of the Nixon Appointment That Redefined the Supreme Court.* New York: Free Press.

Diamond, Sara. 1995. *Roads to Dominion: Right-Wing Movements and Political Power in the United States.* New York: Guilford Press.

Douglas, William O. 1980. *The Court Years, 1939–1975: The Autobiography of William O. Douglas.* New York: Random House.

Dworkin, Ronald. 1996a. "Sex, Death, and the Courts." *New York Review of Books* 43(13) (August 8): 44–50.

———. 1996b. *Freedom's Law: The Moral Reading of the American Constitution.* Cambridge: Harvard University Press.

———. 1992. "The Center Holds!" *New York Review of Books,* August 13, 29.

———. 1978. *Taking Rights Seriously.* Cambridge: Harvard University Press.

———. 1972. "The Jurisprudence of Richard Nixon." *New York Review of Books* 8(18) (May 4): 17–27.

Edelman, Paul H., and Jim Chen. 2001. "The Most Dangerous Justice Rides Again: Revisiting the Power Pageant of the Justices." *Minnesota Law Review* 86:1–88.

Editors of *First Things.* 1996. "Introduction." Reprinted in *The End of Democracy? The Judicial Usurpation of Politics,* ed. Mitchell S. Muncy, 3–9. Dallas: Spence Publishing.

Edsall, Thomas Byrne, and Mary D. Edsall. 1992. *Chain Reaction: The Impact of Race, Rights, and Taxes on American Politics.* New York: Norton.

Ely, John Hart. 1980. *Democracy and Distrust: A Theory of Judicial Review.* Cambridge: Harvard University Press.

Epp, Charles. 1998. *The Rights Revolution: Lawyers, Activists, and Supreme Courts in Comparative Perspective.* Chicago: University of Chicago Press.

Epstein, Lee, and Joseph F. Kobylka. 1992. *The Supreme Court and Legal Change: Abortion and the Death Penalty.* Chapel Hill: University of North Carolina Press.

Epstein, Richard A. 2000. "Undue Restraint: Why Judicial Activism Has Its Place." *National Review* 52(25) (December 31).

———. 1992. *Forbidden Grounds: The Case against Employment Discrimination Laws.* Cambridge: Harvard University Press.

———. 1987. "The Proper Scope of the Commerce Power." *Virginia Law Review* 73(8) (November): 1387–1455.

———. 1985. *Takings: Private Property and the Power of Eminent Domain.* Cambridge: Harvard University Press.

———. 1984. "Toward a Revitalization of the Contract Clause." *The University of Chicago Law Review* 51(3) (Summer): 703–51.

———. 1973. "Substantive Due Process by Any Other Name: The Abortion Cases." *Supreme Court Review* 1973:159–85.

Eskridge, William N., Jr., and Philip P. Frickey. 1994. "An Historical and Critical Introduction to *The Legal Process.*" In *The Legal Process: Basic Problems in the Making and Application of Law,* ed. William N. Eskridge Jr., and Philip P. Frickey, li–cxxxvi. Westbury, N.Y.: Foundation.

Fairman, Charles. 1956. "Foreword: The Attack on the Segregation Cases." *Harvard Law Review* 70:83–94.

———. 1949. "Does the Fourteenth Amendment Incorporate the Bill of Rights? The Original Understanding." *Stanford Law Review* 2 (December): 5–139.

Farber, Daniel A., and Philip P. Frickey. 1991. *Law and Public Choice: A Critical Introduction.* Chicago: University of Chicago Press.

Feeley, Malcolm M., and Edward L. Rubin. 1998. *Judicial Policy Making and the Modern State: How the Courts Reformed America's Prisons.* New York: Cambridge University Press.

Foner, Eric. 1998. *The Story of American Freedom.* New York: Norton.

———. 1988. *Reconstruction: America's Unfinished Revolution, 1863–1877.* New York: Harper and Row.

Frankfurter, Felix. 1947. "Some Reflections on the Reading of Statutes." Lecture before the Association of the Bar of the City of New York, March 18, 1947, reprinted in *Of Law and Men: Papers and Addresses of Felix Frankfurter, 1939–1956,* ed. Philip Elman, 44–71. Hamden, Conn.: Archon Books, 1956.

———. 1937. *The Commerce Clause under Marshall, Taney and Waite.* Chicago: Quadrangle Books.

———. 1925. "Can the Supreme Court Guarantee Toleration?" Unsigned editorial in *New Republic,* June 17, 1925, reprinted in *Law and Politics: Occasional Papers of Felix Frankfurter, 1913 — 1938,* ed. Archibald MacLeish and E. F. Prichard Jr., 195–97. New York: Harcourt, Brace and Co., 1939.

Freund, Paul A. 1952. "Foreword: The Year of the Steel Case." *Harvard Law Review* 66:89–97.

Fried, Charles. 1999. "Uneasy Preferences: Affirmative Action, in Retrospect." *American Prospect* 46 (Sept.–Oct.): 50–56.

———. 1991. *Order and Law: Arguing the Reagan Revolution — A Firsthand Account.* New York: Simon and Schuster.

Frymer, Paul, and John David Skrentny. 1998. "Coalition-Building and the Politics of Electoral Capture during the Nixon Administration: African Americans, Labor, Latinos." *Studies in American Political Development* 12(1) (Spring):131–61.

Garrow, David J. 1997. "From *Brown* to *Casey:* The U.S. Supreme Court and the Burdens of History." In *Race, Law, and Culture: Reflections on Brown v. Board of Education,* ed. Austin Sarat, 74–90. New York: Oxford University Press.

———. 1994. *Liberty and Sexuality: The Right to Privacy and the Making of Roe v. Wade.* New York: Macmillan Publishing.

Gillman, Howard. 2001. *The Votes that Counted: How the Court Decided the 2000 Presidential Election.* Chicago: University of Chicago Press.

———. 1999a. "The Court as an Idea, Not a Building (or a Game): Interpretive Institutionalism and the Analysis of Supreme Court Decision-Making." In *Supreme Court Decision-Making: New Institutionalist Approaches,* ed. Cornell W. Clayton and Howard Gillman, 65–90. Chicago: University of Chicago Press.

———. 1999b. "Reconnecting the Modern Supreme Court to the Historical Evolution of American Capitalism." In *The Supreme Court in American Politics: New Institutionalist Interpretations,* ed. Howard Gillman and Cornell Clayton, 235–56. Lawrence: University Press of Kansas.

———. 1997. "The Collapse of Constitutional Originalism and the Rise of the Notion of the 'Living Constitution' in the Course of American State-Building." *Studies in American Political Development* 11(2) (Fall): 191–247.

———. 1994a. "Preferred Freedoms: The Progressive Expansion of State Power and the Rise of Modern Civil Liberties Jurisprudence." *Political Research Quarterly* 47 (September): 623–53.

———. 1994b. "The Struggle over Marshall and the Politics of Constitutional History." *Political Research Quarterly* 47 (December): 877–86.

———. 1993. *The Constitution Besieged: The Rise and Decline of Lochner Era Police Powers Jurisprudence.* Durham: Duke University Press.

Gillman, Howard, and Cornell Clayton, eds. 1999a. *The Supreme Court in American Politics: New Institutionalist Interpretations.* Lawrence: University Press of Kansas.

———. 1999b. "Beyond Judicial Attitudes: Institutional Approaches to Supreme Court Decision-Making." In *Supreme Court Decision-Making: New Institutionalist Approaches,* ed. Cornell W. Clayton and Howard Gillman, 1–14. Chicago: University of Chicago Press.

Glazer, Nathan. 1975a. "Towards an Imperial Judiciary?" *Public Interest* 41 (Fall): 104–23.

———. 1975b. *Affirmative Discrimination: Ethnic Inequality and Public Policy.* New York: Basic Books.

———. 1972. "Is Busing Necessary?" *Commentary* 53 (March): 39–52.

———. 1971. "The Limits of Social Policy." *Commentary* 52(3) (September): 51–58.

Glendon, Mary Ann. 1993. *Rights Talk: The Impoverishment of Political Discourse.* New York: Free Press.

Goldwater, Barry. 1960. *The Conscience of a Conservative.* Shepherdsville, Ky.: Victor Publishing.

Graber, Mark A. 2003. "Clarence Thomas and the Perils of Amateur History." In *Rehnquist Justice: Understanding the Court Dynamic,* ed. Earl Maltz, 70–102. Lawrence: University Press of Kansas.

———. 2000. "The Jacksonian Origins of Chase Court Activism." *Journal of Supreme Court History* 25:17–39.

———. 1999. "The Problematic Establishment of Judicial Review." In *The Supreme*

Court in American Politics: New Institutionalist Interpretations, ed. Howard Gillman and Cornell W. Clayton, 28–42. Lawrence: University Press of Kansas.

———. 1997. "The Clintonification of American Law: Abortion, Welfare, and Liberal Constitutional Theory." *Ohio State Law Journal* 58:731–818.

———. 1995. "The Passive-Aggressive Virtues: *Cohens v. Virginia* and the Problematic Establishment of Judicial Power." *Constitutional Commentary* 12:67–92.

———. 1991. *Transforming Free Speech: The Ambiguous Legacy of Civil Libertarianism.* Berkeley: University of California Press.

Graglia, Lino A. 1997. "Order in the Court." *National Review,* November 24, 48–64.

———. 1976. *Disaster by Decree: The Supreme Court Decisions on Race and the Schools.* Ithaca: Cornell University Press.

Griffin, Stephen M. 2002. "Judicial Supremacy and Equal Protection in a Democracy of Rights." *University of Pennsylvania Journal of Constitutional Law* 4 (January): 281–313.

———. 1996. *American Constitutionalism: From Theory to Politics.* Princeton: Princeton University Press.

Griswold, Erwin N. 1960. "Foreword: Of Time and Attitudes — Professor Hart and Judge Arnold." *Harvard Law Review* 74:81–94.

Gunther, Gerald. 1994. *Learned Hand: The Man and the Judge.* New York: Knopf.

———. 1964. "The Subtle Vices of the 'Passive Virtues' — A Comment on Principle and Expediency in Judicial Review." *Columbia Law Review* 64(1) (January): 1–25.

Hand, Learned. 1958. *The Bill of Rights: The Oliver Wendell Holmes Lectures, 1958.* Cambridge: Harvard University Press.

———. 1908. "Due Process of Law and the Eight-Hour Day." *Harvard Law Review* 21:495.

Harrington, Michael. 1973. "The Welfare State and Its Neoconservative Critics." In *The New Conservatives: A Critique from the Left,* ed. Lewis A. Coser and Irving Howe, 29–63. New York: Quadrangle.

Hart, Henry M., Jr. 1959. "Foreword: The Time Chart of the Justices." *Harvard Law Review* 73:84.

Hart, Henry M., Jr., and Albert M. Sacks. 1994. *The Legal Process: Basic Problems in the Making and Application of Law.* Prepared for publication from the 1958 Tentative Edition by editors William N. Eskridge Jr. and Philip P. Frickey. Westbury, N.Y.: Foundation Press.

Hart, Henry M., Jr., and Herbert Wechsler. 1953. *The Federal Courts and the Federal System.* Brooklyn: Foundation Press.

Hayek, F. A. 1994. *The Road to Serfdom,* 50th anniversary ed. Chicago: University of Chicago Press.

Heineman, Robert. 1997. "Conservatism in the US: 1976 to the Present." *Choice* 34(9) (May): 1451–58.

Hess, Stephen, and David S. Broder. 1967. *The Republican Establishment: The Present and Future of the G.O.P.* New York: Harper and Row.

Himmelfarb, Gertrude. 1997. "Untitled comment." In *The End of Democracy? The Judicial Usurpation of Politics: The Celebrated* First Things *Debate with Arguments Pro and Con.,* ed. Mitchell S. Muncy, 87–92. Dallas: Spence Publishing. Hirsch, H. N. 1981. *The Enigma of Felix Frankfurter.* New York: Basic Books.

Holmes, Oliver Wendell, Jr. 1897. "The Path of the Law." *Harvard Law Review* 10:457–78. Reprinted in *American Legal Realism,* ed. William W. Fisher III, Morton J. Horwitz, and Thomas A. Reed, 15–24. New York: Oxford University Press, 1993.

Horowitz, Donald L. 1977. *The Courts and Social Policy.* Washington, D.C.: Brookings Institution.

Horwitz, Morton J. 1993. "Foreword: The Constitution of Change: Legal Fundamentality without Fundamentalism." *Harvard Law Review* 107:30–117.

———. 1992. *The Transformation of American Law, 1870–1960: The Crisis of Legal Orthodoxy.* New York: Oxford University Press.

Howard, Robert M., and Jeffrey A. Segal. 2002. "An Original Look at Originalism." *Law and Society Review* 36 (1): 113–37.

Hutchinson, Dennis J. 1989. "The Black–Jackson Feud." *Supreme Court Review* 1989:203–43.

———. 1983. "Hail to the Chief: Earl Warren and the Supreme Court." *Michigan Law Review* 81:922–30.

Jaffe, Louis L. 1951. "Foreword: The Supreme Court, 1950 Term." *Harvard Law Review* 65:107.

Jeffries, John C., Jr. 1994. *Justice Lewis F. Powell Jr.* New York: Charles Scribner's Sons.

Kahn, Ronald. 1994. *The Supreme Court and Constitutional Theory, 1953–1993.* Lawrence: University Press of Kansas.

Kalman, Laura. 1996. *The Strange Career of Legal Liberalism.* New Haven: Yale University Press.

———. 1990. *Abe Fortas: A Biography.* New Haven: Yale University Press.

Kazin, Michael. 1995. *The Populist Persuasion: An American History.* New York: Basic Books.

Keck, Thomas M. 2003. "David H. Souter: Liberal Constitutionalism and the Brennan Seat." In *Rehnquist Justice: Understanding the Court Dynamic,* ed. Earl Maltz, 185–215. Lawrence: University Press of Kansas.

———. 2000. "Race and Rights in the 21st Century: The Conservative Campaign against Affirmative Action and the Politics of Constitutional Rights." Presented at the 2000 annual meeting of the American Political Science Association, Washington, D.C., August 31–September 3.

Keen, Lisa, and Suzanne B. Goldberg. 1998. *Strangers to the Law: Gay People on Trial.* Ann Arbor: University of Michigan Press.

Kelly, Alfred H. 1965. "Clio and the Court: An Illicit Love Affair." *Supreme Court Review* 1965:119–58.

Kelsh, John P. 1999. "The Opinion Delivery Practices of the United States Supreme Court, 1790–1945." *Washington University Law Quarterly* 77 (Spring):137–81.

Kersch, Ken I. 2003. "The Synthetic Progressivism of Stephen G. Breyer." In *Rehnquist Justice: Understanding the Court Dynamic,* ed. Earl Maltz, 241–76. Lawrence: University Press of Kansas.

———. 2002. "The Reconstruction of Constitutional Privacy Rights and the New American State." *Studies in American Political Development* 16 (Spring): 61–87.

Kirkpatrick, Jeane. 1979. "Why We Don't Become Republicans." *Commonsense* 2(3) (Fall): 27–35.

Kluger, Richard. 1975. *Simple Justice: The History of* Brown v. Board of Education *and Black America's Struggle for Equality.* New York: Vintage Books.

Koppelman, Andrew. 1996. *Antidiscrimination Law and Social Equality.* New Haven: Yale University Press.

Kramer, Larry D. 2001. "Foreword: We the Court." *Harvard Law Review* 115 (November): 4–168.

Kristol, Irving. 1976. "What Is a 'Neo-Conservative'"? *Newsweek,* January 19, 17.

———. 1972. "About Equality." *Commentary* 54(5) (November): 41–47.

Kristol, William. 1997. "Untitled." *Commentary* (February): 32–33.

Kritzer, Herbert M. 2001. "The Impact of *Bush v. Gore* on Public Perceptions and Knowledge of the Supreme Court." *Judicature* 85(1) (July August): 32–38.

Kull, Andrew. 1992. *The Color-Blind Constitution.* Cambridge: Harvard University Press.

Kurland, Philip B. 1970a. "Egalitarianism and the Warren Court." *Michigan Law Review* 69:629–82.

———. 1970b. *Politics, the Constitution, and the Warren Court.* Chicago: University of Chicago Press.

———. 1964. "Foreword: 'Equal in Origin and Equal in Title to the Legislative and Executive Branches of the Government.'" *Harvard Law Review* 78:143–76.

Lasser, William. 1988. *The Limits of Judicial Power: The Supreme Court in American Politics.* Chapel Hill: University of North Carolina Press.

Levinson, Sanford. 2003. "Redefining the Center: Liberal Decisions from a Conservative Court." *Village Voice* 8(27) (July 2): 38–40.

———. 2002. "*Bush v. Gore* and the French Revolution: A Tentative List of Some Early Lessons." *Law and Contemporary Problems* 65(3) (Summer): 7–39.

———. 1996. "The Limited Relevance of Originalism in the Actual Performance of Legal Roles." *Harvard Journal of Law and Public Policy* 19:495–508.

———. 1988. "Constitutional Rhetoric and the Ninth Amendment." *Chicago-Kent Law Review* 64:131–61.

Lewis, Anthony. 1997. "Untitled Comment on William J. Brennan Jr." *Harvard Law Review* 111:29–37.

Lewis, Frederick P. 1999. *The Context of Judicial Activism: The Endurance of the Warren*

Court Legacy in a Conservative Age. Lanham, Md.: Rowman and Littlefield Publishers.

Lieberman, Robert C. 2002. "Ideas, Institutions, and Political Order: Explaining Political Change." *American Political Science Review* 96(4) (December): 697–712.

Maltese, John Anthony. 1998. *The Selling of Supreme Court Nominees.* Baltimore: Johns Hopkins University Press.

Maltz, Earl M. 1983. "Some New Thoughts on an Old Problem — The Role of the Intent of the Framers in Constitutional Theory." *Boston University Law Review* 63(4) (July): 811–51.

Martinson, Robert. 1974. "What Works?: Questions and Answers about Prison Reform." *Public Interest* 35 (Spring): 22–44.

Maveety, Nancy. 1987. "The Populist of the Adversary Society: The Jurisprudence of Justice Rehnquist." *Journal of Contemporary Law* 13:221–47.

McCann, Michael. 1996. "Causal versus Constitutive Explanations (or, On the Difficulty of Being so Positive . . .)." *Law and Social Inquiry* 21 (Spring): 457–82.

McCloskey, Robert G. 1994. *The American Supreme Court,* 2d ed. rev. Sanford Levinson. Chicago: University of Chicago Press.

McDowell, Gary L. 1988. *Curbing the Courts: The Constitution and the Limits of Judicial Power.* Baton Rouge: Louisiana State University Press.

McGirr, Lisa. 2001. *Suburban Warriors: The Origins of the New American Right.* Princeton: Princeton University Press.

McMahon, Kevin J. 2000. "Constitutional Vision and Supreme Court Decisions: Reconsidering Roosevelt on Race." *Studies in American Political Development* 14 (Spring): 20–50.

McWilliams, Wilson Carey. 1995. *The Politics of Disappointment: American Elections, 1976–1994.* Chatham, N.J.: Chatham House Publishers.

Meese, Edwin, III. 1990. "Interpreting the Constitution." In *Interpreting the Constitution: The Debate over Original Intent,* ed. Jack Rakove, 13–21. Boston: Northeastern University Press.

———. 1987. "The Law of the Constitution." *Tulane Law Review* 61(5) (April): 979–90.

———. 1986. "The Supreme Court of the United States: Bulwark of a Limited Constitution." *South Texas Law Review* 27:455–66.

Melnick, R. Shep. 2003. "Deregulating the States: Federalism in the Rehnquist Court." In *Evolving Federalisms: The Intergovernmental Balance of Power in America and Europe,* 109–41. Campbell Public Affairs Institute, Maxwell School of Citizenship and Public Affairs, Syracuse University.

Mendelson, Wallace. 1963. "The Neo-Behavioral Approach to the Judicial Process: A Critique." *American Political Science Review* 57:593–603.

Mettler, Suzanne. 2002. "Bringing the State Back In to Civic Engagement: Policy Feedback Effects of the G.I. Bill for World War II Veterans." *American Political Science Review* 96(2) (June): 351–65.

Michelman, Frank I. 1988. "Law's Republic." *Yale Law Journal* 97 (July): 1493–1537.

————. 1977. "States' Rights and States' Roles: Permutations of Sovereignty in *National League of Cities v. Usery.*" *Yale Law Journal* 86:1165–95.

————. 1969. "Foreword: On Protecting the Poor Through the Fourteenth Amendment." *Harvard Law Review* 83 (November): 7–59.

Mosteller, Frederick, and Daniel P. Moynihan. 1972. *On Equality of Educational Opportunity.* New York: Random House.

Moynihan, Daniel P. 1973. *The Politics of a Guaranteed Income: The Nixon Administration and the Family Assistance Plan.* New York: Vintage Books.

————. 1969. *Maximum Feasible Misunderstanding: Community Action in the War on Poverty.* New York: Free Press.

Muncy, Mitchell S., ed. 1997. *The End of Democracy? The Judicial Usurpation of Politics: The Celebrated* First Things *Debate with Arguments Pro and Con.* Dallas: Spence Publishing.

Murphy, Walter F. 1962. *Congress and the Court: A Case Study in the American Political Process.* Chicago: University of Chicago Press.

Murphy, Walter F., James E. Fleming, and Sotirios A. Barber. 1995. *American Constitutional Interpretation,* 2d ed. Westbury, N.Y.: Foundation Press.

Nedelsky, Jennifer. 1990. *Private Property and the Limits of American Constitutionalism.* Chicago: University of Chicago Press.

Orfield, Gary. 1996a. "Turning Back to Segregation." In *Dismantling Desegregation: The Quiet Reversal of* Brown v. Board of Education, ed. Gary Orfield and Susan E. Eaton, 1–22. New York: New Press.

————. 1996b. "*Plessy* Parallels: Back to Traditional Assumptions." In *Dismantling Desegregation: The Quiet Reversal of* Brown v. Board of Education, ed. Gary Orfield and Susan E. Eaton, 23–52. New York: New Press.

————. 1978. *Must We Bus? Segregated Schools and National Policy.* Washington, D.C.: Brookings Institute.

Orren, Karen, and Stephen Skowronek. 2002. "The Study of American Political Development." In *Political Science: State of the Discipline,* ed. Ira Katznelson and Helen V. Milner, 722–54. New York: Norton.

————. 2000. "History and Governance in the Study of American Political Development." Presented at the annual meeting of the American Political Science Association, Washington, D.C., August 30–September 3.

————. 1996. "Institutions and Intercurrence: Theory Building in the Fullness of Time." In *Nomos 38: Political Order,* ed. Ian Shapiro and Russell Hardin, 111–46. New York: New York University Press.

Pell, Terrence. 1998. "Conservatives and the Courts: Judicial Activism on the Right?" *Philanthropy* (May–June): 28–30.

Peller, Gary. 1988. "Neutral Principles in the 1950's." *University of Michigan Journal of Law Reform* 21 (Summer): 561–622.

Peretti, Terri Jennings. 1999. *In Defense of a Political Court.* Princeton: Princeton University Press.

Perlstein, Rick. 2001. *Before the Storm: Barry Goldwater and the Unmaking of the American Consensus.* New York: Hill and Wang.

Peters, Shawn Francis. 2000. *Judging Jehovah's Witnesses: Religious Persecution and the Dawn of the Rights Revolution.* Lawrence: University Press of Kansas.

Phelps, Glenn A., and John B. Gates. 1996. "Intentionalism in Constitutional Opinions." *Political Research Quarterly* 49 (June): 245–61.

———. 1991. "The Myth of Jurisprudence: Interpretive Theory in the Constitutional Opinions of Justices Rehnquist and Brennan." *Santa Clara Law Review* 31:56796.

Phillips, Kevin. 1969. *The Emerging Republican Majority.* New Rochelle, N.Y.: Arlington House.

Pierson, Paul. 2000a. "Increasing Returns, Path Dependence, and the Study of Politics." *American Political Science Review* 94(2) (June): 251–67.

———. 2000b. "Not Just What, but *When:* Timing and Sequence in Political Processes." *Studies in American Political Development* 14 (Spring): 72–92.

———. 1996a. "The New Politics of the Welfare State." *World Politics* 48 (January): 143–79.

———. 1996b. "The Path to European Integration: A Historical Institutionalist Analysis." *Comparative Political Studies* 29(2) (April): 123–63.

———. 1993. "When Effect Becomes Cause: Policy Feedback and Political Change." *World Politics* 45 (July): 595–628.

Pierson, Paul, and Theda Skocpol. 2002. "Historical Institutionalism in Contemporary Political Science." In *Political Science: The State of the Discipline,* ed. Ira Katznelson and Helen V. Milner, 693–721. New York: Norton.

Plotke, David. 1996. *Building a Democratic Political Order: Reshaping American Liberalism in the 1930s and 1940s.* New York: Cambridge University Press.

Posner, Richard A. 2001. *Breaking the Deadlock: The 2000 Election, the Constitution, and the Courts.* Princeton: Princeton University Press.

———. 1996. *The Federal Courts: Challenge and Reform.* Cambridge: Harvard University Press.

———. 1990. *The Problems of Jurisprudence.* Cambridge: Harvard University Press.

———. 1974. "The *DeFunis* Case and the Constitutionality of Preferential Treatment of Racial Minorities." *Supreme Court Review* 1974:1–32.

———. 1972. *Economic Analysis of Law.* Boston: Little, Brown.

Powe, Lucas A., Jr. 2000. *The Warren Court and American Politics.* Cambridge: Harvard University Press.

Purcell, Edward A., Jr. 1976. "Alexander M. Bickel and the Post-Realist Constitution." *Harvard Civil Rights-Civil Liberties Law Review* 11:521–64.

———. 1973. *The Crisis of Democratic Theory: Scientific Naturalism and the Problem of Value.* Lexington: University Press of Kentucky.

Reagan, Ronald. 1964. "A Time for Choosing: Address on Behalf of Senator Barry Goldwater," October 27, 1964. Retrieved July 9, 2002 from www.reaganfoundation .org/reagan/speeches/rendezvous.asp.

Rehnquist, William H. 1980. "Government by Cliche: Keynote Address of the Earl F. Nelson Lecture Series." *Missouri Law Review* 45(3) (Summer): 379–93.

———. 1976. "The Notion of a Living Constitution." *Texas Law Review* 54 (May): 693–706.

Reich, Charles A. 1964. "The New Property." *Yale Law Journal* 73(5) (April): 733–87.

Reynolds, William Bradford. 1984. "Individualism vs. Group Rights: The Legacy of *Brown*." *Yale Law Journal* 93:995–1005.

Rosen, Jeffrey. 2001a. "The Recount Is In, and the Supreme Court Loses." *New York Times,* July 17.

———. 2001b. "A Majority of One." *New York Times,* June 3, sec. 6, 32, col. 1.

———. 2000a. "Disgrace: The Supreme Court Commits Suicide." *New Republic* (December 25).

———. 2000b. "The End of Deference." *New Republic* (November 6).

———. 2000c. "Hyperactive: How the Right Learned to Love Judicial Activism." *New Republic* (January 31): 20–21.

———. 1999. "One Case at a Time." *New Republic* 220(26) (June 28): 43–51.

———. 1997a. "Dual Sovereigns: Who Shall Rule — Congress or the Court?" *New Republic* 217(4) (July 28): 16.

———. 1997b. "Originalist Sin: The Achievement of Antonin Scalia, and Its Intellectual Incoherence." *New Republic* (May 5): 26–36.

———. 1996a. "Sandramandered." *New Republic* 214(2) (July 8): 6–7.

———. 1996b. "Just a Quirk." *New Republic* 214(12) (March 16): 16.

———. 1995. "The Color-Blind Court." *New Republic* 213(5) (July 31): 19.

Rossum, Ralph A. 2003. "Text and Tradition: The Originalist Jurisprudence of Antonin Scalia." In *Rehnquist Justice: Understanding the Court Dynamic,* ed. Earl Maltz, 34–69. Lawrence: University Press of Kansas.

Rubenfeld, Jed. 2002. "The Anti-Antidiscrimination Agenda." *Yale Law Journal* 111 (March):1141–78.

———. 1997. "Affirmative Action." *Yale Law Journal* 107 (November): 427–72.

Scalia, Antonin. 1997. *A Matter of Interpretation: Federal Courts and the Law.* Princeton: Princeton University Press.

———. 1989. "The Rule of Law as a Law of Rules." *University of Chicago Law Review* 56:1175–88.

———. 1979. "The Disease as Cure: 'In Order to Get beyond Racism, We Must First Take Account of Race.'" *Washington University Law Quarterly* 1979:147–57.

Schnapper, Eric. 1985. "Affirmative Action and the Legislative History of the Fourteenth Amendment." *Virginia Law Review* 71:753–98.

Schudson, Michael. 1998. *The Good Citizen: A History of American Civic Life.* Cambridge: Harvard University Press.

Schwartz, Bernard. 1996a. *Decision: How the Supreme Court Decides Cases.* New York: Oxford University Press.

———. 1996b. *The Unpublished Opinions of the Rehnquist Court.* New York: Oxford University Press.

———. 1986. Swann's *Way: The School Busing Case and the Supreme Court.* New York: Oxford University Press.

Segal, Jeffrey A., and Harold J. Spaeth. 2003. "Reply to the Critics of the Supreme Court Attitudinal Model Revisited." *Law and Courts* 13:3 (Summer): 31–38.

———. 2002. *The Supreme Court and the Attitudinal Model Revisited.* New York: Cambridge University Press.

———. 1993. *The Supreme Court and the Attitudinal Model.* New York: Cambridge University Press.

Seidman, Louis Michael. 1996. "*Romer*'s Radicalism: The Unexpected Revival of Warren Court Activism." *Supreme Court Review* 1996: 67–121.

Seidman, Louis Michael, and Mark V. Tushnet. 1996. *Remnants of Belief: Contemporary Constitutional Issues.* New York: Oxford University Press.

Shapiro, Fred R. 1985. "The Most-Cited Law Review Articles." *California Law Review* 73:1540–54.

Shapiro, Martin. 1983. "Fathers and Sons: The Court, The Commentators, and the Search for Values." In *The Burger Court: The Counter-Revolution That Wasn't,* ed. Vincent Blasi, 218–39. New Haven: Yale University Press).

Sherry, Suzanna. 1999. "Taking a Narrow View of Federalism." *The Washington Post– National Weekly Edition,* July 12, 23.

Siegel, Stephen A. 1998. "The Federal Government's Power to Enact Color-Conscious Laws: An Originalist Inquiry." *Northwestern University Law Review* 92 (Winter): 477–590.

Silverstein, Mark. 2003. "Conclusion: Politics and the Rehnquist Court." In *Rehnquist Justice: Understanding the Court Dynamic,* ed. Earl Maltz, 277–92. Lawrence: University Press of Kansas).

———. 1994. *Judicious Choices: The New Politics of Supreme Court Confirmations.* New York: Norton.

Silverstein, Mark, and Benjamin Ginsberg. 1987. "The Supreme Court and the New Politics of Judicial Power." *Political Science Quarterly* 102(3) (Fall): 371–88.

Simon, James F. 1995. *The Center Holds: The Power Struggle Inside the Rehnquist Court.* New York: Simon and Schuster.

———. 1989. *The Antagonists: Hugo Black, Felix Frankfurter and Civil Liberties in Modern America.* New York: Simon and Schuster.

———. 1973. *In His Own Image: The Supreme Court in Richard Nixon's America.* New York: David McKay.

Skocpol, Theda. 2000. "Commentary: Theory Tackles History." *Social Science History* 24:4 (Winter): 669–76.

Skowronek, Stephen. 1993. *The Politics Presidents Make: Leadership from John Adams to George Bush.* Cambridge: Harvard University Press.

Smith, Christopher E. 1993. *Justice Antonin Scalia and the Supreme Court's Conservative Moment.* Westport, Conn.: Praeger.

Smith, Rogers M. 1988. "Political Jurisprudence, the 'New Institutionalism,' and the Future of Public Law." *American Political Science Review* 82 (March): 89–108.

———. 1985. *Liberalism and American Constitutional Law.* Cambridge: Harvard University Press.

Spaeth, Harold J. 1964. "The Judicial Restraint of Mr. Justice Frankfurter — Myth or Reality." *Midwest Journal of Political Science* 8 (February): 22–38.

Spaeth, Harold J., and Stuart H. Teger. 1982. "Activism and Restraint: A Cloak for the Justices' Policy Preferences." In *Supreme Court Activism and Restraint,* ed. Stephen C. Halpern and Charles M. Lamb, 227–301. Lexington, Mass.: Lexington Books.

Stevens, John Paul. 1985. "Judicial Restraint." *San Diego Law Review* 22(2–3) (May–June): 437–52.

Sunstein, Cass R. 2003. "A Hand in the Matter." *Legal Affairs* (March–April): 27–30.

———. 2001. "Order without Law." In *The Vote: Bush, Gore and The Supreme Court,* ed. Cass R. Sunstein and Richard A. Epstein, 205–22. Chicago: University of Chicago Press.

———. 1999. *One Case At a Time: Judicial Minimalism on the Supreme Court.* Cambridge: Harvard University Press.

———. 1996. "Foreword: Leaving Things Undecided." *Harvard Law Review* 110 (November): 4–101.

Thayer, James Bradley. 1893. "The Origin and Scope of the American Doctrine of Constitutional Law." *Harvard Law Review* 7:129.

Thomas, Clarence. 2001. "Be Not Afraid." Delivered as Francis Boyer Lecture at the American Enterprise Institute for Public Policy Research, Washington, D.C., February 13, 2001. Retrieved October 3, 2003 from www.aei.org/news/newsID.15211,filter.social/news_detail.asp.

Tribe, Laurence H. 1977. "Unraveling *National League of Cities:* The New Federalism and Affirmative Rights to Essential Government Services." *Harvard Law Review* 90 (April): 1065–1104.

Tribe, Laurence H., and Dorf, Michael C. 1991. *On Reading the Constitution.* Cambridge: Harvard University Press.

Tushnet, Mark V. 2003. *The New Constitutional Order.* Princeton: Princeton University Press.

———. 1999a. *Taking the Constitution Away from the Courts.* Princeton: Princeton University Press.

———. 1999b. "The Supreme Court, 1998 Term — Foreword: The New Constitutional Order and the Chastening of Constitutional Aspiration." *Harvard Law Review* 113 (November): 29–109.

———. 1998. "The Burger Court in Historical Perspective: The Triumph of Country-

Club Republicanism." In *The Burger Court: Counter-Revolution or Confirmation?*, ed. Bernard Schwartz, 203–15. New York: Oxford University Press.

———. 1994. *Making Civil Rights Law: Thurgood Marshall and the Supreme Court, 1936–1964.* New York: Oxford University Press.

Tushnet, Mark, and Timothy Lynch. 1994–1995. "The Project of the Harvard Forewords: A Social and Intellectual Inquiry." *Constitutional Commentary* 11: 463–500.

Ulmer, Sidney. 1960. "Supreme Court Behavior and Civil Rights." *Western Political Quarterly* 13:288.

Van Alstyne, William. 1965. "The Fourteenth Amendment, the 'Right' to Vote, and the Understanding of the Thirty-ninth Congress." *Supreme Court Review* 1965:33–86.

Volokh, Eugene. 1997. "What Speech Does 'Hostile Work Environment' Harassment Law Restrict?" *Georgetown Law Journal* 85 (February): 627–48.

Weaver, John D. 1967. *Warren: The Man, the Court, the Era.* Boston: Little, Brown.

Wechsler, Herbert. 1965. "The Courts and the Constitution." *Columbia Law Review* 65:1001–14.

———. 1959. "Toward Neutral Principles of Constitutional Law." *Harvard Law Review* 73 (November): 1–35.

———. 1954. "The Political Safeguards of Federalism: The Role of the States in the Composition and Selection of the National Government." *Columbia Law Review* 54:543–60.

White, G. Edward. 1978a. "The Path of American Jurisprudence." In *Patterns of American Legal Thought,* ed. G. Edward White, 18–73. Indianapolis: Bobbs-Merrill.Originally published in *University of Pennsylvania Law Review* 124(5) (1976).

———. 1978b. "The Evolution of Reasoned Elaboration: Jurisprudential Criticism and Social Change." In *Patterns of American Legal Thought,* ed. G. Edward White, 136–62. Indianapolis: Bobbs-Merrill.

Whittington, Keith E. 2003. "William H. Rehnquist: Nixon's Strict Constructionist, Reagan's Chief Justice." In *Rehnquist Justice: Understanding the Court Dynamic,* ed. Earl Maltz, 8–33. Lawrence: University Press of Kansas.

———. 2001a. "Presidential Challenges to Judicial Supremacy and the Politics of Constitutional Meaning." *Polity* 33(3) (Spring): 365–95.

———. 2001b. "Taking What They Give Us: Explaining the Court's Federalism Offensive." *Duke Law Journal* 51 (October): 477–520.

———. 1998a. "Oppositional Presidents and Judicial Negotiations: Judicial Authority in Political Time." Presented at the annual meeting of the American Political Science Association, Boston, Massachusetts, September 3–6.

———. 1998b. "Review of *The End of Democracy? The Judicial Usurpation of Politics: The Celebrated* First Things *Debate with Arguments Pro and Con,* by Mitchell S. Muncy." *Review of Politics* 60(3) (Summer): 597–99.

Wiley, Richard E., and Laurence Bodine. 1985. "Q & A with the Attorney General." *ABA Journal* 71 (July): 44.

Wilkinson, J. Harvie, III. 1979. *From* Brown *to* Bakke: *The Supreme Court and School Integration: 1954–1978.* New York: Oxford University Press.

Woodward, Bob, and Scott Armstrong. 1979. *The Brethren: Inside the Supreme Court.* New York: Avon Books.

Wright, J. Skelly. 1971. "Professor Bickel, the Scholarly Tradition, and the Supreme Court." *Harvard Law Review* 84 (February): 769–805.

Yalof, David Alistair. 1999. *Pursuit of Justices: Presidential Politics and the Selection of Supreme Court Nominees.* Chicago: University of Chicago Press.

Yarbrough, Tinsley E. 2002. *Race and Redistricting: The Shaw-Cromartie Cases.* Lawrence: University Press of Kansas.

Young, James. 1996. *Reconsidering American Liberalism: The Troubled Odyssey of the Liberal Idea.* Boulder: Westview Press.

INDEX

Abingdon School District v. Schempp, 69
abortion, 119, 127–30, 172–75, 218
academic freedom, 45
Ackerman, Bruce, 24, 92, 157, 254, 298n13
Adams, John, 46
Adamson v. California, 33, 34, 43, 48, 55, 69
Adarand Constructors, Inc. v. Pena, 231, 232, 255, 259, 280, 292
affirmative action, 6, 13; color-blind critique of, 181, 186; Kennedy and, 230; neoconservative attacks on, 139–40; Nixon court, 144–50; O'Connor and, 200, 230; race-conscious admissions policies, 199–200, 233–35; Rehnquist Court, 10, 191
Affirmative Discrimination: Ethnic Inequality and Public Policy (Glazer), 141–42, 146, 310n57
Age Discrimination in Employment Act, 2, 190, 239, 291, 315n61
Agostini v. Felton, 226–27
Agricultural Adjustment Act, 22, 299n16
Agricultural Marketing Act, 183
Aguilar v. Felton, 226
Aid to Families with Dependent Children (AFDC), 138
Akron v. Akron Center for Reproductive Health, 172, 309n41
alcohol advertising, 265
Alden v. Maine, 206, 241, 263
Alexander v. Holmes County Board of Education, 308n15
Allied Structural Steel Co. v. Spannaus, 151
Amar, Akhil Reed, 36
American Airlines v. Wolens, 209

American Bar Association, Committee on Communist Strategy, 54
American Center for Law and Justice (ACLJ), 248
American Civil Liberties Union (ACLU), 101, 182
American Enterprise Institute, 193
American Insurance Association v. Garamendi, 214, 322n17
American Revolution, 46
Americans with Disabilities Act, 2, 239, 241, 261, 291
anti-communism, 95, 136
anti-contraception laws, 90
Anti-Defamation League (ADL) of B'nai B'rith, 145
anti-discrimination laws, 267
Apprendi v. New Jersey, 212
Arizona Department of Corrections, 215
Arkes, Hadley, 180
Arrow, Kenneth, 185
Ashcroft v. Free Speech Coalition, 207
Ashwander v. TVA, 21–22, 42
Atkins v. Virginia, 226
at-large districting system, 150
attitudinal model, 44, 268, 270, 290
Austin v. Michigan State Chamber of Commerce, 265

Babbitt v. Youpee, 204
Baker v. Carr, 65, 69, 80–81
Bakke, Allan, 147
Bakker, Jim, 135
Baldwin v. Missouri, 21
Balkin, Jack, 255, 291
Banfield, Edward, 137

Barenblatt, Lloyd, 53
Barenblatt v. United States, 53
Barnett Bank v. Nelson, 209
Bartkus v. Illinois, 43
Bartnicki v. Vopper, 207
Bauer, Gary, 179
Bell, Daniel, 137, 139
Bennett, William, 179
Berger, Raoul: constitutional originalism, 103, 153–54, 156; on incorporation, school segregation, and reapportionment questions, 36, 311n70; research on Reconstruction amendments, 305n36, 305n37
Berns, Walter, 287
Betts v. Brady, 33, 72, 88
Bickel, Alexander: on affirmative action, 145–46, 147; defense of judicial power while emphasizing importance of judicial restraint, 24, 58, 61, 288; denunciation of reapportionment decisions, 307n60; espousal of judicial prudence, 64; *Harvard Law Review* foreword, 59; incorporation debate, 36; *The Least Dangerous Branch: The Supreme Court at the Bar of Politics,* 61–64, 65, 97, 303n34, 310n56; on limits of judicial capacity, 120, 140–41; *The Morality of Consent,* 145–46, 146; passive virtues, 21–22; on race-conscious remedial measures, 188; research memo on school segregation, 48, 49, 51–52; support for *Brown* decision, 97; view of American democracy, 90
Bill of Rights, 19, 32, 33, 134
Bipartisan Campaign Reform Act (McCain-Feingold Bill), 248
Bituminous Coal Conservation Act, 25
Black, Hugo: absolutist conception of textually guaranteed rights, 54, 58, 173, 175, 257; appeal to history, 77; *Barnette,* 32; constitutional equality, 28; constitutional order emphasizing judicial protection of preferred freedoms, 38; defender of Bill of Rights, 18, 32–37, 72; dissent in *Adamson,* 34; dissent in *Goldberg v. Kelly,* 92, 304n19; dissenting opinions throughout the 1960s, 92–93; dissent in *Griswold,* 75, 76; dissent in *In re Winship,* 78; dissent in *Katz v. United States,* 77–78; *Douglas v. California,* 89; on Due Process and Equal Protection Clauses, 79–80; economic equality cases, 88; *Everson,* 46–47; free speech absolutism, 32–33, 53–54; *Gobitis,* 32; *Harper v. Virginia,* 89; incorporation theory, 33–34, 52, 73, 162; influence on judicial conservatism, 69, 102–3, 216; interagreement with other justices, 86–88; *Jones v. Opelika,* 32; leading critic of expanding liberal activism, 67; modifications to Frankfurterian critique, 68; narrow vision of constitutional liberty, 131; opinions of the 1940s and 1950s laid groundwork for Warren Court's landmark decisions, 67; retirement, 113; rights-based activism, 279; *Shapiro v. Thompson,* 92; Warren Court's leading dissenter, 13, 67–68; welfare rights cases, 88, 90; *Wesberry v. Sanders,* 82
Blackmun, Harry: on capital punishment, 127; *Casey,* 173; development into leading judicial liberal, 117; dissent from Court's refusal to hear death penalty appeal, 178; dissent in *Webster,* 173; *National League of Cities,* 190; Nixon's appointment of, 113
Blum, John, 110
Board of Curators of the University of Missouri v. Horowtiz, 147–48, 234
Board of Trustees of the University of Alabama v. Garrett, 241, 255, 294
Bob Jones University v. United States, 180

Boddie v. Connecticut, 90

Bolick, Clint, 181

Bolling v. Sharpe, 48–49

Bork, Robert, 97, 115, 180, 287; *amicus curiae* in *Milliken,* 124; confirmation hearings, 163–64; constitutional originalism, 103, 154, 156; criticism of *Griswold,* 163; "Neutral Principles and Some First Amendment problems," 151–53, 265; proposed constitutional amendment abolishing judicial review, 290, 324n7; Reagan nomination of, 163; *Slouching toward Gomorrah: Modern Liberalism and American Decline,* 287

Bowers v. Hardwick, 166, 172, 216, 218, 272

Bowsher v. Synar, 193

Boy Scouts of America v. Dale, 212, 249, 267

Bradley v. School Board, 308n14

Brady Bill, 2, 238, 240

Branch, Taylor, 306n56

Brandeis, Louis: call for judicial restraint, 20, 21, 288; dissent in *Olmstead,* 46, 63; and freedom of speech, 27; insistence that Court should avoid constitutional decisions whenever possible, 22, 42; opinion in *Ashwander,* 59

Brandwein, Pamela, 36

Brennan, William: *Baker v. Carr,* 65; *Boddie,* 90; on capital punishment, 126; "compelling state interest" approach, 91; defense of individual liberty and minority rights, 4; dissent in *National League of Cities,* 149; *Eisenstadt,* 129; *Frontiero,* 133; *Furman v. Georgia,* 127; *Goldberg v. Kelly,* 91; incorporation theory, 73; living constitution, 48; *Michael H.,* 170, 171; *New York Times v. Sullivan,* 71; retirement, 164; *Shapiro v. Thompson,* 91; upholding of federal affirmative action program designed to increase minority ownership of broadcast licenses, 188–89

"Brennan Court," 133

Brest, Paul, 156

Breyer, Stephen, 201, 234; dissent in *Bush v. Gore,* 288, 325n13; dissent in *United Foods,* 246; on Fourteenth Amendment, 264; *Pottawatomie County v. Earls,* 316n5

Bridges, Harry, 32

Bridges v. California, 32–33, 37

Brisbin, Richard, 223

Broder, David, 95

Brookings Institute, 141

Brown, Edmund "Pat," 110

Brown, Ernest, 302n30

Brown v. Board of Education: conservative critique of, 168; critical reaction to, 54–55; and Fourteenth Amendment's Equal Protection and Due Process Clauses, 38, 48, 69; Frankfurter and, 48; historicist critique of, 51; segregationist critique of, 129; Southern reaction to, 50–51; Thomas on, 231

Brown v. Legal Foundation of Washington, 244, 266

Bryant, Anita, 135

Buchanan, James, 185

Buchanan, Pat, 289, 290, 324n7

Buckley v. American Constitutional Law Foundation, 211

Buckley v. Valeo, 246–47

Burger, Warren: came to oppose *Roe* over time, 130; *Dandridge,* 120; dissent from Court's recognition of a constitutionally protected right for a family to live together, 131; dissent in *Carter v. West Feliciana,* 122; dissent in *Eisenstadt,* 130; inclined to join a majority he disagreed with in an effort to narrow the opinion, 116; on legislative apportionment, 189; Nixon's appointment of, 113;

Burger, Warren (*continued*)
objection to Court's activist decisions
because they were undemocratic and
rooted in liberal social engineering,
124; plurality opinion in *Fullilove,* 186;
retirement, 158, 159, 167; 1967 speech
complaining about *Miranda,* 111;
Swann, 122, 124; welfare rights decisions, 119–20; *Wright v. Emporia,*
122–23
Burger Court, 103, 118; abortion cases,
128–30; approach to liberal rights-
protecting doctrines, 121, 165; and capital punishment, 125–28; conservative
critique constrained liberal activism
at the margins, 119; constitutional protection to "commercial speech," 245;
"Country-Club Republicanism," 3,
297n1; curtailed Warren Court's liberal
activism in some areas and reaffirmed
and extended it in others, 109; equal
protection decisions other than school
cases, 124–25; frequency of solo dissent
during, 116–17; held that statistical
evidence of a racially disparate impact
could support an inference of discriminatory purpose, 176; school desegregation, 121–24; "the counter-revolution
that wasn't," 108
Burke, Edmund, 180
Bush, George H. W.: justices appointed
by, 5; nomination of Souter, 164–65,
173
Bush, George W., 196
Bush v. Gore, 1, 208, 252, 255, 276; attitudinal model, 268; Breyer and, 288; as
conservative activism, 267; expanded
judicial power, 284–85; originalist and
equal protection bases, 286, 293; "reason of state" justification, 295
Bush v. Vera, 210, 233, 318n45

Bussiere, Elizabeth, 91
Bybee, Keith, 147

Calabresi, Dean Guido, 254
California Democratic Party v. Jones, 212
California Supreme Court, striking down
of death penalty on state constitutional
grounds, 126
Callins v. Collins, 178–79
campaign finance regulation, 246–48
*Camps Newfound/Owatonna v. Town of
Harrison,* 211
capital punishment: administered in a
racially discriminatory fashion, 177;
and Burger Court, 119, 125–28; execu-
tion of mentally retarded, 178, 226
Caplan, Lincoln, 160
Cardozo, Benjamin: judicial restraint, 21;
open-ended interpretation of abstract
provisions of the Fourteenth Amendment, 33, 35; "ordered liberty" formulation, 36; *Palko,* 27–28; reasoned judg-
ment, 68
Carmell v. Texas, 212
Carolene Products approach, 29, 40, 147,
151, 169, 188, 220–21
Carswell, G. Harrold, 113
Carter, Jimmy, 158
Carter v. Carter Coal, 25
*Carter v. West Feliciana Parish School
Board,* 122
Center for Individual Rights (CIR): anti-
affirmative action lawsuits, 182, 234;
goal, 181, 314n40; rights-based conser-
vative legal claims, 182–86
Chandler v. Miller, 211
Chemerinsky, Erwin, 254
Chicago v. Morales, 211, 217, 229
child labor cases, 260, 322n6
Child Online Protection Act, 320n82
Child Pornography Prevention Act, 251

Christian Broadcasting Network, 135
Christian Coalition, 179
Christian Legal Society, 248
Christian Right, 109, 135–36, 179
City of Boerne v. Flores, 203, 204, 237, 239, 294
City of Rome v. United States, 150
Civil Rights Act of 1964, 95, 101, 125, 240
Civil Rights Act of 1991, 314n34
Clark, Tom, 37, 38, 69
Clayton, Cornell, 11
Clean Air Act, 243
Clean Water Act, 319n53
Clinton, William Jefferson, 195
Clinton administration, defense of Gun-Free School Zone Act, 236
Clinton v. City of New York, 205, 243
Coal Industry Retiree Health Benefit Act, 244
Coase, Ronald, 185
Cold War, 95, 96
Colegrove v. Green, 31, 65
Coleman Report, 310n51
College Savings Bank v. Florida Prepaid Postsecondary Educ. Exp. Bd., 206
Colorado Republican Campaign Comm. v. FEC, 204, 246
color-blind principle: and aversion to affirmative action, 144, 160, 187, 188–89; conservative version of, 146–48; and Fourteenth Amendment equality, 6; Reagan administration, 181
Commentary, 137, 138, 141, 180
Commerce Clause, 184, 192, 194, 236, 237
commercial speech, 245–46, 265, 267, 322n18
Communications Decency Act, 250
community action programs, 138, 310n51
compelling state interest doctrine, 91, 92, 129

Conference of State Chief Justices, 54
Connecticut contraceptive statute, 74–75, 76
conservatism: comparison of *Roe* to *Lochner,* 161–62; critique of judicial power, 128; denunciation of liberal activism while demanding exercise of judicial power on behalf of conservative principles, 5, 155; federalism-based limits on congressional power, 285; hostility to federal government and critique of national welfare-regulatory state, 134; individualistic, meritocratic conception of equality of opportunity, 5, 143; and judicial power, 156–57, 284–96; use of originalist argument to support judicial restraint, 154–55
conservative evangelical churches, 135
conservative intellectuals, 179–80
conservative judicial activism: birth of, 143–51; evolution over time, 278; flowering of, 230–50; in the 1980s and early 1990s, 186–96; Rehnquist Court, 1–2, 148; tension with commitment to judicial restraint, 184–86
conservative public interest law firms, 158, 181–86, 192
constitutional development, 4; as a "path dependent" historical process, 18; steady entrenchment of rights-based constitutionalism and expansion of judicial power, 19; timing, sequence, and conjuncture in, 8–14
constitutional discourse, inherited traditions of, 7, 8, 199, 279
constitutional equality, 28, 176
constitutional history, scholarly attention to, 84
constitutional litigation, 160
constitutional originalism. *See* originalism

constitutional scholarship, of the 1970s,
    151–55
"constitutive" conception of law, 298n7
content analysis, of Rehnquist's and
    Brennan's opinions from 1973 to 1982,
    270
Contract Clause, 23, 151, 183
"Contract with America," 195
Cook v. Gralike, 213
Cooley Lectures, University of Michigan,
    99
Coolidge, Calvin, 298n1
Cooper v. Aaron, 308n14
counterculture of 1960s, 137
"Country-Club Republicanism," 3, 297n1
Cox, Archibald, 91
Craig v. Boren, 133, 176
Crimes Act of 1790, 127
criminal procedures, 177–78, 224
criminal punishments, 224, 225
Crosby v. National Foreign Trade Council,
    212, 264–65
cross-burning laws, 251
Crosskey, William, 36
Cruel and Unusual Punishment Clause,
    125, 127, 166, 225
Cruzan, Nancy, 171
*Cruzan v. Director, Missouri Department
    of Health,* 171–72, 280
culture of poverty, 138
"culture wars," 289
Curtis, Michael Kent, 36
Cushman, Barry, 298n13

Dahl, Robert, 3, 9, 63, 90, 98, 108
Dandridge v. Williams, 120
Davis v. United States, 46
Dayton Board of Education v. Brinkman,
    124, 309n23
death penalty. *See* capital punishment
Declaration of Independence, 259
DeFunis v. Odegaard, 144–45

DeJonge, Dirk, 27
DeJonge v. Oregon, 27
DeLay, Tom, 196
"democracy of rights," 303n6
Demore v. Hyung Joon Kim, 225, 229
Dennis v. United States, 40–41, 44, 77
*Denver Area Educ. Tel. Consortium v.
    FCC,* 204
deportation orders, 225
Dickerson v. United States, 206
District of Columbia, school segregation,
    50, 51
Doctor's Associates, Inc. v. Casarotto, 210
Doe v. Bolton, 130
Dolan v. City of Tigard, 194–95
double jeopardy, 43, 73
"double standard," post-New Deal, 56,
    76, 194
Douglas, William O.: coining of phrase,
    "one person, one vote," 81; *Davis v.
    United States,* 46; *DeFunis,* 144–45,
    146; on Equal Protection Clause,
    79; *Furman v. Georgia,* 127; *Gray v.
    Sanders,* 82; *Griswold,* 75; *Harper v.
    Virginia,* 88; *Jones v. Opelika,* 32; retire-
    ment, 114; solo dissents, 116; "strict
    scrutiny," 28
Douglas v. California, 89, 231
Downs, Anthony, 185
Dred Scott v. Sandford, 42–43, 158
Drivers Privacy Protection Act, 242
"dual sovereignty," 263
Due Process Clauses, 134; and the Bill of
    Rights, 33, 72–78; Frankfurter on, 22,
    35, 43; Harlan on, 73; Rehnquist Court
    on, 165–66, 173–74, 237
Duncan v. Louisiana, 73
Dworkin, Ronald, 48, 102, 134, 164, 174;
    "The Center Holds," 254

Easley v. Cromartie, 233, 272
East Coast intellectuals, 136

Eastern Enterprises v. Apfel, 205, 244, 245
economic equality, 88, 119, 120–21
educational diversity, as a compelling
state interest, 235
Edwards v. California, 28
egalitarianism: conservative rejection of,
68, 90, 99, 139, 177, 231; Reagan admin-
istration litigation efforts against, 187;
and welfare rights, 86–96
Egelhoff v. Egelhoff, 213
Eisenhower, Dwight D., 53, 69
Eisenstadt v. Baird, 129, 313n26
election of 2000, recount, 1
Eleventh Amendment, 149–50, 238, 241,
263
Ely, John Hart, 72, 175
*Employment Division, Department of
Human Resources of Oregon v. Smith,*
169, 293
"The End of Democracy? The Judicial
Usurpation of Politics," 287
Engel v. Vitale, 69
Environmental Protection Agency (EPA),
243
Epp, Charles, 101, 303n6
Epstein, Richard, 183–84, 194, 271, 288
equality of opportunity, neoconservative
attack on, 5, 139, 143
Equal Protection Clause, 28; color-blind
reading, 6, 143–44; guidelines for, 79;
Kennedy and, 232; Rehnquist Court,
131, 220–21, 237. *See also* Fourteenth
Amendment
Equal Rights Amendment, 135
Escobedo v. Illinois, 69, 71, 73
Eskridge, William, 303n32
Establishment Clause, 46–47, 168, 180,
228
ethical relativism, 152
evangelical Christians, 179
*Everson v. Board of Education of Ewing
Township,* 46

Excessive Fines Clause, 245
exclusionary rule, 43
Ex parte Young, 319n60
Ex Post Facto Clause, 245

Fair Labor Standards Act, 26, 149, 183
Fairman, Charles, 85; endorsing of
Court's anti-historical approach in
Brown, 52; on the original understanding of the Fourteenth Amendment,
35–36, 43, 73, 84, 153, 302n27
Falwell, Jerry, 135, 179
Family and Medical Leave Act, 242, 261,
262
Family Research Council, 179, 248
Federal Election Campaign, 246
federalism, 6, 17, 121, 126, 159, 182; Bur-
ger Court on, 148–50, 190–92; con-
cept of limited government, 17; Frank-
furter on, 42–43; Meese on, 190–91;
O'Connor and Kennedy on, 235–36,
239–40, 273; originalist conceptions of,
183–84; Powell on, 191–92; Rehnquist
Court on, 192, 235–42, 260–65; Rehn-
quist on, 148–50, 191–92; Thomas on,
260
"federalism revolution," 235–43, 264, 278
The Federalist, 82, 261
*Federal Maritime Commission v. South
Carolina State Port Authority,* 263
Feeley, Malcolm, 11
Feltner v. Columbia Pictures Television,
205
Ferguson v. Skrupa, 76
Fifth Amendment, 33, 35, 127, 225
First Amendment, 71, 182, 245–46, 250,
265
First Things, 180, 287, 289, 321n1
flag-burning, 250
*Florida Prepaid Postsecondary Educ. Exp.
Bd. v. College Savings Bank,* 205
Focus on the Family, 248

Ford, Gerald, nomination of John Paul
  Stevens, 115
Fortas, Abe, 107–8; nomination, 307n1;
  retirement, 113
44 Liquormart, Inc. v. Rhode Island, 209,
  245, 319n69, 322n18
Foster v. Love, 211
Fourteenth Amendment: *Brown,* 38, 48,
  69; *Bush v. Gore,* 1; Cardozo's interpretation of, 33, 35; color-blind conception
  of, 6, 187; Fairman's study of, 35–36,
  153, 302n27; Frankfurter on, 25, 33;
  Harlan on, 73–74, 85; inconclusive history, 50; originalist approach to, 33, 51,
  68; protection against violation by the
  states, 27; Reagan administration use to
  protect white "victims" of affirmative
  action, 180–81; Rehnquist Court and,
  191, 239, 258, 264; Section 5 of, 192, 239,
  262, 264, 294; and segregation debate,
  49, 51
Fourth Amendment: exclusionary rule,
  43, 72, 215; Frankfurter on, 77; limits
  on police searches, 224; and Rehnquist
  Court, 225; right to privacy, 46
Franchise Tax Board v. Hyatt, 242
Frankfurter, Felix, 126, 132; *Adamson,* 34–
  37; *Ashwander,* 42; *Bartkus v. Illinois,*
  43; belief that rigid adherence to unchanging text leads to distortion, 258;
  and Bill of Rights, 32–37; *Brown,* 48;
  "Can the Supreme Court Guarantee
  Toleration?", 301n4; Commerce Clause
  lectures, 298n14; as committed civil
  libertarian, 44–45; critique of *Carolene
  Products,* 132; *Davis v. United States,* 46;
  Dennis v. United States, 40–41; denunciation of judicial activism, 13; *Dick v.
  New York Life Insurance Co.,* 302n31;
  dissent in *Baker v. Carr,* 65, 80, 83, 129;
  dissent in *Barnette,* 303n35; on Establishment Clause, 46–47; on federalism,

42–43; First Amendment debate with
  Black, 33; *Gobitis,* 26; judicial restraint,
  4, 5, 24–25, 31, 39–48, 200, 248, 279,
  3818; *Kovacs,* 39–40; *Poe v. Ullman,* 42;
  on racial equality, 47–48; on reapportionment, 189; retirement, 65; *Rochin,*
  43–44; "shocks-the-conscience" test,
  45–46, 77, 217; *Sweezy,* 45; *Trop v.
  Dulles,* 42; *Wieman v. Updegraff,*
  301n13; *Wolf v. Colorado,* 43
Freedmen's Bureau Act, 321n5
freedom of association, 58
freedom of speech, 32, 71, 245, 246, 248,
  250
Free Exercise Clause, 180, 248
Freeman v. Pitts, 176
free speech demonstrations of 1964, 110
Freund, Paul, 67
Frickey, Philip, 303n32
Fried, Charles, 160, 180, 193; *amicus* brief
  in *Wygant,* 181, 187; *amicus* brief urging
  that *Roe* be overturned, 161–62
Frontiero v. Richardson, 4, 133
Fullilove v. Klutznick, 186, 191
Fulton Corp. v. Faulkner, 209
fundamentalist Protestantism, 180

*Garcia v. San Antonio Metropolitan Tran-
  sit Authority,* 190–91, 192, 235, 242
Garrow, David, 48
Gates, John, 270
gay and lesbian rights, 167, 215, 219–21,
  268, 272
gender equality: Burger Court on, 133;
  constitutional guarantee of, 215;
  O'Connor's defense of, 176; Rehnquist
  Court on, 175–76, 272
Gideon v. Wainwright, 72, 73
Gillman, Howard, 11, 12, 19, 23, 303n1
Gingrich, Newt, 196
Ginsburg, Douglas, 164
Ginsburg, Ruth Bader: dissent in *United*

Foods, 246; *United States v. Virginia,* 220, 221

Glazer, Nathan, 137, 147; *Affirmative Discrimination: Ethnic Inequality and Public Policy,* 141–42, 146, 187, 310n57; critique of egalitarianism, 139; critique of the "imperial judiciary," 140–41; "The Limits of Social Policy," 138

Glendon, Mary Ann: *Rights Talk: The Improvishment of Political Discourse,* 102

Goldberg, Arthur, 67, 75

Goldberg v. Kelly, 91, 92, 119, 120

Goldwater, Barry: 1964 campaign, 94, 110; *The Conscience of a Conservative,* 94–95; frequent criticisms of the Supreme Court, 94; libertarian, free market conservatism, 134

Good News Club v. Milford Central School, 213, 248

Gore, Al, 1

"government by judiciary," critique of, 1, 103, 223

Graber, Mark, 12, 265, 279, 324n8; on doctrinal evolution, 102; on judicial power, 250, 300n1; on jurisprudential foundations of poverty rights, 119; on originalism, 266; on "passive virtues," 22

Gratz v. Bollinger, 199, 259, 275

Gray v. Sanders, 65, 81, 82–83

Greater New Orleans Broadcasting Association v. United States, 205, 245

Great Society, conservative critique of, 94, 138

Green v. County School Board, 308n14

Gregg v. Georgia, 128

Greve, Michael, 181

Griffin, Stephen, 12, 24, 102, 303n6

Griffin v. County School Board of Prince Edward County, 308n14

Griffin v. Illinois, 88, 231

Griggs v. Duke Power Co., 125, 177

Griswold, Erwin, 302n30

Griswold v. Connecticut, 75–76, 128–30, 313n26; Black's dissent, 75, 76; Bork's criticism of, 163; Douglas and, 75; Harlan and, 152; Stewart's dissent, 69, 75, 309n37

Grutter v. Bollinger, 199, 234, 252, 256, 259, 272, 292

Gun-Free School Zones Act, 2, 236, 261

Gunther, Gerald, 55, 56, 61, 98

Hand, Learned, 62, 252, 302n29; comparison of justices to "a bevy of Platonic Guardians," 76, 172; critique of judicial power, 55–57; on *Lochner* decision in the *Harvard Law Review,* 302n28; rejection of strict originalist approach to constitutional interpretation, 55; urging of judges to refuse to enforce the Bill of Rights, 55–56

Hans v. Louisiana, 238

Harlan, John Marshall (the first), dissent in *Plessy,* 187

Harlan, John Marshall (the second), 53, 77, 253, 305n36; on capital punishment, 125; critique of egalitarianism, 90; dissenting opinions throughout the 1960s, 13, 92–93; dissent in *Poe v. Ullman,* 73–75, 173; dissents in reapportionment cases, 79–84, 129, 189; *Douglas v. California,* 89; on due process, 43, 73–74, 131; on federalism, 73; on Fourteenth Amendment, 73–74, 85, 305n33; *Goldberg v. Kelly,* 92; *Gray v. Sanders,* 81; *Griswold,* 152; influence on judicial conservatism, 68–69, 102–3; opposition to liberal social engineering, 132; *Oregon v. Mitchell,* 85–86; reasoned judgment, 68, 175, 217, 253, 281; retirement, 113; *In re Winship,* 78; *Shapiro v. Thompson,* 92; voting rights, 84; on Warren Court activism, 67–68; on welfare rights, 88–90

Harper v. Virginia State Board of Elections,
88, 120
Hart, Henry, 59, 64, 98; *The Legal Process:
Basic Problems in Making and Applica-
tion of Law,* 60–61
Harvard Journal of Law and Public Policy,
142
Harvard Law Review, 51, 58–59, 99, 254,
290, 302n30
hate speech, 251
Hayek, Friedrich, 180; *The Road to Serf-
dom,* 137
Haynsworth, Clement, 113
Herrera v. Collins, 178
Hess, Steve, 95
Himmelfarb, Gertrude, 287
"history's Warren Court," 71, 72
Holder v. Hall, 318n44
Holmes, Oliver Wendell, 126, 283; dissent
in *Baldwin v. Missouri,* 21; dissent in
Lochner, 20; and freedom of speech, 27;
influence on generation of scholars, 21;
judicial restraint, 20, 24, 252; *Meyer v.
Nebraska,* 298n4; *Missouri v. Holland,*
21; "regulatory takings" doctrine,
311n65
Holmes Lectures, Harvard Law School,
55–56, 57
*Home Building and Loan Association v.
Blaisdell,* 24
Hope v. Pelzer, 225
Horowitz, Donald, 141; *The Courts and
Social Policy,* 208
Horwitz, Morton, 23–24, 60
House Un-American Activities Commit-
tee, 53
Hughes, Charles Evans: *Blaisdell,* 24;
DeJonge v. Oregon, 27; Holmesian judi-
cial restraint, 21; *Missouri,* 28; *NLRB v.
Jones and Laughlin,* 25; retirement, 32
Hughes Court, 26–27, 278
Hurley v. Irish-American Gay Group, 209

Idaho v. Coeur d'Alene Tribe of Idaho, 240
immigration rights, 224
incorporation of the Bill of Rights:
Berger, 311n70; Black, 33–34, 52, 73, 162;
Brennan, 73; debate about, 34–37, 73;
Fairman, 84
independent counsel statute, 257
Indiana Law Journal, 151
Institute for Justice, 180–81, 182
Institute on Religion and Public Life, 180
INS v. Chadha, 193
INS v. St. Cyr, 225
intermediate scrutiny, 133, 176
Internal Revenue Service (IRS), 180
involuntary sterilization of "habitual
criminals," 28

Jackson, Robert: *Bridges,* 32; dissent in
Everson, 46; impressed by the Texas
brief in *Sweatt,* 51; and Justice Black,
37; overturning of *Gobitis,* 30; on segregation, 84
Jaffe, Harold, 302n30
Japanese Americans, wartime internment, 28
Jarvis, Howard, 134
Jehovah's Witnesses, 30, 32
Jim Crow segregation, 49
Johnson, Frank, 121
Johnson, Lyndon, 93, 96, 107
Jones and Laughlin Steel Corporation, 25
Jones v. Opelika, 32
judicial conservatism, 2–8; appeal to
history, 80; concerned more often
with liberalism than with judicial
power, 289; contradictions, 278; critique of judicial deference to the national welfare-regulatory state, 5; critique of judicial power and New Right
critique of liberalism, 155; defined,
297n3; origins of, 13; overturning *Roe*
as dominant goal, 161; pre-New Deal

conceptions of limited government, 6; rights-based constitutionalism, 182, 282, 286; suspicion of the New Deal / Great Society welfare state, 90

judicial minimalism, 255, 292

judicial power: conservative critique of, 128; denunciations of, 288–90; expansion with *Bush v. Gore,* 284–85; growth of, 19, 282, 285; and judicial minimalism, 292

judicial restraint, 39–48, 146, 184–86, 200, 291; Brandeis, 20, 21; Burger Court, 121, 123; Cardozo, 21; conservative originalist argument for, 1, 154–55; as cover for justices' own predilections, 269–70; defined by O'Connor and Kennedy, 281; defining characteristic of judicial liberalism during New Deal, 22; doctrine of, 3, 121, 144; Frankfurter, 4, 20, 24–25, 31, 38, 39–48, 54–65, 279; Holmes, 20, 24; Hughes, 21; Kennedy, 274; Nixon justices, 127; O'Connor, 274; Rehnquist, 7, 115, 126, 131–33, 165; rise and decline of, 1949–1962, 38–66; Scalia, 167–69, 321n3; Stone, 21; Sutherland, 23

Justice-Centered Rehnquist Court Database (Benesh and Spaeth), 320n79

Justice Department, 101

Kahn, Ronald, 11, 63, 100

Kalman, Laura, 63, 108, 185

Katzenbach, Nicholas, 306n56

Katzenbach v. Morgan, 294

Katz v. United States, 77–78

Kazin, Michael, 111

Kelly, Alfred, "Clio and the Court," 84–85

Kennedy, Anthony, 199–203, 215, 230, 253; *Alden,* 241; *Bush v. Gore,* 293; case-by-case adjudication, 281; *Casey,* 173, 293; color-blind views, 189–90, 232;

confirmation, 164; and conservative rights claims, 271, 272; criminal procedure, 177; and death penalty, 179; deciding votes, 208; dissent in *Shrink Missouri,* 247; on Eighth Amendment, 225; on Establishment Clause, 228, 249; and federalism, 243; and free speech, 247–48, 250–51; *Garrett,* 241; *Herrera,* 178; judicial power, 251–52; judicial restraint, 274; *Lawrence,* 219; and legislative districting, 189–90; limiting of Court's activism, 203, 217, 229, 235, 292; *Lopez,* 239–40, 244; *Michael H.,* 171; as moderate conservative, 274–75; on property rights, 244; *Romer,* 219–20, 272; *Sacramento v. Lewis,* 217; sovereign immunity cases, 240–42; thwarting of conservative constitutional revolution, 254–55; *United Foods,* 246; upholding of liberal statutes, 271; *Weisman,* 170; *Wisconsin v. Southworth,* 320n77; *Zadvydas,* 224

Kennedy, John F., nomination of Arthur Goldberg, 107

Kennedy, Robert, 107, 110

Kennedy-Johnson liberalism, 93

Keyes v. School District No. 1, Denver, Colorado, 123

Kimel v. Florida Board of Regents, 206, 241, 263

King, Martin Luther, Jr., 110

Kirk, Russell, 180

Kirkpatrick, Jeane, 140

Kiryas Joel Village School District v. Grumet, 226–27, 228, 229

Knowles v. Iowa, 211

Korematsu v. United States, 28, 46

Kovacs v. Cooper, 39–40, 132

Kristol, Irving, 137, 139; "About Equality," 140

Kull, Andrew, 321n5

Kurland, Philip: *amicus curiae* brief on

Kurland, Philip (*continued*)
  behalf of Anti-Defamation League,
  145–47, 188; "Egalitarianism and the
  Warren Court," 99, 290; on limits of
  judicial capacity, 140–41, 307n61; recognition that Warren Court revolution
  could not easily be reversed, 101

"law and economics," 184–85
"law office history," 84
Lawrence v. Texas: challenge to state
  criminal sodomy statutes, 199, 214, 219;
  as hallmark of Court's liberal activism,
  253, 256, 271, 275, 285; Kennedy, 219,
  229; Scalia, 222, 285
*The Least Dangerous Branch: The Supreme
  Court at the Bar of Politics* (Bickel), 61–
  64, 65, 97, 303n34, 310n56
Lee, Rex, 160–61
Lee v. Weisman, 169, 170, 174, 228, 254, 280
legal process scholars, 59–60, 60, 61, 64
legal realist movement, 21, 60, 324n5
Legal Services Corp. v. Velazquez, 207
legislative apportionment, 31, 65, 69, 189,
  232, 305n35, 307n60
legislative veto, 193
Lemon v. Kurtzman, 228
Levinson, Sanford, 255, 291; "Redefining
  the Center," 256
Lewis, Frederick, 101
Lewis, Phillip, 217
Lewis v. Casey, 208, 215, 231
liberal activism: constrained at the margins during Burger era, 119–34; in the
  1980s and early 1990s, 165–79; vitality
  of, 215–30
libertarianism: constitutional scholarship, 183; judicial activism in defense
  of limited government, 248; tax revolt,
  109, 134
Libertarian Party, 136, 310n49
limited government, 157; judicial activism

in defense of, 248; neoconservative de-
  mand for, 5, 13, 139, 140, 157; pre-New
  Deal conceptions of, 6; and Rehnquist
  Court, 115, 231
*Lincoln Federal Labor Union v. Northwest-
  ern Iron and Metal Company,* 39
Line Item Veto Act, 243
Lipset, Seymour Martin, 137
Lochner v. New York, 20, 22, 75, 76, 120,
  131, 222, 244, 246
Lorillard Tobacco v. Reilly, 213, 245, 319n69
Los Angeles riots of 1965, 110
Lucas v. Forty-fourth General Assembly, 71
Lucas v. South Carolina Coastal Council,
  194, 243–44
*Lunding v. New York Tax Appeals Tribu-
  nal,* 211
Lynce v. Mathis, 210

Madison, James: "double security" pas-
  sage from *The Federalist* No. 51, 261;
  Fourth Amendment, 46
Maltz, Earl, 311n72
Mapp v. Ohio, 72, 73, 94, 215
marijuana, medical use of, 264
Marshall, Thurgood: on the Constitu-
  tion, 24; dissent in *Bakke,* 321n5; *Fur-
  man v. Georgia,* 127; on Reconstruction
  Congress and Fourteenth Amendment,
  259; retirement, 165
Marshall Court, 22, 285
Martinson, Robert, "What Works?" 138
Maryland v. Craig, 177–78
Masses Publishing Co. v. Patten, 302n28
McCain-Feingold Bill (Bipartisan Cam-
  paign Reform Act), 248
McCleskey, Warren, 177
McCleskey v. Kemp, 177
McCollum v. Board of Education, 47
McConnell v. FEC, 247
McDonald, Michael, 181
McGautha v. California, 127

McGirr, Lisa, 95, 111, 134, 136

McIntyre v. Ohio Elections Commission, 209

McLaurin v. Oklahoma State Regents for Higher Education, 47

McReynolds, James C., 32

Medicaid, 138

Meese, Edwin: on appointing of federal judges, 162; commitment of the administration to originalism, 156, 158–59; on federalism, 190–91; on *Roe,* 163

Mellor, William "Chip," 181

Melnick, Shep, 261, 273

Mendelson, Wallace, 44

mentally retarded, execution of, 178, 226

Metro Broadcasting v. FCC, 232, 233

Miami-Dade County, repeal of gay rights ordinance, 135

Michael H. v. Gerald D., 170–71, 280

Michael M. v. Superior Court, 175

Michelman, Frank, 91

Miller v. Johnson, 209, 232

Milliken v. Bradley, 124

Minersville School District v. Gobitis, 26, 30, 44

Minton, Sherman, 37, 38

Miranda v. Arizona, 4, 69, 71, 73, 94, 111, 208, 215

miscegenation laws, 128

Mississippi University for Women v. Hogan, 176

Missouri ex rel. Gaines v. Canada, 28, 47

Missouri v. Holland, 21, 24

Missouri v. Jenkins, 208, 215, 229, 231, 280

Mitchell v. Helms, 227, 229

M.L.B. v. S.L.J., 210

modern liberalism, emerging critique of, 134–43

Moral Majority, 179

Morrison, Stanley, 302n27

Moynihan, Daniel Patrick, 137, 138, 310n51

Murphy, Frank, 32, 37, 38

Murray, Charles, *Losing Ground: American Social Policy, 1950–1980,* 138

National Association for the Advancement of Colored People (NAACP), 28, 47, 101, 182

National Industrial Recovery Act, 299n16

National Labor Relations Act, 25, 183

National League of Cities v. Usery, 110, 149, 190, 235

National Review, 314n38

neoconservatives, 180; critique of welfare state, 137–39; on egalitarianism, 139; on judicial policymaking, 141; on limited government, 142–43; new argument for judicial activism, 142–43; on school busing, 141

Neuhaus, Richard John, 179, 180

Nevada Department of Human Resources v. Hibbs, 242, 272

Nevada v. Hall, 150, 242

New Deal Constitutionalism, 3, 4, 5, 13, 17–37, 24

New Deal Court, 6, 260

New Deal "switch in time," 25, 39

The New Republic, 61, 97

New Right: critique of liberalism, 5, 109, 137, 180; critique of welfare state, 148; demand for limited government, 5, 13; domination of national politics, 134; establishment of public interest law firms, 181–82; impact on the Supreme Court, 259–60; judicial deference to majoritarian morality, 248; political movements, 109; rise of, 179–86; role in Republican electoral successes, 136; theme that nation's schools are dominated by liberal elites, 249

New York Landmark Preservation Commission, 150

New York Times Co. v. Sullivan, 71

New York v. United States, 192, 238, 261–
      62
Nixon, Richard: appeal to "Middle
      America," 111; blame of Supreme
      Court for rising crime rates, 110–11;
      call for "strict construction," 113, 157,
      159; 1968 campaign, 4, 97, 107–8, 110;
      criticism of Burger Court's decisions
      on school busing and death penalty,
      113; 1972 campaign, 114; on race and
      civil rights, 111–12; "southern strategy,"
      111
*Nixon v. Shrink Missouri Government
      PAC,* 247, 265
Nollan v. California Coastal Commission,
      194
nondelegation doctrine, 193, 194
North, Douglass, 185

obscenity, 71, 93
O'Connor, Sandra Day, 7, 97, 196, 199–
      200, 215, 229, 230, 253, 271, 275, 292; on
      affirmative action, 187–90, 232–35, 273,
      315n49; *Agostini,* 227; *Ashcroft v. Free
      Speech Coalition,* 320n82; *Bush v. Gore,*
      293; campaign finance cases, 247–48;
      case-by-case adjudication, 281; *Casey,*
      173, 293; *Croson,* 188; *Cruzan,* 171–72;
      Davis v. Bandemer, 315n56; death pen-
      alty cases, 178–79, 226; decisive role on
      Rehnquist Court, 203, 208, 284; dissent
      in *City of Boerne,* 325n12; on Eighth
      Amendment, 225; *Employment Division
      v. Smith,* 170; on Equal Protection
      Clause, 272–73; Establishment Clause
      decisions, 170, 228, 249; on federalism,
      190–92, 240–43; frequency in Court
      majority, 201–3; gender equality cases,
      176; *Glucksberg,* 216; *Gregory v. Ashcroft,*
      315n61; *Herrera,* 178; *Kiryas Joel,* 228;
      Lawrence, 219, 272; *Maryland v. Craig,*
      177–78; *Michael H.,* 171; *Mitchell,* 227;

nomination, 158; property rights cases,
      244, 266; racial gerrymandering, 189–
      90, 233; *Romer,* 272; *Rosenberger,* 249;
      Sacramento v. Lewis, 217; *Stenberg,* 218;
      Takings Clause, 244, 319n65; thwarting
      of conservative constitutional revolu-
      tion, 254–55; *Troxel,* 217–18; unwilling-
      ness to overturn *Roe,* 172–73; version
      of judicial restraint, 274; *Zadvydas,* 224;
      Zelman, 227–28
"O'Connor Court," 284, 285, 286, 288,
      291, 292, 295
Office of the Independent Counsel, 193–
      94
Oklahoma, racially discriminatory
      "grandfather clause" for voting rights,
      47
*Oklahoma Tax Commission v. Chickasaw
      Nation,* 209
Olmstead v. United States, 46
Olson, Mancur, 185
Omnibus Crime Control and Safe Streets
      Act, 111
"one person, one vote," 65, 69, 71, 81, 82,
      83, 307n60
Oregon Criminal Syndicalism Law, 27
Oregon v. Mitchell, 85–86
originalism, 23, 33, 69, 153; Bork, 103, 154,
      156; conservative philosophy of, 103,
      156; in defense of segregation, 51; and
      federalism, 260–62; focus on Recon-
      struction-era history, 311n71; intent
      to remove politics from Court, 257;
      Meese, 158–59; Reagan administra-
      tion, 103; reemergence as a politically
      significant constitutional vision in the
      1970s, 151–54; Rehnquist and, 115, 151;
      resemblance to New Right policy
      agenda, 266; roots of, 303n1; Scalia,
      167–69
Orren, Karen, 8–9
Otis, James, 46

Palazzolo, Anthony, 244

Palazzolo v. Rhode Island, 319n66

Palko v. Connecticut, 27–28, 73, 88, 301n12

partial birth abortion, 218

Pasadena Board of Education v. Spangler, 124

"passive virtues," 21–22, 144, 233, 292

Paxton's Case, 46

Pell, Terrence, 184, 185–86

Peller, Gary, 63

Penn Central Transportation Co. v. New York City, 150

Penry v. Lynaugh, 226

Phelps, Glenn, 270

Phillips, Kevin, *The Emerging Republican Majority,* 111, 136

Phillips v. Washington Legal Foundation, 244, 266

physician-assisted suicide, 216

Pierson, Paul, 18

Planned Parenthood of Missouri v. Danforth, 130

Planned Parenthood of Southeastern Pennsylvania v. Casey, 173–74, 218, 219, 230, 254, 285; dissent in, 174, 280; plurality opinion in, 173, 293, 295; Scalia and, 222

Plaut v. Spendthrift Farm, Inc., 204

Pledge of Allegiance, 26

Plessy v. Ferguson, 49

Plotke, David, 297n2

Podhoretz, Norman, 137

Poe v. Ullman, 42, 59, 73–75, 173

police powers, 260

police searches, Fourth Amendment limits on, 224

policy feedback effect, 282, 323n33

political questions doctrine, 56

politics of preemption, 195

poll taxes, 88, 89, 90

pornography, 250, 251

Posner, Richard, 1, 185, 267, 295; *Economic Analysis of Law,* 315n45

poverty rights, jurisprudential foundations of, 119

Powe, Lucas, 53, 71, 72, 91, 93, 120

Powell, Lewis: on abortion, 121, 163; affirmative action cases, 146–48, 186–87; *amicus curiae* brief against court-ordered busing in *Swann,* 123; *Bakke* opinion, 187–88, 234; *Bowers,* 166–67, 312n9; as the Court's swing justice in the 1970s and 1980s, 117; dissent in *City of Rome,* 150; dissent in *Dayton v. Brinkman,* 309n23; dissent in *Furman v. Georgia,* 126–27; dissent in *Garcia,* 191–92; dissent in *Keyes,* 123; on due process, 131; and economic equality, 120–21; *McCleskey,* 177; Nixon appointment of, 114; objection to Court's activist decisions, 124; rejection of the *Carolene Products* model, 147; retirement, 167

prayer in the public schools, 169, 226, 229

"preferred freedoms," 18, 19, 31, 38

Prince Edward County, Virginia schools, 71

Printz v. United States, 205, 238, 240, 262, 280

privacy right, 46, 68, 75, 128, 129

Progressive Era, 260

progressive taxation, 183

pro-life movement, 135

property rights, 6, 17; Rehnquist Court, 150–51, 194–95, 243–45, 266

Proposition 13, 135

public choice scholarship, 185, 192, 261

The Public Interest, 137, 138, 140, 141, 180

Public Works Employment Act, 186

Purcell, Edward, 62, 63

race-conscious gerrymandering, 233, 267

racial equality, 46; Burger Court, 124–25; constitutional conflict in 1970s shifted

racial equality (*continued*)
  from desegregation to affirmative action, 144; Frankfurter, 47–48; Rehnquist Court, 176–77
racially restrictive covenants, 47
racial preferences/quotas, 121, 139, 147, 181, 199–201, 233–35
Railway Express Agency v. New York, 39
rational basis test, 220
"rational choice" ("public choice"), 185, 192, 261
rationality review, 216
Reagan, Ronald: election to presidency, 135; elevation of Rehnquist to chief justice, 157, 160; as governor of California, 110; 1966 gubernatorial campaign, 111; justices appointed by, 5, 164, 170; support of Goldwater, 95–96
Reagan administration: anti-egalitarian litigation efforts, 187; appeal to "Middle America," 111; calls for judicial activism, 180–81, 191; campaign to reshape the Court and the Constitution, 155, 157–58; constitutional litigation, 16–162, 192; efforts to enact the New Right constitutional vision into law, 160; judicial nominenations, 130, 157–60, 162–64; libertarian conservatism, 96, 134, 135; objections to race-conscious policies, 180–81; originalism, 103, 158–59
"Reagan Democrats," 113
reapportionment, 31, 65, 69, 189, 232, 305n35, 307n60
"reasoned elaboration," 60
"reasoned judgment," 68, 174, 175, 217, 253, 281
Reconstruction Congress: and Fourteenth Amendment, 47, 153, 154, 191; race-conscious remedial measures, 259; research on, 305n36, 305n37

"Red Monday," 53
Reed, Ralph, 179
Regents of the University of California v. Bakke, 110, 146, 186, 191, 233; Kennedy on, 232; Marshall's dissent, 321n5; Powell's compromise, 188, 234
Regents of the University of Michigan v. Ewing, 148, 234
"regulatory takings" doctrine, 194, 243, 311n65
Rehnquist, William, 7, 97, 199, 257, 271; abortion dissents, 129–30, 162, 172–73; alienage cases, 131–32; *Boy Scouts v. Dale,* 249–50; *Bush v. Gore,* 286; Commerce Clause, 192; conservative activism, 115, 148, 199; Contract Clause, 245; *Cruzan,* 171; *Dayton v. Brinkman,* 124, 309n23; dissent in *Casey,* 174; dissent in *City of Rome,* 150; dissenting opinions, 116–17, 131, 194, 316n4; dissent in *Hodel v. Virginia,* 316n62; dissent in *Keyes,* 123; dissent in *Sugarman,* 132; dissent in *Weber,* 131; dissent in *Zablocki,* 131; *Dolan,* 195; on equal protection, 123, 131–33, 175; on federalism, 148–50, 235–43; gender equality decisions, 133; *Glucksberg,* 216; *Herrera,* 178; interagreement with during Burger era, 118; legislative districting, 189–90; *Lopez,* 236, 260; *Morrison,* 237, 261; narrow vision of constitutional liberty, 131; Nixon appointment of, 114; objection to Court's activist decisions, 124; opinion in *National League of Cities,* 190; opposition to liberal social engineering, 132; on originalism, 115, 201; property rights, 150–51; religious establishment cases, 228–29; *Romer,* 220; *Seminole Tribe,* 238; separation of powers, 193; state sovereign immunity, 149–50; *Trimble,* 132–33
Rehnquist Court, 103, 157, 172, 208;

affirmative action decisions, 230–35; distinctive constitutional jurisprudence, 291; Establishment Clause cases, 226–28; existing accounts of judicial decisionmaking, 276; failure to overturn landmark decisions of Warren Court, 10; federalism, 2, 192, 246, 255, 265, 28310; federal statutes ruled unconstitutional, 1994–2002 terms, 203, 204–7; First Amendment decisions, 246–47, 250, 265; Fourteenth Amendment decisions, 191, 239, 264; Fourth and Fifth Amendment cases, 225; gay rights, 219–20, 271; law and politics, 254–83; mix of activism and restraint, 165, 199–253; mix of liberal and conservative activism, 1–3, 7–8, 200–203, 250–53; O'Connor and Kennedy role, 175; property rights cases, 194–95; reaffirmation of *Roe*, 215, 230; tools of conservative activism in Burger era decisions, 109; Scalia, Thomas, and Rehnquist against Souter, Stevens, Ginsburg, and Breyer, 201; scholarly assessments of, 254–56; sovereign immunity decisions, 239; state and local statutes ruled unconstitutional, 1994–2002 terms, 209–14; support for judicial review on, 251

Reich, Charles, 90–91

religious broadcasting industry, 135

religious freedom cases, 30, 180, 182, 273–74

Religious Freedom Restoration Act, 237, 291

religious fundamentalism, 135

religious right, 109, 135–36, 179

Reno v. ACLU, 204, 250

Reno v. Condon, 242

Republican Party: 1964 convention, 95; evangelical Christians in, 179; post-1968 electoral successes, 156; rise of conservatism, 110–13; southern and western conservatives, 94, 95; southern strategy, 111, 113, 195

Republican Party of Minnesota v. White, 248

Reynolds, William Bradford, 181

Reynolds v. Sims, 71, 82–83, 85

Rice v. Cayetano, 211

Richmond v. J. A. Croson Co., 188–89, 191, 231, 232, 233, 259, 280

rights-based constitutionalism, 10, 17, 65, 72, 102; entrenched in the American political system by late 1960s, 19, 108–9, 282; and judicial conservatism, 182, 282, 286; Rehnquist Court, 179; Warren Court, 13

"rights revolution," 101, 282

Rights Talk: The Improvishment of Political Discourse (Glendon), 102

right to a speedy trial, 73

right to confront witnesses, 73

right to counsel, 72

"right to die," 171–72, 216

right to livelihood, 91

right to marry, 131

right to trial by jury, 73

Roberts, Owen, 72

Robertson, Pat, 135, 179

Rochin v. California, 43–44, 77

Rockefeller, Nelson, 94

Roe v. Wade, 4, 119, 208; call for the Court to overturn, 161–62; conservative critics of, 168; Meese's denunciation of, 159; Powell and, 121; Rehnquist dissent, 129; response to, 135; Stewart and, 69; upholding of, 313n26

Romer v. Evans, 210, 219–22, 223, 255, 267, 271, 280, 285, 292

Roosevelt, Franklin Delano: Court-packing plan, 17, 20, 24; model of presidential leadership in constitutional change, 25, 157; struggle with

Roosevelt, Franklin Delano (*continued*)
    conservative Court over constitution-
    ality of New Deal legislation, 19
Rosen, Jeffrey, 269, 278, 294, 296
Rosenberger v. University of Virginia, 248,
    249, 273–74
Rostker v. Goldberg, 175–76
Rubin, Edward, 11
Rubin v. Coors Brewing Co., 204, 245
Rutan v. Republican Party in Illinois,
    168
Rutledge, Wiley, 37, 38, 46

Sacks, Albert, 98; *The Legal Process: Basic
    Problems in Making and Application of
    Law,* 60–61, 64
Sacramento v. Lewis, 217, 229
Saenz v. Roe, 211
*San Antonio Independent School District v.
    Rodriguez,* 120–21
*Santa Fe Independent School District v.
    Doe,* 228
Scalia, Antonin, 7, 8, 199, 287; on affir-
    mative action, 188, 231, 235, 315n52;
    Callins v. Collins, 178–79; on campaign
    finance regulation, 246; conservative
    rights claims, 199; conservative statutes
    struck down, 271; constitutional inter-
    pretation through categorical reason-
    ing, 257; critical of O'Connor's case-
    by-case jurisprudence, 292; *Cruzan,*
    171; dissent in *Casey,* 174; dissenting
    rhetoric in the 1990s, 224; dissent in
    Maryland v. Craig, 178; dissent in *Ru-
    tan,* 168; dissent in *United States v. Vir-
    ginia,* 220–24; dissent in *Weisman,* 170;
    Eighth Amendment, 225; *Employment
    Division v. Smith,* 170; on Establish-
    ment Clause, 169, 170, 228–29; on fed-
    eralism, 242; federal statutes struck
    down on constitutional grounds, 250;
    Herrera, 178; judicial restraint, 321n3;
    Lawrence, 220–24; legislative district-
    ing, 189–90; liberal statutes upheld by,
    271; *Michael H.,* 170–71; nomination,
    160; on originalism, 167–69, 201, 221–
    22, 257; *Printz,* 238, 261, 262–63; on
    property rights, 194, 243–44; racial
    gerrymandering, 189–90, 233; *Romer,*
    220–24; *Sacramento v. Lewis,* 217; sepa-
    ration of powers, 193–94, 316n65; Tan-
    ner Lectures, 216; "text and traditions"
    approach, 169, 173, 174; *Troxel,* 218;
    Whitman, 243
*Schechter Poultry Corporation v. United
    States,* 299n16
Schlafly, Phyllis, 135
school busing, 6, 121, 123, 141–42
school desegregation, 6; Burger Court,
    121–24; late Rehnquist Court, 208
school prayer, 69, 93, 135, 215
school vouchers, 227
Segal, Jeffrey, 3, 251, 268, 269–70, 271, 275
Seidman, Louis, 220, 223, 288–89
self-incrimination, 73
Seminole Tribe of Florida v. Florida, 204,
    238, 239
Senate Judiciary Committee, on Bork, 163
separation of powers, 126, 193–94, 243,
    316n65
Service v. Dulles, 53
700 Club, 135
sexual harassment policies, 182, 320n78
Shapiro, Martin, 3, 65–66, 278–79
Shapiro v. Thompson, 4, 91, 92, 119, 120,
    215
Shaw v. Hunt, 210
Shaw v. Reno (Shaw I), 189, 191, 232, 233,
    259
Sherry, Suzanna, 261
Silverstein, Mark, 22
Simon, James, 108, 254
sit-ins, 71
Sixth Amendment, 33, 72, 177

Skinner v. Oklahoma, 28, 29

Skocpol, Theda, 18

Skowronek, Stephen, 8–9, 195, 323n34

Slouching toward Gomorrah: Modern Liberalism and American Decline (Bork), 287

Smith, Rogers, 82

Smith, William French, 180

Smith Act, 40, 44

"social engineering," 5, 124, 132, 136, 140, 177

socialism, 137

Social Security, 96, 183

sodomy laws, 166, 199, 200, 219, 222

Solid Waste Agency v. U.S. Army Corps of Engineers, 319n53

solo dissent: Douglas, 116; frequency of on Burger Court, 116–17; Rehnquist, 116, 316n4

Souter, David: *Agostini,* 227; defense of substantive due process, 216; leader of the Court's liberal wing, 174, 217; nomination, 164; plurality opinion in *Casey,* 173; prohibition of state funding of religious activities, 249; rates of agreement with O'Connor, 313n27; *Sacramento v. Lewis,* 217; sometimes abandons liberals, 203; thwarting of conservative constitutional revolution, 254–55

South Central Bell Tel. Co. v. Alabama, 211

"The Southern Manifesto: A Declaration of Constitutional Principles," 50

southern strategy, 111, 113, 195

sovereign immunity, 149–50, 238, 239, 240–42, 263–64, 268

Spaeth, Harold, 3, 44, 251, 268, 269–70, 271, 275

Stanford Law Review, 36

stare decisis, 126, 149, 256, 313n26

Stenberg v. Carhart, 212, 218, 229

Stevens, John Paul: dissent in *Ward's Cove,* 177; *Gregg v. Georgia,* 128; leading

judicial liberal, 117; *Michigan v. Ewing,* 234; *National League of Cities,* 190; nomination, 115; striking down state and local statutes, 250; support of abortion rights, 173; *Washington v. Davis,* 124–25

Stewart, Potter: *Baker v. Carr,* 69; *Dandridge,* 120; dissent from Court's recognition of a constitutionally protected right for a family to live together, 131; dissent in *Carter v. West Feliciana,* 122; dissent in *City of Rome,* 150; dissent in *Griswold,* 69, 75; *Furman v. Georgia,* 127; *Gregg,* 128; reapportionment decisions, 305n35; retirement, 158; *Roe,* 69, 309n37

Stogner v. California, 214

Stone, Harlan Fiske: *Carolene Products* footnote, 40, 72, 93, 151; dissent in *Butler,* 126; dissent in *Gobitis,* 26, 29–30; elevation to chief justice, 298n11; *Jones v. Opelika,* 32; and judicial restraint, 21, 288; and "preferred freedoms," 18, 19, 38; protection of individual liberty and minority rights, 4, 28–30, 37, 219, 279

Stone Court, 278

Sugarman v. Dougall, 132, 310n57

Sunstein, Cass, 216, 255, 274, 292, 293, 297n5

Supreme Court: approval ratings, 323n1; constitutional revolution in 1937, 24; decisions striking down federal statutes on constitutional grounds, 40; decisions striking down state and local statutes on constitutional grounds, 41; dramatic increase in support among Republicans, 284; formal and informal rules of operation, 10–11; mutually constitutive legal and political influences, 277; standard conservative view of, 1; successful institutionalization of judicial activism, 156

Sutherland, George: *Carter Coal,* 25; dissent in *Blaisdell,* 23–24; dissent in *West Coast Hotel,* 23
Swann v. Charlotte-Mecklenburg Board of Education, 121, 122
Sweatt v. Painter, 47, 51
Sweezy v. New Hampshire, 45, 53

Takings Clause, 183, 184, 194, 195, 244–45, 266, 319n65
taxpayer revolt of the 1970s, 134–35
Tenth Amendment, 13, 149, 190, 192, 238, 263
Texas brief, in *Sweatt,* 51
Texas Democratic Party, effort to hold a whites-only primary election, 47
Thayer, James Bradley, 21, 25, 45, 55, 83
Thomas, Clarence, 7–8, 201, 257; on affirmative action, 231, 235, 259; *Agostini,* 227; *Bajakajian,* 245; on campaign finance regulation, 246, 265; on commercial speech, 245, 265; confirmation battle, 165; conservative rights claims, 199; conservative statutes struck down, 271; dissent in *Farmer v. Brennan,* 317n31; on Eight Amendment, 225; on Establishment Clause, 227–29, 249; on federalism, 240, 242, 250, 260; *Glucksberg,* 216; *Herrera,* 178; on judicial restraint, 208, 215; liberal statutes upheld, 271; *Lopez,* 260; originalism, 258, 260; racial gerrymandering, 189–90, 233; rejection of liberal egalitarianism, 231; *Romer,* 220; *Sacramento v. Lewis,* 217; on sovereign immunity, 263–64; *Whitman,* 319n64
Thompson v. Western States Medical Center, 207, 245, 319n69
Thornberry, Homer, 107
Thornburgh v. American College of Obstetricians and Gynecologists, 161, 163, 166, 309n41

Thurmond, Strom, 96–97, 107, 108
Title VII discrimination, 177
tobacco advertising, 265
Tocqueville, Alexis de, *Democracy in America,* 265
Trimble v. Gordon, 132
Trop v. Dulles, 42, 127
Troxel v. Granville, 212, 217–18
Truman, David, 63
Tushnet, Mark, 3, 51, 252, 255–56, 292, 294

Ulmer, Sidney, "Supreme Court Behavior and Civil Rights," 290
United States v. Bajakajian, 205, 245
United States v. Butler, 28, 126, 299n16
United States v. Carolene Products, 29, 147, 169, 188, 220–21
United States v. Darby, 25
United States v. Hatter, 206
United States v. IBM Corp., 204
United States v. Locke, 212
United States v. Lopez, 204, 236, 239–40, 242, 244, 260, 280
United States v. Montgomery County, 121
United States v. Morrison, 206, 236, 237, 261, 280
United States v. National Treasury Employees Union, 204
United States v. Oakland Cannabis Buyers' Cooperative, 264
United States v. Playboy Entertainment Group, 206
United States v. Quinones, 318n37
United States v. United Auto Workers, 42
United States v. United Foods, 207, 246
United States v. United States Shoe Corp., 205
United States v. Virginia, 210, 220, 255, 280
university admissions policies, 144–48, 199–200, 233–35
University of Alabama v. Garrett, 206

University of California–Davis, 147

University of Oklahoma School of Law, whites-only admissions policy, 47

University of Texas Law School, 234

University of Washington School of Law, preferential admissions program, 144–45

university speech codes, 182

unreasonable searches and seizures, 77

urban riots, 110

U.S. Sentencing Commission, 193

U.S. Term Limits v. Thornton, 209, 242

Van Alstyne, William, 305n36

Vinson, Fred, 47

Violence against Women Act, 2, 236–37, 239, 261, 291

violent crime, 110

Virginia Law Review, 183

Virginia Military Institute, 220

Virginia v. Black, 214, 251

Voting Rights Act of 1965, 150

Wagner Act. *See* National Labor Relations Act

Wallace, George, 94, 108, 110–11, 306n56

Wards Cove Packing Co. v. Atonio, 177

War on Poverty, 138

Warren, Earl: and *Brown,* 49–50; individual liberty and minority rights, 4; joined the Court in 1953, 38; resignation, 107; resigned membership in the ABA, 54; retirement, 113; *Reynolds,* 82–83

Warren Court: conservative backlash against, 53, 97–102; conservative critique of, 1; criminal procedure, 72, 94; equal protection decisions, 88, 90, 128; interagreement with Black during, 86–88; judicial activism, 2, 4, 5, 13, 17, 39, 64, 65, 72, 305n36; and the political system in the 1960s, 93–97; scholarly cri-

tique of activism in late 1950s, 54–65; school desegregation, 48, 53, 71, 121

Washington Legal Foundation, 266

Washington Supreme Court, 144

Washington v. Davis, 124–25, 176

Washington v. Glucksberg, 215–17, 218, 229, 255, 292

Watchtower Bible and Tract Society of New York v. Stratton, 213

Watergate scandal, 114

Watkins v. United States, 53

Weber v. Aetna Casualty & Surety Co., 131

Webster, William, 172

Webster v. Reproductive Health Services, 172

Wechsler, Herbert: argument regarding "the political safeguards of federalism," 149; famous response to Hand, 57–58; Holmes Lectures, 151; "neutral principles" formulation, 60, 64; "political safeguards" argument, 190

welfare assistance: and egalitarianism, 86–96; as a form of "new property," 91; residency requirements, 91; rights, 91, 100, 119–20

welfare-regulatory state, 5, 13, 17, 137, 148

Wesberry v. Sanders, 71, 81, 82–83

West Coast Hotel v. Parrish, 22, 23, 25

West Virginia v. Barnette, 30, 31, 37, 44

White, Byron: abortion dissents, 130, 162; agreement with Rehnquist, 129–30; *Bowers,* 166–67; dissenting opinions, 69; dissent in *Moore,* 131; *Furman v. Georgia,* 127; *Gregg,* 128; *Pasadena v. Spangler,* 124; rejection of constitutionally guaranteed right to adequate housing, 131; *Washington v. Davis,* 124–25

Whitman v. American Trucking Associations, 243, 280

Whittington, Keith, 9, 115, 297n6

Wickard v. Filburn, 26, 236

Wiggins v. Smith, 226

Williamson v. Lee Optical, 39, 81
Wilson, James Q., 137
In re Winship, 78, 304n18
wire-tapping, 63, 77–78
Wolf v. Colorado, 43, 72
Wright, J. Skelly, 98
Wright v. Council of City of Emporia,
   122–23
writs of assistance, 46

Wygant v. Jackson Board of Education, 181,
   187, 191

Yarbrough, Tinsley, 233
Yates v. United States, 53

Zablocki v. Redhail, 131
Zadvydas v. Davis, 224–25
Zelman v. Simmons-Harris, 227, 229